1178

COMPLETE MORTGAGE PAYMENT TABLES

Showing the monthly payment required to amortize a loan in a given number of years. Complete and simple.

PUBLICATION NO. ISBN 0-8209-0597-6

Computed and Published by

INSTITUTE FOR CONSUMER INFORMATION

P.O. Box 12643
Knoxville, TN 37912

PRINTED IN THE
UNITED STATES OF AMERICA

PUBLICATION NO. ISBN 0-8209-0597-6

COWELL-MEAD PUBLISHERS
HAS TAKEN EXTREME CARE TO MAKE THESE
AMORTIZATION SCHEDULES CORRECT,
THOUGH THERE IS NO GUARANTEE OF
COMPLETE ACCURACY.

OUR GUARANTEE: Complete satisfaction or your money back.

CONTENTS

INTEREST RATES:
5% to 10% by 1/2%
10% to 20% by 1/4%
20% to 25% by 1/2%

TERMS:
1 year to 40 years

AMOUNTS:
$500 to $500,000 and any amount beyond

METHOD OF COMPUTING TOTAL INTEREST IS ON PAGE 3.

METHOD OF COMPUTING AMOUNTS NOT EXACTLY LISTED ON PAGE 4.

Easy method for computing the interest charged on any given loan.

EXAMPLE: On a $40,000 at 14 3/4%, 20-year loan, how much interest will you pay?

SOLUTION: Take the monthly payment, $519.35, and multiply it by the number of payments for 20 years, 240. Subtract from the total paid, $124,644, the amount of the original loan, $40,000, and you have the total amount of interest paid, $84,644.

$40,000 original loan
mo. payments $519.35 × 240 total payments

$124,644.00	total amount paid
– 40,000.00	original loan
$ 84,644.00	interest charged

How to compute the payment for amounts which are not listed exactly.

EXAMPLE:
amount $38,000.00 for 10 years at 14%

amount $35,000.00 = $543.44 per mo.
amount $ 3,000.00 = $ 46.58 per mo.
$38,000.00 = $590.02 total mo. payment

EXAMPLE:
amount $7,600.00 for 10 years at 14%

amount $7,000.00 = $108.69 per mo.
amount $ 600.00 = $ 9.32 per mo.
$7,600.00 = $117.91 total mo. payment

EXAMPLE:
The monthly mortgage payment for a sum of one million dollars can be known simply by doubling the mo. payment for $500,000.

5%

MONTHLY PAYMENT

Necessary to amortize a loan

TERM / AMOUNT	1 YEAR	2 YEARS	3 YEARS	4 YEARS	5 YEARS	6 YEARS
500	42.80	21.94	14.99	11.51	9.44	8.05
600	51.36	26.32	17.98	13.82	11.32	9.66
700	59.92	30.71	20.98	16.12	13.21	11.27
800	68.48	35.10	23.98	18.42	15.10	12.88
900	77.05	39.48	26.97	20.73	16.98	14.49
1000	85.61	43.87	29.97	23.03	18.87	16.10
2000	171.21	87.74	59.94	46.06	37.74	32.21
3000	256.82	131.61	89.91	69.09	56.61	48.31
4000	342.42	175.48	119.88	92.12	75.48	64.42
5000	428.03	219.35	149.85	115.14	94.35	80.52
6000	513.64	263.22	179.82	138.17	113.23	96.63
7000	599.24	307.09	209.79	161.20	132.10	112.73
8000	684.85	350.97	239.76	184.23	150.97	128.84
9000	770.45	394.84	269.73	207.26	169.84	144.94
10000	856.06	438.71	299.70	230.29	188.71	161.05
11000	941.66	482.58	329.67	253.32	207.58	177.15
12000	1027.27	526.45	359.64	276.35	226.45	193.26
13000	1112.88	570.32	389.62	299.38	245.32	209.36
14000	1198.48	614.19	419.59	322.40	264.19	225.47
15000	1284.09	658.06	449.56	345.43	283.06	241.57
16000	1369.69	701.93	479.53	368.46	301.94	257.68
17000	1455.30	745.80	509.50	391.49	320.81	273.78
18000	1540.90	789.67	539.47	414.52	339.68	289.88
19000	1626.51	833.54	569.44	437.55	358.55	305.99
20000	1712.12	877.41	599.41	460.58	377.42	322.09
21000	1797.72	921.28	629.38	483.61	396.29	338.20
22000	1883.33	965.15	659.35	506.64	415.16	354.30
23000	1968.93	1009.02	689.32	529.66	434.03	370.41
24000	2054.54	1052.89	719.29	552.69	452.90	386.51
25000	2140.14	1096.76	749.26	575.72	471.77	402.62
30000	2568.17	1316.12	899.11	690.87	566.13	483.14
35000	2996.20	1535.47	1048.96	806.01	660.48	563.66
40000	3424.23	1754.82	1198.81	921.16	754.84	644.19
45000	3852.26	1974.18	1348.67	1036.30	849.19	724.71
50000	4280.29	2193.53	1498.52	1151.44	943.55	805.23
55000	4708.32	2412.88	1648.37	1266.59	1037.90	885.76
60000	5136.35	2632.23	1798.22	1381.73	1132.25	966.28
65000	5564.38	2851.59	1948.07	1496.88	1226.61	1046.80
70000	5992.40	3070.94	2097.93	1612.02	1320.96	1127.33
75000	6420.43	3290.29	2247.78	1727.17	1415.32	1207.85
80000	6848.46	3509.65	2397.63	1842.31	1509.67	1288.37
85000	7276.49	3729.00	2547.48	1957.46	1604.03	1368.90
90000	7704.52	3948.35	2697.33	2072.60	1698.38	1449.42
95000	8132.55	4167.70	2847.18	2187.74	1792.74	1529.94
100000	8560.58	4387.06	2997.04	2302.89	1887.09	1610.47
200000	17121.20	8774.11	5994.07	4605.78	3774.18	3220.93
300000	25681.70	13161.20	8991.11	6908.67	5661.27	4831.40
400000	34242.30	17548.20	11988.10	9211.56	7548.36	6441.86
500000	42802.90	21935.30	14985.20	11514.40	9435.45	8052.33

MONTHLY PAYMENT

Necessary to amortize a loan

5%

TERM / AMOUNT	7 YEARS	8 YEARS	9 YEARS	10 YEARS	11 YEARS	12 YEARS
500	7.07	6.33	5.76	5.30	4.93	4.62
600	8.48	7.60	6.91	6.36	5.92	5.55
700	9.89	8.86	8.06	7.42	6.91	6.47
800	11.31	10.13	9.21	8.49	7.89	7.40
900	12.72	11.39	10.37	9.55	8.88	8.32
1000	14.13	12.66	11.52	10.61	9.86	9.25
2000	28.27	25.32	23.03	21.21	19.73	18.50
3000	42.40	37.98	34.55	31.82	29.59	27.75
4000	56.53	50.64	46.07	42.43	39.46	37.00
5000	70.67	63.30	57.59	53.03	49.32	46.24
6000	84.80	75.96	69.10	63.64	59.19	55.49
7000	98.94	88.62	80.62	74.24	69.05	64.74
8000	113.07	101.28	92.14	84.85	78.91	73.99
9000	127.20	113.94	103.65	95.46	88.78	83.24
10000	141.34	126.60	115.17	106.06	98.64	92.49
11000	155.47	139.26	126.69	116.67	108.51	101.74
12000	169.60	151.92	138.21	127.28	118.37	110.99
13000	183.74	164.58	149.72	137.88	128.24	120.23
14000	197.87	177.24	161.24	148.49	138.10	129.48
15000	212.01	189.90	172.76	159.10	147.97	138.73
16000	226.14	202.56	184.27	169.70	157.83	147.98
17000	240.27	215.22	195.79	180.31	167.69	157.23
18000	254.41	227.88	207.31	190.92	177.56	166.48
19000	268.54	240.54	218.83	201.52	187.42	175.73
20000	282.67	253.19	230.34	212.13	197.29	184.98
21000	296.81	265.85	241.86	222.73	207.15	194.22
22000	310.94	278.51	253.38	233.34	217.02	203.47
23000	325.08	291.17	264.89	243.95	226.88	212.72
24000	339.21	303.83	276.41	254.55	236.74	221.97
25000	353.34	316.49	287.93	265.16	246.61	231.22
30000	424.01	379.79	345.51	318.19	295.93	277.46
35000	494.68	443.09	403.10	371.22	345.25	323.71
40000	565.35	506.39	460.68	424.26	394.57	369.95
45000	636.02	569.69	518.27	477.29	443.90	416.20
50000	706.68	632.99	575.86	530.32	493.22	462.44
55000	777.35	696.29	633.44	583.35	542.54	508.68
60000	848.02	759.58	691.03	636.38	591.86	554.93
65000	918.69	822.88	748.61	689.42	641.18	601.17
70000	989.36	886.18	806.20	742.45	690.50	647.41
75000	1060.03	949.48	863.78	795.48	739.83	693.66
80000	1130.69	1012.78	921.37	848.51	789.15	739.90
85000	1201.36	1076.08	978.95	901.54	838.47	786.15
90000	1272.03	1139.37	1036.54	954.58	887.79	832.39
95000	1342.70	1202.67	1094.12	1007.61	937.11	878.63
100000	1413.37	1265.97	1151.71	1060.64	986.43	924.88
200000	2826.74	2541.94	2303.42	2121.28	1972.87	1849.75
300000	4240.10	3797.92	3455.13	3181.92	2959.30	2774.63
400000	5653.47	5063.89	4606.84	4242.56	3945.74	3699.51
500000	7066.84	6329.86	5758.55	5303.20	4932.17	4624.39

5%

MONTHLY PAYMENT

Necessary to amortize a loan

TERM / AMOUNT	13 YEARS	14 YEARS	15 YEARS	16 YEARS	17 YEARS	18 YEARS
500	4.37	4.14	3.95	3.79	3.64	3.52
600	5.24	4.97	4.74	4.55	4.37	4.22
700	6.11	5.80	5.54	5.30	5.10	4.92
800	6.98	6.63	6.33	6.06	5.83	5.62
900	7.86	7.46	7.12	6.82	6.56	6.33
1000	8.73	8.29	7.91	7.58	7.29	7.03
2000	17.46	16.58	15.82	15.15	14.57	14.06
3000	26.19	24.87	23.72	22.73	21.86	21.09
4000	34.92	33.15	31.63	30.31	29.15	28.12
5000	43.65	41.44	39.54	37.88	36.43	35.15
6000	52.38	49.73	47.45	45.46	43.72	42.18
7000	61.11	58.02	55.35	53.04	51.01	49.21
8000	69.84	66.31	63.26	60.61	58.29	56.24
9000	78.57	74.60	71.17	68.19	65.58	63.27
10000	87.30	82.89	79.08	75.77	72.86	70.30
11000	96.04	91.17	86.99	83.34	80.15	77.33
12000	104.77	99.46	94.89	90.92	87.44	84.36
13000	113.50	107.75	102.80	98.50	94.72	91.39
14000	122.23	116.04	110.71	106.07	102.01	98.42
15000	130.96	124.33	118.62	113.65	109.30	105.45
16000	139.69	132.62	126.53	121.23	116.58	112.48
17000	148.42	140.91	134.43	128.80	123.87	119.51
18000	157.15	149.20	142.34	136.38	131.16	126.55
19000	165.88	157.48	150.25	143.96	138.44	133.58
20000	174.61	165.77	158.16	151.53	145.73	140.61
21000	183.34	174.06	166.07	159.11	153.02	147.64
22000	192.07	182.35	173.97	166.69	160.30	154.67
23000	200.80	190.64	181.88	174.26	167.59	161.70
24000	209.53	198.93	189.79	181.84	174.88	168.73
25000	218.26	207.22	197.70	189.42	182.16	175.76
30000	261.91	248.66	237.24	227.30	218.59	210.91
35000	305.57	290.10	276.77	265.19	255.03	246.06
40000	349.22	331.54	316.31	303.07	291.46	281.21
45000	392.87	372.99	355.85	340.95	327.89	316.36
50000	436.52	414.43	395.39	378.84	364.32	351.51
55000	480.18	455.87	434.93	416.72	400.76	386.66
60000	523.83	497.32	474.47	454.60	437.19	421.82
65000	567.48	538.76	514.01	492.49	473.62	456.97
70000	611.13	580.20	553.55	530.37	510.05	492.12
75000	654.79	621.65	593.09	568.25	546.49	527.27
80000	698.44	663.09	632.63	606.14	582.92	562.42
85000	742.09	704.53	672.17	644.02	619.35	597.57
90000	785.74	745.97	711.71	681.90	655.78	632.72
95000	829.40	787.42	751.24	719.79	692.21	667.87
100000	873.05	828.86	790.78	757.67	728.65	703.03
200000	1746.10	1657.72	1581.57	1515.34	1457.29	1406.05
300000	2619.14	2486.58	2372.35	2273.01	2185.94	2109.08
400000	3492.19	3315.44	3163.13	3030.69	2914.59	2812.10
500000	4365.24	4144.30	3953.92	3788.36	3643.23	3515.13

MONTHLY PAYMENT

Necessary to amortize a loan

5%

TERM / AMOUNT	19 YEARS	20 YEARS	25 YEARS	30 YEARS	35 YEARS	40 YEARS
500	3.40	3.30	2.92	2.68	2.52	2.41
600	4.08	3.96	3.51	3.22	3.03	2.89
700	4.76	4.62	4.09	3.76	3.53	3.38
800	5.44	5.28	4.68	4.29	4.04	3.86
900	6.12	5.94	5.26	4.83	4.54	4.34
1000	6.80	6.60	5.85	5.37	5.05	4.82
2000	13.61	13.20	11.69	10.74	10.09	9.64
3000	20.41	19.80	17.54	16.10	15.14	14.47
4000	27.21	26.40	23.38	21.47	20.19	19.29
5000	34.01	33.00	29.23	26.84	25.23	24.11
6000	40.82	39.60	35.08	32.21	30.28	28.93
7000	47.62	46.20	40.92	37.58	35.33	33.75
8000	54.42	52.80	46.77	42.95	40.37	38.58
9000	61.22	59.40	52.61	48.31	45.42	43.40
10000	68.03	65.99	58.46	53.68	50.47	48.22
11000	74.83	72.59	64.30	59.05	55.52	53.04
12000	81.63	79.19	70.15	64.42	60.56	57.86
13000	88.44	85.79	76.00	69.79	65.61	62.69
14000	95.24	92.39	81.84	75.15	70.66	67.51
15000	102.04	98.99	87.69	80.52	75.70	72.33
16000	108.84	105.59	93.53	85.89	80.75	77.15
17000	115.65	112.19	99.38	91.26	85.80	81.97
18000	122.45	118.79	105.23	96.63	90.84	86.79
19000	129.25	125.39	111.07	102.00	95.89	91.62
20000	136.05	131.99	116.92	107.36	100.94	96.44
21000	142.86	138.59	122.76	112.73	105.98	101.26
22000	149.66	145.19	128.61	118.10	111.03	106.08
23000	156.46	151.79	134.46	123.47	116.08	110.91
24000	163.27	158.39	140.30	128.84	121.12	115.73
25000	170.07	164.99	146.15	134.20	126.17	120.55
30000	204.08	197.98	175.38	161.05	151.41	144.66
35000	238.09	230.98	204.61	187.89	176.64	168.77
40000	272.11	263.98	233.83	214.73	201.87	192.88
45000	306.12	296.98	263.06	241.57	227.11	216.99
50000	340.14	329.97	292.29	268.41	252.34	241.10
55000	374.15	362.97	321.52	295.25	277.58	265.21
60000	408.16	395.97	350.75	322.09	302.81	289.32
65000	442.18	428.97	379.98	348.93	328.05	313.43
70000	476.19	461.96	409.21	375.77	353.28	337.54
75000	510.20	494.96	438.44	402.61	378.51	361.65
80000	544.22	527.96	467.67	429.45	403.75	385.76
85000	578.23	560.96	496.90	456.30	428.98	409.87
90000	612.24	593.95	526.13	483.14	454.22	433.98
95000	646.26	626.95	555.36	509.98	479.45	458.08
100000	680.27	659.95	584.59	536.82	504.69	482.19
200000	1360.54	1319.90	1169.17	1073.64	1009.37	964.39
300000	2040.81	1979.84	1753.76	1610.45	1514.05	1446.58
400000	2721.08	2639.79	2338.34	2147.27	2018.74	1928.78
500000	3401.35	3299.74	2922.93	2684.09	2523.42	2410.97

5 1/2%

MONTHLY PAYMENT

Necessary to amortize a loan

TERM / AMOUNT	1 YEAR	2 YEARS	3 YEARS	4 YEARS	5 YEARS	6 YEARS
500	42.92	22.05	15.10	11.63	9.55	8.17
600	51.50	26.46	18.12	13.95	11.46	9.80
700	60.09	30.87	21.14	16.28	13.37	11.44
800	68.67	35.28	24.16	18.61	15.28	13.07
900	77.25	39.69	27.18	20.93	17.19	14.70
1000	85.84	44.10	30.20	23.26	19.10	16.34
2000	171.67	88.19	60.39	46.51	38.20	32.68
3000	257.51	132.29	90.59	69.77	57.30	49.01
4000	343.35	176.38	120.78	93.03	76.40	65.35
5000	429.18	220.48	150.98	116.28	95.51	81.69
6000	515.02	264.57	181.18	139.54	114.61	98.03
7000	600.86	308.67	211.37	162.80	133.71	114.37
8000	686.69	352.76	241.57	186.05	152.81	130.70
9000	772.53	396.86	271.76	209.31	171.91	147.04
10000	858.37	440.96	301.96	232.56	191.01	163.38
11000	944.20	485.05	332.15	255.82	210.11	179.72
12000	1030.04	529.15	362.35	279.08	229.21	196.05
13000	1115.87	573.24	392.55	302.33	248.31	212.39
14000	1201.71	617.34	422.74	325.59	267.42	228.73
15000	1287.55	661.43	452.94	348.85	286.52	245.07
16000	1373.38	705.53	483.13	372.10	305.62	261.41
17000	1459.22	749.62	513.33	395.36	324.72	277.74
18000	1545.06	793.72	543.53	418.62	343.82	294.08
19000	1630.89	837.82	573.72	441.87	362.92	310.42
20000	1716.73	881.91	603.92	465.13	382.02	326.76
21000	1802.57	926.01	634.11	488.39	401.12	343.10
22000	1888.40	970.10	664.31	511.64	420.22	359.43
23000	1974.24	1014.20	694.50	534.90	439.33	375.77
24000	2060.08	1058.29	724.70	558.15	458.43	392.11
25000	2145.91	1102.39	754.90	581.41	477.53	408.45
30000	2575.09	1322.87	905.87	697.69	573.03	490.14
35000	3004.28	1543.34	1056.85	813.97	668.54	571.82
40000	3433.46	1763.82	1207.83	930.26	764.04	653.51
45000	3862.64	1984.30	1358.81	1046.54	859.55	735.20
50000	4291.82	2204.78	1509.79	1162.82	955.06	816.89
55000	4721.01	2425.25	1660.77	1279.10	1050.56	898.58
60000	5150.19	2645.73	1811.75	1395.38	1146.07	980.27
65000	5579.37	2866.21	1962.73	1511.67	1241.57	1061.96
70000	6008.55	3086.69	2113.71	1627.95	1337.08	1143.65
75000	6437.74	3307.17	2264.69	1744.23	1432.58	1225.34
80000	6866.92	3527.64	2415.66	1860.51	1528.09	1307.03
85000	7296.10	3748.12	2566.64	1976.79	1623.59	1388.72
90000	7725.28	3968.60	2717.62	2093.08	1719.10	1470.41
95000	8154.46	4189.08	2868.60	2209.36	1814.61	1552.10
100000	8583.65	4409.55	3019.58	2325.64	1910.11	1633.78
200000	17167.30	8819.11	6039.16	4651.28	3820.22	3267.57
300000	25750.90	13228.70	9058.74	6976.92	5730.33	4901.35
400000	34334.60	17638.20	12078.30	9302.56	7640.44	6535.14
500000	42918.20	22047.80	15097.90	11628.20	9550.55	8168.92

MONTHLY PAYMENT

Necessary to amortize a loan

5 1/2%

TERM / AMOUNT	7 YEARS	8 YEARS	9 YEARS	10 YEARS	11 YEARS	12 YEARS
500	7.19	6.45	5.88	5.43	5.06	4.75
600	8.62	7.74	7.06	6.51	6.07	5.70
700	10.06	9.03	8.23	7.60	7.08	6.65
800	11.50	10.32	9.41	8.68	8.09	7.60
900	12.93	11.61	10.58	9.77	9.10	8.55
1000	14.37	12.90	11.76	10.85	10.11	9.50
2000	28.74	25.80	23.52	21.71	20.23	19.00
3000	43.11	38.70	35.28	32.56	30.34	28.51
4000	57.48	51.60	47.04	43.41	40.46	38.01
5000	71.85	64.50	58.80	54.26	50.57	47.51
6000	86.22	77.40	70.56	65.12	60.68	57.01
7000	100.59	90.30	82.32	75.97	70.80	66.51
8000	114.96	103.19	94.08	86.82	80.91	76.01
9000	129.33	116.09	105.84	97.67	91.03	85.52
10000	143.70	128.99	117.60	108.53	101.14	95.02
11000	158.07	141.89	129.36	119.38	111.25	104.52
12000	172.44	154.79	141.12	130.23	121.37	114.02
13000	186.81	167.69	152.88	141.08	131.48	123.52
14000	201.18	180.59	164.64	151.94	141.60	133.02
15000	215.55	193.49	176.40	162.79	151.71	142.53
16000	229.92	206.39	188.16	173.64	161.82	152.03
17000	244.29	219.29	199.92	184.49	171.94	161.53
18000	258.66	232.19	211.68	195.35	182.05	171.03
19000	273.03	245.09	223.44	206.20	192.16	180.53
20000	287.40	257.99	235.20	217.05	202.28	190.03
21000	301.77	270.89	246.96	227.91	212.39	199.54
22000	316.14	283.78	258.72	238.76	222.51	209.04
23000	330.51	296.68	270.48	249.61	232.62	218.54
24000	344.88	309.58	282.24	260.46	242.73	228.04
25000	359.25	322.48	294.00	271.32	252.85	237.54
30000	431.10	386.98	352.80	325.58	303.42	285.05
35000	502.95	451.48	411.60	379.84	353.99	332.56
40000	574.80	515.97	470.40	434.10	404.56	380.07
45000	646.65	580.47	529.20	488.37	455.13	427.58
50000	718.50	644.96	588.00	542.63	505.70	475.09
55000	790.35	709.46	646.80	596.89	556.27	522.59
60000	862.20	773.96	705.60	651.16	606.83	570.10
65000	934.05	838.45	764.40	705.42	657.40	617.61
70000	1005.90	902.95	823.20	759.68	707.97	665.12
75000	1077.75	967.45	882.00	813.95	758.54	712.63
80000	1149.60	1031.94	940.80	868.21	809.11	760.14
85000	1221.45	1096.44	999.60	922.47	859.68	807.64
90000	1293.30	1160.94	1058.40	976.73	910.25	855.15
95000	1365.15	1225.43	1117.20	1031.00	960.82	902.66
100000	1437.00	1289.93	1176.00	1085.26	1011.39	950.17
200000	2874.00	2579.86	2351.99	2170.52	2022.78	1900.34
300000	4311.00	3869.79	3527.99	3255.78	3034.17	2850.51
400000	5748.00	5159.72	4703.99	4341.04	4045.56	3800.68
500000	7185.00	6449.64	5879.98	5426.30	5056.95	4750.85

5 1/2%

MONTHLY PAYMENT

Necessary to amortize a loan

TERM AMOUNT	13 YEARS	14 YEARS	15 YEARS	16 YEARS	17 YEARS	18 YEARS
500	4.49	4.27	4.09	3.92	3.78	3.65
600	5.39	5.13	4.90	4.71	4.53	4.38
700	6.29	5.98	5.72	5.49	5.29	5.11
800	7.19	6.84	6.54	6.27	6.04	5.84
900	8.09	7.69	7.35	7.06	6.80	6.57
1000	8.99	8.55	8.17	7.84	7.56	7.30
2000	17.97	17.10	16.34	15.69	15.11	14.61
3000	26.96	25.64	24.51	23.53	22.67	21.91
4000	35.95	34.19	32.68	31.37	30.22	29.21
5000	44.93	42.74	40.85	39.22	37.78	36.52
6000	53.92	51.29	49.02	47.06	45.34	43.82
7000	62.91	59.84	57.20	54.90	52.89	51.12
8000	71.89	68.39	65.37	62.74	60.45	58.43
9000	80.88	76.93	73.54	70.59	68.00	65.73
10000	89.87	85.48	81.71	78.43	75.56	73.03
11000	98.85	94.03	89.88	86.27	83.12	80.33
12000	107.84	102.58	98.05	94.12	90.67	87.64
13000	116.83	111.13	106.22	101.96	98.23	94.94
14000	125.82	119.68	114.39	109.80	105.79	102.24
15000	134.80	128.22	122.56	117.65	113.64	109.55
16000	143.79	136.77	130.73	125.49	120.90	116.85
17000	152.78	145.32	138.90	133.33	128.45	124.15
18000	161.76	153.87	147.08	141.17	136.01	131.46
19000	170.75	162.42	155.25	149.02	143.57	138.76
20000	179.74	170.97	163.42	156.86	151.12	146.06
21000	188.72	179.51	171.59	164.70	158.68	153.37
22000	197.71	188.06	179.76	172.55	166.23	160.67
23000	206.70	196.61	187.93	180.39	173.79	167.97
24000	215.68	205.16	196.10	188.23	181.35	175.28
25000	224.67	213.71	204.27	196.08	188.90	182.58
30000	269.60	256.45	245.13	235.29	226.68	219.09
35000	314.54	299.19	285.98	274.51	264.46	255.61
40000	359.47	341.93	326.83	313.72	302.24	292.13
45000	404.40	384.67	367.69	352.94	340.02	328.64
50000	449.34	427.41	408.54	392.15	377.80	365.16
55000	494.27	470.15	449.40	431.37	415.58	401.67
60000	539.21	512.89	490.25	470.58	453.37	438.19
65000	584.14	555.64	531.10	509.80	491.15	474.71
70000	629.07	598.38	571.96	549.01	528.93	511.22
75000	674.01	641.12	612.81	588.23	566.71	547.74
80000	718.94	683.86	653.67	627.44	604.49	584.25
85000	763.88	726.60	694.52	666.66	642.27	620.77
90000	808.81	769.34	735.37	705.87	680.05	657.28
95000	853.74	812.08	776.23	745.09	717.83	693.80
100000	898.68	854.82	817.08	784.30	755.61	730.32
200000	1797.35	1709.65	1634.16	1568.60	1511.22	1460.63
300000	2696.03	2564.47	2451.25	2352.91	2266.82	2190.94
400000	3594.71	3419.30	3268.33	3137.21	3022.43	2921.26
500000	4493.38	4274.12	4085.41	3921.51	3778.04	3651.57

MONTHLY PAYMENT

Necessary to amortize a loan

5 1/2%

TERM / AMOUNT	19 YEARS	20 YEARS	25 YEARS	30 YEARS	35 YEARS	40 YEARS
500	3.54	3.44	3.07	2.84	2.69	2.58
600	4.25	4.13	3.68	3.41	3.22	3.09
700	4.96	4.82	4.30	4.97	3.76	3.61
800	5.66	5.50	4.91	4.54	4.30	4.13
900	6.37	6.19	5.53	5.11	4.83	4.64
1000	7.08	6.88	6.14	5.68	5.37	5.16
2000	14.16	13.76	12.28	11.36	10.74	10.32
3000	21.24	20.64	18.42	17.03	16.11	15.47
4000	28.32	27.52	24.56	22.71	21.48	20.63
5000	35.39	34.39	30.70	28.39	26.85	25.79
6000	42.47	41.27	36.85	34.07	32.22	30.95
7000	49.55	48.15	42.99	39.75	37.59	36.10
8000	56.63	55.03	49.13	45.42	42.96	41.26
9000	63.71	61.91	55.27	51.10	48.33	46.42
10000	70.79	68.79	61.41	56.78	53.70	51.58
11000	77.87	75.67	67.55	62.46	59.07	56.73
12000	84.95	82.55	73.69	68.13	64.44	61.89
13000	92.03	89.43	79.83	73.81	69.81	67.05
14000	99.10	96.30	85.97	79.49	75.18	72.21
15000	106.18	103.18	92.11	85.17	80.55	77.37
16000	113.26	110.06	98.25	90.85	85.92	82.52
17000	120.34	116.94	104.39	96.52	91.29	87.68
18000	127.42	123.82	110.54	102.20	96.66	92.84
19000	134.50	130.70	116.68	107.88	102.03	98.00
20000	141.58	137.58	122.82	113.56	107.40	103.15
21000	148.66	144.46	128.96	119.24	112.77	108.31
22000	155.74	151.34	135.10	124.91	118.14	113.47
23000	162.81	158.21	141.24	130.59	123.51	118.63
24000	169.89	165.09	147.38	136.27	128.88	123.78
25000	176.97	171.97	153.52	141.95	134.25	128.94
30000	212.37	206.37	184.23	170.34	161.10	154.73
35000	247.76	240.76	214.93	198.73	187.96	180.52
40000	283.15	275.15	245.63	227.11	214.81	206.31
45000	318.55	309.55	276.34	255.50	241.66	232.10
50000	353.94	343.94	307.04	283.89	268.51	257.88
55000	389.34	378.34	337.75	312.28	295.36	283.67
60000	424.73	412.73	368.45	340.67	322.21	309.46
65000	460.13	447.13	399.15	369.06	349.06	335.25
70000	495.52	481.52	429.86	397.45	375.91	361.04
75000	530.91	515.92	460.56	425.84	402.76	386.83
80000	566.31	550.31	491.27	454.23	429.61	412.62
85000	601.70	584.70	521.97	482.62	456.46	438.40
90000	637.10	619.10	552.68	511.01	483.31	464.19
95000	672.49	653.49	583.38	539.40	510.16	489.98
100000	707.89	687.89	614.08	567.79	537.01	515.77
200000	1415.77	1375.77	1228.17	1135.57	1074.03	1031.54
300000	2123.65	2063.66	1842.25	1703.36	1611.04	1547.30
400000	2831.54	2751.54	2456.33	2271.14	2148.05	2063.07
500000	3539.42	3439.43	3070.42	2838.93	2685.07	2578.84

6%

MONTHLY PAYMENT

Necessary to amortize a loan

TERM / AMOUNT	1 YEAR	2 YEARS	3 YEARS	4 YEARS	5 YEARS	6 YEARS
500	43.03	22.16	15.21	11.74	9.67	8.29
600	51.64	26.59	18.25	14.09	11.60	9.94
700	60.25	31.02	21.30	16.44	13.53	11.60
800	68.85	35.46	24.34	18.79	15.47	13.26
900	77.46	39.89	27.38	21.14	17.40	14.92
1000	86.07	44.32	30.42	23.49	19.33	16.57
2000	172.13	88.64	60.84	46.97	38.67	33.15
3000	258.20	132.96	91.27	70.46	58.00	49.72
4000	344.27	177.28	121.69	93.94	77.33	66.29
5000	430.33	221.60	152.11	117.43	96.66	82.86
6000	516.40	265.92	182.53	140.91	116.00	99.44
7000	602.46	310.24	212.95	164.40	135.33	116.01
8000	688.53	354.56	243.38	187.88	154.66	132.58
9000	774.60	398.89	273.80	211.37	174.00	149.16
10000	860.66	443.21	304.22	234.85	193.33	165.73
11000	946.73	487.53	334.64	258.34	212.66	182.30
12000	1032.80	531.85	365.06	281.82	231.99	198.88
13000	1118.86	576.17	395.49	305.31	251.33	215.45
14000	1204.93	620.49	425.91	328.79	270.66	232.02
15000	1290.99	664.81	456.33	352.28	289.99	248.59
16000	1377.06	709.13	486.75	375.76	309.33	265.17
17000	1463.13	753.45	517.17	399.25	328.66	281.74
18000	1549.19	797.77	547.60	422.73	347.99	298.31
19000	1635.26	842.09	578.02	446.22	367.32	314.89
20000	1721.33	886.41	608.44	469.70	386.66	331.46
21000	1807.39	930.73	638.86	493.19	405.99	348.03
22000	1893.46	975.05	669.28	516.67	425.32	364.60
23000	1979.53	1019.37	699.70	540.16	444.65	381.18
24000	2065.59	1063.69	730.13	563.64	463.99	397.75
25000	2151.66	1108.01	760.55	587.13	483.32	414.32
30000	2581.99	1329.62	912.66	704.55	579.98	497.19
35000	3012.32	1551.22	1064.77	821.98	676.65	580.05
40000	3442.65	1772.82	1216.88	939.40	773.31	662.92
45000	3872.98	1994.42	1368.99	1056.83	869.98	745.78
50000	4303.32	2216.03	1521.10	1174.25	966.64	828.64
55000	4733.65	2437.63	1673.21	1291.68	1063.30	911.51
60000	5163.98	2659.23	1825.32	1409.10	1159.97	994.37
65000	5594.31	2880.84	1977.42	1526.53	1256.63	1077.24
70000	6024.64	3102.44	2129.53	1643.95	1353.29	1160.10
75000	6454.97	3324.04	2281.64	1761.38	1449.96	1242.97
80000	6885.31	3545.64	2433.75	1878.80	1546.62	1325.83
85000	7315.64	3767.25	2585.86	1996.23	1643.29	1408.69
90000	7745.97	3988.85	2737.97	2113.65	1739.95	1491.56
95000	8176.30	4210.45	2890.08	2231.08	1836.61	1574.42
100000	8606.63	4432.05	3042.19	2348.50	1933.28	1657.29
200000	17213.30	8864.11	6084.38	4697.00	3866.56	3314.58
300000	25819.90	13296.20	9126.58	7045.50	5799.84	4971.86
400000	34426.50	17728.20	12168.80	9394.00	7733.11	6629.15
500000	43033.20	22160.30	15211.00	11742.50	9666.39	8286.44

MONTHLY PAYMENT

Necessary to amortize a loan

6%

TERM / AMOUNT	7 YEARS	8 YEARS	9 YEARS	10 YEARS	11 YEARS	12 YEARS
500	7.30	6.57	6.00	5.55	5.18	4.88
600	8.77	7.88	7.20	6.66	6.22	5.86
700	10.23	9.20	8.40	7.77	7.26	6.83
800	11.69	10.51	9.60	8.88	8.29	7.81
900	13.15	11.83	10.81	9.99	9.33	8.78
1000	14.61	13.14	12.01	11.10	10.37	9.76
2000	29.22	26.28	24.01	22.20	20.73	19.52
3000	43.83	39.42	36.02	33.31	31.10	29.28
4000	58.43	52.57	48.02	44.41	41.47	39.03
5000	73.04	65.71	60.03	55.51	51.84	48.79
6000	87.65	78.85	72.03	66.61	62.20	58.55
7000	102.26	91.99	84.04	77.71	72.57	68.31
8000	116.87	105.13	96.05	88.82	82.94	78.07
9000	131.48	118.27	108.05	99.92	93.30	87.83
10000	146.09	131.41	120.06	111.02	103.67	97.59
11000	160.69	144.56	132.06	122.12	114.04	107.34
12000	175.30	157.70	144.07	133.23	124.40	117.10
13000	189.91	170.84	156.08	144.33	134.77	126.86
14000	204.52	183.98	168.08	155.43	145.14	136.62
15000	219.13	197.12	180.09	166.53	155.51	146.38
16000	233.74	210.26	192.09	177.63	165.87	156.14
17000	248.35	223.40	204.10	188.74	176.24	165.89
18000	262.95	236.55	216.10	199.84	186.61	175.65
19000	277.56	249.69	228.11	210.94	196.97	185.41
20000	292.17	262.83	240.12	222.04	207.34	195.17
21000	306.78	275.97	252.12	233.14	217.71	204.93
22000	321.39	289.11	264.13	244.25	228.08	214.69
23000	336.00	302.25	276.13	255.35	238.44	224.45
24000	350.61	315.39	288.14	266.45	248.81	234.20
25000	365.21	328.54	300.14	277.55	259.18	243.96
30000	438.26	394.24	360.17	333.06	311.01	292.76
35000	511.30	459.95	420.20	388.57	362.85	341.55
40000	584.34	525.66	480.23	444.08	414.68	390.34
45000	657.39	591.36	540.26	499.59	466.52	439.13
50000	730.43	657.07	600.29	555.10	518.35	487.93
55000	803.47	722.78	660.32	610.61	570.19	536.72
60000	876.51	788.49	720.35	666.12	622.02	585.51
65000	949.56	854.19	780.37	721.63	673.86	634.30
70000	1022.60	919.90	840.40	777.14	725.69	683.10
75000	1095.64	985.61	900.43	832.65	777.53	731.89
80000	1168.68	1051.31	960.46	888.16	829.36	780.68
85000	1241.73	1117.02	1020.49	943.67	881.20	829.47
90000	1314.77	1182.73	1080.52	999.18	933.03	878.27
95000	1387.81	1248.44	1140.55	1054.69	984.87	927.06
100000	1460.85	1314.14	1200.57	1110.20	1036.70	975.85
200000	2921.71	2628.28	2401.15	2220.41	2073.41	1951.70
300000	4382.56	3942.43	3601.72	3330.61	3110.11	2927.55
400000	5843.42	5256.57	4802.30	4440.82	4146.81	3903.40
500000	7304.27	6570.71	6002.87	5551.02	5183.51	4879.25

6% MONTHLY PAYMENT

Necessary to amortize a loan

TERM / AMOUNT	13 YEARS	14 YEARS	15 YEARS	16 YEARS	17 YEARS	18 YEARS
500	4.62	4.41	4.22	4.06	3.92	3.79
600	5.55	5.29	5.06	4.87	4.70	4.55
700	6.47	6.17	5.91	5.68	5.48	5.31
800	7.40	7.05	6.75	6.49	6.26	6.07
900	8.32	7.93	7.59	7.30	7.05	6.82
1000	9.25	8.81	8.44	8.11	7.83	7.58
2000	18.49	17.62	16.88	16.23	15.66	15.16
3000	27.74	26.44	25.32	24.34	23.49	22.74
4000	36.99	35.25	33.75	32.46	31.32	30.33
5000	46.24	44.06	42.19	40.57	39.16	37.91
6000	55.48	52.87	50.63	48.69	46.99	45.49
7000	64.73	61.69	59.07	56.80	54.82	53.07
8000	73.98	70.50	67.51	64.92	62.65	60.65
9000	83.23	79.31	75.95	73.03	70.48	68.23
10000	92.47	88.12	84.39	81.14	78.31	75.82
11000	101.72	96.94	92.82	89.26	86.14	83.40
12000	110.97	105.75	101.26	97.37	93.97	90.98
13000	120.21	114.56	109.70	105.49	101.80	98.56
14000	129.46	123.37	118.14	113.60	109.63	106.14
15000	138.71	132.19	126.58	121.72	117.47	113.72
16000	147.96	141.00	135.02	129.83	125.30	121.31
17000	157.20	149.81	143.46	137.94	133.13	128.89
18000	166.45	158.62	151.89	146.06	140.96	136.47
19000	175.70	167.44	160.33	154.17	148.79	144.05
20000	184.95	176.25	168.77	162.29	156.62	151.63
21000	194.19	185.06	177.21	170.40	164.45	159.21
22000	203.44	193.87	185.65	178.52	172.28	166.80
23000	212.69	202.68	194.09	186.63	180.11	174.38
24000	221.93	211.50	202.53	194.75	187.94	181.96
25000	231.18	220.31	210.96	202.86	195.78	189.54
30000	277.42	264.37	253.16	243.43	234.93	227.45
35000	323.65	308.43	295.35	284.00	274.09	265.36
40000	369.89	352.49	337.54	324.58	313.24	303.27
45000	416.13	396.56	379.74	365.15	352.40	341.17
50000	462.36	440.62	421.93	405.72	391.55	379.08
55000	508.60	484.68	464.12	446.29	430.71	416.99
60000	554.83	528.74	506.31	486.86	469.86	454.90
65000	601.07	572.80	548.51	527.43	509.02	492.81
70000	647.31	616.87	590.70	568.01	548.17	530.71
75000	693.54	660.93	632.89	608.58	587.33	568.62
80000	739.78	704.99	675.09	649.15	626.48	606.53
85000	786.01	749.05	717.28	689.72	665.64	644.44
90000	832.25	793.11	759.47	730.29	704.79	682.35
95000	878.49	837.17	801.66	770.87	743.95	720.25
100000	924.72	881.24	843.86	811.44	783.10	758.16
200000	1849.45	1762.47	1687.71	1622.88	1566.20	1516.32
300000	2774.17	2643.71	2531.57	2434.31	2349.30	2274.49
400000	3698.89	3524.94	3375.43	3245.75	3132.40	3032.65
500000	4623.61	4406.18	4219.28	4057.19	3915.50	3790.81

MONTHLY PAYMENT

Necessary to amortize a loan

6%

TERM / AMOUNT	19 YEARS	20 YEARS	25 YEARS	30 YEARS	35 YEARS	40 YEARS
500	3.68	3.58	3.22	3.00	2.85	2.75
600	4.42	4.30	3.87	3.60	3.42	3.30
700	5.15	5.02	4.51	4.20	3.99	3.85
800	5.89	5.73	5.15	4.80	4.56	4.40
900	6.62	6.45	5.80	5.40	5.13	4.95
1000	7.36	7.16	6.44	6.00	5.70	5.50
2000	14.72	14.33	12.89	11.99	11.40	11.00
3000	22.08	21.49	19.33	17.99	17.11	16.51
4000	29.44	28.66	25.77	23.98	22.81	22.01
5000	36.80	35.82	32.22	29.98	28.51	27.51
6000	44.17	42.99	38.66	35.97	34.21	33.01
7000	51.53	50.15	45.10	41.97	39.91	38.52
8000	58.89	57.31	51.54	47.96	45.62	44.02
9000	66.25	64.48	57.99	53.96	51.32	49.52
10000	73.61	71.64	64.43	59.96	57.02	55.02
11000	80.97	78.81	70.87	65.95	62.72	60.52
12000	88.33	85.97	77.32	71.95	68.42	66.03
13000	95.69	93.14	83.76	77.94	74.12	71.53
14000	103.05	100.30	90.20	83.94	79.83	77.03
15000	110.41	107.47	96.65	89.93	85.53	82.53
16000	117.77	114.63	103.09	95.93	91.23	88.03
17000	125.13	121.79	109.53	101.92	96.93	93.54
18000	132.50	128.96	115.97	107.92	102.63	99.04
19000	139.86	136.12	122.42	113.92	108.34	104.54
20000	147.22	143.29	128.86	119.91	114.04	110.04
21000	154.58	150.45	135.30	125.91	119.74	115.55
22000	161.94	157.62	141.75	131.90	125.44	121.05
23000	169.30	164.78	148.19	137.90	131.14	126.55
24000	176.66	171.94	154.63	143.89	136.85	132.05
25000	184.02	179.11	161.08	149.89	142.55	137.55
30000	220.83	214.93	193.29	179.87	171.06	165.06
35000	257.63	250.75	225.51	209.84	199.57	192.58
40000	294.43	286.57	257.72	239.82	228.08	220.09
45000	331.24	322.39	289.94	269.80	256.59	247.60
50000	368.04	358.22	322.15	299.78	285.10	275.11
55000	404.85	394.04	354.37	329.75	313.60	302.62
60000	441.65	429.86	386.58	359.73	342.11	330.13
65000	478.45	465.68	418.80	389.71	370.62	357.64
70000	515.26	501.50	451.01	419.69	399.13	385.15
75000	552.06	537.32	483.23	449.66	427.64	412.66
80000	588.87	573.15	515.44	479.64	456.15	440.17
85000	625.67	608.97	547.66	509.62	484.66	467.68
90000	662.47	644.79	579.87	539.60	513.17	495.19
95000	699.28	680.61	612.09	569.57	541.68	522.70
100000	736.08	716.43	644.30	599.55	570.19	550.21
200000	1472.17	1432.86	1288.60	1199.10	1140.38	1100.43
300000	2208.25	2149.29	1932.90	1798.65	1710.57	1650.64
400000	2944.33	2865.72	2577.21	2398.20	2280.76	2200.86
500000	3680.41	3582.15	3221.51	2997.75	2850.95	2751.07

6 1/2%

MONTHLY PAYMENT

Necessary to amortize a loan

TERM AMOUNT	1 YEAR	2 YEARS	3 YEARS	4 YEARS	5 YEARS	6 YEARS
500	43.15	22.27	15.32	11.86	9.78	8.41
600	51.78	26.73	18.39	14.23	11.74	10.09
700	60.41	31.18	21.45	16.60	13.70	11.77
800	69.04	35.64	24.52	18.97	15.65	13.45
900	77.67	40.09	27.58	21.34	17.61	15.13
1000	86.30	44.55	30.65	23.72	19.57	16.81
2000	172.59	89.09	61.30	47.43	39.13	33.62
3000	258.89	133.64	91.95	71.15	58.70	50.43
4000	345.19	178.19	122.60	94.86	78.27	67.24
5000	431.49	222.73	153.25	118.58	97.83	84.05
6000	517.78	267.28	183.90	142.29	117.40	100.86
7000	604.08	311.83	214.55	166.01	136.96	117.67
8000	690.38	356.37	245.19	189.72	156.53	134.48
9000	776.67	400.92	275.84	213.44	176.10	151.29
10000	862.97	445.47	306.49	237.15	195.66	168.10
11000	949.27	490.01	337.14	260.87	215.23	184.91
12000	1035.56	534.56	367.79	284.58	234.80	201.72
13000	1121.86	579.11	398.44	308.30	254.36	218.53
14000	1208.16	623.65	429.09	332.01	273.93	235.34
15000	1294.46	668.20	459.74	355.73	293.49	252.15
16000	1380.75	712.75	490.39	379.44	313.06	268.96
17000	1467.05	757.29	521.04	403.16	332.63	285.77
18000	1553.35	801.84	551.69	426.87	352.19	302.58
19000	1639.64	846.39	582.34	450.59	371.76	319.39
20000	1725.94	890.93	612.99	474.30	391.33	336.20
21000	1812.24	935.48	643.63	498.02	410.89	353.01
22000	1898.54	980.03	674.28	521.73	430.46	369.82
23000	1984.83	1024.57	704.93	545.45	450.03	386.63
24000	2071.13	1069.12	735.58	569.16	469.59	403.44
25000	2157.43	1113.66	766.23	592.88	489.16	420.25
30000	2588.91	1336.40	919.48	711.45	586.99	504.30
35000	3020.40	1559.13	1072.72	830.03	684.82	588.35
40000	3451.88	1781.86	1225.97	948.61	782.65	672.40
45000	3883.37	2004.60	1379.22	1067.18	880.48	756.45
50000	4314.85	2227.33	1532.46	1185.76	978.31	840.50
55000	4746.34	2450.06	1685.71	1304.33	1076.15	924.55
60000	5177.82	2672.79	1838.95	1422.91	1173.98	1008.60
65000	5609.31	2895.53	1992.20	1541.48	1271.81	1092.65
70000	6040.79	3118.26	2145.45	1660.06	1369.64	1176.70
75000	6472.28	3340.99	2298.69	1778.63	1467.47	1260.75
80000	6903.77	3563.73	2451.94	1897.21	1565.30	1344.80
85000	7335.25	3786.46	2605.18	2015.79	1663.13	1428.85
90000	7766.74	4009.19	2758.43	2134.36	1760.97	1512.90
95000	8198.22	4231.93	2911.68	2252.94	1858.80	1596.95
100000	8629.71	4454.66	3064.92	2371.51	1956.63	1681.00
200000	17259.40	8909.32	6129.85	4743.02	3913.26	3362.01
300000	25889.10	13364.00	9194.77	7114.54	5869.89	5043.01
400000	34518.80	17818.60	12259.70	9486.05	7826.52	6724.02
500000	43148.50	22273.30	15324.60	11857.60	9783.14	8405.02

MONTHLY PAYMENT

Necessary to amortize a loan

6 1/2%

TERM / AMOUNT	7 YEARS	8 YEARS	9 YEARS	10 YEARS	11 YEARS	12 YEARS
500	7.42	6.69	6.13	5.68	5.31	5.01
600	8.91	8.03	7.35	6.81	6.37	6.01
700	10.39	9.37	8.58	7.95	7.44	7.01
800	11.88	10.71	9.80	9.08	8.50	8.02
900	13.36	12.05	11.03	10.22	9.56	9.02
1000	14.85	13.39	12.25	11.35	10.62	10.02
2000	29.70	26.77	24.51	22.71	21.25	20.04
3000	44.55	40.16	36.76	34.06	31.87	30.06
4000	59.40	53.55	49.02	45.42	42.50	40.08
5000	74.25	66.93	61.27	56.77	53.12	50.10
6000	89.10	80.32	73.53	68.13	63.74	60.12
7000	103.95	93.70	85.78	79.48	74.37	70.13
8000	118.80	107.09	98.04	90.84	84.99	80.15
9000	133.65	120.48	110.29	102.19	95.61	90.17
10000	148.50	133.86	122.55	113.55	106.24	100.19
11000	163.35	147.25	134.80	124.90	116.86	110.21
12000	178.19	160.64	147.06	136.26	127.49	120.23
13000	193.04	174.02	159.31	147.61	138.11	130.25
14000	207.89	187.41	171.56	158.97	148.73	140.27
15000	222.74	200.80	183.82	170.32	159.36	150.29
16000	237.59	214.18	196.07	181.68	169.98	160.31
17000	252.44	227.57	208.33	193.03	180.61	170.33
18000	267.29	240.95	220.58	204.39	191.23	180.35
19000	282.14	254.34	232.84	215.74	201.85	190.37
20000	296.99	267.73	245.09	227.10	212.48	200.39
21000	311.84	281.11	257.35	238.45	223.10	210.41
22000	326.69	294.50	269.60	249.81	233.72	220.42
23000	341.54	307.89	281.86	261.16	244.35	230.44
24000	356.39	321.27	294.11	272.52	254.97	240.46
25000	371.24	334.66	306.37	283.87	265.60	250.48
30000	445.49	401.59	367.64	340.65	318.72	300.58
35000	519.73	468.52	428.91	397.42	371.83	350.67
40000	593.98	535.45	490.18	454.20	424.95	400.77
45000	668.23	602.38	551.46	510.97	478.07	450.87
50000	742.48	669.32	612.73	567.74	531.19	500.96
55000	816.72	736.25	674.00	624.52	584.31	551.06
60000	890.97	803.18	735.28	681.29	637.43	601.16
65000	965.22	870.11	796.55	738.07	690.55	651.25
70000	1039.47	937.04	857.82	794.84	743.67	701.35
75000	1113.71	1003.97	919.09	851.62	796.79	751.45
80000	1187.96	1070.91	980.37	908.39	849.91	801.54
85000	1262.21	1137.84	1041.64	965.16	903.03	851.64
90000	1336.46	1204.77	1102.91	1021.94	956.14	901.73
95000	1410.71	1271.70	1164.19	1078.71	1009.26	951.83
100000	1484.95	1338.63	1225.46	1135.49	1062.38	1001.93
200000	2969.91	2677.26	2450.92	2270.97	2124.77	2003.85
300000	4454.86	4015.89	3676.38	3406.46	3187.15	3005.78
400000	5939.81	5354.53	4901.84	4541.95	4249.53	4007.71
500000	7424.77	6693.16	6127.30	5677.43	5311.91	5009.63

6 1/2% MONTHLY PAYMENT

Necessary to amortize a loan

TERM / AMOUNT	13 YEARS	14 YEARS	15 YEARS	16 YEARS	17 YEARS	18 YEARS
500	4.76	4.54	4.36	4.20	4.06	3.93
600	5.71	5.45	5.23	5.03	4.87	4.72
700	6.66	6.36	6.10	5.87	5.68	5.51
800	7.61	7.26	6.97	6.71	6.49	6.29
900	8.56	8.17	7.84	7.55	7.30	7.08
1000	9.51	9.08	8.71	8.39	8.11	7.87
2000	19.02	18.16	17.42	16.78	16.22	15.73
3000	28.54	27.24	26.13	25.17	24.33	23.60
4000	38.05	36.32	34.84	33.56	32.45	31.46
5000	47.56	45.41	43.56	41.95	40.56	39.33
6000	57.07	54.49	52.27	50.34	48.67	47.19
7000	66.58	63.57	60.98	58.74	56.78	55.06
8000	76.10	72.65	69.69	67.13	64.89	62.93
9000	85.61	81.73	78.40	75.52	73.00	70.79
10000	95.12	90.81	87.11	83.91	81.11	78.66
11000	104.63	99.89	95.82	92.30	89.22	86.52
12000	114.14	108.97	104.53	100.69	97.34	94.39
13000	123.66	118.05	113.24	109.08	105.45	102.25
14000	133.17	127.13	121.96	117.47	113.56	110.12
15000	142.68	136.22	130.67	125.86	121.67	117.99
16000	152.19	145.30	139.38	134.25	129.78	125.85
17000	161.70	154.38	148.09	142.64	137.89	133.72
18000	171.22	163.46	156.80	151.03	146.00	141.58
19000	180.73	172.54	165.51	159.43	154.11	149.45
20000	190.24	181.62	174.22	167.82	162.23	157.31
21000	199.75	190.70	182.93	176.21	170.34	165.18
22000	209.26	199.78	191.65	184.60	178.45	173.04
23000	218.78	208.86	200.36	192.99	186.56	180.91
24000	228.29	217.94	209.07	201.38	194.67	188.78
25000	237.80	227.03	217.78	209.77	202.78	196.64
30000	285.36	272.43	261.33	251.72	243.34	235.97
35000	332.92	317.84	304.89	293.68	283.89	275.30
40000	380.48	363.24	348.45	335.63	324.45	314.63
45000	428.04	408.65	392.00	377.59	365.01	353.95
50000	475.60	454.05	435.56	419.54	405.56	393.28
55000	523.16	499.46	479.11	461.49	446.12	432.61
60000	570.72	544.86	522.67	503.45	486.68	471.94
65000	618.28	590.27	566.22	545.40	527.23	511.27
70000	665.84	635.67	609.78	587.36	567.79	550.60
75000	713.40	681.08	653.33	629.31	608.34	589.92
80000	760.96	726.48	696.89	671.26	648.90	629.25
85000	808.52	771.89	740.45	713.22	689.46	668.58
90000	856.08	817.29	784.00	755.17	730.01	707.91
95000	903.64	862.70	827.56	797.13	770.57	747.24
100000	951.20	908.10	871.11	839.08	811.13	786.57
200000	1902.39	1816.20	1742.22	1678.16	1622.25	1573.13
300000	2853.59	2724.30	2613.33	2517.24	2433.37	2359.69
400000	3804.78	3632.40	3484.45	3356.32	3244.50	3146.26
500000	4755.98	4540.50	4355.56	4195.40	4055.62	3932.82

MONTHLY PAYMENT

Necessary to amortize a loan

6 1/2%

TERM / AMOUNT	19 YEARS	20 YEARS	25 YEARS	30 YEARS	35 YEARS	40 YEARS
500	3.82	3.73	3.38	3.16	3.02	2.93
600	4.59	4.47	4.05	3.79	3.62	3.51
700	5.35	5.22	4.73	4.42	4.23	4.10
800	6.12	5.96	5.40	5.06	4.83	4.68
900	6.88	6.71	6.08	5.69	5.44	5.27
1000	7.65	7.46	6.75	6.32	6.04	5.85
2000	15.30	14.91	13.50	12.64	12.08	11.71
3000	22.95	22.37	20.26	18.96	18.12	17.56
4000	30.59	29.82	27.01	25.28	24.17	23.42
5000	38.24	37.28	33.76	31.60	30.21	29.27
6000	45.89	44.73	40.51	37.92	36.25	35.13
7000	53.54	52.19	47.26	44.24	42.29	40.98
8000	61.19	59.65	54.02	50.57	48.33	46.84
9000	68.84	67.10	60.77	56.89	54.37	52.69
10000	76.49	74.56	67.52	63.21	60.42	58.55
11000	84.13	82.01	74.27	69.53	66.46	64.40
12000	91.78	89.47	81.03	75.85	72.50	70.25
13000	99.43	96.92	87.78	82.17	78.54	76.11
14000	107.08	104.38	94.53	88.49	84.58	81.96
15000	114.73	111.84	101.28	94.81	90.62	87.82
16000	122.38	119.29	108.03	101.13	96.66	93.67
17000	130.03	126.75	114.79	107.45	102.71	99.53
18000	137.68	134.20	121.54	113.77	108.75	105.38
19000	145.32	141.66	128.29	120.09	114.79	111.24
20000	152.97	149.12	135.04	126.41	120.83	117.09
21000	160.62	156.57	141.79	132.73	126.87	122.95
22000	168.27	164.03	148.55	139.06	132.91	128.80
23000	175.92	171.48	155.30	145.38	138.96	134.66
24000	183.57	178.94	162.05	151.70	145.00	140.51
25000	191.22	186.39	168.80	158.02	151.04	146.36
30000	229.46	223.67	202.56	189.62	181.25	175.64
35000	267.70	260.95	236.32	221.22	211.45	204.91
40000	305.94	298.23	270.08	252.83	241.66	234.18
45000	344.19	335.51	303.84	284.43	271.87	263.46
50000	382.43	372.79	337.60	316.03	302.08	292.73
55000	420.67	410.07	371.36	347.64	332.29	322.00
60000	458.92	447.35	405.13	379.24	362.49	351.27
65000	497.16	484.62	438.89	410.85	392.70	380.55
70000	535.40	521.90	472.65	442.45	422.91	409.82
75000	573.64	559.18	506.41	474.05	453.12	439.09
80000	611.89	596.46	540.17	505.66	483.32	468.37
85000	650.13	633.74	573.93	537.26	513.53	497.64
90000	688.37	671.02	607.69	568.86	543.74	526.91
95000	726.62	708.30	641.45	600.47	573.95	556.18
100000	764.86	745.58	675.21	632.07	604.16	585.46
200000	1529.72	1491.15	1350.42	1264.14	1208.31	1170.91
300000	2294.58	2236.73	2025.62	1896.21	1812.46	1756.37
400000	3059.44	2982.30	2700.83	2528.28	2416.62	2341.83
500000	3824.30	3727.88	3376.04	3160.34	3020.77	2927.29

7% MONTHLY PAYMENT

Necessary to amortize a loan

TERM / AMOUNT	1 YEAR	2 YEARS	3 YEARS	4 YEARS	5 YEARS	6 YEARS
500	43.26	22.39	15.44	11.97	9.90	8.52
600	51.92	26.86	18.53	14.37	11.88	10.23
700	60.57	31.34	21.61	16.76	13.86	11.93
800	69.22	35.82	24.70	19.16	15.84	13.64
900	77.87	40.30	27.79	21.55	17.82	15.34
1000	86.53	44.77	30.88	23.95	19.80	17.05
2000	173.05	89.54	61.75	47.89	39.60	34.10
3000	259.58	134.32	92.63	71.84	59.40	51.15
4000	346.11	179.09	123.51	95.78	79.20	68.20
5000	432.63	223.86	154.39	119.73	99.01	85.24
6000	519.16	268.64	185.26	143.68	118.81	102.29
7000	605.69	313.41	216.14	167.62	138.61	119.34
8000	692.21	358.18	247.02	191.57	158.41	136.39
9000	778.74	402.95	277.89	215.52	178.21	153.44
10000	865.27	447.73	308.77	239.46	198.01	170.49
11000	951.79	492.50	339.65	263.41	217.81	187.54
12000	1038.32	537.27	370.52	287.35	237.61	204.59
13000	1124.84	582.04	401.40	311.30	257.42	221.64
14000	1211.37	626.81	432.28	335.25	277.22	238.69
15000	1297.90	671.59	463.16	359.19	297.02	255.73
16000	1384.42	716.36	494.03	383.14	316.82	272.78
17000	1470.95	761.13	524.91	407.09	336.62	289.83
18000	1557.48	805.90	555.79	431.03	356.42	306.88
19000	1644.00	850.68	586.66	454.98	376.22	323.93
20000	1730.53	895.45	617.54	478.92	396.02	340.98
21000	1817.06	940.22	648.42	502.87	415.82	358.03
22000	1903.58	984.99	679.29	526.82	435.63	375.08
23000	1990.11	1029.77	710.17	550.76	455.43	392.13
24000	2076.64	1074.54	741.05	574.71	475.23	409.18
25000	2163.16	1119.31	771.93	598.66	495.03	426.22
30000	2595.79	1343.17	926.31	718.39	594.03	511.47
35000	3028.43	1567.04	1080.70	838.12	693.04	596.71
40000	3461.06	1790.90	1235.08	957.85	792.05	681.96
45000	3893.69	2014.76	1389.47	1077.58	891.05	767.20
50000	4326.32	2238.62	1543.85	1197.31	990.06	852.45
55000	4758.96	2462.49	1698.24	1317.04	1089.06	937.69
60000	5191.59	2686.35	1852.62	1436.77	1188.07	1022.94
65000	5624.22	2910.21	2007.01	1556.50	1287.07	1108.18
70000	6056.85	3134.07	2161.39	1676.23	1386.08	1193.43
75000	6489.49	3357.93	2315.78	1795.96	1485.09	1278.67
80000	6922.12	3581.80	2470.16	1915.69	1584.09	1363.92
85000	7354.75	3805.66	2624.55	2035.43	1683.10	1449.16
90000	7787.38	4029.52	2778.93	2155.16	1782.10	1534.41
95000	8220.02	4253.38	2933.32	2274.89	1881.11	1619.65
100000	8652.65	4477.25	3087.70	2394.62	1980.11	1704.90
200000	17305.30	8954.49	6175.40	4789.24	3960.23	3409.79
300000	25957.90	13431.70	9263.10	7183.86	5940.34	5114.69
400000	34610.60	17909.00	12350.80	9578.47	7920.46	6819.59
500000	43263.20	22386.20	15438.50	11973.10	9900.57	8524.48

MONTHLY PAYMENT

Necessary to amortize a loan

7%

TERM / AMOUNT	7 YEARS	8 YEARS	9 YEARS	10 YEARS	11 YEARS	12 YEARS
500	7.55	6.82	6.25	5.81	5.44	5.14
600	9.06	8.18	7.50	6.97	6.53	6.17
700	10.56	9.54	8.75	8.13	7.62	7.20
800	12.07	10.91	10.01	9.29	8.71	8.23
900	13.58	12.27	11.26	10.45	9.80	9.26
1000	15.09	13.63	12.51	11.61	10.88	10.28
2000	30.19	27.27	25.01	23.22	21.77	20.57
3000	45.28	40.90	37.52	34.83	32.65	30.85
4000	60.37	54.53	50.03	46.44	43.54	41.14
5000	75.46	68.17	62.53	58.05	54.42	51.42
6000	90.56	81.80	75.04	69.66	65.30	61.70
7000	105.65	95.44	87.54	81.28	76.19	71.99
8000	120.74	109.07	100.05	92.89	87.07	82.27
9000	135.83	122.70	112.56	104.50	97.96	92.55
10000	150.93	136.34	125.06	116.11	108.84	102.84
11000	166.02	149.97	137.57	127.72	119.73	113.12
12000	181.11	163.60	150.08	139.33	130.61	123.41
13000	196.20	177.24	162.58	150.94	141.49	133.69
14000	211.30	190.87	175.09	162.55	152.38	143.97
15000	226.39	204.51	187.59	174.16	163.26	154.26
16000	241.48	218.14	200.10	185.77	174.15	164.54
17000	256.58	231.77	212.61	197.38	185.03	174.82
18000	271.67	245.41	225.11	209.00	195.91	185.11
19000	286.76	259.04	237.62	220.61	206.80	195.39
20000	301.85	272.67	250.13	232.22	217.68	205.68
21000	316.95	286.31	262.63	243.83	228.57	215.95
22000	332.04	299.94	275.14	255.44	239.45	226.24
23000	347.13	313.58	287.64	267.05	250.33	236.53
24000	362.22	327.21	300.15	278.66	261.22	246.81
25000	377.32	340.84	312.66	290.27	272.10	257.10
30000	452.78	409.01	375.19	348.33	326.52	308.51
35000	528.24	477.18	437.72	406.38	380.94	359.93
40000	603.71	545.35	500.25	464.43	435.36	411.35
45000	679.17	613.52	562.78	522.49	489.78	462.77
50000	754.63	681.68	625.31	580.54	544.20	514.19
55000	830.10	749.85	687.84	638.60	598.62	565.61
60000	905.56	818.02	750.38	696.65	653.05	617.03
65000	981.02	886.19	812.91	754.70	707.47	668.45
70000	1056.49	954.36	875.44	812.76	761.89	719.87
75000	1131.95	1022.53	937.97	870.81	816.31	771.28
80000	1207.41	1090.70	1000.50	928.87	870.73	822.70
85000	1282.87	1158.86	1063.03	986.92	925.15	874.12
90000	1358.34	1227.03	1125.56	1044.97	979.57	925.54
95000	1433.80	1295.20	1188.09	1103.03	1033.99	976.96
100000	1509.26	1363.37	1250.63	1161.08	1088.41	1028.38
200000	3018.53	2726.74	2501.25	2322.17	2176.82	2056.76
300000	4527.79	4090.11	3751.88	3483.25	3265.22	3085.14
400000	6037.06	5453.48	5002.50	4644.33	4353.63	4113.52
500000	7546.32	6816.84	6253.13	5805.41	5442.04	5141.90

7%

MONTHLY PAYMENT

Necessary to amortize a loan

TERM / AMOUNT	13 YEARS	14 YEARS	15 YEARS	16 YEARS	17 YEARS	18 YEARS
500	4.89	4.68	4.49	4.34	4.20	4.08
600	5.87	5.61	5.39	5.20	5.04	4.89
700	6.85	6.55	6.29	6.07	5.88	5.71
800	7.82	7.48	7.19	6.94	6.72	6.52
900	8.80	8.42	8.09	7.80	7.56	7.34
1000	9.78	9.35	8.99	8.67	8.40	8.16
2000	19.56	18.71	17.98	17.34	16.79	16.31
3000	29.34	28.06	26.96	26.02	25.19	24.47
4000	39.12	37.42	35.95	34.69	33.59	32.62
5000	48.90	46.77	44.94	43.36	41.98	40.78
6000	58.68	56.12	53.93	52.03	50.38	48.93
7000	68.47	65.48	62.92	60.70	58.78	57.09
8000	78.25	74.83	71.91	69.38	67.17	65.24
9000	88.03	84.19	80.89	78.05	75.57	73.40
10000	97.81	93.54	89.88	86.72	83.97	81.55
11000	107.59	102.89	98.87	95.39	92.36	89.71
12000	117.37	112.25	107.86	104.07	100.76	97.86
13000	127.15	121.60	116.85	112.74	109.16	106.02
14000	136.93	130.96	125.84	121.41	117.55	114.17
15000	146.71	140.31	134.82	130.08	125.95	122.33
16000	156.49	149.66	143.81	138.75	134.35	130.48
17000	166.27	159.02	152.80	147.43	142.74	138.64
18000	176.05	168.37	161.79	156.10	151.14	146.79
19000	185.83	177.73	170.78	164.77	159.54	154.95
20000	195.61	187.08	179.77	173.44	167.93	163.10
21000	205.40	196.43	188.75	182.11	176.33	171.26
22000	215.18	205.79	197.74	190.79	184.73	179.41
23000	224.96	215.14	206.73	199.46	193.12	187.57
24000	234.74	224.50	215.72	208.13	201.52	195.72
25000	244.52	233.85	224.71	216.80	209.92	203.88
30000	293.42	280.62	269.65	260.16	251.90	244.65
35000	342.33	327.39	314.59	303.52	293.88	285.43
40000	391.23	374.16	359.53	346.88	335.86	326.20
45000	440.13	420.93	404.47	390.24	377.85	366.98
50000	489.04	467.70	449.41	433.60	419.83	407.75
55000	537.94	514.47	494.36	476.96	461.81	448.53
60000	586.84	561.24	539.30	520.32	503.80	489.30
65000	635.75	608.01	584.24	563.68	545.78	530.08
70000	684.65	654.78	629.18	607.05	587.76	570.85
75000	733.55	701.55	674.12	650.41	629.75	611.63
80000	782.46	748.32	719.06	693.77	671.73	652.40
85000	831.36	795.09	764.00	737.13	713.71	693.18
90000	880.27	841.86	808.94	780.49	755.69	733.95
95000	929.17	888.63	853.89	823.85	797.68	774.73
100000	978.07	935.40	898.83	867.21	839.66	815.50
200000	1956.14	1870.80	1797.65	1734.41	1679.32	1631.00
300000	2934.22	2806.20	2696.48	2601.62	2518.98	2446.50
400000	3912.29	3741.60	3595.31	3468.83	3358.64	3262.00
500000	4890.36	4676.99	4494.13	4336.03	4198.30	4077.50

MONTHLY PAYMENT

Necessary to amortize a loan

7%

TERM / AMOUNT	19 YEARS	20 YEARS	25 YEARS	30 YEARS	35 YEARS	40 YEARS
500	3.97	3.88	3.53	3.33	3.19	3.11
600	4.77	4.65	4.24	3.99	3.83	3.73
700	5.56	5.43	4.95	4.66	4.47	4.35
800	6.35	6.20	5.65	5.32	5.11	4.97
900	7.15	6.98	6.36	5.99	5.75	5.59
1000	7.94	7.75	7.07	6.65	6.39	6.21
2000	15.88	15.51	14.14	13.31	12.78	12.43
3000	23.83	23.26	21.20	19.96	19.17	18.64
4000	31.77	31.01	28.27	26.61	25.55	24.86
5000	39.71	38.76	35.34	33.27	31.94	31.07
6000	47.65	46.52	42.41	39.92	38.33	37.29
7000	55.59	54.27	49.47	46.57	44.72	43.50
8000	63.54	62.02	56.54	53.22	51.11	49.71
9000	71.48	69.78	63.61	59.88	57.50	55.93
10000	79.42	77.53	70.68	66.53	63.89	62.14
11000	87.36	85.28	77.75	73.18	70.27	68.36
12000	95.30	93.04	84.81	79.84	76.66	74.57
13000	103.25	100.79	91.88	86.49	83.05	80.79
14000	111.19	108.54	98.95	93.14	89.44	87.00
15000	119.13	116.30	106.02	99.80	95.83	93.21
16000	127.07	124.05	113.08	106.45	102.22	99.43
17000	135.01	131.80	120.15	113.10	108.61	105.64
18000	142.95	139.55	127.22	119.75	114.99	111.86
19000	150.90	147.31	134.22	126.41	121.38	118.07
20000	158.84	155.06	141.36	133.06	127.77	124.29
21000	166.78	162.81	148.42	139.71	134.16	130.50
22000	174.72	170.57	155.49	146.37	140.55	136.72
23000	182.66	178.32	162.56	153.02	146.94	142.93
24000	190.61	186.07	169.63	159.67	153.33	149.14
25000	198.55	193.82	176.69	166.33	159.71	155.36
30000	238.26	232.59	212.03	199.59	191.66	186.43
35000	277.97	271.35	247.37	232.86	223.60	217.50
40000	317.68	310.12	282.71	266.12	255.54	248.57
45000	357.39	348.88	318.05	299.39	287.49	279.64
50000	397.10	387.65	353.39	332.65	319.43	310.72
55000	436.81	426.41	388.73	365.92	351.37	341.79
60000	476.52	465.18	424.07	399.18	383.31	372.86
65000	516.22	503.94	459.40	432.45	415.26	403.93
70000	555.93	542.71	494.74	465.71	447.20	435.00
75000	595.64	581.47	530.08	498.98	479.14	466.07
80000	635.35	620.24	565.42	532.24	511.08	497.14
85000	675.06	659.00	600.76	565.51	543.03	528.22
90000	714.77	697.77	636.10	598.77	574.97	559.29
95000	754.48	736.53	671.44	632.04	606.91	590.36
100000	794.19	775.30	706.78	665.30	638.85	621.43
200000	1588.38	1550.60	1413.55	1330.60	1277.71	1242.86
300000	2382.57	2325.89	2120.33	1995.90	1916.56	1864.29
400000	3176.77	3101.19	2827.10	2661.20	2555.42	2485.72
500000	3970.96	3876.49	3533.88	3326.50	3194.27	3107.15

7 1/2%

MONTHLY PAYMENT

Necessary to amortize a loan

TERM / AMOUNT	1 YEAR	2 YEARS	3 YEARS	4 YEARS	5 YEARS	6 YEARS
500	43.38	22.50	15.55	12.09	10.02	8.65
600	52.05	27.00	18.66	14.51	12.02	10.37
700	60.73	31.50	21.77	16.93	14.03	12.10
800	69.41	36.00	24.88	19.34	16.03	13.83
900	78.08	40.50	28.00	21.76	18.03	15.56
1000	86.76	45.00	31.11	24.18	20.04	17.29
2000	173.51	90.00	62.21	48.36	40.08	34.58
3000	260.27	135.00	93.32	72.54	60.11	51.87
4000	347.03	180.00	124.42	96.72	80.15	69.16
5000	433.78	225.00	155.53	120.89	100.19	86.45
6000	520.54	270.00	186.64	145.07	120.23	103.74
7000	607.30	315.00	217.74	169.25	140.27	121.03
8000	694.06	360.00	248.85	193.43	160.30	138.32
9000	780.81	404.99	279.95	217.61	180.34	155.61
10000	867.57	449.99	311.06	241.79	200.38	172.90
11000	954.33	494.99	342.17	265.97	220.42	190.19
12000	1041.08	539.99	373.27	290.15	240.45	207.48
13000	1127.84	584.99	404.38	314.32	260.49	224.77
14000	1214.60	629.99	435.49	338.50	280.53	242.06
15000	1301.35	674.99	466.59	362.68	300.57	259.35
16000	1388.11	719.99	497.70	386.86	320.61	276.64
17000	1474.87	764.99	528.80	411.04	340.64	293.93
18000	1561.62	809.99	559.91	435.22	360.68	311.22
19000	1648.38	854.99	591.02	459.40	380.72	328.51
20000	1735.14	899.99	622.12	483.58	400.76	345.80
21000	1821.89	944.99	653.23	507.75	420.80	363.09
22000	1908.65	989.99	684.33	531.93	440.83	380.38
23000	1995.41	1034.98	715.44	556.11	460.87	397.67
24000	2082.16	1079.98	746.55	580.29	480.91	414.96
25000	2168.92	1124.98	777.65	604.47	500.95	432.25
30000	2602.70	1349.98	933.18	725.36	601.14	518.70
35000	3036.49	1574.98	1088.71	846.26	701.33	605.15
40000	3470.27	1799.97	1244.24	967.15	801.51	691.60
45000	3904.06	2024.97	1399.77	1088.04	901.70	778.05
50000	4337.84	2249.97	1555.30	1208.94	1001.89	864.50
55000	4771.63	2474.96	1710.83	1329.83	1102.08	950.95
60000	5205.41	2699.96	1866.36	1450.73	1202.27	1037.40
65000	5639.19	2924.96	2021.89	1571.62	1302.46	1123.85
70000	6072.98	3149.95	2177.42	1692.51	1402.65	1210.30
75000	6506.76	3374.95	2332.95	1813.41	1502.84	1296.75
80000	6940.55	3599.95	2488.48	1934.30	1603.03	1383.20
85000	7374.33	3824.94	2644.01	2055.20	1703.22	1469.65
90000	7808.11	4049.94	2799.54	2176.09	1803.41	1556.10
95000	8241.90	4274.94	2955.07	2296.98	1903.60	1642.55
100000	8675.68	4499.93	3110.60	2417.88	2003.78	1729.00
200000	17351.40	8999.86	6221.21	4835.75	4007.57	3458.00
300000	26027.00	13499.80	9331.81	7253.63	6011.35	5187.01
400000	34702.70	17999.70	12442.40	9671.51	8015.14	6916.01
500000	43378.40	22499.70	15553.00	12089.40	10018.90	8645.01

MONTHLY PAYMENT

Necessary to amortize a loan

7 1/2%

TERM / AMOUNT	7 YEARS	8 YEARS	9 YEARS	10 YEARS	11 YEARS	12 YEARS
500	7.67	6.94	6.38	5.94	5.57	5.28
600	9.20	8.33	7.66	7.12	6.69	6.33
700	10.74	9.72	8.93	8.31	7.80	7.39
800	12.27	11.11	10.21	9.50	8.92	8.44
900	13.80	12.50	11.48	10.68	10.03	9.50
1000	15.34	13.88	12.76	11.87	11.15	10.55
2000	30.68	27.77	25.52	23.74	22.30	21.10
3000	46.01	41.65	38.28	35.61	33.44	31.66
4000	61.35	55.54	51.04	47.48	44.59	42.21
5000	76.69	69.42	63.80	59.35	55.74	52.76
6000	92.03	83.30	76.57	71.22	66.89	63.31
7000	107.37	97.19	89.33	83.09	78.04	73.87
8000	122.71	111.07	102.09	94.96	89.18	84.42
9000	138.04	124.95	114.85	106.83	100.33	94.97
10000	153.38	138.84	127.61	118.70	111.48	105.52
11000	168.72	152.72	140.37	130.57	122.63	116.07
12000	184.06	166.61	153.13	142.44	133.78	126.63
13000	199.40	180.49	165.89	154.31	144.92	137.18
14000	214.74	194.37	178.65	166.18	156.07	147.73
15000	230.07	208.26	191.41	178.05	167.22	158.28
16000	245.41	222.14	204.18	189.92	178.37	168.84
17000	260.75	236.03	216.94	201.79	189.52	179.39
18000	276.09	249.91	229.70	213.66	200.66	189.94
19000	291.43	263.79	242.46	225.53	211.81	200.49
20000	306.76	277.68	255.22	237.40	222.96	211.04
21000	322.10	291.56	267.98	249.27	234.11	221.60
22000	337.44	305.44	280.74	261.14	245.26	232.15
23000	352.78	319.33	293.50	273.01	256.40	242.70
24000	368.12	333.21	306.26	284.88	267.55	253.25
25000	383.46	347.10	319.02	296.75	278.70	263.81
30000	460.15	416.51	382.83	356.10	334.44	316.57
35000	536.84	485.93	446.63	415.45	390.18	369.33
40000	613.53	555.35	510.44	474.81	445.92	422.09
45000	690.22	624.77	574.24	534.16	501.66	474.85
50000	766.91	694.19	638.05	593.51	557.40	527.61
55000	843.60	763.61	701.85	652.86	613.14	580.37
60000	920.29	833.03	765.66	712.21	668.88	633.13
65000	996.98	902.45	829.46	771.56	724.62	685.89
70000	1073.67	971.87	893.27	830.91	780.36	738.66
75000	1150.37	1041.29	957.07	890.26	836.10	791.42
80000	1227.06	1110.70	1020.88	949.61	891.84	844.18
85000	1303.75	1180.12	1084.68	1008.96	947.58	896.94
90000	1380.44	1249.54	1148.49	1068.31	1003.32	949.70
95000	1457.13	1318.96	1212.29	1127.66	1059.06	1002.46
100000	1533.82	1388.38	1276.10	1187.01	1114.80	1055.22
200000	3067.64	2776.76	2552.19	2374.03	2229.59	2110.44
300000	4601.46	4165.14	3828.29	3561.04	3344.39	3165.67
400000	6135.28	5553.52	5104.38	4748.05	4459.18	4220.89
500000	7669.10	6941.90	6380.48	5935.06	5573.98	5276.11

7 1/2%

MONTHLY PAYMENT

Necessary to amortize a loan

TERM AMOUNT	13 YEARS	14 YEARS	15 YEARS	16 YEARS	17 YEARS	18 YEARS
500	5.03	4.82	4.64	4.48	4.34	4.22
600	6.03	5.78	5.56	5.37	5.21	5.07
700	7.04	6.74	6.49	6.27	6.08	5.91
800	8.04	7.71	7.42	7.17	6.95	6.76
900	9.05	8.67	8.34	8.06	7.82	7.60
1000	10.05	9.63	9.27	8.96	8.69	8.45
2000	20.11	19.26	18.54	17.92	17.37	16.90
3000	30.16	28.89	27.81	26.87	26.06	25.35
4000	40.21	38.53	37.08	35.83	34.75	33.80
5000	50.27	48.16	46.35	44.79	43.44	42.25
6000	60.32	57.79	55.62	53.75	52.12	50.70
7000	70.38	67.42	64.89	62.71	60.81	59.15
8000	80.43	77.05	74.16	71.67	69.50	67.60
9000	90.48	86.68	83.43	80.62	78.18	76.05
10000	100.54	96.31	92.70	89.58	86.87	84.50
11000	110.59	105.95	101.97	98.54	95.56	92.95
12000	120.64	115.58	111.24	107.50	104.25	101.40
13000	130.70	125.21	120.51	116.46	112.93	109.85
14000	140.75	134.84	129.78	125.42	121.62	118.30
15000	150.81	144.47	139.05	134.37	130.31	126.75
16000	160.86	154.10	148.32	143.33	138.99	135.20
17000	170.91	163.73	157.59	152.29	147.68	143.65
18000	180.97	173.37	166.86	161.25	156.37	152.10
19000	191.02	183.00	176.13	170.21	165.05	160.54
20000	201.07	192.63	185.40	179.17	173.74	168.99
21000	211.13	202.26	194.67	188.12	182.43	177.44
22000	221.18	211.89	203.94	197.08	191.12	185.89
23000	231.23	221.52	213.21	206.04	199.80	194.34
24000	241.29	231.15	222.48	215.00	208.49	202.79
25000	251.34	240.79	231.75	223.96	217.18	211.24
30000	301.61	288.94	278.10	268.75	260.61	253.49
35000	351.88	337.10	324.45	313.54	304.05	295.74
40000	402.15	385.26	370.80	358.33	347.48	337.99
45000	452.42	433.41	417.15	403.12	390.92	380.24
50000	502.68	481.57	463.51	447.91	434.35	422.49
55000	552.95	529.73	509.86	492.70	477.79	464.73
60000	603.22	577.88	556.21	537.50	521.22	506.98
65000	653.49	626.04	602.56	582.29	564.66	549.23
70000	703.76	674.20	648.91	627.08	608.10	591.48
75000	754.03	722.36	695.26	671.87	651.53	633.73
80000	804.29	770.51	741.61	716.66	694.97	675.98
85000	854.56	818.67	787.96	761.45	738.40	718.23
90000	904.83	866.83	834.31	806.24	781.84	760.47
95000	955.10	914.98	880.66	851.03	825.27	802.72
100000	1005.37	963.14	927.01	895.83	868.71	844.97
200000	2010.73	1926.28	1854.02	1791.65	1737.41	1689.94
300000	3016.10	2889.42	2781.03	2687.47	2606.12	2534.91
400000	4021.47	3852.56	3708.04	3583.30	3474.83	3379.88
500000	5026.83	4815.70	4635.05	4479.12	4343.53	4224.85

MONTHLY PAYMENT

Necessary to amortize a loan

7 1/2%

TERM / AMOUNT	19 YEARS	20 YEARS	25 YEARS	30 YEARS	35 YEARS	40 YEARS
500	4.12	4.03	3.69	3.50	3.37	3.29
600	4.94	4.83	4.43	4.20	4.05	3.95
700	5.77	5.64	5.17	4.89	4.72	4.61
800	6.59	6.44	5.91	5.59	5.39	5.26
900	7.42	7.25	6.65	6.29	6.07	5.92
1000	8.24	8.06	7.39	6.99	6.74	6.58
2000	16.48	16.11	14.78	13.98	13.48	13.16
3000	24.72	24.17	22.17	20.98	20.23	19.74
4000	32.96	32.22	29.56	27.97	26.97	26.32
5000	41.20	40.28	36.95	34.96	33.71	32.90
6000	49.44	48.34	44.34	41.95	40.45	39.48
7000	57.69	56.39	51.73	48.94	47.20	46.06
8000	65.93	64.45	59.12	55.94	53.94	52.65
9000	74.17	72.50	66.51	62.93	60.68	59.23
10000	82.41	80.56	73.90	69.92	67.42	65.81
11000	90.65	88.62	81.29	76.91	74.17	72.39
12000	98.89	96.67	88.68	83.91	80.91	78.97
13000	107.13	104.73	96.07	90.90	87.65	85.55
14000	115.37	112.78	103.46	97.89	94.39	92.13
15000	123.61	120.84	110.85	104.88	101.14	98.71
16000	131.85	128.90	118.24	111.87	107.88	105.29
17000	140.09	136.95	125.63	118.87	114.62	111.87
18000	148.33	145.01	133.02	125.86	121.36	118.45
19000	156.58	153.06	140.41	132.85	128.11	125.03
20000	164.82	161.12	147.80	139.84	134.85	131.61
21000	173.06	169.17	155.19	146.84	141.59	138.20
22000	181.30	177.23	162.58	153.83	148.33	144.78
23000	189.54	185.29	169.97	160.82	155.08	151.36
24000	197.78	193.34	177.36	167.81	161.82	157.94
25000	206.02	201.40	184.75	174.80	168.56	164.52
30000	247.22	241.68	221.70	209.76	202.27	197.42
35000	288.43	281.96	258.65	244.73	235.99	230.32
40000	329.63	322.24	295.60	279.69	269.70	263.23
45000	370.83	362.52	332.55	314.65	303.41	296.13
50000	412.04	402.80	369.50	349.61	337.12	329.04
55000	453.24	443.08	406.44	384.57	370.83	361.94
60000	494.45	483.36	443.39	419.53	404.55	394.84
65000	535.65	523.63	480.34	454.49	438.26	427.75
70000	576.85	563.91	517.29	489.45	471.97	460.65
75000	618.06	604.19	554.24	524.41	505.68	493.55
80000	659.26	644.47	591.19	559.37	539.39	526.46
85000	700.47	684.75	628.14	594.33	573.11	559.36
90000	741.67	725.03	665.09	629.29	606.82	592.26
95000	782.87	765.31	702.04	664.25	640.53	625.17
100000	824.08	805.59	738.99	699.21	674.24	658.07
200000	1648.15	1611.18	1477.98	1398.43	1348.48	1316.14
300000	2472.23	2416.77	2216.97	2097.64	2022.73	1974.21
400000	3296.31	3222.36	2955.96	2796.85	2696.97	2632.28
500000	4120.38	4027.95	3694.95	3496.07	3371.21	3290.35

8%

MONTHLY PAYMENT

Necessary to amortize a loan

TERM / AMOUNT	1 YEAR	2 YEARS	3 YEARS	4 YEARS	5 YEARS	6 YEARS
500	43.49	22.61	15.67	12.21	10.14	8.77
600	52.19	27.14	18.80	14.65	12.17	10.52
700	60.89	31.66	21.94	17.09	14.19	12.27
800	69.59	36.18	25.07	19.53	16.22	14.03
900	78.29	40.70	28.20	21.97	18.25	15.78
1000	86.99	45.23	31.34	24.41	20.28	17.53
2000	173.98	90.45	62.67	48.83	40.55	35.07
3000	260.97	135.68	94.01	73.24	60.83	52.60
4000	347.95	180.91	125.35	97.65	81.11	70.13
5000	434.94	226.14	156.68	122.07	101.38	87.67
6000	521.93	271.36	188.02	146.48	121.66	105.20
7000	608.92	316.59	219.35	170.89	141.94	122.73
8000	695.91	361.82	250.69	195.30	162.21	140.27
9000	782.90	407.05	282.03	219.72	182.49	157.80
10000	869.89	452.27	313.36	244.13	202.76	175.33
11000	956.87	497.50	344.70	268.54	223.04	192.87
12000	1043.86	542.73	376.04	292.96	243.32	210.40
13000	1130.85	587.95	407.37	317.37	263.59	227.93
14000	1217.84	633.18	438.71	341.78	283.87	245.47
15000	1304.83	678.41	470.05	366.19	304.15	263.00
16000	1391.82	723.64	501.38	390.61	324.42	280.53
17000	1478.80	768.86	532.72	415.02	344.70	298.07
18000	1565.79	814.09	564.05	439.43	364.98	315.60
19000	1652.78	859.32	595.39	463.85	385.25	333.13
20000	1739.77	904.55	626.73	488.26	405.53	350.67
21000	1826.76	949.77	658.06	512.67	425.80	368.20
22000	1913.75	995.00	689.40	537.08	446.08	385.73
23000	2000.73	1040.23	720.74	561.50	466.36	403.26
24000	2087.72	1085.45	752.07	585.91	486.63	420.80
25000	2174.71	1130.68	783.41	610.32	506.91	438.33
30000	2609.65	1356.82	940.09	732.39	608.29	526.00
35000	3044.60	1582.95	1096.77	854.45	709.67	613.66
40000	3479.54	1809.09	1253.45	976.52	811.06	701.33
45000	3914.48	2035.23	1410.14	1098.58	912.44	789.00
50000	4349.42	2261.36	1566.82	1220.65	1013.82	876.66
55000	4784.37	2487.50	1723.50	1342.71	1115.20	964.33
60000	5219.31	2713.64	1880.18	1464.77	1216.58	1051.99
65000	5654.25	2939.77	2036.86	1586.84	1317.97	1139.66
70000	6089.19	3165.91	2193.54	1708.90	1419.35	1227.33
75000	6524.13	3392.04	2350.23	1830.97	1520.73	1314.99
80000	6959.08	3618.18	2506.91	1953.03	1622.11	1402.66
85000	7394.02	3844.32	2663.59	2075.10	1723.49	1490.33
90000	7828.96	4070.45	2820.27	2197.16	1824.87	1577.99
95000	8263.90	4296.59	2976.95	2319.23	1926.26	1665.66
100000	8698.85	4522.73	3133.63	2441.29	2027.64	1753.32
200000	17397.70	9045.45	6267.27	4882.58	4055.28	3506.65
300000	26096.50	13568.20	9400.90	7323.87	6082.92	5259.97
400000	34795.40	18090.90	12534.50	9765.17	8110.55	7013.29
500000	43494.20	22613.60	15668.20	12206.50	10138.20	8766.62

MONTHLY PAYMENT

Necessary to amortize a loan

8%

TERM / AMOUNT	7 YEARS	8 YEARS	9 YEARS	10 YEARS	11 YEARS	12 YEARS
500	7.79	7.07	6.51	6.07	5.71	5.41
600	9.35	8.48	7.81	7.28	6.85	6.49
700	10.91	9.90	9.11	8.49	7.99	7.58
800	12.47	11.31	10.42	9.71	9.13	8.66
900	14.03	12.72	11.72	10.92	10.27	9.74
1000	15.59	14.14	13.02	12.13	11.42	10.82
2000	31.17	28.27	26.04	24.27	22.83	21.65
3000	46.76	42.41	39.06	36.40	34.25	32.47
4000	62.34	56.55	52.07	48.53	45.66	43.30
5000	77.93	70.68	65.09	60.66	57.08	54.12
6000	93.52	84.82	78.11	72.80	68.49	64.95
7000	109.10	98.96	91.13	84.93	79.91	75.77
8000	124.69	113.09	104.15	97.06	91.32	86.60
9000	140.28	127.23	117.17	109.20	102.74	97.42
10000	155.86	141.37	130.19	121.33	114.15	108.25
11000	171.45	155.50	143.21	133.46	125.57	119.07
12000	187.04	169.64	156.23	145.59	136.99	129.89
13000	202.62	183.78	169.24	157.73	148.40	140.72
14000	218.21	197.91	182.26	169.86	159.82	151.54
15000	233.79	212.05	195.28	181.99	171.23	162.37
16000	249.38	226.19	208.30	194.12	182.65	173.19
17000	264.97	240.32	221.32	206.26	194.06	184.02
18000	280.55	254.46	234.34	218.39	205.48	194.84
19000	296.14	268.60	247.36	230.52	216.89	205.67
20000	311.72	282.73	260.37	242.66	228.31	216.49
21000	327.31	296.87	273.39	254.79	239.72	227.32
22000	342.90	311.01	286.41	266.92	251.14	238.14
23000	358.48	325.14	299.43	279.05	262.56	248.96
24000	374.07	339.28	312.45	291.19	273.97	259.79
25000	389.66	353.42	325.47	303.32	285.39	270.61
30000	467.59	424.10	390.56	363.98	342.46	324.74
35000	545.52	494.78	455.66	424.65	399.54	378.86
40000	623.45	565.47	520.75	485.31	456.62	432.98
45000	701.38	636.15	585.84	545.97	513.70	487.10
50000	779.31	706.83	650.94	606.64	570.77	541.23
55000	857.24	777.52	716.03	667.30	627.85	595.35
60000	935.17	848.20	781.12	727.97	684.93	649.47
65000	1013.10	918.88	846.22	788.63	742.00	703.59
70000	1091.03	989.57	911.31	849.29	799.08	757.72
75000	1168.97	1060.25	976.40	909.96	856.16	811.84
80000	1246.90	1130.93	1041.50	970.62	913.24	865.96
85000	1324.83	1201.62	1106.59	1031.28	970.31	920.08
90000	1402.76	1272.30	1171.68	1091.95	1027.39	974.21
95000	1480.69	1342.98	1236.78	1152.61	1084.47	1028.33
100000	1558.62	1413.67	1301.87	1213.28	1141.54	1082.45
200000	3117.24	2827.33	2603.74	2426.55	2283.09	2164.90
300000	4675.86	4241.00	3905.61	3639.83	3424.63	3247.36
400000	6234.48	5654.67	5207.48	4853.10	4566.18	4329.81
500000	7793.10	7068.34	6509.36	6066.38	5707.72	5412.26

8%

MONTHLY PAYMENT

Necessary to amortize a loan

TERM / AMOUNT	13 YEARS	14 YEARS	15 YEARS	16 YEARS	17 YEARS	18 YEARS
500	5.17	4.96	4.78	4.62	4.49	4.37
600	6.20	5.95	5.73	5.55	5.39	5.25
700	7.23	6.94	6.69	6.47	6.29	6.12
800	8.26	7.93	7.65	7.40	7.19	7.00
900	9.30	8.92	8.60	8.32	8.08	7.87
1000	10.33	9.91	9.56	9.25	8.98	8.75
2000	20.66	19.83	19.11	18.50	17.97	17.50
3000	30.99	29.74	28.67	27.75	26.95	26.25
4000	41.32	39.65	38.23	37.00	35.93	35.00
5000	51.65	49.57	47.78	46.25	44.91	43.75
6000	61.98	59.48	57.34	55.50	53.90	52.50
7000	72.32	69.39	66.90	64.74	62.88	61.25
8000	82.65	79.31	76.45	73.99	71.86	70.00
9000	92.98	89.22	86.01	83.24	80.84	78.75
10000	103.31	99.13	95.57	92.49	89.83	87.50
11000	113.64	109.05	105.12	101.74	98.81	96.25
12000	123.97	118.96	114.68	110.99	107.79	105.00
13000	134.30	128.87	124.24	120.24	116.77	113.75
14000	144.63	138.78	133.79	129.49	125.76	122.50
15000	154.96	148.70	143.35	138.74	134.74	131.24
16000	165.29	158.61	152.90	147.99	143.72	139.99
17000	175.62	168.52	162.46	157.24	152.70	148.74
18000	185.95	178.44	172.02	166.49	161.69	157.49
19000	196.28	188.35	181.57	175.74	170.67	166.24
20000	206.62	198.26	191.13	184.99	179.65	174.99
21000	216.95	208.18	200.69	194.23	188.63	183.74
22000	227.28	218.09	210.24	203.48	197.62	192.49
23000	237.61	228.00	219.80	212.73	206.60	201.24
24000	247.94	237.92	229.36	221.98	215.58	209.99
25000	258.27	247.83	238.91	231.23	224.56	218.74
30000	309.92	297.40	286.70	277.48	269.48	262.49
35000	361.58	346.96	334.48	323.72	314.39	306.24
40000	413.23	396.53	382.26	369.97	359.30	349.99
45000	464.88	446.09	430.04	416.22	404.22	393.73
50000	516.54	495.66	477.83	462.46	449.13	437.48
55000	568.19	545.23	525.61	508.71	494.04	481.23
60000	619.84	594.79	573.39	554.96	538.95	524.98
65000	671.50	644.36	621.17	601.20	583.87	568.73
70000	723.15	693.92	668.96	647.45	628.78	612.47
75000	774.81	743.49	716.74	693.69	673.69	656.22
80000	826.46	793.05	764.52	739.94	718.61	699.97
85000	878.11	842.62	812.30	786.19	763.52	743.72
90000	929.77	892.19	860.09	832.43	808.43	787.47
95000	981.42	941.75	907.87	878.68	853.34	831.21
100000	1033.07	991.32	955.65	924.93	898.26	874.96
200000	2066.15	1982.64	1911.30	1849.85	1796.51	1749.92
300000	3099.22	2973.95	2866.96	2774.77	2694.77	2624.89
400000	4132.29	3965.27	3822.61	3699.70	3593.03	3499.85
500000	5165.37	4956.59	4778.26	4624.62	4491.28	4374.81

MONTHLY PAYMENT

Necessary to amortize a loan

8%

TERM / AMOUNT	19 YEARS	20 YEARS	25 YEARS	30 YEARS	35 YEARS	40 YEARS
500	4.27	4.18	3.86	3.67	3.55	3.48
600	5.13	5.02	4.63	4.40	4.26	4.17
700	5.98	5.86	5.40	5.14	4.97	4.87
800	6.84	6.69	6.17	5.87	5.68	5.56
900	7.69	7.53	6.95	6.60	6.39	6.26
1000	8.55	8.36	7.72	7.34	7.10	6.95
2000	17.09	16.73	15.44	14.68	14.21	13.91
3000	25.64	25.09	23.15	22.01	21.31	20.86
4000	34.18	33.46	30.87	29.35	28.41	27.81
5000	42.73	41.82	38.59	36.69	35.51	34.77
6000	51.27	50.19	46.31	44.03	42.62	41.72
7000	59.82	58.55	54.03	51.36	49.72	48.67
8000	68.36	66.92	61.75	58.70	56.82	55.62
9000	76.91	75.28	69.46	66.04	63.92	62.58
10000	85.45	83.64	77.18	73.38	71.03	69.53
11000	94.00	92.01	84.90	80.71	78.13	76.48
12000	102.54	100.37	92.62	88.05	85.23	83.44
13000	111.09	108.74	100.34	95.39	92.33	90.39
14000	119.63	117.10	108.05	102.73	99.44	97.34
15000	128.18	125.47	115.77	110.07	106.54	104.30
16000	136.72	133.83	123.49	117.40	113.64	111.25
17000	145.27	142.20	131.21	124.74	120.74	118.20
18000	153.81	150.56	138.93	132.08	127.85	125.16
19000	162.36	158.92	146.65	139.42	134.95	132.11
20000	170.90	167.29	154.36	146.75	142.05	139.06
21000	179.45	175.65	162.08	154.09	149.16	146.02
22000	187.99	184.02	169.80	161.43	156.26	152.97
23000	196.54	192.38	177.52	168.77	163.36	159.92
24000	205.08	200.75	185.24	176.10	170.46	166.88
25000	213.63	209.11	192.95	183.44	177.57	173.83
30000	256.35	250.93	231.55	220.13	213.08	208.59
35000	299.08	292.75	270.14	256.82	248.59	243.36
40000	341.80	334.58	308.73	293.51	284.10	278.13
45000	384.53	376.40	347.32	330.19	319.62	312.89
50000	427.25	418.22	385.91	366.88	355.13	347.66
55000	469.98	460.04	424.50	403.57	390.64	382.42
60000	512.70	501.86	463.09	440.26	426.16	417.19
65000	555.43	543.69	501.68	476.95	461.67	451.95
70000	598.15	585.51	540.27	513.64	497.18	486.72
75000	640.88	627.33	578.86	550.32	532.70	521.48
80000	683.60	669.15	617.45	587.01	568.21	556.25
85000	726.33	710.97	656.04	623.70	603.72	591.02
90000	769.05	752.80	694.63	660.39	639.24	625.78
95000	811.78	794.62	733.23	697.08	674.75	660.55
100000	854.50	836.44	771.82	733.76	710.26	695.31
200000	1709.00	1672.88	1543.63	1467.53	1420.52	1390.62
300000	2563.50	2509.32	2315.45	2201.29	2130.78	2085.93
400000	3418.00	3345.76	3087.26	2935.06	2841.04	2781.25
500000	4272.51	4182.20	3859.08	3668.82	3551.30	3476.56

8 1/2%

MONTHLY PAYMENT

Necessary to amortize a loan

TERM / AMOUNT	1 YEAR	2 YEARS	3 YEARS	4 YEARS	5 YEARS	6 YEARS
500	43.61	22.73	15.78	12.32	10.26	8.89
600	52.33	27.27	18.94	14.79	12.31	10.67
700	61.05	31.82	22.10	17.25	14.36	12.44
800	69.78	36.36	25.25	19.72	16.41	14.22
900	78.50	40.91	28.41	22.18	18.47	16.00
1000	87.22	45.46	31.57	24.65	20.52	17.78
2000	174.44	90.91	63.14	49.30	41.03	35.56
3000	261.66	136.37	94.70	73.95	61.55	53.34
4000	348.88	181.82	126.27	98.59	82.07	71.11
5000	436.10	227.28	157.84	123.24	102.58	88.89
6000	523.32	272.74	189.41	147.89	123.10	106.67
7000	610.54	318.19	220.97	172.54	143.62	124.45
8000	697.76	363.65	252.54	197.19	164.13	142.23
9000	784.98	409.10	284.11	221.84	184.65	160.01
10000	872.20	454.56	315.68	246.48	205.17	177.79
11000	959.42	500.02	347.25	271.13	225.68	195.56
12000	1046.64	545.47	378.81	295.78	246.20	213.34
13000	1133.86	590.93	410.38	320.43	266.72	231.12
14000	1221.08	636.38	441.95	345.08	287.23	248.90
15000	1308.30	681.84	473.52	369.73	307.75	266.68
16000	1395.52	727.29	505.08	394.38	328.27	284.46
17000	1482.75	772.75	536.65	419.02	348.78	302.23
18000	1569.97	818.21	568.22	443.67	369.30	320.01
19000	1657.19	863.66	599.79	468.32	389.82	337.79
20000	1744.41	909.12	631.35	492.97	410.33	355.57
21000	1831.63	954.57	662.92	517.62	430.85	373.35
22000	1918.85	1000.03	694.49	542.27	451.37	391.13
23000	2006.07	1045.49	726.06	566.91	471.88	408.91
24000	2093.29	1090.94	757.63	591.56	492.40	426.68
25000	2180.51	1136.40	789.19	616.21	512.92	444.46
30000	2616.61	1363.68	947.03	739.45	615.50	533.35
35000	3052.71	1590.96	1104.87	862.70	718.08	622.25
40000	3488.81	1818.24	1262.71	985.94	820.67	711.14
45000	3924.91	2045.52	1420.55	1109.18	923.25	800.03
50000	4361.01	2272.79	1578.38	1232.42	1025.83	888.92
55000	4797.12	2500.07	1736.22	1355.66	1128.41	977.82
60000	5233.22	2727.35	1894.06	1478.91	1231.00	1066.71
65000	5669.32	2954.63	2051.90	1602.15	1333.58	1155.60
70000	6105.42	3181.91	2209.74	1725.39	1436.16	1244.49
75000	6541.52	3409.19	2367.58	1848.63	1538.75	1333.38
80000	6977.62	3636.47	2525.42	1971.87	1641.33	1422.28
85000	7413.73	3863.75	2683.25	2095.12	1743.91	1511.17
90000	7849.83	4091.03	2841.09	2218.36	1846.50	1600.06
95000	8285.93	4318.31	2998.93	2341.60	1949.08	1688.95
100000	8722.03	4545.59	3156.77	2464.84	2051.66	1777.85
200000	17444.10	9091.18	6313.54	4929.68	4103.33	3555.69
300000	26166.10	13636.80	9470.31	7394.52	6154.99	5333.54
400000	34888.10	18182.40	12627.10	9859.37	8206.65	7111.38
500000	43610.10	22727.90	15783.80	12324.20	10258.30	8889.23

MONTHLY PAYMENT

Necessary to amortize a loan

8 1/2%

TERM / AMOUNT	7 YEARS	8 YEARS	9 YEARS	10 YEARS	11 YEARS	12 YEARS
500	7.92	7.20	6.64	6.20	5.84	5.55
600	9.50	8.64	7.97	7.44	7.01	6.66
700	11.09	10.07	9.30	8.68	8.18	7.77
800	12.67	11.51	10.62	9.92	9.35	8.88
900	14.25	12.95	11.95	11.16	10.52	9.99
1000	15.84	14.39	13.28	12.40	11.69	11.10
2000	31.67	28.78	26.56	24.80	23.37	22.20
3000	47.51	43.18	39.84	37.20	35.06	33.30
4000	63.35	57.57	53.12	49.59	46.75	44.40
5000	79.18	71.96	66.40	61.99	58.43	55.50
6000	95.02	86.35	79.68	74.39	70.12	66.60
7000	110.86	100.75	92.96	86.79	81.81	77.70
8000	126.69	115.14	106.24	99.19	93.49	88.80
9000	142.53	129.53	119.52	111.59	105.18	99.91
10000	158.37	143.92	132.79	123.99	116.86	111.01
11000	174.20	158.31	146.07	136.39	128.55	122.11
12000	190.04	172.71	159.35	148.78	140.24	133.21
13000	205.88	187.10	172.63	161.18	151.92	144.31
14000	221.71	201.49	185.91	173.58	163.61	155.41
15000	237.55	215.88	199.19	185.98	175.30	166.51
16000	253.39	230.28	212.47	198.38	186.98	177.61
17000	269.22	244.67	225.75	210.78	198.67	188.71
18000	285.06	259.06	239.03	223.18	210.36	199.81
19000	300.90	273.45	252.31	235.57	222.04	210.91
20000	316.73	287.84	265.59	247.97	233.73	222.01
21000	332.57	302.24	278.87	260.37	245.42	233.11
22000	348.40	316.63	292.15	272.77	257.10	244.21
23000	364.24	331.02	305.43	285.17	268.79	255.31
24000	380.08	345.41	318.71	297.57	280.47	266.41
25000	395.91	359.81	331.99	309.97	292.16	277.52
30000	475.10	431.77	398.38	371.96	350.59	333.02
35000	554.28	503.73	464.78	433.95	409.03	388.52
40000	633.46	575.69	531.18	495.94	467.46	444.02
45000	712.65	647.65	597.57	557.94	525.89	499.53
50000	791.83	719.61	663.97	619.93	584.32	555.03
55000	871.01	791.57	730.37	681.92	642.75	610.53
60000	950.19	863.53	796.76	743.92	701.19	666.04
65000	1029.38	935.49	863.16	805.91	759.62	721.54
70000	1108.56	1007.45	929.56	867.90	818.05	777.04
75000	1187.74	1079.41	995.96	929.90	876.48	832.54
80000	1266.92	1151.37	1062.35	991.89	934.92	888.05
85000	1346.11	1223.34	1128.75	1053.88	993.35	943.55
90000	1425.29	1295.30	1195.15	1115.88	1051.78	999.05
95000	1504.47	1367.26	1261.54	1177.87	1110.21	1054.56
100000	1583.66	1439.22	1327.94	1239.86	1168.64	1110.06
200000	3167.31	2878.44	2655.88	2479.72	2337.29	2220.12
300000	4750.97	4317.66	3983.82	3719.58	3505.93	3330.18
400000	6334.62	5756.87	5311.76	4959.44	4674.57	4440.24
500000	7918.28	7196.09	6639.70	6199.31	5843.22	5550.30

8 1/2% MONTHLY PAYMENT

Necessary to amortize a loan

TERM / AMOUNT	13 YEARS	14 YEARS	15 YEARS	16 YEARS	17 YEARS	18 YEARS
500	5.31	5.10	4.92	4.77	4.64	4.53
600	6.37	6.12	5.91	5.73	5.57	5.43
700	7.43	7.14	6.89	6.68	6.50	6.34
800	8.49	8.16	7.88	7.64	7.43	7.24
900	9.55	9.18	8.86	8.59	8.35	8.15
1000	10.61	10.20	9.85	9.54	9.28	9.05
2000	21.22	20.40	19.69	19.09	18.57	18.11
3000	31.84	30.60	29.54	28.63	27.85	27.16
4000	42.45	40.80	39.39	38.18	37.13	36.22
5000	53.06	51.00	49.24	47.72	46.41	45.27
6000	63.67	61.20	59.08	57.27	55.70	54.33
7000	74.28	71.39	68.93	66.81	64.98	63.38
8000	84.89	81.59	78.78	76.36	74.26	72.44
9000	95.51	91.79	88.63	85.90	83.55	81.49
10000	106.12	101.99	98.47	95.45	92.83	90.55
11000	116.73	112.19	108.32	104.99	102.11	99.60
12000	127.34	122.39	118.17	114.54	111.40	108.66
13000	137.95	132.59	128.02	124.08	120.68	117.71
14000	148.57	142.79	137.86	133.63	129.96	126.76
15000	159.18	152.99	147.71	143.17	139.24	135.82
16000	169.79	163.19	157.56	152.72	148.53	144.87
17000	180.40	173.39	167.41	162.26	157.81	153.93
18000	191.01	183.59	177.25	171.81	167.09	162.98
19000	201.63	193.79	187.10	181.35	176.38	172.04
20000	212.24	203.98	196.95	190.90	185.66	181.09
21000	222.85	214.18	206.80	200.44	194.94	190.15
22000	233.46	224.38	216.64	209.99	204.23	199.20
23000	244.07	234.58	226.49	219.53	213.51	208.26
24000	254.68	244.78	236.34	229.08	222.79	217.31
25000	265.30	254.98	246.19	238.62	232.07	226.37
30000	318.36	305.98	295.42	286.35	278.49	271.64
35000	371.41	356.97	344.66	334.07	324.90	316.91
40000	424.47	407.97	393.90	381.80	371.32	362.18
45000	477.53	458.97	443.13	429.52	417.73	407.46
50000	530.59	509.96	492.37	477.25	464.15	452.73
55000	583.65	560.96	541.61	524.97	510.56	498.00
60000	636.71	611.95	590.85	572.70	556.98	543.28
65000	689.77	662.95	640.08	620.42	603.39	588.55
70000	742.83	713.95	689.32	668.15	649.81	633.82
75000	795.89	764.94	738.56	715.87	696.22	679.10
80000	848.95	815.94	787.79	763.60	742.64	724.37
85000	902.01	866.93	837.03	811.32	789.05	769.64
90000	955.06	917.93	886.27	859.04	835.47	814.91
95000	1008.12	968.93	935.51	906.77	881.88	860.19
100000	1061.18	1019.92	984.74	954.49	928.29	905.46
200000	2122.36	2039.84	1969.48	1908.99	1856.59	1810.92
300000	3183.55	3059.76	2954.23	2863.48	2784.88	2716.38
400000	4244.73	4079.69	3938.97	3817.97	3713.18	3621.84
500000	5305.91	5099.61	4923.71	4772.47	4641.47	4527.30

MONTHLY PAYMENT

Necessary to amortize a loan

8 1/2%

TERM / AMOUNT	19 YEARS	20 YEARS	25 YEARS	30 YEARS	35 YEARS	40 YEARS
500	4.43	4.34	4.03	3.84	3.73	3.67
600	5.31	5.21	4.83	4.61	4.48	4.40
700	6.20	6.07	5.64	5.38	5.23	5.13
800	7.08	6.94	6.44	6.15	5.97	5.86
900	7.97	7.81	7.25	6.92	6.72	6.60
1000	8.85	8.68	8.05	7.69	7.47	7.33
2000	17.71	17.36	16.10	15.38	14.94	14.66
3000	26.56	26.03	24.16	23.07	22.41	21.99
4000	35.42	34.71	32.21	30.76	29.87	29.32
5000	44.27	43.39	40.26	38.45	37.34	36.65
6000	53.13	52.07	48.31	46.13	44.81	43.99
7000	61.98	60.75	56.37	53.82	52.28	51.32
8000	70.84	69.43	64.42	61.51	59.75	58.65
9000	79.69	78.10	72.47	69.20	67.22	65.98
10000	88.54	86.78	80.52	76.89	74.69	73.31
11000	97.40	95.46	88.58	84.58	82.15	80.64
12000	106.25	104.14	96.63	92.27	89.62	87.97
13000	115.11	112.82	104.68	99.96	97.09	95.30
14000	123.96	121.50	112.73	107.65	104.56	102.63
15000	132.82	130.17	120.78	115.34	112.03	109.96
16000	141.67	138.85	128.84	123.03	119.50	117.30
17000	150.53	147.53	136.89	130.72	126.97	124.63
18000	159.38	156.21	144.94	138.41	134.44	131.96
19000	168.24	164.89	152.99	146.09	141.90	139.29
20000	177.09	173.57	161.05	153.78	149.37	146.62
21000	185.94	182.24	169.10	161.47	156.84	153.95
22000	194.80	190.92	177.15	169.16	164.31	161.28
23000	203.65	199.60	185.20	176.85	171.78	168.61
24000	212.51	208.28	193.26	184.54	179.25	175.94
25000	221.36	216.96	201.31	192.23	186.72	183.27
30000	265.63	260.35	241.57	230.67	224.06	219.93
35000	309.91	303.74	281.83	269.12	261.40	256.58
40000	354.18	347.13	322.09	307.57	298.75	293.24
45000	398.45	390.52	362.35	346.01	336.09	329.89
50000	442.72	433.91	402.61	384.46	373.43	366.55
55000	487.00	477.30	442.88	422.90	410.77	403.20
60000	531.27	520.70	483.14	461.35	448.12	439.86
65000	575.54	564.09	523.40	499.79	485.46	476.51
70000	619.81	607.48	563.66	538.24	522.80	513.17
75000	664.09	650.87	603.92	576.69	560.15	549.82
80000	708.36	694.26	644.18	615.13	597.49	586.48
85000	752.63	737.65	684.44	653.58	634.83	623.13
90000	796.90	781.04	724.71	692.02	672.18	659.79
95000	841.18	824.43	764.97	730.47	709.52	696.44
100000	885.45	867.83	805.23	768.92	746.86	733.10
200000	1770.90	1735.65	1610.46	1537.83	1493.72	1466.19
300000	2656.34	2603.48	2415.69	2306.74	2240.58	2199.28
400000	3541.79	3471.30	3220.91	3075.66	2987.45	2932.38
500000	4427.24	4339.13	4026.14	3844.57	3734.31	3665.47

9%

MONTHLY PAYMENT

Necessary to amortize a loan

TERM / AMOUNT	1 YEAR	2 YEARS	3 YEARS	4 YEARS	5 YEARS	6 YEARS
500	43.73	22.84	15.90	12.44	10.38	9.01
600	52.47	27.41	19.08	14.93	12.45	10.82
700	61.22	31.98	22.26	17.42	14.53	12.62
800	69.96	36.55	25.44	19.91	16.61	14.42
900	78.71	41.12	28.62	22.40	18.68	16.22
1000	87.45	45.68	31.80	24.88	20.76	18.03
2000	174.90	91.37	63.60	49.77	41.52	36.05
3000	262.35	137.05	95.40	74.65	62.27	54.08
4000	349.80	182.74	127.20	99.54	83.03	72.10
5000	437.25	228.42	159.00	124.42	103.79	90.13
6000	524.70	274.11	190.80	149.31	124.55	108.15
7000	612.16	319.79	222.60	174.19	145.31	126.18
8000	699.61	365.47	254.40	199.08	166.07	144.20
9000	787.06	411.16	286.20	223.96	186.82	162.23
10000	874.51	456.84	317.99	248.85	207.58	180.25
11000	961.96	502.53	349.79	273.73	228.34	198.28
12000	1049.41	548.21	381.59	298.62	249.10	216.31
13000	1136.86	593.90	413.39	323.50	269.86	234.33
14000	1224.31	639.58	445.19	348.39	290.62	252.36
15000	1311.76	685.27	476.99	373.27	311.37	270.38
16000	1399.21	730.95	508.79	398.16	332.13	288.41
17000	1486.66	776.63	540.59	423.04	352.89	306.43
18000	1574.11	822.32	572.39	447.93	373.65	324.46
19000	1661.56	868.00	604.19	472.81	394.41	342.48
20000	1749.01	913.69	635.99	497.70	415.16	360.51
21000	1836.46	959.37	667.79	522.58	435.92	378.53
22000	1923.92	1005.05	699.59	547.47	456.68	396.56
23000	2011.37	1050.74	731.39	572.35	477.44	414.58
24000	2098.82	1096.42	763.19	597.24	498.20	432.61
25000	2186.27	1142.11	794.99	622.12	518.96	450.64
30000	2623.52	1370.53	953.98	746.55	622.75	540.76
35000	3060.77	1598.95	1112.98	870.97	726.54	630.89
40000	3498.03	1827.37	1271.98	995.39	830.33	721.02
45000	3935.28	2055.79	1430.98	1119.82	934.12	811.14
50000	4372.53	2284.22	1589.97	1244.24	1037.91	901.27
55000	4809.79	2512.64	1748.97	1368.67	1141.70	991.40
60000	5247.04	2741.06	1907.97	1493.09	1245.49	1081.52
65000	5684.29	2969.48	2066.96	1617.51	1349.28	1171.65
70000	6121.55	3197.90	2225.96	1741.94	1453.07	1261.78
75000	6558.80	3426.32	2384.96	1866.36	1556.86	1351.90
80000	6996.06	3654.74	2543.96	1990.79	1660.65	1442.03
85000	7433.31	3883.17	2702.95	2115.21	1764.45	1532.16
90000	7870.56	4111.59	2861.95	2239.63	1868.24	1622.29
95000	8307.82	4340.01	3020.95	2364.06	1972.03	1712.41
100000	8745.07	4568.43	3179.94	2488.48	2075.82	1802.54
200000	17490.10	9136.86	6359.89	4976.97	4151.64	3605.08
300000	26235.20	13705.30	9539.83	7465.45	6227.46	5407.62
400000	34980.30	18273.70	12719.80	9953.93	8303.27	7210.16
500000	43725.30	22842.20	15899.70	12442.40	10379.10	9012.70

MONTHLY PAYMENT

Necessary to amortize a loan

9%

TERM / AMOUNT	7 YEARS	8 YEARS	9 YEARS	10 YEARS	11 YEARS	12 YEARS
500	8.04	7.33	6.77	6.33	5.98	5.69
600	9.65	8.79	8.13	7.60	7.18	6.83
700	11.26	10.26	9.48	8.87	8.37	7.97
800	12.87	11.72	10.83	10.13	9.57	9.10
900	14.48	13.19	12.19	11.40	10.76	10.24
1000	16.09	14.65	13.54	12.67	11.96	11.38
2000	32.18	29.30	27.09	25.34	23.92	22.76
3000	48.27	43.95	40.63	38.00	35.88	34.14
4000	64.36	58.60	54.17	50.67	47.84	45.52
5000	80.44	73.25	67.71	63.34	59.80	56.90
6000	96.53	87.90	81.26	76.01	71.76	68.28
7000	112.62	102.55	94.80	88.67	83.73	79.66
8000	128.71	117.20	108.34	101.34	95.69	91.04
9000	144.80	131.85	121.89	114.01	107.65	102.42
10000	160.89	146.50	135.43	126.68	119.61	113.80
11000	176.98	161.15	148.97	139.34	131.57	125.18
12000	193.07	175.80	162.51	152.01	143.53	136.56
13000	209.16	190.45	176.06	164.68	155.49	147.94
14000	225.25	205.10	189.60	177.35	167.45	159.32
15000	241.33	219.75	203.14	190.01	179.41	170.70
16000	257.42	234.40	216.69	202.68	191.37	182.08
17000	273.51	249.05	230.23	215.35	203.33	193.46
18000	289.60	263.70	243.77	228.02	215.29	204.84
19000	305.69	278.35	257.31	240.68	227.25	216.23
20000	321.78	293.00	270.86	253.35	239.22	227.61
21000	337.87	307.65	284.40	266.02	251.18	238.99
22000	353.96	322.30	297.94	278.69	263.14	250.37
23000	370.05	336.95	311.49	291.35	275.10	261.75
24000	386.14	351.60	325.03	304.02	287.06	273.13
25000	402.22	366.25	338.57	316.69	299.02	284.51
30000	482.67	439.50	406.29	380.03	358.82	341.41
35000	563.11	512.75	474.00	443.36	418.63	398.31
40000	643.56	586.00	541.71	506.70	478.43	455.21
45000	724.00	659.25	609.43	570.04	538.23	512.11
50000	804.45	732.51	677.14	633.38	598.04	569.01
55000	884.89	805.76	744.86	696.71	657.84	625.91
60000	965.34	879.01	812.57	760.05	717.64	682.81
65000	1045.78	952.26	880.28	823.39	777.45	739.72
70000	1126.23	1025.51	948.00	886.73	837.25	796.62
75000	1206.67	1098.76	1015.71	950.06	897.06	853.52
80000	1287.12	1172.01	1083.43	1013.40	956.86	910.42
85000	1367.56	1245.26	1151.14	1076.74	1016.66	967.32
90000	1448.01	1318.51	1218.85	1140.07	1076.47	1024.22
95000	1528.45	1391.76	1286.57	1203.41	1136.27	1081.12
100000	1608.90	1465.01	1354.28	1266.75	1196.07	1138.02
200000	3217.79	2930.02	2708.56	2533.50	2392.15	2276.05
300000	4826.69	4395.03	4062.84	3800.25	3588.22	3414.07
400000	6435.58	5860.04	5417.13	5067.00	4784.29	4552.10
500000	8044.48	7325.05	6771.41	6333.75	5980.37	5690.12

9%

MONTHLY PAYMENT

Necessary to amortize a loan

TERM / AMOUNT	13 YEARS	14 YEARS	15 YEARS	16 YEARS	17 YEARS	18 YEARS
500	5.45	5.24	5.07	4.92	4.79	4.68
600	6.54	6.29	6.09	5.91	5.75	5.62
700	7.63	7.34	7.10	6.89	6.71	6.56
800	8.72	8.39	8.11	7.88	7.67	7.49
900	9.81	9.44	9.13	8.86	8.63	8.43
1000	10.90	10.49	10.14	9.85	9.59	9.36
2000	21.79	20.98	20.29	19.69	19.18	18.73
3000	32.69	31.47	30.43	29.54	28.76	28.09
4000	43.59	41.96	40.57	39.38	38.35	37.46
5000	54.48	52.45	50.71	49.23	47.94	46.82
6000	65.38	62.94	60.86	59.07	57.53	56.19
7000	76.28	73.43	71.00	68.92	67.12	65.55
8000	87.17	83.91	81.14	78.76	76.70	74.92
9000	98.07	94.40	91.28	88.61	86.29	84.28
10000	108.97	104.89	101.43	98.45	95.88	93.64
11000	119.86	115.38	111.57	108.30	105.47	103.01
12000	130.76	125.87	121.71	118.14	115.06	112.37
13000	141.66	136.36	131.84	127.99	124.64	121.74
14000	152.55	146.85	142.00	137.83	134.23	131.10
15000	163.45	157.34	152.14	147.68	143.82	140.47
16000	174.35	167.83	162.28	157.52	153.41	149.83
17000	185.25	178.32	172.42	167.37	163.00	159.20
18000	196.14	188.81	182.57	177.21	172.58	168.56
19000	207.04	199.30	192.71	187.06	182.17	177.92
20000	217.94	209.79	202.85	196.90	191.76	187.29
21000	228.83	220.28	213.00	206.75	201.35	196.65
22000	239.73	230.77	223.14	216.59	210.94	206.02
23000	250.63	241.25	233.28	226.44	220.52	215.38
24000	261.52	251.74	243.42	236.28	230.11	224.75
25000	272.42	262.23	253.57	246.13	239.70	234.11
30000	326.90	314.68	304.28	295.35	287.64	280.93
35000	381.39	367.13	354.99	344.58	335.58	327.75
40000	435.87	419.57	405.71	393.80	383.52	374.58
45000	490.35	472.02	456.42	443.03	431.46	421.40
50000	544.84	524.47	507.13	492.26	479.40	468.22
55000	599.32	576.91	557.84	541.48	527.34	515.04
60000	653.81	629.36	608.56	590.71	575.28	561.87
65000	708.29	681.81	659.27	639.93	623.22	608.69
70000	762.77	734.25	709.98	689.16	671.16	655.51
75000	817.26	786.70	760.70	738.38	719.10	702.33
80000	871.74	839.15	811.41	787.61	767.04	749.15
85000	926.22	891.59	862.12	836.84	814.98	795.98
90000	980.71	944.04	912.84	886.06	862.92	842.80
95000	1035.19	996.49	963.55	935.29	910.86	889.62
100000	1089.67	1048.93	1014.26	984.51	958.80	936.44
200000	2179.35	2097.86	2028.52	1969.02	1917.60	1872.88
300000	3269.02	3146.80	3042.78	2953.53	2876.40	2809.32
400000	4358.70	4195.73	4057.05	3938.04	3835.20	3745.76
500000	5448.37	5244.66	5071.31	4922.56	4794.00	4682.20

MONTHLY PAYMENT

Necessary to amortize a loan

9%

TERM / AMOUNT	19 YEARS	20 YEARS	25 YEARS	30 YEARS	35 YEARS	40 YEARS
500	4.58	4.50	4.20	4.02	3.92	3.86
600	5.50	5.40	5.04	4.83	4.70	4.63
700	6.42	6.30	5.87	5.63	5.49	5.40
800	7.34	7.20	6.71	6.44	6.27	6.17
900	8.25	8.10	7.55	7.24	7.06	6.94
1000	9.17	9.00	8.39	8.05	7.84	7.71
2000	18.34	17.99	16.78	16.09	15.68	15.43
3000	27.51	26.99	25.18	24.14	23.52	23.14
4000	36.68	35.99	33.57	32.18	31.36	30.85
5000	45.84	44.99	41.96	40.23	39.20	38.57
6000	55.01	53.98	50.35	48.28	47.04	46.28
7000	64.18	62.98	58.74	56.32	54.88	54.00
8000	73.35	71.98	67.14	64.37	62.72	61.71
9000	82.52	80.98	75.53	72.42	70.56	69.42
10000	91.69	89.97	83.92	80.46	78.40	77.14
11000	100.86	98.97	92.31	88.51	86.24	84.85
12000	110.03	107.97	100.70	96.55	94.08	92.56
13000	119.20	116.96	109.10	104.60	101.92	100.28
14000	128.37	125.96	117.49	112.65	109.76	107.99
15000	137.53	134.96	125.88	120.69	117.60	115.70
16000	146.70	143.96	134.27	128.74	125.44	123.42
17000	155.87	152.95	142.66	136.79	133.28	131.13
18000	165.04	161.95	151.06	144.83	141.12	138.85
19000	174.21	170.95	159.45	152.88	148.96	146.56
20000	183.38	179.95	167.84	160.92	156.80	154.27
21000	192.55	188.94	176.23	168.97	164.64	161.99
22000	201.72	197.94	184.62	177.02	172.48	169.70
23000	210.89	206.94	193.02	185.06	180.32	177.41
24000	220.05	215.93	201.41	193.11	188.16	185.13
25000	229.22	224.92	209.80	201.16	196.00	192.84
30000	275.07	269.92	251.76	241.39	235.20	231.41
35000	320.91	314.90	293.72	281.62	274.40	269.98
40000	366.76	359.89	335.68	321.85	313.60	308.54
45000	412.60	404.88	377.64	362.08	352.80	347.11
50000	458.45	449.86	419.60	402.31	392.00	385.68
55000	504.29	494.85	461.56	442.54	431.20	424.25
60000	550.14	539.83	503.52	482.77	470.40	462.82
65000	595.98	584.82	545.48	523.00	509.60	501.38
70000	641.83	629.81	587.44	563.24	548.79	539.95
75000	687.67	674.79	629.40	603.47	587.99	578.52
80000	733.52	719.78	671.36	643.70	627.19	617.09
85000	779.36	764.76	713.32	683.93	666.39	655.66
90000	825.20	809.75	755.28	724.16	705.59	694.23
95000	871.05	854.74	797.23	764.39	744.79	732.79
100000	916.89	899.72	839.19	804.62	783.99	771.36
200000	1833.79	1799.45	1678.39	1609.24	1567.98	1542.72
300000	2750.68	2699.17	2517.58	2413.86	2351.98	2314.08
400000	3667.57	3598.89	3356.78	3218.48	3135.97	3085.44
500000	4584.47	4498.61	4195.97	4023.10	3919.96	3856.80

9 1/2%

MONTHLY PAYMENT
Necessary to amortize a loan

TERM AMOUNT	1 YEAR	2 YEARS	3 YEARS	4 YEARS	5 YEARS	6 YEARS
500	43.84	22.96	16.02	12.56	10.50	9.14
600	52.61	27.55	19.22	15.07	12.60	10.96
700	61.38	32.14	22.42	17.59	14.70	12.79
800	70.15	36.73	25.63	20.10	16.80	14.62
900	78.91	41.32	38.83	22.61	18.90	16.45
1000	87.68	45.91	32.03	25.12	21.00	18.27
2000	175.37	91.83	64.07	50.25	42.00	36.55
3000	263.05	137.74	96.10	75.37	63.01	54.82
4000	350.73	183.66	128.13	100.49	84.01	73.10
5000	438.42	229.57	160.16	125.62	105.01	91.37
6000	526.10	275.49	192.20	150.74	126.01	109.65
7000	613.78	321.40	224.23	175.86	147.01	127.92
8000	701.46	367.31	256.26	200.98	168.01	146.20
9000	789.15	413.23	288.30	226.11	189.02	164.47
10000	876.83	459.14	320.33	251.23	210.02	182.75
11000	964.51	505.06	352.36	276.35	231.02	201.02
12000	1052.20	550.97	384.39	301.48	252.02	219.30
13000	1139.88	596.89	416.43	326.60	273.02	237.57
14000	1227.56	642.80	448.46	351.72	294.03	255.85
15000	1315.25	688.71	480.49	376.85	315.03	274.12
16000	1402.93	734.63	512.53	401.97	336.03	292.39
17000	1490.61	780.54	544.56	427.09	357.03	310.67
18000	1578.29	826.46	576.59	452.21	378.03	328.94
19000	1665.98	872.37	608.62	477.34	399.03	347.22
20000	1753.66	918.29	640.66	502.46	420.04	365.49
21000	1841.34	964.20	672.69	527.58	441.04	383.77
22000	1929.03	1010.11	704.72	552.71	462.04	402.04
23000	2016.71	1056.03	736.75	577.83	483.04	420.32
24000	2104.39	1101.94	768.79	602.95	504.04	438.59
25000	2192.08	1147.86	800.82	628.08	525.04	456.87
30000	2630.49	1377.43	960.98	753.69	630.05	548.24
35000	3068.91	1607.00	1121.15	879.31	735.06	639.61
40000	3507.32	1836.57	1281.31	1004.92	840.07	730.99
45000	3945.74	2066.14	1441.48	1130.54	945.08	822.36
50000	4384.15	2295.71	1601.64	1256.15	1050.09	913.73
55000	4822.57	2525.28	1761.80	1381.77	1155.10	1005.10
60000	5260.98	2754.85	1921.97	1507.38	1260.11	1096.48
65000	5699.40	2984.43	2082.13	1633.00	1365.12	1187.85
70000	6137.81	3214.00	2242.30	1758.61	1470.12	1279.22
75000	6576.23	3443.57	2402.46	1884.23	1575.13	1370.60
80000	7014.64	3673.14	2562.62	2009.84	1680.14	1461.97
85000	7453.06	3902.71	2722.79	2135.46	1785.15	1553.34
90000	7891.47	4132.28	2882.95	2261.07	1890.16	1644.72
95000	8329.89	4361.85	3043.12	2386.69	1995.17	1736.09
100000	8768.30	4591.42	3203.28	2512.30	2100.18	1827.46
200000	17536.60	9182.85	6406.56	5024.60	4200.35	3654.92
300000	26304.90	13774.30	9609.84	7536.91	6300.53	5482.38
400000	35073.20	18365.70	12813.10	10049.20	8400.71	7309.85
500000	43841.50	22957.10	16016.40	12561.50	10500.90	9137.31

MONTHLY PAYMENT

Necessary to amortize a loan

9 1/2%

TERM / AMOUNT	7 YEARS	8 YEARS	9 YEARS	10 YEARS	11 YEARS	12 YEARS
500	8.17	7.46	6.90	6.47	6.12	5.83
600	9.81	8.95	8.29	7.76	7.34	7.00
700	11.44	10.44	9.67	9:06	8.57	8.16
800	13.08	11.93	11.05	10.35	9.79	9.33
900	14.71	13.42	12.43	11.65	11.01	10.50
1000	16.34	14.91	13.81	12.94	12.24	11.66
2000	32.69	29.82	27.62	25.88	24.48	23.33
3000	49.03	44.73	41.43	38.82	36.72	34.99
4000	65.38	59.64	55.24	51.76	48.95	46.65
5000	81.72	74.55	69.05	64.70	61.19	58.32
6000	98.06	89.47	82.86	77.64	73.43	69.98
7000	114.41	104.38	96.67	90.58	85.67	81.65
8000	130.75	119.29	110.47	103.52	97.91	93.31
9000	147.10	134.20	124.28	116.46	110.15	104.97
10000	163.44	149.11	138.09	129.40	122.39	116.64
11000	179.78	164.02	151.90	142.34	134.63	128.30
12000	196.13	178.93	165.71	155.28	146.86	139.96
13000	212.47	193.84	179.52	168.22	159.10	151.63
14000	228.82	208.75	193.33	181.16	171.34	163.29
15000	245.16	223.66	207.14	194.10	183.58	174.96
16000	261.50	238.57	220.95	207.04	195.82	186.62
17000	277.85	253.48	234.76	219.98	208.06	198.28
18000	294.19	268.40	248.57	232.92	220.30	209.95
19000	310.53	283.31	262.38	245.86	232.53	221.61
20000	326.88	298.22	276.19	258.79	244.77	233.27
21000	343.22	313.13	290.00	271.73	257.01	244.94
22000	359.57	328.04	303.81	284.67	269.25	256.60
23000	375.91	342.95	317.61	297.61	281.49	268.27
24000	392.25	357.86	331.42	310.55	293.73	279.93
25000	408.60	372.77	345.23	323.49	305.97	291.59
30000	490.32	447.33	414.28	388.19	367.16	349.91
35000	572.04	521.88	483.33	452.89	428.35	408.23
40000	653.76	596.43	552.37	517.59	489.54	466.55
45000	735.48	670.99	621.42	582.29	550.74	524.87
50000	817.20	745.54	690.47	646.99	611.93	583.19
55000	898.92	820.10	759.51	711.68	673.12	641.50
60000	980.64	894.65	828.56	776.38	734.32	699.82
65000	1062.35	969.20	897.61	841.08	795.51	758.14
70000	1144.07	1043.76	966.65	905.78	856.70	816.46
75000	1225.79	1118.31	1035.70	970.48	917.90	874.78
80000	1307.51	1192.87	1104.74	1035.18	979.09	933.10
85000	1389.23	1267.42	1173.79	1099.88	1040.28	991.41
90000	1470.95	1341.97	1242.84	1164.57	1101.47	1049.73
95000	1552.67	1416.53	1311.88	1229.27	1162.67	1108.05
100000	1634.39	1491.08	1380.93	1293.97	1223.86	1166.37
200000	3268.78	2982.17	2761.86	2587.94	2447.72	2332.74
300000	4903.17	4473.25	4142.79	3881.91	3671.58	3499.11
400000	6537.57	5964.33	5523.72	5175.88	4895.44	4665.48
500000	8171.96	7455.42	6904.66	6469.86	6119.30	5831.85

9 1/2% MONTHLY PAYMENT

Necessary to amortize a loan

TERM / AMOUNT	13 YEARS	14 YEARS	15 YEARS	16 YEARS	17 YEARS	18 YEARS
500	5.59	5.39	5.22	5.07	4.95	4.84
600	6.71	6.47	6.27	6.09	5.94	5.81
700	7.83	7.55	7.31	7.10	6.93	6.78
800	8.95	8.63	8.35	8.12	7.92	7.74
900	10.07	9.71	9.40	9.13	8.91	8.71
1000	11.19	10.78	10.44	10.15	9.90	9.68
2000	22.37	21.57	20.88	20.30	19.80	19.36
3000	33.56	32.35	31.33	30.45	29.69	29.04
4000	44.74	43.13	41.77	40.60	39.59	38.72
5000	55.93	53.92	52.21	50.75	49.49	48.40
6000	67.11	64.70	62.65	60.90	59.39	58.07
7000	78.30	75.49	73.10	71.05	69.28	67.75
8000	89.49	86.27	83.54	81.20	79.18	77.43
9000	100.67	97.05	93.98	91.35	89.08	87.11
10000	111.86	107.84	104.42	101.50	98.98	96.79
11000	123.04	118.62	114.86	111.65	108.88	106.47
12000	134.23	129.40	125.31	121.80	118.77	116.15
13000	145.41	140.19	135.75	131.95	128.67	125.83
14000	156.60	150.97	146.19	142.10	138.57	135.51
15000	167.79	161.76	156.63	152.25	148.47	145.19
16000	178.97	172.54	167.08	162.40	158.37	154.87
17000	190.16	183.32	177.52	172.55	168.26	164.55
18000	201.34	194.11	187.96	182.70	178.16	174.22
19000	212.53	204.89	198.40	192.85	188.06	183.90
20000	223.71	215.67	208.84	203.00	197.96	193.58
21000	234.90	226.46	219.29	213.15	207.85	203.26
22000	246.09	237.24	229.73	223.30	217.75	212.94
23000	257.27	248.02	240.17	233.45	227.65	222.62
24000	268.46	258.81	250.61	243.60	237.55	232.30
25000	279.64	269.59	261.06	253.75	247.45	241.98
30000	335.57	323.51	313.27	304.50	296.93	290.37
35000	391.50	377.43	365.48	355.25	346.42	338.77
40000	447.43	431.35	417.69	406.00	395.91	387.16
45000	503.36	485.26	469.90	456.74	445.40	435.56
50000	559.28	539.18	522.11	507.49	494.89	483.96
55000	615.21	593.10	574.32	558.24	544.38	532.35
60000	671.14	647.02	626.53	608.99	593.87	580.75
65000	727.07	700.94	678.74	659.74	643.36	629.14
70000	783.00	754.86	730.96	710.49	692.85	677.54
75000	838.93	808.77	783.17	761.24	742.33	725.93
80000	894.86	862.69	835.38	811.99	791.82	774.33
85000	950.78	916.61	887.59	862.74	841.31	822.72
90000	1006.71	970.53	939.80	913.49	890.80	871.12
95000	1062.64	1024.45	992.01	964.24	940.29	919.51
100000	1118.57	1078.37	1044.22	1014.99	989.78	967.91
200000	2237.14	2156.73	2088.44	2029.97	1979.56	1935.82
300000	3355.71	3235.10	3132.67	3044.96	2969.33	2903.73
400000	4474.28	4313.46	4176.89	4059.95	3959.11	3871.64
500000	5592.84	5391.83	5221.11	5074.94	4948.89	4839.55

MONTHLY PAYMENT

Necessary to amortize a loan

9 1/2%

TERM / AMOUNT	19 YEARS	20 YEARS	25 YEARS	30 YEARS	35 YEARS	40 YEARS
500	4.74	4.66	4.37	4.20	4.11	4.05
600	5.69	5.59	5.24	5.05	4.93	4.86
700	6.64	6.52	6.12	5.89	5.75	5.67
800	7.59	7.46	6.99	6.73	6.57	6.48
900	8.54	8.39	7.86	7.57	7.39	7.29
1000	9.49	9.32	8.74	8.41	8.22	8.10
2000	18.98	18.64	17.47	16.82	16.43	16.20
3000	28.47	27.96	26.21	25.23	24.65	24.30
4000	37.95	37.29	34.95	33.63	32.86	32.40
5000	47.44	46.61	43.68	42.04	41.08	40.50
6000	56.93	55.93	52.42	50.45	49.30	48.60
7000	66.42	65.25	61.16	58.86	57.51	56.70
8000	75.91	74.57	69.90	67.27	65.73	64.80
9000	85.40	83.89	78.63	75.68	73.95	72.91
10000	94.88	93.21	87.37	84.09	82.16	81.01
11000	104.37	102.53	96.11	92.49	90.38	89.11
12000	113.86	111.86	104.84	100.90	98.59	97.21
13000	123.35	121.18	113.58	109.31	106.81	105.31
14000	132.84	130.50	122.32	117.72	115.03	113.41
15000	142.33	139.82	131.05	126.13	123.24	121.51
16000	151.81	149.14	139.79	134.54	131.46	129.61
17000	161.30	158.46	148.53	142.95	139.67	137.71
18000	170.79	167.78	157.27	151.35	147.89	145.81
19000	180.28	177.11	166.00	159.76	156.11	153.91
20000	189.77	186.43	174.74	168.17	164.32	162.01
21000	199.26	195.75	183.48	176.58	172.54	170.11
22000	208.74	205.07	192.21	184.99	180.75	178.21
23000	218.23	214.39	200.95	193.40	188.97	186.31
24000	227.72	223.71	209.69	201.81	197.19	194.42
25000	237.21	233.03	218.42	210.21	205.40	202.52
30000	284.65	279.64	262.11	252.26	246.48	243.02
35000	332.09	326.25	305.79	294.30	287.56	283.52
40000	379.54	372.85	349.48	336.34	328.65	324.03
45000	426.98	419.46	393.16	378.38	369.73	364.53
50000	474.42	466.07	436.85	420.43	410.81	405.03
55000	521.86	512.67	480.53	462.47	451.89	445.53
60000	569.30	559.28	524.22	504.51	492.97	486.04
65000	616.75	605.88	567.90	546.56	534.05	526.54
70000	664.19	652.49	611.59	588.60	575.13	567.04
75000	711.63	699.10	655.27	630.64	616.21	607.55
80000	759.07	745.70	698.96	672.68	657.29	648.05
85000	806.51	792.31	742.64	714.73	698.37	688.55
90000	853.95	838.92	786.33	756.77	739.45	729.06
95000	901.40	885.52	830.01	798.81	780.53	769.56
100000	948.84	932.13	873.70	840.85	821.61	810.06
200000	1897.68	1864.26	1747.39	1681.71	1643.22	1620.12
300000	2846.51	2796.39	2621.09	2522.56	2464.83	2430.18
400000	3795.35	3728.52	3494.78	3363.42	3286.45	3240.25
500000	4744.19	4660.65	4368.48	4204.27	4108.06	4050.31

10%

MONTHLY PAYMENT

Necessary to amortize a loan

TERM / AMOUNT	1 YEAR	2 YEARS	3 YEARS	4 YEARS	5 YEARS	6 YEARS
500	43.96	23.07	16.13	12.68	10.62	9.26
600	52.75	27.69	19.36	15.22	12.75	11.12
700	61.54	32.30	22.59	17.75	14.87	12.97
800	70.33	36.92	25.81	20.29	17.00	14.82
900	79.12	41.53	29.04	22.83	19.12	16.67
1000	87.92	46.14	32.27	25.36	21.25	18.53
2000	175.83	92.29	64.53	50.73	42.49	37.05
3000	263.75	138.43	96.80	76.09	63.74	55.58
4000	351.66	184.58	129.07	101.45	84.99	74.10
5000	439.58	230.72	161.34	126.81	106.24	92.63
6000	527.49	276.87	193.60	152.18	127.48	111.16
7000	615.41	323.01	225.87	177.54	148.73	129.68
8000	703.32	369.16	258.14	202.90	169.98	148.21
9000	791.24	415.30	290.40	228.26	191.22	166.73
10000	879.16	461.45	322.67	253.63	212.47	185.26
11000	967.07	507.59	354.94	278.99	233.72	203.78
12000	1054.99	553.74	387.21	304.35	254.96	222.31
13000	1142.90	599.88	419.47	329.71	276.21	240.84
14000	1230.82	646.03	451.74	355.08	297.46	259.36
15000	1318.73	692.17	484.01	380.44	318.71	277.89
16000	1406.65	738.32	516.27	405.80	339.95	296.41
17000	1494.56	784.46	548.54	431.16	361.20	314.94
18000	1582.48	830.61	580.81	456.53	382.45	333.46
19000	1670.40	876.75	613.07	481.89	403.69	351.99
20000	1758.31	922.90	645.34	507.25	424.94	370.52
21000	1846.23	969.04	677.61	532.61	446.19	389.04
22000	1934.14	1015.18	709.88	557.98	467.43	407.57
23000	2022.06	1061.33	742.14	583.34	488.68	426.09
24000	2109.97	1107.47	774.41	608.70	509.93	444.62
25000	2197.89	1153.62	806.68	634.06	531.17	463.15
30000	2637.47	1384.34	968.01	760.88	637.41	555.77
35000	3077.04	1615.07	1129.35	887.69	743.64	648.40
40000	3516.62	1845.79	1290.68	1014.50	849.88	741.03
45000	3956.20	2076.51	1452.02	1141.31	956.11	833.66
50000	4395.78	2307.24	1613.35	1268.13	1062.35	926.29
55000	4835.35	2537.96	1774.69	1394.94	1168.58	1018.92
60000	5274.93	2768.68	1936.02	1521.75	1274.82	1111.55
65000	5714.51	2999.41	1097.36	1648.56	1381.05	1204.18
70000	6154.09	3230.13	2258.70	1775.37	1487.29	1296.80
75000	6593.67	3460.86	2420.03	1902.19	1593.52	1389.43
80000	7033.24	3691.58	2581.37	2029.00	1699.76	1482.06
85000	7472.82	3922.30	2742.70	2155.81	1805.99	1574.69
90000	7912.40	4153.03	2904.04	2282.63	1912.23	1667.32
95000	8351.98	4383.75	3065.37	2409.44	2018.46	1759.95
100000	8791.55	4614.47	3226.71	2536.25	2124.70	1852.58
200000	17583.10	9228.95	6453.42	5072.50	4249.40	3705.16
300000	26374.70	13843.40	9680.12	7608.75	6374.09	5557.73
400000	35166.20	18457.90	12906.80	10145.00	8498.79	7410.31
500000	43957.80	23072.40	16133.50	12681.30	10623.50	9262.89

MONTHLY PAYMENT

Necessary to amortize a loan

10%

TERM / AMOUNT	7 YEARS	8 YEARS	9 YEARS	10 YEARS	11 YEARS	12 YEARS
500	8.30	7.59	7.04	6.61	6.26	5.98
600	9.96	9.10	8.45	7.93	7.51	7.17
700	11.62	10.62	9.86	9.25	8.76	8.37
800	13.28	12.14	11.26	10.57	10.02	9.56
900	14.94	13.66	12.67	11.89	11.27	10.76
1000	16.60	15.17	14.08	13.22	12.52	11.95
2000	33.20	30.35	28.16	26.43	25.04	23.90
3000	49.80	45.52	42.24	39.65	37.56	35.85
4000	66.40	60.70	56.31	52.86	50.08	47.80
5000	83.01	75.87	70.39	66.08	62.60	59.75
6000	99.61	91.04	84.47	79.29	75.12	71.70
7000	116.21	106.22	98.55	92.51	87.64	83.66
8000	132.81	121.39	112.63	105.72	100.16	95.61
9000	149.41	136.57	126.71	118.94	112.68	107.56
10000	166.01	151.74	140.79	132.15	125.20	119.51
11000	182.61	166.92	154.87	145.37	137.72	131.46
12000	199.21	182.09	168.94	158.58	150.24	143.41
13000	215.82	197.26	183.02	171.80	162.76	155.36
14000	232.42	212.44	197.10	185.01	175.28	167.31
15000	249.02	227.61	211.18	198.23	187.80	179.26
16000	265.62	242.79	225.26	211.44	200.32	191.21
17000	282.22	257.96	239.34	224.66	212.84	203.16
18000	298.82	273.13	153.42	237.87	225.36	215.11
19000	315.42	288.31	267.49	251.09	237.88	227.06
20000	332.02	303.48	281.57	264.30	250.40	239.02
21000	348.62	318.66	295.65	277.52	262.92	250.97
22000	365.23	333.83	309.73	290.73	275.44	262.92
23000	381.83	349.01	323.81	303.95	287.96	274.87
24000	398.43	364.18	337.89	317.16	300.48	286.82
25000	415.03	379.35	351.97	330.38	313.00	298.77
30000	498.03	455.22	422.36	396.45	375.60	358.52
35000	581.04	531.09	492.75	462.53	438.20	418.28
40000	664.05	606.97	563.15	528.60	500.79	478.03
45000	747.05	682.84	633.54	594.68	563.39	537.78
50000	830.06	758.71	703.93	660.75	625.99	597.54
55000	913.06	834.58	774.33	726.83	688.59	657.29
60000	996.07	910.45	844.72	792.90	751.19	717.05
65000	1079.07	986.32	915.11	858.98	813.79	776.80
70000	1162.08	1062.19	985.51	925.05	876.39	836.55
75000	1245.09	1138.06	1055.90	991.13	938.99	896.31
80000	1328.09	1213.93	1126.29	1057.20	1001.59	956.06
85000	1411.10	1289.80	1196.69	1123.28	1064.19	1015.81
90000	1494.10	1365.67	1267.08	1189.35	1126.79	1075.57
95000	1577.11	1441.54	1337.47	1255.43	1189.39	1135.32
100000	1660.11	1517.41	1407.87	1321.50	1251.98	1195.08
200000	3320.23	3034.82	2815.73	2643.01	2503.97	2390.15
300000	4980.34	4552.24	4223.59	3964.51	3755.95	3585.23
400000	6640.45	6069.65	5631.46	5286.02	5007.94	4780.30
500000	8300.57	7587.06	7039.32	6607.52	6259.92	5975.38

10%

MONTHLY PAYMENT

Necessary to amortize a loan

TERM / AMOUNT	13 YEARS	14 YEARS	15 YEARS	16 YEARS	17 YEARS	18 YEARS
500	5.74	5.54	5.37	5.23	5.11	5.00
600	6.89	6.65	6.45	6.28	6.13	6.00
700	8.03	7.76	7.52	7.32	7.15	7.00
800	9.18	8.87	8.60	8.37	8.17	8.00
900	10.33	9.97	9.67	9.41	9.19	9.00
1000	11.48	11.08	10.75	10.46	10.21	10.00
2000	22.96	22.16	21.49	20.92	20.42	20.00
3000	34.44	33.25	32.24	31.38	30.64	30.00
4000	45.91	44.33	42.98	41.84	40.85	39.99
5000	57.39	55.41	53.73	52.30	51.06	49.99
6000	68.87	66.49	64.48	62.75	61.27	59.99
7000	80.35	77.57	75.22	73.21	71.48	69.99
8000	91.83	88.66	85.97	83.67	81.70	79.99
9000	103.31	99.74	96.71	94.13	91.91	89.99
10000	114.79	110.82	107.46	104.59	102.12	99.98
11000	126.26	121.90	118.21	115.05	112.33	109.98
12000	137.74	132.98	128.95	125.51	122.55	119.98
13000	149.22	144.07	139.70	135.97	132.76	129.98
14000	160.70	155.15	150.44	146.43	142.97	139.98
15000	172.18	166.23	161.19	156.89	153.18	149.98
16000	183.66	177.31	171.94	167.34	163.39	159.98
17000	195.13	188.39	182.68	177.80	173.61	169.97
18000	206.61	199.48	193.43	188.26	183.82	179.97
19000	218.09	210.56	204.18	198.72	194.03	189.97
20000	229.57	221.64	214.92	209.18	204.24	199.97
21000	241.05	232.72	225.67	219.64	214.45	209.97
22000	252.53	243.80	236.41	230.10	224.67	219.97
23000	264.01	254.89	247.16	240.56	234.88	229.96
24000	275.48	265.97	257.91	251.02	245.09	239.96
25000	286.96	277.05	268.65	261.48	255.30	249.96
30000	344.35	332.46	322.38	313.77	306.36	299.95
35000	401.75	387.87	376.11	366.07	357.42	349.95
40000	459.14	443.28	429.84	418.36	408.48	399.94
45000	516.53	498.69	483.57	470.66	459.54	449.93
50000	573.92	554.10	537.30	522.95	510.60	499.92
55000	631.32	609.51	591.03	575.25	561.67	549.91
60000	688.71	664.92	644.76	627.54	612.73	599.91
65000	746.10	720.33	698.49	679.84	663.79	649.90
70000	803.49	775.74	752.22	732.13	714.85	699.89
75000	860.88	831.15	805.95	784.43	765.91	749.88
80000	918.28	886.56	859.68	836.72	816.97	799.87
85000	975.67	941.97	913.41	889.02	868.03	849.87
90000	1033.06	997.38	967.14	941.31	919.09	899.86
95000	1090.45	1052.79	1020.87	993.61	970.15	949.85
100000	1147.85	1108.20	1074.60	1045.90	1021.21	999.84
200000	2295.69	2216.40	2149.21	2091.80	2042.42	1999.68
300000	3443.54	3324.60	3223.81	3137.70	3063.63	2999.53
400000	4591.38	4432.80	4298.41	4183.60	4084.84	3999.37
500000	5739.23	5541.00	5373.02	5229.50	5106.04	4999.21

MONTHLY PAYMENT

Necessary to amortize a loan

10%

TERM / AMOUNT	19 YEARS	20 YEARS	25 YEARS	30 YEARS	35 YEARS	40 YEARS
500	4.91	4.83	4.54	4.39	4.30	4.25
600	5.89	5.79	5.45	5.27	5.16	5.09
700	6.87	6.76	6.36	6.14	6.02	5.94
800	7.85	7.72	7.27	7.02	6.88	6.79
900	8.83	8.69	8.18	7.90	7.74	7.64
1000	9.81	9.65	9.09	8.78	8.60	8.49
2000	19.63	19.30	18.17	17.55	17.19	16.98
3000	29.44	28.95	27.26	26.33	25.79	25.47
4000	39.25	38.60	36.35	35.10	34.39	33.97
5000	49.06	48.25	45.44	43.88	42.98	42.46
6000	58.88	57.90	54.52	52.65	51.58	50.95
7000	68.69	67.55	63.61	61.43	60.18	59.44
8000	78.50	77.20	72.70	70.21	68.77	67.93
9000	88.31	86.85	81.78	78.98	77.37	76.42
10000	98.13	96.50	90.87	87.76	85.97	84.91
11000	107.94	106.15	99.96	96.53	94.56	93.41
12000	117.75	115.80	109.04	105.31	103.16	101.90
13000	127.56	125.45	118.13	114.08	111.76	110.39
14000	137.38	135.10	127.22	122.86	120.35	118.88
15000	147.19	144.75	136.31	131.64	128.95	127.37
16000	157.00	154.40	145.39	140.41	137.55	135.86
17000	166.81	164.05	154.48	149.19	146.14	144.36
18000	176.63	173.70	163.57	157.96	154.74	152.85
19000	186.44	183.35	172.65	166.74	163.34	161.34
20000	196.25	193.00	181.74	175.51	171.93	169.83
21000	206.06	202.65	190.83	184.29	180.53	178.32
22000	215.88	212.30	199.91	193.07	189.13	186.81
23000	225.69	221.96	209.00	201.84	197.73	195.30
24000	235.50	231.61	218.09	210.62	206.32	203.80
25000	245.31	241.26	227.18	219.39	214.92	212.29
30000	294.38	289.51	272.61	263.27	257.90	254.74
35000	343.44	337.76	318.05	307.15	300.89	297.20
40000	392.50	386.01	363.48	351.03	343.87	339.66
45000	441.57	434.26	408.92	394.91	386.85	382.12
50000	490.63	482.51	454.35	438.79	429.84	424.57
55000	539.69	530.76	499.79	482.66	472.82	467.03
60000	588.76	579.01	545.22	526.54	515.80	509.49
65000	637.82	627.26	590.66	570.42	558.79	551.95
70000	686.88	675.51	636.09	614.30	601.77	594.40
75000	735.94	723.77	681.53	658.18	644.75	636.86
80000	785.01	772.02	726.96	702.06	687.74	679.32
85000	834.07	820.27	772.40	745.94	730.72	721.77
90000	883.13	868.52	817.83	789.81	773.71	764.23
95000	932.20	916.77	863.27	833.69	816.69	806.69
100000	981.26	965.02	908.70	877.57	859.67	849.15
200000	1962.52	1930.04	1817.40	1755.14	1719.34	1698.29
300000	2943.77	2895.06	2726.10	2632.71	2579.02	2547.44
400000	3925.03	3860.08	3634.80	3510.29	3438.69	3396.58
500000	4906.29	4825.10	4543.50	4387.86	4298.36	4245.73

10 1/4% MONTHLY PAYMENT

Necessary to amortize a loan

TERM / AMOUNT	1 YEAR	2 YEARS	3 YEARS	4 YEARS	5 YEARS	6 YEARS
500	44.02	23.13	16.19	12.74	10.69	9.33
600	52.82	27.76	19.43	15.29	12.82	11.19
700	61.62	32.38	22.67	17.84	14.96	13.06
800	70.43	37.01	25.91	20.39	17.10	14.92
900	79.23	41.63	29.15	22.93	19.23	16.79
1000	88.03	46.26	32.38	25.48	21.37	18.65
2000	176.06	92.52	64.77	50.97	42.74	37.30
3000	264.10	138.78	97.15	76.45	64.11	55.96
4000	352.13	185.04	129.54	101.93	85.48	74.61
5000	440.16	231.30	161.92	127.41	106.85	93.26
6000	528.19	277.56	194.31	152.90	128.22	111.91
7000	616.22	323.82	226.69	178.38	149.59	130.57
8000	704.26	370.08	259.08	203.86	170.96	149.22
9000	792.29	416.34	291.46	229.35	192.33	167.87
10000	880.32	462.60	323.85	254.83	213.70	186.52
11000	968.35	508.86	356.23	280.31	235.07	205.17
12000	1056.38	555.12	388.62	305.79	256.44	223.83
13000	1144.41	601.38	421.00	331.28	277.81	242.48
14000	1232.45	647.64	453.38	356.76	299.18	261.13
15000	1320.48	693.90	485.77	382.24	320.55	279.78
16000	1408.51	740.16	518.15	407.72	341.92	298.43
17000	1496.54	786.42	550.54	433.21	363.29	317.09
18000	1584.57	832.68	582.92	458.69	384.66	335.74
19000	1672.61	878.94	615.31	484.17	406.03	354.39
20000	1760.64	925.21	647.69	509.66	427.40	373.04
21000	1848.67	971.47	680.08	535.14	448.77	391.69
22000	1936.70	1017.73	712.46	560.62	470.14	410.35
23000	2024.73	1063.99	744.85	586.10	491.51	429.00
24000	2112.76	1110.25	777.23	611.59	512.89	447.65
25000	2200.80	1156.51	809.61	637.07	534.26	466.30
30000	2640.96	1387.81	971.54	764.48	641.11	559.56
35000	3081.12	1619.11	1133.46	891.90	747.96	652.82
40000	3521.27	1850.41	1295.38	1019.31	854.81	746.08
45000	3961.43	2081.71	1457.31	1146.72	961.66	839.34
50000	4401.59	2313.01	1619.23	1274.14	1068.51	932.61
55000	4841.75	2544.31	1781.15	1401.55	1175.36	1025.87
60000	5281.91	2775.61	1943.07	1528.96	1282.21	1119.13
65000	5722.07	3006.91	2105.00	1656.38	1389.06	1212.39
70000	6162.23	3238.22	2266.92	1783.79	1495.91	1305.65
75000	6602.39	3469.52	2428.84	1911.20	1602.76	1398.91
80000	7042.55	3700.82	2590.77	2038.62	1709.62	1492.17
85000	7482.71	3932.12	2752.69	2166.03	1816.47	1585.43
90000	7922.87	4163.42	2914.61	2293.45	1923.32	1678.69
95000	8363.03	4394.72	3076.53	2420.86	2030.17	1771.95
100000	8803.19	4626.02	3238.46	2548.27	2137.02	1865.21
200000	17606.40	9252.04	6476.91	5096.55	4274.04	3730.42
300000	26409.60	13878.10	9715.37	7644.82	6411.06	5595.63
400000	35212.70	18504.10	12953.80	10193.10	8548.08	7460.84
500000	44015.90	23130.10	16192.30	12741.40	10685.10	9326.05

MONTHLY PAYMENT

Necessary to amortize a loan

10 1/4%

TERM / AMOUNT	7 YEARS	8 YEARS	9 YEARS	10 YEARS	11 YEARS	12 YEARS
500	8.37	7.65	7.11	6.68	6.33	6.05
600	10.04	9.18	8.53	8.01	7.60	7.26
700	11.71	10.71	9.95	9.35	8.86	8.47
800	13.38	12.25	11.37	10.68	10.13	9.68
900	15.06	13.78	12.79	12.02	11.40	10.89
1000	16.73	15.31	14.21	13.35	12.66	12.10
2000	33.46	30.61	28.43	26.71	25.32	24.19
3000	50.19	45.92	42.64	40.06	37.99	36.29
4000	66.92	61.23	58.86	53.42	50.65	48.38
5000	83.65	76.53	71.07	66.77	63.31	60.48
6000	100.38	91.84	85.29	80.12	75.97	72.57
7000	117.11	107.15	99.50	93.48	88.63	84.67
8000	133.85	122.45	113.72	106.83	101.29	96.77
9000	150.58	137.76	127.93	120.19	113.96	108.86
10000	167.31	153.07	142.14	133.54	126.62	120.96
11000	184.04	168.37	156.36	146.89	139.28	133.05
12000	200.77	183.68	170.57	160.25	151.94	145.15
13000	217.50	198.99	184.79	173.60	164.60	157.24
14000	234.23	214.29	199.00	186.95	177.26	169.34
15000	250.96	229.60	213.22	200.31	189.93	181.43
16000	267.69	244.91	227.43	213.66	202.59	193.53
17000	284.42	260.21	241.65	227.02	215.25	205.63
18000	301.15	275.52	255.86	240.37	227.91	217.72
19000	317.88	290.83	270.07	253.72	240.57	229.82
20000	334.61	306.14	284.29	267.08	253.23	241.91
21000	351.34	321.44	298.50	280.43	265.90	254.01
22000	368.07	336.75	312.72	293.79	278.56	266.10
23000	384.80	352.06	326.93	307.14	291.22	278.20
24000	401.53	367.36	341.15	320.49	303.88	290.30
25000	418.27	382.67	355.36	333.85	316.54	302.39
30000	501.92	459.20	426.43	400.62	379.85	362.87
35000	585.57	535.74	497.50	467.39	443.16	423.35
40000	669.22	612.27	568.58	534.16	506.47	483.83
45000	752.88	688.80	639.65	600.92	569.78	544.30
50000	836.53	765.34	710.72	667.69	633.09	604.78
55000	920.18	841.87	781.79	734.46	696.40	665.26
60000	1003.84	918.40	852.86	801.23	759.70	725.74
65000	1087.49	994.94	923.94	868.00	823.01	786.22
70000	1171.14	1071.47	995.01	934.77	886.32	846.69
75000	1254.79	1148.00	1066.08	1001.54	949.63	907.17
80000	1338.45	1224.54	1137.15	1068.31	1012.94	967.65
85000	1422.10	1301.07	1208.22	1135.08	1076.25	1028.13
90000	1505.75	1377.61	1279.29	1201.85	1139.56	1088.61
95000	1589.41	1454.14	1350.37	1268.62	1202.86	1149.08
100000	1673.06	1530.67	1421.44	1335.39	1266.17	1209.56
200000	3346.12	3061.35	2842.88	2670.77	2532.34	2419.13
300000	5019.18	4592.02	4264.31	4006.16	3798.52	3628.69
400000	6692.24	6122.69	5685.75	5341.55	5064.69	4838.25
500000	8365.30	7653.36	7107.19	6676.93	6330.86	6047.81

10 1/4% MONTHLY PAYMENT

Necessary to amortize a loan

TERM / AMOUNT	13 YEARS	14 YEARS	15 YEARS	16 YEARS	17 YEARS	18 YEARS
500	5.81	5.62	5.45	5.31	5.19	5.08
600	6.98	6.74	6.54	6.37	6.22	6.10
700	8.14	7.86	7.63	7.43	7.26	7.11
800	9.30	8.99	8.72	8.49	8.30	8.13
900	10.46	10.11	9.81	9.55	9.33	9.14
1000	11.63	11.23	10.90	10.62	10.37	10.16
2000	23.25	22.47	21.80	21.23	20.74	20.32
3000	34.88	33.70	32.70	31.85	31.11	30.48
4000	46.51	44.93	43.60	42.46	41.48	40.64
5000	58.13	56.16	54.50	53.08	51.85	50.80
6000	69.76	67.40	65.40	63.69	62.23	60.96
7000	81.38	78.63	76.30	74.31	72.60	71.12
8000	93.01	89.86	87.20	84.92	82.97	81.28
9000	104.64	101.09	98.10	95.54	93.34	91.44
10000	116.26	112.33	109.00	106.15	103.71	101.60
11000	127.89	123.56	119.89	116.77	114.08	111.76
12000	139.52	134.79	130.79	127.38	124.45	121.92
13000	151.14	146.03	141.69	138.00	134.82	132.08
14000	162.77	157.26	152.59	148.61	145.19	142.24
15000	174.39	168.49	163.49	159.23	155.56	152.40
16000	186.02	179.72	174.39	169.84	165.93	162.56
17000	197.65	190.96	185.29	180.46	176.31	172.72
18000	209.27	202.19	196.19	191.07	186.68	182.88
19000	220.90	213.42	207.09	201.69	197.05	193.04
20000	232.53	224.65	217.99	212.30	207.42	203.20
21000	244.15	235.89	228.89	222.92	217.79	213.36
22000	255.78	247.12	239.79	233.53	228.16	223.52
23000	267.40	258.35	250.69	244.15	238.53	233.68
24000	279.03	269.58	261.59	254.76	248.90	243.84
25000	290.66	280.82	272.49	265.38	259.27	254.00
30000	348.79	336.98	326.99	318.46	311.13	304.79
35000	406.92	393.14	381.48	371.53	362.98	355.59
40000	465.05	449.31	435.98	424.61	414.84	406.39
45000	523.18	505.47	490.48	477.68	466.69	457.19
50000	581.31	561.63	544.97	530.76	518.55	507.99
55000	639.44	617.80	599.47	583.84	570.40	558.79
60000	697.58	673.97	653.97	636.91	622.25	609.59
65000	755.71	730.12	708.47	689.99	674.11	660.39
70000	813.84	786.29	762.96	743.06	725.96	711.19
75000	871.97	842.45	817.46	796.14	777.82	761.98
80000	930.10	898.61	871.96	849.21	829.67	812.78
85000	988.23	954.78	926.46	902.29	881.53	863.58
90000	1046.36	1010.94	980.95	955.37	933.38	914.38
95000	1104.49	1067.10	1035.45	1008.44	985.24	965.18
100000	1162.63	1123.27	1089.95	1061.52	1037.09	1015.98
200000	2325.25	2246.53	2179.90	2123.04	2074.18	2031.96
300000	3487.88	3369.80	3269.85	3184.55	3111.27	3047.94
400000	4650.50	4493.07	4359.80	4246.07	4148.36	4063.91
500000	5813.13	5616.34	5449.75	5307.59	5185.45	5079.89

MONTHLY PAYMENT

Necessary to amortize a loan

10 1/4%

TERM → AMOUNT	19 YEARS	20 YEARS	25 YEARS	30 YEARS	35 YEARS	40 YEARS
500	4.99	4.91	4.63	4.48	4.39	4.34
600	5.99	5.89	5.56	5.38	5.27	5.21
700	6.98	6.87	6.48	6.27	6.15	6.08
800	7.98	7.85	7.41	7.17	7.03	6.95
900	8.98	8.83	8.34	8.06	7.91	7.82
1000	9.98	9.82	9.26	8.96	8.79	8.69
2000	19.95	19.63	18.53	17.92	17.58	17.38
3000	29.93	29.45	27.79	26.88	26.37	26.06
4000	39.91	39.27	37.06	35.84	35.15	34.75
5000	49.88	49.08	46.32	44.81	43.94	43.44
6000	59.86	58.90	55.58	53.77	52.73	52.13
7000	69.83	68.72	64.85	62.73	61.52	60.82
8000	79.81	78.53	74.11	71.69	70.31	69.51
9000	89.79	88.35	83.37	80.65	79.10	78.19
10000	99.76	98.16	92.64	89.61	87.89	86.88
11000	109.74	107.98	101.90	98.57	96.67	95.57
12000	119.72	117.80	111.17	107.53	105.46	104.26
13000	129.69	127.61	120.43	116.49	114.25	112.95
14000	139.67	137.43	129.69	125.45	123.04	121.64
15000	149.65	147.25	138.96	134.42	131.83	130.32
16000	159.62	157.06	148.22	143.38	140.62	139.01
17000	169.60	166.88	157.49	152.34	149.41	147.70
18000	179.58	176.70	166.75	161.30	158.19	156.39
19000	189.55	186.51	176.01	170.26	166.98	165.08
20000	199.53	196.33	185.28	179.22	175.77	173.76
21000	209.51	206.15	194.54	188.18	184.56	182.45
22000	219.48	215.96	203.80	197.14	193.35	191.14
23000	229.46	225.78	213.07	206.10	202.14	199.83
24000	239.43	235.59	222.33	215.06	210.93	208.52
25000	249.41	245.41	231.60	224.03	219.71	217.21
30000	299.29	294.49	277.92	268.83	263.66	260.65
35000	349.17	343.58	324.23	313.64	307.60	304.09
40000	399.06	392.66	370.55	358.44	351.54	347.53
45000	448.94	441.74	416.87	403.25	395.49	390.97
50000	498.82	490.82	463.19	448.05	439.43	434.41
55000	548.70	539.90	509.51	492.86	483.37	477.85
60000	598.59	588.99	555.83	537.66	527.31	521.29
65000	648.47	638.07	602.15	582.47	571.26	564.73
70000	698.35	687.15	648.47	627.27	615.20	608.17
75000	748.23	736.23	694.79	672.08	659.14	651.61
80000	798.11	785.31	741.11	716.88	703.08	695.06
85000	848.00	834.40	787.43	761.69	747.03	738.50
90000	897.88	883.48	833.75	806.49	790.97	781.94
95000	947.76	932.56	880.06	851.30	834.91	825.38
100000	997.64	981.64	926.38	896.10	878.86	868.82
200000	1995.28	1963.28	1852.77	1792.20	1757.71	1737.64
300000	2992.92	2944.93	2779.15	2688.30	2636.57	2606.45
400000	3990.56	3926.57	3705.53	3584.40	3515.42	3475.27
500000	4988.20	4908.21	4631.92	4480.51	4394.28	4344.09

10 1/2%

MONTHLY PAYMENT

Necessary to amortize a loan

TERM / AMOUNT	1 YEAR	2 YEARS	3 YEARS	4 YEARS	5 YEARS	6 YEARS
500	44.07	23.19	16.25	12.80	10.75	9.39
600	52.89	27.83	19.50	15.36	12.90	11.27
700	61.70	32.46	22.75	17.92	15.05	13.15
800	70.52	37.10	26.00	20.48	17.20	15.02
900	79.33	41.74	29.25	23.04	19.34	16.90
1000	88.15	46.38	32.50	25.60	21.49	18.78
2000	176.30	92.75	65.01	51.21	42.99	37.56
3000	264.45	139.13	97.51	76.81	64.48	56.34
4000	352.60	185.51	130.01	102.41	85.98	75.12
5000	440.75	231.88	162.51	128.02	107.47	93.90
6000	528.90	278.26	195.02	153.62	128.96	112.67
7000	617.05	324.63	227.52	179.23	150.46	131.45
8000	705.19	371.01	260.02	204.83	171.95	150.23
9000	793.34	417.39	292.52	230.43	193.45	169.01
10000	881.49	463.76	325.03	256.04	214.94	187.79
11000	969.64	510.14	357.53	281.64	236.43	206.57
12000	1057.79	556.52	390.03	307.24	257.93	225.35
13000	1145.94	602.89	422.53	332.85	279.42	244.13
14000	1234.09	649.27	455.04	358.45	300.92	262.91
15000	1322.24	695.65	487.54	384.05	322.41	281.69
16000	1410.39	742.02	520.04	409.66	343.90	300.47
17000	1498.54	788.40	552.55	435.26	365.40	319.24
18000	1586.69	834.77	585.05	460.86	386.89	338.02
19000	1674.84	881.15	617.55	486.47	408.39	356.80
20000	1762.98	927.53	650.05	512.07	429.88	375.58
21000	1851.13	973.90	682.56	537.67	451.37	394.36
22000	1939.28	1020.28	715.06	563.28	472.87	413.14
23000	2027.43	1066.66	747.56	588.88	494.36	431.92
24000	2115.58	1113.03	780.06	614.49	515.86	450.70
25000	2203.73	1159.41	812.57	640.09	537.35	469.48
30000	2644.48	1391.29	975.08	768.11	644.82	563.37
35000	3085.22	1623.17	1137.59	896.12	752.29	657.27
40000	3525.97	1855.05	1300.11	1024.14	859.76	751.16
45000	3966.72	2086.94	1462.62	1152.16	967.23	845.06
50000	4407.46	2318.82	1625.13	1280.18	1074.70	938.95
55000	4848.21	2550.70	1787.65	1408.19	1182.17	1032.85
60000	5288.95	2782.58	1950.16	1536.21	1289.64	1126.74
65000	5729.70	3014.46	2112.67	1664.23	1397.11	1220.64
70000	6170.45	3246.34	2275.19	1792.25	1504.58	1314.53
75000	6611.19	3478.23	2437.70	1920.27	1612.05	1408.43
80000	7051.94	3710.11	2600.21	2048.28	1719.52	1502.33
85000	7492.68	3941.99	2762.72	2176.30	1826.99	1596.22
90000	7933.43	4173.87	2925.24	2304.32	1934.46	1690.12
95000	8374.18	4405.75	3087.75	2432.34	2041.93	1784.01
100000	8814.92	4637.64	3250.26	2560.35	2149.40	1877.91
200000	17629.80	9275.27	6500.53	5120.71	4298.80	3755.81
300000	26444.80	13912.90	9750.79	7681.06	6448.21	5633.72
400000	35259.70	18550.50	13001.10	10241.40	8597.61	7511.63
500000	44074.60	23188.20	16251.30	12801.80	10747.00	9389.54

MONTHLY PAYMENT

Necessary to amortize a loan

10 1/2%

TERM / AMOUNT	7 YEARS	8 YEARS	9 YEARS	10 YEARS	11 YEARS	12 YEARS
500	8.43	7.72	7.18	6.75	6.40	6.12
600	10.12	9.26	8.61	8.10	7.68	7.34
700	11.80	10.81	10.05	9.45	8.96	8.57
800	13.49	12.35	11.48	10.79	10.24	9.79
900	15.17	13.90	12.92	12.14	11.52	11.02
1000	16.86	15.44	14.35	13.49	12.80	12.24
2000	33.72	30.88	28.70	26.99	25.61	24.48
3000	50.58	46.32	43.05	40.48	38.41	36.72
4000	67.44	61.76	57.40	53.97	51.22	48.97
5000	84.30	77.20	71.75	67.47	64.02	61.21
6000	101.17	92.64	86.11	80.96	76.83	73.45
7000	118.03	108.08	100.46	94.45	89.63	85.69
8000	134.89	123.52	114.81	107.95	102.44	97.93
9000	151.75	138.96	129.16	121.44	115.24	110.17
10000	168.61	154.40	143.51	134.94	128.05	122.42
11000	185.47	169.84	157.86	148.43	140.85	134.66
12000	202.33	185.28	172.21	161.92	153.65	146.90
13000	219.19	200.72	186.56	175.42	166.46	159.14
14000	236.05	216.16	200.91	188.91	179.26	171.38
15000	252.91	231.60	215.26	202.40	192.07	183.62
16000	269.77	247.04	229.62	215.90	204.87	195.86
17000	286.63	262.48	243.97	229.39	217.68	208.11
18000	303.49	277.92	258.32	242.88	230.48	220.35
19000	320.35	293.36	272.67	256.38	243.29	232.59
20000	337.22	308.80	287.02	269.87	256.09	244.83
21000	354.08	324.24	301.37	283.37	268.90	257.07
22000	370.94	339.68	315.72	296.86	281.70	269.31
23000	387.80	355.12	330.07	310.35	294.50	281.55
24000	404.66	370.56	344.42	323.85	307.31	293.80
25000	421.52	386.00	358.77	337.34	320.11	306.04
30000	505.82	463.20	430.53	404.81	384.14	367.24
35000	590.13	540.40	502.28	472.27	448.16	428.45
40000	674.43	617.60	574.04	539.74	512.18	489.66
45000	758.73	694.80	645.79	607.21	576.20	550.87
50000	843.04	772.00	717.55	674.68	640.23	612.07
55000	927.34	849.21	789.30	742.15	704.25	673.28
60000	1011.65	926.41	861.06	809.61	768.27	734.49
65000	1095.95	1003.61	932.81	877.08	832.29	795.69
70000	1180.25	1080.81	1004.56	955.66	896.32	856.90
75000	1264.56	1158.01	1076.32	1012.02	960.34	918.11
80000	1348.86	1235.21	1148.07	1079.48	1024.36	979.32
85000	1433.16	1312.41	1219.83	1146.95	1088.38	1040.52
90000	1517.47	1389.61	1291.58	1214.42	1152.41	1101.73
95000	1601.77	1466.81	1363.34	1281.89	1216.43	1162.94
100000	1686.08	1544.01	1435.09	1349.36	1280.45	1224.15
200000	3372.15	3088.02	2870.19	2698.71	2560.90	2448.29
300000	5058.23	4632.03	4305.28	4048.07	3841.35	3672.44
400000	6744.30	6176.04	5740.37	5397.42	5121.80	4896.58
500000	8430.38	7720.04	7175.46	6746.78	6402.25	6120.73

10 1/2%

MONTHLY PAYMENT

Necessary to amortize a loan

TERM / AMOUNT	13 YEARS	14 YEARS	15 YEARS	16 YEARS	17 YEARS	18 YEARS
500	5.89	5.69	5.53	5.39	5.27	5.16
600	7.07	6.83	6.63	6.46	6.32	6.19
700	8.24	7.97	7.74	7.54	7.37	7.23
800	9.42	9.11	8.84	8.62	8.42	8.26
900	10.60	10.25	9.95	9.70	9.48	9.29
1000	11.78	11.38	11.05	10.77	10.53	10.32
2000	23.55	22.77	22.11	21.54	21.06	20.64
3000	35.33	34.15	33.16	32.32	31.59	30.97
4000	47.10	45.54	44.22	43.09	42.12	41.29
5000	58.88	56.92	55.27	53.86	52.65	51.61
6000	70.65	68.31	66.32	64.63	63.19	61.93
7000	82.43	79.69	77.38	75.41	73.72	72.26
8000	94.20	91.08	88.43	86.18	84.25	82.58
9000	105.98	102.46	99.49	96.95	94.78	92.90
10000	117.75	113.84	110.54	107.73	105.31	103.22
11000	129.53	125.23	121.59	118.50	115.84	113.55
12000	141.30	136.61	132.65	129.27	126.37	123.87
13000	153.08	148.00	143.70	140.04	136.90	134.19
14000	164.85	159.38	154.76	150.81	147.43	144.51
15000	176.63	170.77	165.81	161.59	157.96	154.84
16000	188.40	182.15	176.86	172.36	168.49	165.16
17000	200.18	193.53	187.92	183.13	179.02	175.48
18000	211.95	204.92	198.97	193.90	189.56	185.80
19000	223.73	216.30	210.03	204.68	200.09	196.12
20000	235.50	227.69	221.08	215.45	210.62	206.45
21000	247.28	239.07	232.13	226.22	221.15	216.77
22000	259.05	250.46	243.19	236.99	231.68	227.09
23000	270.83	261.84	254.24	247.77	242.21	237.41
24000	282.60	273.23	265.30	258.54	252.74	247.74
25000	294.38	284.61	276.35	269.31	263.27	258.06
30000	353.25	341.53	331.62	323.17	315.93	309.67
35000	412.13	398.45	386.89	377.04	368.58	361.28
40000	471.00	455.38	442.16	430.90	421.23	412.89
45000	529.88	512.30	497.43	484.76	473.89	464.50
50000	588.75	569.22	552.70	538.62	526.54	516.12
55000	647.63	626.14	607.97	592.49	579.20	567.73
60000	706.50	683.06	663.24	646.35	631.85	619.34
65000	765.38	739.98	718.51	700.21	684.51	670.95
70000	824.25	796.91	773.78	754.07	737.16	722.56
75000	883.13	853.83	829.05	807.93	789.81	774.17
80000	942.01	910.75	884.32	861.80	842.47	825.78
85000	1000.88	967.67	939.59	915.66	895.12	877.40
90000	1059.76	1024.59	994.86	969.52	947.78	929.01
95000	1118.63	1081.52	1050.13	1023.38	1000.43	980.62
100000	1177.51	1138.44	1105.40	1077.25	1053.08	1032.23
200000	2355.01	2276.88	2210.80	2154.49	2106.17	2064.46
300000	3532.52	3415.31	3316.21	3231.74	3159.25	3096.69
400000	4710.02	4553.75	4421.61	4308.98	4212.34	4128.92
500000	5887.53	5692.19	5527.01	5386.23	5265.42	5161.15

MONTHLY PAYMENT

Necessary to amortize a loan

10 1/2%

TERM / AMOUNT	19 YEARS	20 YEARS	25 YEARS	30 YEARS	35 YEARS	40 YEARS
500	5.07	4.99	4.72	4.57	4.49	4.44
600	6.08	5.99	5.67	5.49	5.39	5.33
700	7.10	6.99	6.61	6.40	6.29	6.22
800	8.11	7.99	7.55	7.32	7.19	7.11
900	9.13	8.99	8.50	8.23	8.08	8.00
1000	10.14	9.98	9.44	9.15	8.98	8.89
2000	20.28	19.97	18.88	18.29	17.96	17.77
3000	30.42	29.95	28.33	27.44	26.94	26.66
4000	40.57	39.94	37.77	36.59	35.93	35.54
5000	50.71	49.92	47.21	45.74	44.91	44.43
6000	60.85	59.90	56.65	54.88	53.89	53.31
7000	70.99	69.89	66.09	64.03	62.87	62.20
8000	81.13	79.87	75.53	73.18	71.85	71.09
9000	91.27	89.85	84.98	82.33	80.83	79.97
10000	101.41	99.84	94.42	91.47	89.81	88.86
11000	111.56	109.82	103.86	100.62	98.79	97.74
12000	121.70	119.81	113.30	109.77	107.78	106.63
13000	131.84	129.79	122.74	118.92	116.76	115.51
14000	141.98	139.77	132.19	128.06	125.74	124.40
15000	152.12	149.76	141.63	137.21	134.72	133.29
16000	162.26	159.74	151.07	146.36	143.70	142.17
17000	172.40	169.73	160.51	155.51	152.68	151.06
18000	182.55	179.71	169.95	164.65	161.66	159.94
19000	192.69	189.69	179.40	173.80	170.65	168.83
20000	202.83	199.68	188.84	182.95	179.63	177.71
21000	212.97	209.66	198.28	192.10	188.61	186.60
22000	223.11	219.64	207.72	201.24	197.59	195.49
23000	233.25	229.63	217.16	210.39	206.57	204.37
24000	243.39	239.61	226.60	219.54	215.55	213.26
25000	253.54	249.60	236.05	228.69	224.53	222.14
30000	304.24	299.52	283.26	274.42	269.44	266.57
35000	354.95	349.43	330.46	320.16	314.35	311.00
40000	405.66	399.35	377.67	365.90	359.25	355.43
45000	456.36	449.27	424.88	411.63	404.16	399.86
50000	507.07	499.19	472.09	457.37	449.07	444.29
55000	557.78	549.11	519.30	503.11	493.97	488.71
60000	608.49	599.03	566.51	548.84	538.88	533.14
65000	659.19	648.95	613.72	594.58	583.79	577.57
70000	709.90	698.87	660.93	640.32	628.69	622.00
75000	760.61	748.79	708.14	686.06	673.60	666.43
80000	811.31	798.71	755.35	731.79	718.51	710.86
85000	862.02	848.63	802.56	777.53	763.41	755.29
90000	912.73	898.54	849.77	823.27	808.32	799.71
95000	963.43	948.46	896.97	869.00	853.23	844.14
100000	1014.14	998.38	944.18	914.74	898.14	888.57
200000	2028.28	1996.76	1888.37	1829.48	1796.27	1777.14
300000	3042.42	2995.15	2832.55	2744.22	2694.40	2665.71
400000	4056.57	3993.53	3776.73	3658.96	3592.54	3554.28
500000	5070.71	4991.91	4720.92	4573.70	4490.67	4442.85

10 3/4%

MONTHLY PAYMENT

Necessary to amortize a loan

TERM / AMOUNT	1 YEAR	2 YEARS	3 YEARS	4 YEARS	5 YEARS	6 YEARS
500	44.13	23.25	16.31	12.86	10.81	9.45
600	52.96	27.90	19.57	15.43	12.97	11.34
700	61.79	32.54	22.83	18.01	15.13	13.23
800	70.61	37.19	26.10	20.58	17.29	15.13
900	79.44	41.84	29.36	23.15	19.46	17.02
1000	88.27	46.49	32.62	25.72	21.62	18.91
2000	176.53	92.98	65.24	51.45	43.24	37.81
3000	264.80	139.48	97.86	77.17	64.85	56.72
4000	353.06	185.97	130.48	102.90	86.47	75.63
5000	441.33	232.46	163.10	128.62	108.09	94.53
6000	529.59	278.95	195.72	154.35	129.71	113.44
7000	617.86	325.44	228.34	180.07	151.33	132.34
8000	706.12	371.94	260.96	205.80	172.94	151.25
9000	794.39	418.43	293.58	231.52	194.56	170.16
10000	882.65	464.92	326.21	257.24	216.18	189.06
11000	970.92	511.41	358.83	282.97	237.80	207.97
12000	1059.18	557.90	391.45	308.69	259.42	226.88
13000	1147.45	604.40	424.07	334.42	281.03	245.78
14000	1235.71	650.89	456.69	360.14	302.65	264.69
15000	1323.98	697.38	489.31	385.87	324.27	283.59
16000	1412.24	743.87	521.93	411.59	345.89	302.50
17000	1500.51	790.36	554.55	437.31	367.51	321.41
18000	1588.77	836.85	587.17	463.04	389.12	340.31
19000	1677.04	883.35	619.79	488.76	410.74	359.22
20000	1765.30	929.84	652.41	514.49	432.36	378.13
21000	1853.57	976.33	685.03	540.21	453.98	397.03
22000	1941.83	1022.82	717.65	565.94	475.60	415.94
23000	2030.10	1069.31	750.27	591.66	497.21	434.85
24000	2118.36	1115.81	782.89	617.38	518.83	453.75
25000	2206.63	1162.30	815.51	643.11	540.45	472.66
30000	2647.95	1394.76	978.62	771.73	648.54	567.19
35000	3089.28	1627.22	1141.72	900.35	756.63	661.72
40000	3530.60	1859.68	1304.82	1028.97	864.72	756.25
45000	3971.93	2092.14	1467.92	1157.59	972.81	850.78
50000	4413.26	2324.59	1631.02	1286.22	1080.90	945.32
55000	4854.58	2557.05	1794.13	1414.84	1188.99	1039.85
60000	5295.91	2789.51	1957.23	1543.46	1297.08	1134.38
65000	5737.23	3021.97	2120.33	1672.08	1405.17	1228.91
70000	6178.56	3254.43	2283.43	1800.70	1513.26	1323.44
75000	6619.88	3486.89	2446.54	1929.32	1621.35	1417.97
80000	7061.21	3719.35	2609.64	2057.95	1729.44	1512.50
85000	7502.53	3951.81	2772.74	2186.57	1837.53	1607.04
90000	7943.86	4184.27	2935.84	2315.19	1945.62	1701.57
95000	8385.19	4416.73	3098.95	2443.81	2053.71	1796.10
100000	8826.51	4649.19	3262.05	2572.43	2161.80	1890.63
200000	17653.00	9298.38	6524.10	5144.86	4323.59	3781.26
300000	26479.50	13947.60	9786.15	7717.29	6485.39	5671.89
400000	35306.00	18596.80	13048.20	10289.70	8647.19	7562.52
500000	44132.60	23245.90	16310.20	12862.20	10809.00	9453.15

MONTHLY PAYMENT

Necessary to amortize a loan

10 3/4%

TERM AMOUNT	7 YEARS	8 YEARS	9 YEARS	10 YEARS	11 YEARS	12 YEARS
500	8.50	7.79	7.24	6.82	6.47	6.19
600	10.19	9.34	8.69	8.18	7.77	7.43
700	11.89	10.90	10.14	9.54	9.06	8.67
800	13.59	12.46	11.59	10.91	10.36	9.91
900	15.29	14.02	13.04	12.27	11.65	11.15
1000	16.99	15.57	14.49	13.63	12.95	12.39
2000	33.98	31.15	28.98	27.27	25.90	24.78
3000	50.97	46.72	43.46	40.90	38.84	37.16
4000	67.97	62.30	57.95	54.54	51.79	49.55
5000	84.96	77.87	72.44	68.17	64.74	61.94
6000	101.95	93.44	86.93	81.80	77.69	74.33
7000	118.94	109.02	101.42	95.44	90.64	86.72
8000	135.93	124.59	115.90	109.07	103.58	99.10
9000	152.92	140.17	130.39	122.71	116.53	111.49
10000	169.91	155.74	144.88	136.34	129.48	123.88
11000	186.90	171.31	159.37	149.97	142.43	136.27
12000	203.90	186.89	173.86	163.61	155.38	148.66
13000	220.89	202.46	188.34	177.24	168.32	161.05
14000	237.88	218.04	202.83	190.87	181.27	173.43
15000	254.87	233.61	217.32	204.51	194.22	185.82
16000	271.86	249.18	231.81	218.14	207.17	198.21
17000	288.85	264.76	246.30	231.78	220.12	210.60
18000	305.84	280.33	260.78	245.41	233.06	222.99
19000	322.83	295.90	275.27	259.04	246.01	235.37
20000	339.83	311.48	289.76	272.68	258.96	247.76
21000	356.82	327.05	304.25	286.31	271.91	260.15
22000	373.81	342.63	318.74	299.95	284.86	272.54
23000	390.80	358.20	333.22	313.58	297.80	284.93
24000	407.79	373.77	347.71	327.21	310.75	297.31
25000	424.78	389.35	362.20	340.85	323.70	309.70
30000	509.74	467.22	434.64	409.02	388.44	371.64
35000	594.70	545.09	507.08	477.19	453.18	433.58
40000	679.65	622.96	579.52	545.36	517.92	495.52
45000	764.61	700.83	651.96	613.53	582.66	557.46
50000	849.56	778.70	724.40	681.69	647.40	619.40
55000	934.52	856.57	796.84	749.86	712.14	681.34
60000	1019.48	934.44	869.28	818.03	776.88	743.28
65000	1104.43	1012.30	941.72	886.20	841.62	805.22
70000	1189.39	1090.17	1014.16	954.37	906.36	867.16
75000	1274.35	1168.04	1086.60	1022.54	971.10	929.10
80000	1359.30	1245.91	1159.04	1090.71	1035.84	991.04
85000	1444.26	1323.78	1231.48	1158.88	1100.58	1052.98
90000	1529.22	1401.65	1303.92	1227.05	1165.32	1114.92
95000	1614.17	1479.52	1376.36	1295.22	1230.06	1176.86
100000	1699.13	1557.39	1448.80	1363.39	1294.80	1238.81
200000	3398.26	3114.78	2897.60	2726.78	2589.60	2477.61
300000	5097.39	4672.18	4346.41	4090.16	3884.40	3716.42
400000	6796.51	6229.57	5795.21	5453.55	5179.20	4955.22
500000	8495.64	7786.96	7244.01	6816.94	6474.00	6194.03

10 3/4% MONTHLY PAYMENT

Necessary to amortize a loan

TERM / AMOUNT	13 YEARS	14 YEARS	15 YEARS	16 YEARS	17 YEARS	18 YEARS
500	5.96	5.77	5.60	5.47	5.35	5.24
600	7.15	6.92	6.73	6.56	6.42	6.29
700	8.35	8.08	7.85	7.65	7.48	7.34
800	9.54	9.23	8.97	8.74	8.55	8.39
900	10.73	10.38	10.09	9.84	9.62	9.44
1000	11.92	11.54	11.21	10.93	10.69	10.49
2000	23.85	23.07	22.42	21.86	21.38	20.97
3000	35.77	34.61	33.63	32.79	32.08	31.46
4000	47.70	46.15	44.84	43.72	42.77	41.94
5000	59.62	57.68	56.05	54.65	53.46	52.43
6000	71.55	69.22	67.26	65.58	64.15	62.92
7000	83.47	80.76	78.47	76.51	74.84	73.40
8000	95.40	92.30	89.68	87.45	85.53	83.89
9000	107.32	103.83	100.89	98.38	96.23	94.37
10000	119.25	115.37	112.10	109.31	106.92	104.86
11000	131.17	126.91	123.30	120.24	117.61	115.34
12000	143.10	138.44	134.51	131.17	128.30	125.83
13000	155.02	149.98	145.72	142.10	138.99	136.32
14000	166.95	161.52	156.93	153.03	149.69	146.80
15000	178.87	173.05	168.14	163.96	160.38	157.29
16000	190.80	184.59	179.35	174.89	171.07	167.77
17000	202.72	196.13	190.56	185.82	181.76	178.26
18000	214.64	207.67	201.77	196.75	192.45	188.75
19000	226.57	219.20	212.98	207.68	203.14	199.23
20000	238.49	230.74	224.19	218.61	213.84	209.72
21000	250.42	242.28	235.40	229.55	224.53	220.20
22000	262.34	253.81	246.61	240.48	235.22	230.69
23000	274.27	265.35	257.82	251.41	245.91	241.18
24000	286.19	276.89	269.03	262.34	256.60	251.66
25000	298.12	288.42	280.24	273.27	267.30	262.15
30000	357.74	346.11	336.29	327.92	320.75	314.58
35000	417.36	403.79	392.33	382.58	374.21	367.01
40000	476.99	461.48	448.38	437.23	427.67	419.43
45000	536.61	519.16	504.43	491.88	481.13	471.86
50000	596.24	576.85	560.47	546.54	534.59	524.29
55000	655.86	634.53	616.52	601.19	588.05	576.72
60000	715.48	692.22	672.57	655.84	641.51	629.15
65000	775.11	749.90	728.62	710.50	694.97	681.58
70000	834.73	807.59	784.66	765.15	748.43	734.01
75000	894.35	865.27	840.71	819.80	801.88	786.44
80000	953.98	922.96	896.76	874.46	855.34	838.87
85000	1013.60	980.64	952.81	929.11	908.80	891.30
90000	1073.22	1038.33	1008.85	983.76	962.26	943.73
95000	1132.85	1096.01	1064.90	1038.42	1015.72	996.16
100000	1192.47	1153.70	1120.95	1093.07	1069.18	1048.59
200000	2384.94	2307.39	2241.90	2186.14	2138.36	2097.17
300000	3577.41	3461.09	3362.85	3279.21	3207.54	3145.76
400000	4769.88	4614.79	4483.79	4372.28	4276.71	4194.34
500000	5962.35	5768.48	5604.74	5465.35	5345.89	5242.93

MONTHLY PAYMENT

Necessary to amortize a loan

10 3/4%

TERM / AMOUNT	19 YEARS	20 YEARS	25 YEARS	30 YEARS	35 YEARS	40 YEARS
500	5.15	5.08	4.81	4.67	4.59	4.54
600	6.18	6.09	5.77	5.60	5.51	5.45
700	7.22	7.11	6.73	6.53	6.42	6.36
800	8.25	8.12	7.70	7.47	7.34	7.27
900	9.28	9.14	8.66	8.40	8.26	8.18
1000	10.31	10.15	9.62	9.33	9.18	9.08
2000	20.61	20.30	19.24	18.67	18.35	18.17
3000	30.92	30.46	28.86	28.00	27.53	27.25
4000	41.23	40.61	38.48	37.34	36.70	36.34
5000	51.54	50.76	48.10	46.67	45.88	45.42
6000	61.84	60.91	57.73	56.01	55.05	54.50
7000	72.15	71.07	67.35	65.34	64.23	63.59
8000	82.46	81.22	76.97	74.68	73.40	72.67
9000	92.77	91.37	86.59	84.01	82.58	81.76
10000	103.08	101.52	96.21	93.35	91.75	90.84
11000	113.38	111.68	105.83	102.68	100.93	99.92
12000	123.69	121.83	115.45	112.02	110.10	109.01
13000	134.00	131.98	125.07	121.35	119.28	118.09
14000	144.31	142.13	134.69	130.69	128.45	127.18
15000	154.61	152.28	144.31	140.02	137.63	136.26
16000	164.92	162.44	153.94	149.36	146.80	145.34
17000	175.23	172.59	163.56	158.69	155.98	154.54
18000	185.53	182.74	173.18	168.03	165.15	163.51
19000	195.84	192.89	182.80	177.36	174.33	172.60
20000	206.15	203.05	192.42	186.70	183.50	181.68
21000	216.46	213.20	202.04	196.03	192.68	190.76
22000	226.76	223.35	211.66	205.37	201.85	199.85
23000	237.07	233.50	221.28	214.70	211.03	208.93
24000	247.38	243.66	230.90	224.04	220.20	218.02
25000	257.69	253.81	240.52	233.37	229.38	227.10
30000	309.22	304.57	288.63	280.04	275.25	272.52
35000	360.76	355.33	336.73	326.72	321.13	317.94
40000	412.30	406.09	384.84	373.39	367.00	363.36
45000	463.84	456.85	432.94	420.07	412.88	408.78
50000	515.37	507.62	481.05	466.74	458.75	454.20
55000	566.91	558.38	529.15	513.42	504.63	499.62
60000	618.45	609.14	577.26	560.09	550.50	545.04
65000	669.99	659.90	625.36	606.76	596.38	590.46
70000	721.52	710.66	673.47	653.44	642.25	635.88
75000	773.06	761.42	721.57	700.11	688.13	681.30
80000	824.60	812.18	769.67	746.79	734.00	726.72
85000	876.14	862.95	817.78	793.46	779.88	772.14
90000	927.67	913.71	865.88	840.13	825.75	817.56
95000	979.21	964.47	913.99	886.81	871.63	862.98
100000	1030.75	1015.23	962.09	933.48	917.50	908.40
200000	2061.49	2030.46	1924.18	1866.96	1835.01	1816.79
300000	3092.24	3045.69	2886.28	2800.44	2752.51	2725.19
400000	4122.99	4060.92	3848.37	3733.92	3670.01	3633.59
500000	5153.74	5076.15	4810.46	4667.41	4587.51	4541.99

11 %

MONTHLY PAYMENT
Necessary to amortize a loan

TERM / AMOUNT	1 YEAR	2 YEARS	3 YEARS	4 YEARS	5 YEARS	6 YEARS
500	44.19	23.30	16.37	12.92	10.87	9.52
600	53.03	27.96	19.64	15.51	13.05	11.42
700	61.87	32.63	22.92	18.09	15.22	13.32
800	70.71	37.29	26.19	20.68	17.39	15.23
900	79.54	41.95	29.46	23.26	19.57	17.13
1000	88.38	46.61	32.74	25.85	21.74	19.03
2000	176.76	93.22	65.48	51.69	43.48	38.07
3000	265.14	139.82	98.22	77.54	65.23	57.10
4000	353.53	186.43	130.95	103.38	86.97	76.14
5000	441.91	233.04	163.69	129.23	108.71	95.17
6000	530.29	279.65	196.43	155.07	130.45	114.20
7000	618.67	326.25	229.17	180.92	152.20	133.24
8000	707.05	372.86	261.91	206.76	173.94	152.27
9000	795.43	419.47	294.65	232.61	195.68	171.31
10000	883.81	466.08	327.39	258.45	217.42	190.34
11000	972.19	512.68	360.13	284.30	239.17	209.37
12000	1060.58	559.29	392.86	310.15	260.91	228.41
13000	1148.96	605.90	425.60	335.99	282.65	247.44
14000	1237.34	652.51	458.34	361.84	304.39	266.48
15000	1325.72	699.12	491.08	387.68	326.14	285.51
16000	1414.10	745.72	523.82	413.53	347.88	304.54
17000	1502.48	792.33	556.56	439.37	369.62	323.58
18000	1590.86	838.94	589.30	465.22	391.36	342.61
19000	1679.24	885.55	622.03	491.06	413.11	361.65
20000	1767.62	932.15	654.77	516.91	434.85	380.68
21000	1856.01	978.76	687.51	542.75	456.59	399.71
22000	1944.39	1025.37	720.25	568.60	478.33	418.75
23000	2032.77	1071.98	752.99	594.45	500.07	437.78
24000	2121.15	1118.58	785.73	620.29	521.82	456.82
25000	2209.53	1165.19	818.47	646.14	543.56	475.85
30000	2651.44	1398.23	982.16	775.36	652.27	571.02
35000	3093.34	1631.27	1145.85	904.59	760.98	666.19
40000	3535.25	1864.31	1309.54	1033.82	869.69	761.36
45000	3977.16	2097.35	1473.24	1163.04	978.41	856.53
50000	4419.06	2330.38	1636.93	1292.27	1087.12	951.70
55000	4860.97	2563.42	1800.62	1421.50	1195.83	1046.87
60000	5302.87	2796.46	1964.32	1550.73	1304.54	1142.04
65000	5744.78	3029.50	2128.01	1679.95	1413.25	1237.21
70000	6186.69	3262.54	2291.70	1809.18	1521.96	1332.38
75000	6628.59	3495.58	2455.39	1938.41	1630.68	1427.55
80000	7070.50	3728.61	2619.09	2067.63	1739.39	1522.72
85000	7512.41	3961.65	2782.78	2196.86	1848.10	1617.89
90000	7954.31	4194.69	2946.47	2326.09	1956.81	1713.06
95000	8396.22	4427.73	3110.17	2455.32	2065.52	1808.23
100000	8838.12	4660.77	3273.86	2584.54	2174.23	1903.40
200000	17676.20	9321.53	6547.72	5169.09	4348.47	3806.80
300000	26514.40	13982.30	9821.58	7753.63	6522.70	5710.21
400000	35352.50	18643.10	13095.40	10338.20	8696.94	7613.61
500000	44190.60	23303.80	16369.30	12922.70	10871.20	9517.01

MONTHLY PAYMENT

Necessary to amortize a loan

11%

TERM / AMOUNT	7 YEARS	8 YEARS	9 YEARS	10 YEARS	11 YEARS	12 YEARS
500	8.56	7.85	7.31	6.89	6.55	6.27
600	10.27	9.43	8.78	8.26	7.86	7.52
700	11.99	11.00	10.24	9.64	9.16	8.77
800	13.70	12.57	11.70	11.02	10.47	10.03
900	15.41	14.14	13.16	12.40	11.78	11.28
1000	17.12	15.71	14.63	13.78	13.09	12.54
2000	34.24	31.42	29.25	27.55	26.18	25.07
3000	51.37	47.13	43.88	41.32	39.28	37.61
4000	68.49	62.83	58.50	55.10	52.37	50.14
5000	85.61	78.54	73.13	68.87	65.46	62.68
6000	102.73	94.25	87.75	82.65	78.55	75.21
7000	119.86	109.96	102.38	96.42	91.65	87.75
8000	136.98	125.67	117.01	110.20	104.74	100.28
9000	154.10	141.38	131.63	123.98	117.83	112.82
10000	171.22	157.08	146.26	137.75	130.92	125.36
11000	188.35	172.79	160.88	151.53	144.02	137.89
12000	205.47	188.50	175.51	165.30	157.11	150.43
13000	222.59	204.21	190.14	179.08	170.20	162.96
14000	239.71	219.92	204.76	192.85	183.29	175.50
15000	256.84	235.63	219.39	206.63	196.39	188.03
16000	273.96	251.33	234.01	220.40	209.48	200.57
17000	291.08	267.04	248.64	234.17	222.57	213.10
18000	308.20	282.75	263.27	247.95	235.66	225.64
19000	325.33	298.46	277.89	261.72	248.75	238.18
20000	342.45	314.17	292.52	275.50	261.85	250.71
21000	359.57	329.88	307.14	289.27	274.94	263.25
22000	376.69	345.58	321.77	303.05	288.03	275.78
23000	393.82	361.29	336.39	316.82	301.12	288.32
24000	410.94	377.00	351.02	330.60	314.22	300.85
25000	428.06	392.71	365.65	344.37	327.31	313.39
30000	513.67	471.25	438.78	413.25	392.77	376.07
35000	599.28	549.79	511.90	482.12	458.23	438.74
40000	684.90	628.34	585.03	551.00	523.69	501.42
45000	770.51	706.88	658.16	619.87	589.15	564.10
50000	856.12	785.42	731.29	688.75	654.62	626.78
55000	941.73	863.96	804.42	757.62	720.08	689.45
60000	1027.34	942.50	877.55	826.50	785.54	752.13
65000	1112.96	1021.04	950.68	895.37	851.00	814.81
70000	1198.57	1099.59	1023.81	964.25	916.46	877.49
75000	1284.18	1178.13	1096.94	1033.12	981.92	940.16
80000	1369.79	1256.67	1170.07	1102.00	1047.39	1002.84
85000	1455.40	1335.21	1243.20	1170.87	1112.85	1065.52
90000	1541.01	1413.75	1316.32	1239.75	1178.31	1128.20
95000	1626.63	1492.30	1389.45	1308.62	1243.77	1190.88
100000	1712.24	1570.84	1462.58	1377.50	1309.23	1253.55
200000	3424.48	3141.68	2925.16	2754.99	2618.46	2507.11
300000	5136.72	4712.52	4387.75	4132.49	3927.70	3760.66
400000	6848.95	6283.35	5850.33	5509.99	5236.93	5014.21
500000	8561.19	7854.19	7312.91	6887.48	6546.16	6267.76

11% MONTHLY PAYMENT
Necessary to amortize a loan

TERM / AMOUNT	13 YEARS	14 YEARS	15 YEARS	16 YEARS	17 YEARS	18 YEARS
500	6.04	5.85	5.68	5.54	5.43	5.33
600	7.25	7.01	6.82	6.65	6.51	6.39
700	8.45	8.18	7.96	7.76	7.60	7.46
800	9.66	9.35	9.09	8.87	8.68	8.52
900	10.87	10.52	10.23	9.98	9.77	9.59
1000	12.08	11.69	11.37	11.09	10.85	10.65
2000	24.15	23.38	22.73	22.18	21.71	21.30
3000	36.23	35.07	34.10	33.27	32.56	31.95
4000	48.30	46.76	45.46	44.36	43.42	42.60
5000	60.38	58.45	56.83	55.45	54.27	53.25
6000	72.45	70.14	68.20	66.54	65.12	63.90
7000	84.53	81.83	79.56	77.63	75.98	74.55
8000	96.60	93.52	90.93	88.72	86.83	85.20
9000	108.68	105.22	102.29	99.81	97.68	95.85
10000	120.75	116.91	113.66	110.90	108.54	106.51
11000	132.83	128.60	125.03	121.99	119.39	117.16
12000	144.90	140.29	136.39	133.08	130.25	127.81
13000	156.98	151.98	147.76	144.17	141.10	138.46
14000	169.05	163.67	159.12	155.26	151.95	149.11
15000	181.13	175.36	170.49	166.35	162.81	159.76
16000	193.20	187.05	181.86	177.44	173.66	170.41
17000	205.28	198.74	193.22	188.53	184.51	181.06
18000	217.35	210.43	204.59	199.62	195.37	191.71
19000	229.43	222.12	215.95	210.71	206.22	202.36
20000	241.51	233.81	227.32	221.80	217.08	213.01
21000	253.58	245.50	238.69	232.89	227.93	223.66
22000	265.66	257.19	250.05	243.98	238.78	234.31
23000	277.73	268.88	261.42	255.07	249.64	244.96
24000	289.81	280.57	272.78	266.16	160.49	255.61
25000	301.88	292.26	284.15	277.25	271.35	266.26
30000	362.26	350.72	340.98	332.70	325.61	319.51
35000	422.63	409.17	397.81	388.15	379.88	372.77
40000	483.01	467.62	454.64	443.60	434.15	426.02
45000	543.39	526.07	511.47	499.05	488.42	479.27
50000	603.76	584.53	568.30	554.50	542.69	532.52
55000	664.14	642.98	625.13	609.95	596.96	585.78
60000	724.52	701.43	681.96	665.40	651.23	639.03
65000	784.89	759.88	738.79	720.85	705.50	692.28
70000	845.27	818.34	795.62	776.30	759.77	745.53
75000	905.64	876.79	852.45	831.75	814.03	798.79
80000	966.02	935.24	909.28	887.20	868.30	852.04
85000	1026.40	993.69	966.11	942.65	922.57	905.29
90000	1086.77	1052.15	1022.94	998.10	976.84	958.54
95000	1147.15	1110.60	1079.77	1053.55	1031.11	1011.80
100000	1207.52	1169.05	1136.59	1109.00	1085.38	1065.05
200000	2415.05	2338.10	2273.19	2218.00	2170.76	2130.10
300000	3622.57	3507.16	3409.78	3327.00	3256.14	3195.14
400000	4830.10	4676.21	4546.38	4435.99	4341.52	4260.19
500000	6037.62	5845.26	5682.97	5544.99	5426.89	5325.24

MONTHLY PAYMENT

Necessary to amortize a loan

11%

TERM / AMOUNT	19 YEARS	20 YEARS	25 YEARS	30 YEARS	35 YEARS	40 YEARS
500	5.24	5.16	4.90	4.76	4.68	4.64
600	6.28	6.19	5.88	5.71	5.62	5.57
700	7.33	7.23	6.86	6.67	6.56	6.50
800	8.38	8.26	7.84	7.62	7.50	7.43
900	9.43	9.29	8.82	8.57	8.43	8.35
1000	10.47	10.32	9.80	9.52	9.37	9.28
2000	20.95	20.64	19.60	19.05	18.74	18.57
3000	31.42	30.97	29.40	28.57	28.11	27.85
4000	41.90	41.29	39.20	38.09	37.48	37.13
5000	52.37	51.61	49.01	47.62	46.85	46.41
6000	62.85	61.93	58.81	57.14	56.22	55.70
7000	73.32	72.25	68.61	66.66	65.59	64.98
8000	83.80	82.58	78.41	76.19	74.96	74.26
9000	94.27	92.90	88.21	85.71	84.33	83.55
10000	104.75	103.22	98.01	95.23	93.70	92.83
11000	115.22	113.54	107.81	104.76	103.07	102.11
12000	125.70	123.86	117.61	114.28	112.44	111.40
13000	136.17	134.18	127.41	123.80	121.80	120.68
14000	146.65	144.51	137.22	133.33	131.17	129.96
15000	157.12	154.83	147.02	142.85	140.54	139.24
16000	167.59	165.15	156.82	152.37	149.91	148.53
17000	178.07	175.47	166.62	161.90	159.28	157.81
18000	188.54	185.79	176.42	171.42	168.65	167.09
19000	199.02	196.12	186.22	180.94	178.02	176.38
20000	209.49	206.44	196.02	190.46	187.39	185.66
21000	219.97	216.76	205.82	199.99	196.76	194.94
22000	230.44	227.08	215.62	209.51	206.13	204.23
23000	240.92	237.40	225.43	219.03	215.50	213.51
24000	251.39	247.73	235.23	228.56	224.87	222.79
25000	261.87	258.05	245.03	238.08	234.24	232.07
30000	314.24	309.66	294.03	285.70	281.09	278.49
35000	366.61	361.27	343.04	333.31	327.94	324.90
40000	418.99	412.88	392.05	380.93	374.78	371.32
45000	471.36	464.48	441.05	428.55	421.63	417.73
50000	523.73	516.09	490.06	476.16	468.48	464.15
55000	576.10	567.70	539.06	523.78	515.33	510.56
60000	628.48	619.31	588.07	571.39	562.17	556.98
65000	680.85	670.92	637.07	619.01	609.02	603.39
70000	733.22	722.53	686.08	666.63	655.87	649.81
75000	785.60	774.14	735.08	714.24	702.72	696.22
80000	837.97	825.75	784.09	761.86	749.57	742.64
85000	890.34	877.36	833.10	809.47	796.41	789.05
90000	942.72	928.97	882.10	857.09	843.26	835.46
95000	995.09	980.58	931.11	904.71	890.11	881.88
100000	1047.46	1032.19	980.11	952.32	936.96	928.29
200000	2094.93	2064.37	1960.22	1904.64	1873.91	1856.59
300000	3142.39	3096.56	2940.33	2856.97	2810.87	2784.88
400000	4189.85	4128.75	3920.44	3809.29	3747.83	3713.18
500000	5237.31	5160.94	4900.56	4761.61	4684.78	4641.47

11 1/4%

MONTHLY PAYMENT

Necessary to amortize a loan

TERM / AMOUNT	1 YEAR	2 YEARS	3 YEARS	4 YEARS	5 YEARS	6 YEARS
500	44.25	23.36	16.43	12.98	10.93	9.58
600	53.10	28.03	19.71	15.58	13.12	11.50
700	61.95	32.71	23.00	18.18	15.31	13.41
800	70.80	37.38	26.29	20.77	17.49	15.33
900	79.65	42.05	29.57	23.37	19.68	17.25
1000	88.50	46.72	32.86	25.97	21.87	19.16
2000	177.00	93.45	65.71	51.93	43.73	38.32
3000	265.50	140.17	98.57	77.90	65.60	57.49
4000	353.99	186.90	131.43	103.87	87.47	76.65
5000	442.49	233.62	164.29	129.84	109.34	95.81
6000	530.99	280.35	197.14	155.80	131.20	114.97
7000	619.49	327.07	230.00	181.77	153.07	134.14
8000	707.99	373.79	262.86	207.74	174.94	153.30
9000	796.49	420.52	295.72	233.70	196.81	172.46
10000	884.99	467.24	328.57	259.67	218.67	191.62
11000	973.48	513.97	361.43	285.64	240.54	210.79
12000	1061.98	560.69	394.29	311.61	262.41	229.95
13000	1150.48	607.41	427.15	337.57	284.28	249.11
14000	1238.98	654.14	460.00	363.54	306.14	268.27
15000	1327.48	700.86	492.86	389.51	328.01	287.44
16000	1415.98	747.59	525.72	415.47	349.88	306.60
17000	1504.48	794.31	558.57	441.44	371.75	325.76
18000	1592.97	841.03	591.43	467.41	393.61	344.92
19000	1681.47	887.76	624.29	493.38	415.48	364.09
20000	1769.97	934.48	657.15	519.34	437.35	383.25
21000	1858.47	981.21	690.00	545.31	459.21	402.41
22000	1946.97	1027.93	722.86	571.28	481.08	421.57
23000	2035.47	1074.65	755.72	597.25	502.95	440.74
24000	2123.97	1121.38	788.58	623.21	524.82	459.90
25000	2212.46	1168.10	821.43	649.18	546.68	479.06
30000	2654.96	1401.72	985.72	779.02	656.02	574.87
35000	3097.45	1635.34	1150.01	908.85	765.36	670.68
40000	3539.94	1868.96	1314.29	1038.69	874.69	766.50
45000	3982.44	2102.59	1478.58	1168.52	984.03	862.31
50000	4424.93	2336.21	1642.87	1298.36	1093.37	958.12
55000	4867.42	2569.83	1807.15	1428.19	1202.70	1053.93
60000	5309.91	2803.45	1971.44	1558.03	1312.04	1149.74
65000	5752.41	3037.07	2135.73	1687.86	1421.38	1245.56
70000	6194.90	3270.69	2300.01	1817.70	1530.71	1341.37
75000	6637.39	3504.31	2464.30	1947.54	1640.05	1437.18
80000	7079.89	3737.93	2628.59	2077.37	1749.39	1532.99
85000	7522.38	3971.55	2792.87	2207.21	1858.73	1628.80
90000	7964.87	4205.17	2957.16	2337.04	1968.06	1724.62
95000	8407.37	4438.79	3121.44	2466.88	2077.40	1820.43
100000	8849.86	4672.41	3285.73	2596.72	2186.74	1916.24
200000	17699.70	9344.82	6571.46	5193.43	4373.47	3832.48
300000	26549.60	14017.20	9857.19	7790.15	6560.21	5748.72
400000	35399.40	18689.60	13142.90	10386.90	8746.94	7664.96
500000	44249.30	23362.10	16428.70	12983.60	10933.70	9581.21

MONTHLY PAYMENT

Necessary to amortize a loan

11 1/4%

TERM / AMOUNT	7 YEARS	8 YEARS	9 YEARS	10 YEARS	11 YEARS	12 YEARS
500	8.63	7.92	7.38	6.96	6.62	6.34
600	10.35	9.51	8.86	8.35	7.94	7.61
700	12.08	11.09	10.34	9.74	9.27	8.88
800	13.80	12.67	11.81	11.13	10.59	10.15
900	15.53	14.26	13.29	12.53	11.91	11.42
1000	17.25	15.84	14.76	13.92	13.24	12.68
2000	34.51	31.69	29.53	27.83	26.48	25.37
3000	51.76	47.53	44.29	41.75	39.71	38.05
4000	69.02	63.37	59.06	55.67	52.95	50.74
5000	86.27	79.22	73.82	69.58	66.19	63.42
6000	103.53	95.06	88.59	83.50	79.43	76.10
7000	120.78	110.91	103.35	97.42	92.66	88.79
8000	138.03	126.75	118.12	111.34	105.90	101.47
9000	155.29	142.59	132.88	125.25	119.14	114.16
10000	172.54	158.44	147.64	139.17	132.38	126.84
11000	189.80	174.28	162.41	153.09	145.61	139.52
12000	207.05	190.12	177.17	167.00	158.85	152.21
13000	224.31	205.97	191.94	180.92	172.09	164.89
14000	241.56	221.81	206.70	194.84	185.33	177.58
15000	258.81	237.65	221.47	208.75	198.56	190.26
16000	276.07	253.50	236.23	222.67	211.80	202.94
17000	293.32	269.34	251.00	236.59	225.04	215.63
18000	310.58	285.19	265.76	250.50	238.28	228.31
19000	327.83	301.03	280.52	264.42	251.51	241.00
20000	345.08	316.87	295.29	278.34	264.75	253.68
21000	362.34	332.72	310.05	292.26	277.99	266.36
22000	379.59	348.56	324.82	306.17	291.23	279.05
23000	396.85	364.40	339.58	320.09	304.46	291.73
24000	414.10	380.25	354.35	334.01	317.70	304.42
25000	431.36	396.09	369.11	347.92	330.94	317.10
30000	517.63	475.31	442.93	417.51	397.13	380.52
35000	603.90	554.53	516.76	487.09	463.31	443.94
40000	690.17	633.74	590.58	556.68	529.50	507.36
45000	776.44	712.96	664.40	626.26	595.69	570.78
50000	862.71	792.18	738.22	695.85	661.88	634.20
55000	948.98	871.40	812.04	765.43	728.07	697.62
60000	1035.25	950.62	885.87	835.02	794.25	761.04
65000	1121.52	1029.83	959.69	904.60	860.44	824.46
70000	1207.79	1109.05	1033.51	974.18	926.63	887.88
75000	1294.06	1188.27	1107.33	1043.77	992.82	951.30
80000	1380.34	1267.49	1181.15	1113.35	1059.00	1014.72
85000	1466.61	1346.71	1254.98	1182.94	1125.19	1078.14
90000	1552.88	1425.92	1328.80	1252.52	1191.38	1141.56
95000	1639.15	1505.14	1402.62	1322.11	1257.57	1204.97
100000	1725.42	1584.36	1476.44	1391.69	1323.75	1268.39
200000	3450.84	3168.72	2952.89	2783.38	2647.51	2536.79
300000	5176.26	4753.08	4429.33	4175.07	3971.26	3805.18
400000	6901.68	6337.44	5905.77	5566.77	5295.02	5073.58
500000	8627.10	7921.81	7382.22	6958.46	6618.77	6341.97

11 1/4%

MONTHLY PAYMENT

Necessary to amortize a loan

TERM / AMOUNT	13 YEARS	14 YEARS	15 YEARS	16 YEARS	17 YEARS	18 YEARS
500	6.11	5.92	5.76	5.63	5.51	5.41
600	7.34	7.11	6.91	6.75	6.61	6.49
700	8.56	8.29	8.07	7.88	7.71	7.57
800	9.78	9.48	9.22	9.00	8.81	8.65
900	11.00	10.66	10.37	10.13	9.92	9.73
1000	12.23	11.85	11.52	11.25	11.02	10.82
2000	24.45	23.69	23.05	22.50	22.03	21.63
3000	36.68	35.54	34.57	33.75	33.05	32.45
4000	48.91	47.38	46.09	45.00	44.07	43.26
5000	61.13	59.23	57.62	56.25	55.08	54.08
6000	73.36	71.07	69.14	67.50	66.10	64.90
7000	85.59	82.92	80.66	78.75	77.12	75.71
8000	97.81	94.76	92.19	90.00	88.14	86.53
9000	110.04	106.61	103.71	101.25	99.15	97.35
10000	122.27	118.45	115.24	112.50	110.17	108.16
11000	134.50	130.30	126.76	123.75	121.19	118.98
12000	146.72	142.14	138.28	135.00	132.20	129.80
13000	158.95	153.99	149.81	146.25	143.22	140.61
14000	171.18	165.83	161.33	157.51	154.24	151.43
15000	183.40	177.68	172.85	168.76	165.25	162.24
16000	195.63	189.52	184.38	180.01	176.27	173.06
17000	207.86	201.37	195.90	191.26	187.29	183.88
18000	220.08	213.21	207.42	202.51	198.30	194.69
19000	232.31	225.06	218.95	213.76	209.32	205.51
20000	244.54	236.90	230.47	225.01	220.34	216.32
21000	256.76	248.75	241.99	236.26	231.36	227.14
22000	268.99	260.59	253.52	247.51	242.37	237.96
23000	281.22	272.44	265.04	258.76	253.39	248.77
24000	293.44	284.28	276.56	270.01	264.41	259.59
25000	305.67	296.13	288.09	281.26	275.42	270.41
30000	366.80	355.35	345.70	337.51	330.51	324.49
35000	427.94	414.58	403.32	393.76	385.59	378.57
40000	489.07	473.80	460.94	450.01	440.68	432.65
45000	550.21	533.03	518.56	506.27	495.76	486.73
50000	611.34	592.26	576.17	562.52	550.84	540.81
55000	672.47	651.48	633.79	618.77	605.93	594.89
60000	733.61	710.71	691.41	675.02	661.01	648.97
65000	794.74	769.93	749.03	731.27	716.10	703.05
70000	855.88	829.16	806.64	787.52	771.18	757.14
75000	917.01	888.38	864.26	843.78	826.27	811.22
80000	978.14	947.61	921.88	900.03	881.35	865.30
85000	1039.28	1006.83	979.49	956.28	936.44	919.38
90000	1100.41	1066.06	1037.11	1012.53	991.52	973.46
95000	1161.54	1125.28	1094.73	1068.78	1046.60	1027.54
100000	1222.68	1184.51	1152.35	1125.03	1101.69	1081.62
200000	2445.36	2369.02	2304.69	2250.07	2203.38	2163.24
300000	3668.04	3553.53	3457.04	3375.10	3305.06	3244.86
400000	4890.71	4738.04	4609.38	4500.13	4406.75	4326.48
500000	6113.39	5922.54	5761.73	5625.17	5508.44	5408.11

MONTHLY PAYMENT

Necessary to amortize a loan

11 1/4%

TERM / AMOUNT	19 YEARS	20 YEARS	25 YEARS	30 YEARS	35 YEARS	40 YEARS
500	5.32	5.25	4.99	4.86	4.78	4.74
600	6.39	6.30	5.99	5.83	5.74	5.69
700	7.45	7.34	6.99	6.80	6.70	6.64
800	8.51	8.39	7.99	7.77	7.65	7.59
900	9.58	9.44	8.98	8.74	8.61	8.53
1000	10.64	10.49	9.98	9.71	9.56	9.48
2000	21.29	20.99	19.96	19.43	19.13	18.97
3000	31.93	31.48	29.95	29.14	28.69	18.45
4000	42.57	41.97	39.93	38.85	38.26	37.93
5000	53.21	52.46	49.91	48.56	47.82	47.41
6000	63.86	62.96	59.89	58.28	57.39	56.90
7000	74.50	73.45	69.88	67.99	66.95	66.38
8000	85.14	83.94	79.86	77.70	76.52	75.86
9000	95.79	94.43	89.84	87.41	86.08	85.34
10000	106.43	104.93	99.82	97.13	95.65	94.83
11000	117.07	115.42	109.81	106.84	105.21	104.31
12000	127.72	125.91	119.79	116.55	114.78	113.79
13000	138.36	136.40	129.77	126.26	124.34	123.27
14000	149.00	146.90	139.75	135.98	133.91	132.76
15000	159.64	157.39	149.74	145.69	143.47	142.24
16000	170.29	167.88	159.72	155.40	153.04	151.72
17000	180.93	178.37	169.70	165.11	162.60	161.20
18000	191.57	188.87	179.68	174.83	172.17	170.69
19000	202.22	199.36	189.67	184.54	181.73	180.17
20000	212.86	209.85	199.65	194.25	191.30	189.65
21000	223.50	220.34	209.63	203.97	200.86	199.13
22000	234.14	230.84	219.61	213.68	210.43	208.62
23000	244.79	241.33	229.60	223.39	219.99	218.10
24000	255.43	251.82	239.58	233.10	229.56	227.58
25000	266.07	262.31	249.56	242.82	239.12	237.06
30000	319.29	314.78	299.47	291.38	286.95	284.48
35000	372.50	367.24	349.38	339.94	334.77	331.89
40000	425.72	419.70	399.30	388.50	382.60	379.30
45000	478.93	472.17	449.21	437.07	430.42	426.72
50000	532.15	524.63	499.12	485.63	478.25	474.13
55000	585.36	577.09	549.03	534.19	526.07	521.54
60000	638.57	629.55	598.94	582.76	573.90	568.95
65000	691.79	682.02	648.86	631.32	621.72	616.37
70000	745.00	734.48	698.77	679.88	669.55	663.78
75000	798.22	786.94	748.68	728.45	717.37	711.19
80000	851.43	839.41	798.59	777.01	765.20	758.61
85000	904.65	891.87	848.50	825.57	813.02	806.02
90000	957.86	944.33	898.42	874.14	860.84	853.43
95000	1011.07	996.79	948.33	922.70	908.67	900.84
100000	1064.29	1049.26	998.24	971.26	956.49	948.26
200000	2128.58	2098.51	1996.48	1942.52	1912.99	1896.51
300000	3192.87	3147.77	2994.72	2913.78	2869.48	2844.77
400000	4257.16	4197.03	3992.96	3885.04	3825.97	3793.03
500000	5321.45	5246.28	4991.20	4856.31	4782.47	4741.29

11 1/2%

MONTHLY PAYMENT
Necessary to amortize a loan

TERM / AMOUNT	1 YEAR	2 YEARS	3 YEARS	4 YEARS	5 YEARS	6 YEARS
500	44.31	23.42	16.49	13.04	11.00	9.65
600	53.17	28.10	19.79	15.65	13.20	11.57
700	62.03	32.79	23.08	18.26	15.39	13.50
800	70.89	37.47	26.38	20.87	17.59	15.43
900	79.75	42.16	29.68	23.48	19.79	17.36
1000	88.62	46.84	32.98	26.09	21.99	19.29
2000	177.23	93.68	65.95	52.18	43.99	38.58
3000	265.85	140.52	98.93	78.27	65.98	57.87
4000	354.46	187.36	131.90	104.36	87.97	77.16
5000	443.08	234.20	164.88	130.45	109.96	96.46
6000	531.69	281.04	197.86	156.53	131.96	115.75
7000	620.31	327.88	230.83	182.62	153.95	135.04
8000	708.92	374.72	263.81	208.71	175.94	154.33
9000	797.54	421.56	296.78	234.80	197.93	173.62
10000	886.15	468.40	329.76	260.89	219.93	192.91
11000	974.77	515.24	362.74	286.98	241.92	212.20
12000	1063.38	562.08	395.71	313.07	263.91	231.49
13000	1152.00	608.93	428.69	339.16	285.90	250.79
14000	1240.61	655.77	461.66	365.25	307.90	270.08
15000	1329.23	702.61	494.64	391.34	329.89	289.37
16000	1417.84	749.45	527.62	417.42	351.88	308.66
17000	1506.46	796.29	560.59	443.51	373.88	327.95
18000	1595.07	843.13	593.57	469.60	395.87	347.24
19000	1683.69	889.97	626.54	495.69	417.86	355.53
20000	1772.30	936.81	659.52	521.78	439.85	385.82
21000	1860.92	983.65	692.50	547.87	461.85	405.11
22000	1949.53	1030.49	725.47	573.96	483.84	424.41
23000	2038.15	1077.33	758.45	600.05	505.83	443.70
24000	2126.76	1124.17	791.43	626.14	527.82	462.99
25000	2215.38	1171.01	824.40	652.23	549.82	482.28
30000	2658.45	1405.21	989.28	782.67	659.78	578.74
35000	3101.53	1639.41	1154.16	913.12	769.74	675.19
40000	3544.60	1873.61	1319.04	1043.56	879.71	771.65
45000	3987.68	2107.82	1483.92	1174.01	989.67	868.10
50000	4430.76	2342.02	1648.80	1304.45	1099.63	964.56
55000	4873.83	2576.22	1813.68	1434.90	1209.59	1061.01
60000	5316.91	2810.42	1978.56	1565.34	1319.56	1157.47
65000	5759.98	3044.62	2143.44	1695.79	1429.52	1253.93
70000	6203.06	3278.82	2308.32	1826.23	1539.48	1350.38
75000	6646.13	3513.03	2473.20	1956.68	1649.45	1446.84
80000	7089.21	3747.23	2638.08	2087.12	1759.41	1543.29
85000	7532.28	3981.43	2802.96	2217.57	1869.37	1639.75
90000	7975.36	4215.63	2967.84	2348.01	1979.34	1736.20
95000	8418.44	4449.83	3132.72	2478.46	2089.30	1832.66
100000	8861.51	4684.03	3297.60	2608.90	2199.26	1929.12
200000	17723.00	9368.07	6595.20	5217.80	4398.52	3858.23
300000	26584.50	14052.10	9892.81	7826.71	6597.79	5787.35
400000	35446.00	18736.10	13190.40	10435.60	8797.05	7716.47
500000	44307.60	23420.20	16488.00	13044.50	10996.30	9645.58

MONTHLY PAYMENT

Necessary to amortize a loan

11 1/2%

TERM / AMOUNT	7 YEARS	8 YEARS	9 YEARS	10 YEARS	11 YEARS	12 YEARS
500	8.69	7.99	7.45	7.03	6.69	6.42
600	10.43	9.59	8.94	8.44	8.03	7.70
700	12.17	11.19	10.43	9.84	9.37	8.98
800	13.91	12.78	11.92	11.25	10.71	10.27
900	15.65	14.38	13.41	12.65	12.05	11.55
1000	17.39	15.98	14.90	14.06	13.38	12.83
2000	34.77	31.96	29.81	28.12	26.77	25.67
3000	52.16	47.94	44.71	42.18	40.15	38.50
4000	69.55	63.92	59.61	56.24	53.53	51.33
5000	86.93	79.90	74.52	70.30	66.92	64.17
6000	104.32	95.88	89.42	84.36	80.30	77.00
7000	121.71	111.86	104.33	98.42	93.68	89.83
8000	139.09	127.84	119.23	112.48	107.07	102.67
9000	156.48	143.81	134.13	126.54	120.45	115.50
10000	173.87	159.79	149.04	140.60	133.84	128.33
11000	191.25	175.77	163.94	154.66	147.22	141.17
12000	208.64	191.75	178.84	168.72	160.60	154.00
13000	226.02	207.73	193.75	182.77	173.99	166.83
14000	243.41	223.71	208.65	196.83	187.37	179.66
15000	260.80	239.69	223.56	210.89	200.75	192.50
16000	278.18	255.67	238.46	224.95	214.14	205.33
17000	295.57	271.65	253.36	239.01	227.52	218.16
18000	312.96	287.63	268.27	253.07	240.90	231.00
19000	330.34	303.61	283.17	267.13	254.29	243.83
20000	347.73	319.59	298.07	281.19	267.67	256.66
21000	365.12	335.57	312.98	295.25	281.05	269.50
22000	382.50	351.55	327.88	309.31	294.44	282.33
23000	399.89	367.53	342.78	323.37	307.82	295.16
24000	417.28	383.51	357.69	337.43	321.20	308.00
25000	434.66	399.48	372.59	351.49	334.59	320.83
30000	521.59	479.38	447.11	421.79	401.51	385.00
35000	608.53	559.28	521.63	492.08	468.42	449.16
40000	695.46	639.18	596.15	562.38	535.34	513.33
45000	782.39	719.07	670.67	632.68	602.26	577.49
50000	869.32	798.97	745.18	702.98	669.18	641.66
55000	956.26	878.87	819.70	773.28	736.09	705.82
60000	1043.19	958.76	894.22	843.57	803.01	769.99
65000	1130.12	1038.66	968.74	913.87	869.93	834.16
70000	1217.05	1118.56	1043.26	984.17	936.85	898.32
75000	1303.99	1198.45	1117.77	1054.47	1003.76	962.49
80000	1390.92	1278.35	1192.29	1124.76	1070.68	1026.65
85000	1477.85	1358.25	1266.81	1195.06	1137.60	1090.82
90000	1564.78	1438.14	1341.33	1265.36	1204.52	1154.99
95000	1651.71	1518.04	1415.85	1335.66	1271.43	1219.15
100000	1738.65	1597.94	1490.37	1405.95	1338.35	1283.32
200000	3477.29	3195.88	2980.73	2811.91	2676.70	2566.63
300000	5215.94	4793.81	4471.10	4217.86	4015.05	3849.95
400000	6954.59	6391.75	5961.47	5623.82	5353.40	5133.27
500000	8693.23	7989.69	7451.83	7029.77	6691.75	6416.58

11 1/2%

MONTHLY PAYMENT

Necessary to amortize a loan

TERM / AMOUNT	13 YEARS	14 YEARS	15 YEARS	16 YEARS	17 YEARS	18 YEARS
500	6.19	6.00	5.84	5.71	5.59	5.49
600	7.43	7.20	7.01	6.85	6.71	6.59
700	8.67	8.40	8.18	7.99	7.83	7.69
800	9.90	9.60	9.35	9.13	8.94	8.79
900	11.14	10.80	10.51	10.27	10.06	9.88
1000	12.38	12.00	11.68	11.41	11.18	10.98
2000	24.76	24.00	23.36	22.82	22.36	21.97
3000	37.14	36.00	35.05	34.24	33.54	32.95
4000	49.52	48.00	46.73	45.65	44.72	43.93
5000	61.90	60.00	58.41	57.06	55.90	54.91
6000	74.28	72.00	70.09	68.47	67.09	65.90
7000	86.65	84.00	81.77	79.88	78.27	76.88
8000	99.03	96.00	93.46	91.29	89.45	87.86
9000	111.41	108.01	105.14	102.71	100.63	98.85
10000	123.79	120.01	116.82	114.12	111.81	109.83
11000	136.17	132.01	128.50	125.53	122.99	120.81
12000	148.55	144.01	140.18	136.94	134.17	131.80
13000	160.93	156.01	151.87	148.35	145.35	142.78
14000	173.31	168.01	163.55	159.76	156.53	153.76
15000	185.69	180.01	175.23	171.18	167.71	164.74
16000	198.07	192.01	186.91	182.59	178.90	175.73
17000	210.45	204.01	198.59	194.00	190.08	186.71
18000	222.83	216.01	210.27	205.41	201.26	197.69
19000	235.20	228.01	221.96	216.82	212.44	208.68
20000	247.58	240.01	233.64	228.23	223.62	219.66
21000	259.96	252.01	245.32	239.65	234.80	230.64
22000	272.34	264.01	257.00	251.06	245.98	241.63
23000	284.72	276.01	268.68	262.47	257.16	252.61
24000	297.10	288.01	280.37	273.88	268.34	263.59
25000	309.48	300.01	292.05	285.29	279.52	274.57
30000	371.38	360.02	350.46	342.35	335.43	329.49
35000	433.27	420.02	408.87	399.41	391.33	384.40
40000	495.17	480.02	467.28	456.47	447.24	439.32
45000	557.06	540.03	525.69	513.52	503.14	494.23
50000	618.96	600.03	584.10	570.58	559.05	549.15
55000	680.86	660.03	642.51	627.64	614.95	604.06
60000	742.75	720.03	700.91	684.70	670.86	658.98
65000	804.65	780.04	759.32	741.76	726.76	713.89
70000	866.54	840.04	817.73	798.82	782.67	768.81
75000	928.44	900.04	876.14	855.87	838.57	823.72
80000	990.33	960.05	934.55	912.93	894.48	878.64
85000	1052.23	1020.05	992.96	969.99	950.38	933.55
90000	1114.13	1080.05	1051.37	1027.05	1006.29	988.47
95000	1176.02	1140.05	1109.78	1084.11	1062.19	1043.38
100000	1237.92	1200.06	1168.19	1141.17	1118.10	1098.30
200000	2475.84	2400.11	2336.38	2282.33	2236.19	2196.59
300000	3713.75	3600.17	3504.57	3423.50	3354.29	3294.89
400000	4951.67	4800.22	4672.76	4564.66	4472.39	4393.18
500000	6189.59	6000.28	5840.95	5705.83	5590.48	5491.48

MONTHLY PAYMENT

Necessary to amortize a loan

11 1/2%

TERM / AMOUNT	19 YEARS	20 YEARS	25 YEARS	30 YEARS	35 YEARS	40 YEARS
500	5.41	5.33	5.08	4.95	4.88	4.84
600	6.49	6.40	6.10	5.94	5.86	5.81
700	7.57	7.47	7.12	6.93	6.83	6.78
800	8.65	8.53	8.13	7.92	7.81	7.75
900	9.73	9.60	9.15	8.91	8.78	8.71
1000	10.81	10.66	10.16	9.90	9.76	9.68
2000	21.62	21.33	20.33	19.81	19.52	19.37
3000	32.44	31.99	30.49	29.71	29.28	29.05
4000	43.25	42.66	40.66	39.61	39.04	38.73
5000	54.06	53.32	50.82	49.51	48.81	48.41
6000	64.87	63.99	60.99	59.42	58.57	58.10
7000	75.69	74.65	71.15	69.32	68.33	67.78
8000	86.50	85.31	81.32	79.22	78.09	77.46
9000	97.31	95.98	91.48	89.13	87.85	87.15
10000	108.12	106.64	101.65	99.03	97.61	96.83
11000	118.93	117.31	111.81	108.93	107.37	106.51
12000	129.75	127.97	121.98	118.84	117.13	116.19
13000	140.56	138.64	132.14	128.74	126.89	125.88
14000	151.37	149.30	142.31	138.64	136.66	135.56
15000	162.18	159.96	152.47	148.54	146.42	145.24
16000	173.00	170.63	162.64	158.45	156.18	154.93
17000	183.81	181.29	172.80	168.35	165.94	164.61
18000	194.62	191.96	182.96	178.25	175.70	174.29
19000	205.43	202.62	193.13	188.16	185.46	183.97
20000	216.24	213.29	203.29	198.06	195.22	193.66
21000	227.06	223.95	213.46	207.96	204.98	203.34
22000	237.87	234.62	223.62	217.86	214.74	213.02
23000	248.68	245.28	233.79	227.77	224.51	222.71
24000	259.49	255.94	243.95	237.67	234.27	232.39
25000	270.31	266.61	254.12	247.57	244.03	242.07
30000	324.37	319.93	304.94	297.09	292.83	290.48
35000	378.43	373.25	355.76	346.60	341.64	338.90
40000	432.49	426.57	406.59	396.12	390.44	387.31
45000	486.55	479.89	457.41	445.63	439.25	435.73
50000	540.61	533.22	508.23	495.15	488.05	484.14
55000	594.67	586.54	559.06	544.66	536.86	532.56
60000	648.73	639.86	609.88	594.18	585.66	580.97
65000	702.79	693.18	660.70	643.69	634.47	629.38
70000	756.85	746.50	711.53	693.20	683.28	677.80
75000	810.91	799.82	762.35	742.72	732.08	726.21
80000	864.98	853.14	813.17	792.23	780.89	774.63
85000	919.04	906.47	864.00	841.75	829.69	823.04
90000	973.10	959.79	914.82	891.26	878.50	871.45
95000	1027.16	1013.11	965.65	940.78	927.30	919.87
100000	1081.22	1066.43	1016.47	990.29	976.11	968.28
200000	2162.44	2132.86	2032.94	1980.58	1952.21	1936.56
300000	3243.65	3199.29	3049.40	2970.87	2928.32	2904.84
400000	4324.87	4265.72	4065.87	3961.16	3904.43	3873.13
500000	5406.09	5332.15	5082.34	4951.45	4880.53	4841.41

11 3/4%

MONTHLY PAYMENT
Necessary to amortize a loan

TERM / AMOUNT	1 YEAR	2 YEARS	3 YEARS	4 YEARS	5 YEARS	6 YEARS
500	44.37	23.48	16.55	13.11	11.06	9.71
600	53.24	28.17	19.86	15.73	13.27	11.65
700	62.11	32.87	23.17	18.35	15.48	13.59
800	70.99	37.57	26.48	20.97	17.69	15.54
900	79.86	42.26	29.79	23.59	19.91	17.48
1000	88.73	46.96	33.10	26.21	22.12	19.42
2000	177.47	93.91	66.19	52.42	44.24	38.84
3000	266.20	140.87	99.29	78.63	66.36	58.26
4000	354.93	187.83	132.38	104.85	88.47	77.68
5000	443.66	234.79	165.48	131.06	110.59	97.10
6000	532.39	281.74	198.57	157.27	132.71	116.52
7000	621.13	328.70	231.67	183.48	154.83	135.94
8000	709.86	375.66	264.76	209.69	176.95	155.36
9000	798.59	422.61	297.86	235.90	199.07	174.79
10000	887.32	469.57	330.95	262.11	221.18	194.21
11000	976.06	516.53	364.05	288.33	243.30	213.63
12000	1064.79	563.49	397.14	314.54	265.42	233.05
13000	1153.52	610.44	430.24	340.75	287.54	252.47
14000	1242.25	657.40	463.33	366.96	309.66	271.89
15000	1330.99	704.36	496.43	393.17	331.78	291.31
16000	1419.72	751.31	529.52	419.38	353.90	310.73
17000	1508.45	798.27	562.62	445.59	376.01	330.15
18000	1597.18	845.23	595.71	471.81	398.13	349.57
19000	1685.92	892.19	628.81	498.02	420.25	368.99
20000	1774.65	939.14	661.90	524.23	442.37	388.41
21000	1863.38	986.10	695.00	550.44	464.49	407.83
22000	1952.11	1033.06	728.10	576.65	486.61	427.25
23000	2040.84	1080.01	761.19	602.86	508.72	446.67
24000	2129.58	1126.97	794.29	629.07	530.84	466.09
25000	2218.31	1173.93	827.38	655.29	552.96	485.51
30000	2661.97	1408.71	992.86	786.34	663.55	582.62
35000	3105.63	1643.50	1158.33	917.40	774.15	679.72
40000	3549.30	1878.28	1323.81	1048.46	884.74	776.82
45000	3992.96	2113.07	1489.28	1179.51	995.33	873.92
50000	4436.62	2347.85	1654.76	1310.57	1105.92	971.03
55000	4880.28	2582.64	1820.24	1441.63	1216.51	1068.13
60000	5323.94	2817.42	1985.71	1572.68	1327.11	1165.23
65000	5767.60	3052.21	2151.19	1703.74	1437.70	1262.33
70000	6211.27	3287.00	2316.66	1834.80	1548.29	1359.44
75000	6654.93	3521.78	2482.14	1965.85	1658.88	1456.54
80000	7098.59	3756.57	2647.62	2096.91	1769.47	1553.64
85000	7542.25	3991.35	2813.09	2227.97	1880.07	1650.74
90000	7985.91	4226.14	2978.57	2359.02	1990.66	1747.85
95000	8429.58	4460.92	3144.04	2490.08	2101.25	1844.95
100000	8873.24	4695.71	3309.52	2621.14	2211.84	1942.05
200000	17746.50	9391.42	6619.04	5242.28	4423.68	3884.10
300000	26619.70	14087.10	9928.56	7863.42	6635.53	5826.15
400000	35493.00	18782.80	13238.10	10484.60	8847.37	7768.21
500000	44366.20	23478.50	16547.60	13105.70	11059.20	9710.26

MONTHLY PAYMENT

Necessary to amortize a loan

11 3/4%

TERM / AMOUNT	7 YEARS	8 YEARS	9 YEARS	10 YEARS	11 YEARS	12 YEARS
500	8.76	8.06	7.52	7.10	6.77	6.49
600	10.51	9.67	9.03	8.52	8.12	7.79
700	12.26	11.28	10.53	9.94	9.47	9.09
800	14.02	12.89	12.03	11.36	10.82	10.39
900	15.77	14.50	13.54	12.78	12.18	11.69
1000	17.52	16.12	15.04	14.20	13.53	12.98
2000	35.04	32.23	30.09	28.41	27.06	25.97
3000	52.56	48.35	45.13	42.61	40.59	38.95
4000	70.08	64.46	60.17	56.81	54.12	51.93
5000	87.60	80.58	75.22	71.02	67.65	64.92
6000	105.12	96.70	90.26	85.22	81.18	77.90
7000	122.64	112.81	105.31	99.42	94.71	90.88
8000	140.16	128.93	120.35	113.62	108.24	103.87
9000	157.67	145.04	135.39	127.83	121.77	116.85
10000	175.19	161.16	150.44	142.03	135.30	129.83
11000	192.71	177.27	165.48	156.23	148.83	142.82
12000	210.23	193.39	180.52	170.44	162.36	155.80
13000	227.75	209.51	195.57	184.64	175.89	168.78
14000	245.27	225.62	210.61	198.84	189.43	181.77
15000	262.79	241.74	225.66	213.05	202.96	194.75
16000	280.31	257.85	240.70	227.25	216.49	207.73
17000	297.83	273.97	255.74	241.45	230.02	220.72
18000	315.35	290.09	270.79	255.65	243.55	233.70
19000	332.87	306.20	285.83	269.86	257.08	246.68
20000	350.39	322.32	300.87	284.06	270.61	259.67
21000	367.91	338.43	315.92	298.26	284.14	272.65
22000	385.43	354.55	330.96	312.47	297.67	285.63
23000	402.95	370.67	346.00	326.67	311.20	298.62
24000	420.47	386.78	361.05	340.87	324.73	311.60
25000	437.99	402.90	376.09	355.08	338.26	324.58
30000	525.58	483.48	451.31	426.09	405.91	389.50
35000	613.18	564.06	526.53	497.11	473.56	454.42
40000	700.78	644.63	601.75	568.12	541.21	519.33
45000	788.37	725.21	676.96	639.14	608.87	584.25
50000	875.97	805.79	752.18	710.15	676.52	649.17
55000	963.57	886.37	827.40	781.17	744.17	714.08
60000	1051.16	966.95	902.62	852.18	811.82	779.00
65000	1138.76	1047.53	977.84	923.19	879.47	843.91
70000	1226.36	1128.11	1053.06	994.21	947.12	908.83
75000	1313.95	1208.69	1128.27	1065.22	1014.78	973.75
80000	1401.55	1289.27	1203.49	1136.24	1082.43	1038.66
85000	1489.15	1369.85	1278.71	1207.25	1150.08	1103.58
90000	1576.74	1450.43	1353.93	1278.27	1217.73	1168.50
95000	1664.34	1531.01	1429.15	1349.28	1285.38	1233.41
100000	1751.94	1611.59	1504.37	1420.30	1353.03	1298.33
200000	3503.88	3223.17	3008.73	2840.60	2706.07	2596.66
300000	5255.82	4834.76	4513.10	4260.90	4059.10	3894.99
400000	7007.75	6446.34	6017.46	5681.20	5412.13	5193.32
500000	8759.69	8057.93	7521.83	7101.50	6765.17	6491.65

11 3/4%

MONTHLY PAYMENT

Necessary to amortize a loan

TERM / AMOUNT	13 YEARS	14 YEARS	15 YEARS	16 YEARS	17 YEARS	18 YEARS
500	6.27	6.08	5.92	5.79	5.67	5.58
600	7.52	7.29	7.10	6.94	6.81	6.69
700	8.77	8.51	8.29	8.10	7.94	7.81
800	10.03	9.73	9.47	9.26	9.08	8.92
900	11.28	10.94	10.66	10.42	10.21	10.04
1000	12.53	12.16	11.84	11.57	11.35	11.15
2000	25.07	24.31	23.68	23.15	22.69	22.30
3000	37.60	36.47	35.52	34.72	34.04	33.45
4000	50.13	48.63	47.37	46.30	45.38	44.60
5000	62.66	60.79	59.21	57.87	56.73	55.75
6000	75.20	72.94	71.05	69.44	68.08	66.90
7000	87.73	85.10	82.89	81.02	79.42	78.06
8000	100.26	97.26	94.73	92.59	90.77	89.21
9000	112.79	109.41	106.57	104.17	102.12	100.36
10000	125.33	121.57	118.41	115.74	113.46	111.51
11000	137.86	133.73	130.26	127.31	124.81	122.66
12000	150.39	145.88	142.10	138.89	136.15	133.81
13000	162.92	158.04	153.94	150.46	147.50	144.96
14000	175.46	170.20	165.78	162.04	158.85	156.11
15000	187.99	182.36	177.62	173.61	170.19	167.26
16000	200.52	194.51	189.46	185.18	181.54	178.41
17000	213.05	206.67	201.30	196.76	192.88	189.56
18000	225.59	218.83	213.14	208.33	204.23	200.71
19000	238.12	230.98	224.99	219.91	215.58	211.86
20000	250.65	243.14	236.83	231.48	226.92	223.02
21000	263.18	255.30	248.67	243.05	238.27	234.17
22000	275.72	267.45	260.51	254.63	249.61	245.32
23000	288.25	279.61	272.35	266.20	260.96	256.47
24000	300.78	291.77	284.19	277.78	272.31	267.62
25000	313.31	303.93	296.03	289.35	283.65	278.77
30000	375.98	364.71	355.24	347.22	340.38	334.52
35000	438.64	425.50	414.45	405.09	397.11	390.28
40000	501.30	486.28	473.65	462.96	453.84	446.03
45000	563.96	547.07	532.86	520.83	510.57	501.78
50000	626.63	607.85	592.07	578.70	567.30	557.54
55000	689.29	668.64	651.27	636.57	624.04	613.29
60000	751.95	729.42	710.48	694.44	680.77	669.05
65000	814.61	790.21	769.69	752.31	737.50	724.80
70000	877.28	850.99	828.89	810.18	794.23	780.55
75000	939.94	911.78	888.10	868.05	850.96	836.31
80000	1002.60	972.56	947.31	925.92	907.69	892.06
85000	1065.26	1033.34	1006.51	983.79	964.42	947.81
90000	1127.93	1094.13	1065.72	1041.66	1021.15	1003.57
95000	1190.59	1154.91	1124.93	1099.53	1077.88	1059.32
100000	1253.25	1215.70	1184.13	1157.40	1134.61	1115.07
200000	2506.50	2431.40	2368.27	2314.80	2269.22	2230.15
300000	3759.75	3647.10	3552.40	3472.20	3403.83	3345.22
400000	5013.00	4862.80	4736.54	4629.59	4538.43	4460.30
500000	6266.25	6078.50	5920.67	5786.99	5673.04	5575.37

MONTHLY PAYMENT

Necessary to amortize a loan

11 3/4%

TERM / AMOUNT	19 YEARS	20 YEARS	25 YEARS	30 YEARS	35 YEARS	40 YEARS
500	5.49	5.42	5.17	5.05	4.98	4.94
600	6.59	6.50	6.21	6.06	5.97	5.93
700	7.69	7.59	7.24	7.07	6.97	6.92
800	8.79	8.67	8.28	8.08	7.97	7.91
900	9.88	9.75	9.31	9.08	8.96	8.90
1000	10.98	10.84	10.35	10.09	9.96	9.88
2000	21.97	21.67	20.70	20.19	19.92	19.77
3000	32.95	32.51	31.04	30.28	29.87	29.65
4000	43.93	43.35	41.39	40.38	39.83	39.53
5000	54.91	54.19	51.74	50.47	49.79	49.42
6000	65.90	65.02	62.09	60.56	59.75	59.30
7000	76.88	75.86	72.44	70.66	69.71	69.19
8000	87.86	86.70	82.78	80.75	79.66	79.07
9000	98.84	97.53	93.13	90.85	89.62	88.95
10000	109.83	108.37	103.48	100.94	99.58	98.84
11000	120.81	119.21	113.83	111.04	109.54	108.72
12000	131.79	130.05	124.18	121.13	119.50	118.60
13000	142.77	140.88	134.52	131.22	129.45	128.49
14000	153.76	151.72	144.87	141.32	139.41	138.37
15000	164.74	162.56	155.22	151.41	149.37	148.26
16000	175.72	173.39	165.57	161.51	159.33	158.14
17000	186.70	184.23	175.92	171.60	169.29	168.02
18000	197.69	195.07	186.26	181.69	179.24	177.91
19000	208.67	205.91	196.61	191.79	189.20	187.79
20000	219.65	216.74	206.96	201.88	199.16	197.67
21000	230.63	227.58	217.31	211.98	209.12	207.56
22000	241.62	238.42	227.66	222.07	219.08	217.44
23000	252.60	249.25	238.00	232.16	229.03	227.32
24000	263.58	260.09	248.35	242.26	238.99	237.21
25000	274.56	270.93	258.70	252.35	248.95	247.09
30000	329.48	325.11	310.44	302.82	298.74	296.51
35000	384.39	379.30	362.18	353.29	348.53	345.93
40000	439.30	433.48	413.92	403.76	398.32	395.35
45000	494.21	487.67	465.66	454.24	448.11	444.76
50000	549.13	541.85	517.40	504.71	497.90	494.18
55000	604.04	596.04	569.14	555.18	547.69	543.60
60000	658.95	650.23	620.88	605.65	597.48	593.02
65000	713.87	704.41	672.62	656.12	647.27	642.44
70000	768.78	758.60	724.36	706.59	697.06	691.86
75000	823.69	812.78	776.10	757.06	746.85	741.27
80000	878.60	866.97	827.84	807.53	796.64	790.69
85000	933.52	921.15	879.58	858.00	846.43	840.11
90000	988.43	975.34	931.32	908.47	896.22	889.53
95000	1043.34	1029.52	983.06	958.94	946.01	938.95
100000	1098.25	1083.71	1034.80	1009.41	995.79	988.36
200000	2196.51	2167.42	2069.60	2018.82	1991.59	1976.73
300000	3294.76	3251.13	3104.40	3028.23	2987.38	2965.09
400000	4393.01	4334.83	4139.20	4037.64	3983.18	3953.46
500000	5491.27	5418.54	5174.00	5047.05	4978.97	4941.82

12%

MONTHLY PAYMENT

Necessary to amortize a loan

TERM / AMOUNT	1 YEAR	2 YEARS	3 YEARS	4 YEARS	5 YEARS	6 YEARS
500	44.42	23.54	16.61	13.17	11.12	9.78
600	53.31	28.24	19.93	15.80	13.35	11.73
700	62.19	32.95	23.25	18.43	15.57	13.69
800	71.08	37.66	26.57	21.07	17.80	15.64
900	79.96	42.37	29.89	23.70	20.02	17.60
1000	88.85	47.07	33.21	26.33	22.24	19.55
2000	177.70	94.15	66.43	52.67	44.49	39.10
3000	266.55	141.22	99.64	79.00	66.73	58.65
4000	355.40	188.29	132.86	105.34	88.98	78.20
5000	444.24	235.37	166.07	131.67	111.22	97.75
6000	533.09	282.44	199.29	158.00	133.47	117.30
7000	621.94	329.51	232.50	184.34	155.71	136.85
8000	710.79	376.59	265.72	210.67	177.96	156.40
9000	799.64	423.66	298.93	237.01	200.20	175.95
10000	888.49	470.74	332.14	263.34	222.45	195.50
11000	977.34	517.81	365.36	289.67	244.69	215.05
12000	1066.19	564.88	398.57	316.01	266.93	234.60
13000	1155.03	611.96	431.79	342.34	289.18	254.15
14000	1243.88	659.03	465.00	368.67	311.42	273.70
15000	1332.73	706.10	498.22	395.01	333.67	293.25
16000	1421.58	753.18	531.43	421.34	355.91	312.80
17000	1510.43	800.25	564.64	447.68	378.16	332.35
18000	1599.28	847.32	597.86	474.01	400.40	351.90
19000	1688.13	894.40	631.07	500.34	422.65	371.45
20000	1776.98	941.47	664.29	526.68	444.89	391.00
21000	1865.83	988.54	697.50	553.01	467.13	410.55
22000	1954.67	1035.62	730.72	579.35	489.38	430.10
23000	2043.52	1082.69	763.93	605.68	511.62	449.66
24000	2132.37	1129.76	797.14	632.01	533.87	469.21
25000	2221.22	1176.84	830.36	658.35	556.11	488.76
30000	2665.46	1412.21	996.43	790.02	667.33	586.51
35000	3109.71	1647.57	1162.50	921.69	778.56	684.26
40000	3553.95	1882.94	1328.57	1053.35	889.78	782.01
45000	3998.20	2118.31	1494.64	1185.02	1001.00	879.76
50000	4442.44	2353.67	1660.72	1316.69	1112.22	977.51
55000	4886.69	2589.04	1826.79	1448.36	1223.45	1075.26
60000	5330.93	2824.41	1992.86	1580.03	1334.67	1173.01
65000	5775.17	3059.78	2158.93	1711.70	1445.89	1270.76
70000	6219.42	3295.14	2325.00	1843.37	1557.11	1368.51
75000	6663.66	3530.51	2491.07	1975.04	1668.33	1466.26
80000	7107.91	3765.88	2657.15	2106.71	1779.56	1564.02
85000	7552.15	4001.25	2823.22	2238.38	1890.78	1661.77
90000	7996.39	4236.61	2989.29	2370.05	2002.00	1759.52
95000	8440.64	4471.98	3155.36	2501.72	2113.22	1857.27
100000	8884.88	4707.35	3321.43	2633.38	2224.45	1955.02
200000	17769.80	9414.70	6642.86	5266.77	4448.89	3910.04
300000	26654.60	14122.00	9964.29	7900.15	6673.34	5865.06
400000	35539.50	18829.40	13285.70	10533.50	8897.78	7820.08
500000	44424.40	23536.70	16607.20	13166.90	11122.20	9775.10

MONTHLY PAYMENT

Necessary to amortize a loan

12%

TERM / AMOUNT	7 YEARS	8 YEARS	9 YEARS	10 YEARS	11 YEARS	12 YEARS
500	8.83	8.13	7.59	7.17	6.84	6.57
600	10.59	9.75	9.11	8.61	8.21	7.88
700	12.36	11.38	10.63	10.04	9.57	9.19
800	14.12	13.00	12.15	11.48	10.94	10.51
900	15.89	14.63	13.67	12.91	12.31	11.82
1000	17.65	16.25	15.18	14.35	13.68	13.13
2000	35.31	32.51	30.37	28.69	27.36	26.27
3000	52.96	48.76	45.55	43.04	41.03	39.40
4000	70.61	65.01	60.74	57.39	54.71	52.54
5000	88.26	81.26	75.92	71.74	68.39	65.67
6000	105.92	97.52	91.11	86.08	82.07	78.81
7000	123.57	113.77	106.29	100.43	95.75	91.94
8000	141.22	130.02	121.47	114.78	109.42	105.07
9000	158.88	146.28	136.66	129.12	123.10	118.21
10000	176.53	162.53	151.84	143.47	136.78	131.34
11000	194.18	178.78	167.03	157.82	150.46	144.48
12000	211.83	195.03	182.21	172.17	164.14	157.61
13000	229.49	211.29	197.40	186.51	177.81	170.74
14000	247.14	227.54	212.58	200.86	191.49	183.88
15000	264.79	243.79	227.76	215.21	205.17	197.01
16000	282.44	260.05	242.95	229.55	218.85	210.15
17000	300.10	276.30	258.13	243.90	232.52	223.28
18000	317.75	292.55	273.32	258.25	246.20	236.42
19000	335.40	308.80	288.50	272.60	259.88	249.55
20000	353.06	325.06	303.69	286.94	273.56	262.68
21000	370.71	341.31	318.87	301.29	287.24	275.82
22000	388.36	357.56	334.05	315.64	300.91	288.95
23000	406.01	373.82	349.24	329.98	314.59	302.09
24000	423.67	390.07	364.42	344.33	328.27	315.22
25000	441.32	406.32	379.61	358.68	341.95	328.36
30000	529.58	487.59	455.53	430.41	410.34	394.03
35000	617.85	568.85	531.45	502.15	478.73	459.70
40000	706.11	650.11	607.37	573.88	547.12	525.37
45000	794.37	731.38	683.29	645.62	615.51	591.04
50000	882.64	812.64	759.21	717.36	683.89	656.71
55000	970.90	893.91	835.13	789.09	752.28	722.38
60000	1059.16	975.17	911.05	860.83	820.67	788.05
65000	1147.43	1056.43	986.98	932.56	889.06	853.72
70000	1235.69	1137.70	1062.90	1004.30	957.45	919.39
75000	1323.96	1218.96	1138.82	1076.03	1025.84	985.06
80000	1412.22	1300.23	1214.74	1147.77	1094.23	1050.74
85000	1500.48	1381.49	1290.66	1219.50	1162.62	1116.41
90000	1588.75	1462.76	1366.58	1291.24	1231.01	1182.08
95000	1677.01	1544.02	1442.50	1362.97	1299.40	1247.75
100000	1765.27	1625.28	1518.42	1434.71	1367.79	1313.42
200000	3530.55	3250.57	3036.85	2869.42	2735.58	2626.84
300000	5295.82	4875.85	4555.27	4304.13	4103.36	3940.26
400000	7061.09	6501.14	6073.69	5738.84	5471.15	5253.68
500000	8826.37	8126.42	7592.12	7173.55	6838.94	6567.10

12%

MONTHLY PAYMENT
Necessary to amortize a loan

TERM / AMOUNT	13 YEARS	14 YEARS	15 YEARS	16 YEARS	17 YEARS	18 YEARS
500	6.34	6.16	6.00	5.87	5.76	5.66
600	7.61	7.39	7.20	7.04	6.91	6.79
700	8.88	8.62	8.40	8.22	8.06	7.92
800	10.15	9.85	9.60	9.39	9.21	9.06
900	11.42	11.08	10.80	10.56	10.36	10.19
1000	12.69	12.31	12.00	11.74	11.51	11.32
2000	25.37	24.63	24.00	23.47	23.02	22.64
3000	38.06	36.94	36.01	35.21	34.54	33.96
4000	50.75	49.26	48.01	46.95	46.05	45.28
5000	63.43	61.57	60.01	58.69	57.56	56.60
6000	76.12	73.89	72.01	70.42	69.07	67.92
7000	88.81	86.20	84.01	82.16	80.59	79.24
8000	101.49	98.51	96.01	93.90	92.10	90.56
9000	114.18	110.83	108.02	105.64	103.61	101.88
10000	126.87	123.14	120.02	117.37	115.12	113.20
11000	139.55	135.46	132.02	129.11	126.63	124.52
12000	152.24	147.77	144.02	140.85	138.15	135.83
13000	164.93	160.09	156.02	152.58	149.66	147.15
14000	177.61	172.40	168.02	164.32	161.17	158.47
15000	190.30	184.71	180.03	176.06	172.68	169.79
16000	202.99	197.03	192.03	187.80	184.20	181.11
17000	215.67	209.34	204.03	199.53	195.71	192.43
18000	228.36	221.66	216.03	211.27	207.22	203.75
19000	241.05	233.97	228.03	223.01	218.73	215.07
20000	253.73	246.29	240.03	234.75	230.24	226.39
21000	266.42	258.60	252.04	246.48	241.76	237.71
22000	279.11	270.92	264.04	258.22	253.27	249.03
23000	291.79	283.23	276.04	269.96	264.78	260.35
24000	304.48	295.54	288.04	281.69	276.29	271.67
25000	317.17	307.86	300.04	293.43	287.80	282.99
30000	380.60	369.43	360.05	352.12	345.37	339.59
35000	444.03	431.00	420.06	410.80	402.93	396.18
40000	507.47	492.57	480.07	469.49	460.49	452.78
45000	570.90	554.14	540.08	528.18	518.05	509.38
50000	634.33	615.72	600.08	586.86	575.61	565.98
55000	697.77	677.29	660.09	645.55	633.17	622.57
60000	761.20	738.86	720.10	704.24	690.73	679.17
65000	824.63	800.43	780.11	762.92	748.29	735.77
70000	888.07	862.00	840.12	821.61	805.85	792.37
75000	951.50	923.57	900.13	880.29	863.41	848.96
80000	1014.93	985.14	960.14	938.98	920.97	905.56
85000	1078.37	1046.72	1020.14	997.67	978.53	962.16
90000	1141.80	1108.29	1080.15	1056.35	1036.09	1018.76
95000	1205.23	1169.86	1140.16	1115.04	1093.65	1075.35
100000	1268.67	1231.43	1200.17	1173.73	1151.22	1131.95
200000	2537.33	2462.86	2400.34	2347.45	2302.43	2263.90
300000	3806.00	3694.29	3600.50	3521.18	3453.65	3395.85
400000	5074.67	4925.72	4800.67	4694.90	4604.86	4527.80
500000	6343.33	6157.15	6000.84	5868.63	5756.08	5659.75

MONTHLY PAYMENT

Necessary to amortize a loan

12%

TERM / AMOUNT	19 YEARS	20 YEARS	25 YEARS	30 YEARS	35 YEARS	40 YEARS
500	5.58	5.51	5.27	5.14	5.08	5.04
600	6.69	6.61	6.32	6.17	6.09	6.05
700	7.81	7.71	7.37	7.20	7.11	7.06
800	8.92	8.81	8.43	8.23	8.12	8.07
900	10.04	9.91	9.48	9.26	9.14	9.08
1000	11.15	11.01	10.53	10.29	10.16	10.09
2000	22.31	22.02	21.06	20.57	20.31	20.17
3000	33.46	33.03	31.60	30.86	30.47	30.26
4000	44.62	44.04	42.13	41.14	40.62	40.34
5000	55.77	55.05	52.66	51.43	50.78	50.43
6000	66.92	66.07	63.19	61.72	60.93	60.51
7000	78.08	77.08	73.73	72.00	71.09	70.60
8000	89.23	88.09	84.26	82.29	81.24	80.68
9000	100.39	99.10	94.79	92.58	91.40	90.77
10000	111.54	110.11	105.32	102.86	101.56	100.85
11000	122.69	121.12	115.86	113.15	111.71	110.94
12000	133.85	132.13	126.39	123.43	121.87	121.02
13000	145.00	143.14	136.92	133.72	132.02	131.11
14000	156.15	154.15	147.45	144.01	142.18	141.19
15000	167.31	165.16	157.98	154.29	152.33	151.28
16000	178.46	176.17	168.52	164.58	162.49	161.36
17000	189.62	187.19	179.05	174.86	172.64	171.45
18000	200.77	198.20	189.58	185.15	182.80	181.53
19000	211.92	209.21	200.11	195.44	192.95	191.62
20000	223.08	220.22	210.65	205.72	203.11	201.70
21000	234.23	231.23	221.18	216.01	213.27	211.79
22000	245.39	242.24	231.71	226.30	223.42	221.87
23000	256.54	253.25	242.24	236.58	233.58	231.96
24000	267.69	264.26	252.77	246.87	243.73	242.04
25000	278.85	275.27	263.31	257.15	253.89	253.13
30000	334.62	330.33	315.97	308.58	304.67	302.55
35000	390.39	385.38	368.63	360.01	355.44	352.98
40000	446.15	440.43	421.29	411.45	406.22	403.40
45000	501.92	495.49	473.95	462.88	457.00	453.83
50000	557.69	550.54	526.61	514.31	507.78	504.25
55000	613.46	605.60	579.27	565.74	558.55	554.68
60000	669.23	660.65	631.93	617.17	609.33	605.10
65000	725.00	715.71	684.60	668.60	660.11	655.53
70000	780.77	770.76	737.26	720.03	710.89	705.95
75000	836.54	825.82	789.92	771.46	761.66	756.38
80000	892.31	880.87	842.58	822.89	812.44	806.80
85000	948.08	935.92	895.24	874.32	863.22	857.23
90000	1003.85	990.98	947.90	925.75	914.00	907.65
95000	1059.62	1046.03	1000.56	977.18	964.77	958.08
100000	1115.39	1101.09	1053.22	1028.61	1015.55	1008.50
200000	2230.77	2202.17	2106.45	2057.22	2031.10	2017.00
300000	3346.16	3303.26	3159.67	3085.84	3046.65	3025.50
400000	4461.54	4404.34	4212.90	4114.45	4062.20	4034.00
500000	5576.93	5505.43	5266.12	5143.06	5077.75	5042.50

12 1/4%

MONTHLY PAYMENT
Necessary to amortize a loan

TERM / AMOUNT	1 YEAR	2 YEARS	3 YEARS	4 YEARS	5 YEARS	6 YEARS
500	44.48	23.60	16.67	13.23	11.19	9.84
600	53.38	28.31	20.00	15.87	13.42	11.81
700	62.28	33.03	23.33	18.52	15.66	13.78
800	71.17	37.75	26.67	21.17	17.90	15.74
900	80.07	42.47	30.00	23.81	20.13	17.71
1000	88.97	47.19	33.33	26.46	22.37	19.68
2000	177.93	94.38	66.67	52.91	44.74	39.36
3000	266.90	141.57	100.00	79.37	67.11	59.04
4000	355.86	188.76	133.34	105.83	89.48	78.72
5000	444.83	235.95	166.67	132.28	111.86	98.40
6000	533.79	283.14	200.00	158.74	134.23	118.08
7000	622.76	330.33	233.34	185.20	156.60	137.76
8000	711.72	377.52	266.67	211.65	178.97	157.44
9000	800.69	424.71	300.00	238.11	201.34	177.12
10000	889.66	471.90	333.34	264.57	223.71	196.80
11000	978.62	519.09	366.67	291.02	246.08	216.48
12000	1067.59	566.28	400.01	317.48	268.45	236.17
13000	1156.55	613.47	433.34	343.94	290.82	255.85
14000	1245.52	660.66	466.67	370.39	313.19	275.53
15000	1334.48	707.85	500.01	396.85	335.56	295.21
16000	1423.45	755.04	533.34	423.31	357.94	314.89
17000	1512.41	802.23	566.67	449.76	380.31	334.57
18000	1601.38	849.42	600.01	476.22	402.68	354.25
19000	1690.34	896.61	633.34	502.68	425.05	373.93
20000	1779.31	943.80	666.68	529.13	447.42	393.61
21000	1868.27	990.99	700.01	555.59	469.79	413.29
22000	1957.24	1038.18	733.34	582.05	492.16	432.97
23000	2046.21	1085.37	766.68	608.50	514.53	452.65
24000	2135.17	1132.56	800.01	634.96	536.90	472.33
25000	2224.14	1179.75	833.34	661.42	559.27	492.01
30000	2668.96	1415.70	1000.01	793.70	671.13	590.41
35000	3113.79	1651.65	1166.68	925.98	782.98	688.81
40000	3558.62	1887.61	1333.35	1058.27	894.84	787.22
45000	4003.45	2123.56	1500.02	1190.55	1006.69	885.62
50000	4448.27	2359.51	1666.69	1322.83	1118.55	984.02
55000	4893.10	2595.46	1833.36	1455.12	1230.40	1082.42
60000	5337.93	2831.41	2000.02	1587.40	1342.26	1180.82
65000	5782.76	3067.36	2166.69	1719.68	1454.11	1279.23
70000	6227.58	3303.31	2333.36	1851.97	1565.96	1377.63
75000	6672.41	3539.26	2500.03	1984.25	1677.82	1476.03
80000	7117.24	3775.21	2666.70	2116.53	1789.67	1574.43
85000	7562.06	4011.16	2833.37	2248.82	1901.53	1672.83
90000	8006.89	4247.11	3000.04	2381.10	2013.38	1771.23
95000	8451.72	4483.06	3166.70	2513.38	2125.24	1869.64
100000	8896.55	4719.01	3333.37	2645.67	2237.09	1968.04
200000	17793.10	9438.03	6666.75	5291.33	4474.18	3936.08
300000	26689.60	14157.00	10000.10	7937.00	6711.28	5904.12
400000	35586.20	18876.10	13333.50	10582.70	8948.37	7872.15
500000	44482.70	23595.10	16666.90	13228.30	11185.50	9840.19

MONTHLY PAYMENT

Necessary to amortize a loan

12 1/4%

TERM / AMOUNT	7 YEARS	8 YEARS	9 YEARS	10 YEARS	11 YEARS	12 YEARS
500	8.89	8.20	7.66	7.25	6.91	6.64
600	10.67	9.83	9.20	8.70	8.30	7.97
700	12.45	11.47	10.73	10.14	9.68	9.30
800	14.23	13.11	12.26	11.59	11.06	10.63
900	16.01	14.75	13.79	13.04	12.44	11.96
1000	17.79	16.39	15.33	14.49	13.83	13.29
2000	35.57	32.78	30.65	28.98	27.65	26.57
3000	53.36	49.17	45.98	43.48	41.48	39.86
4000	71.15	65.56	61.30	57.97	55.30	53.14
5000	88.93	81.95	76.63	72.46	69.13	66.43
6000	106.72	98.34	91.95	86.95	82.96	79.72
7000	124.51	114.73	107.28	101.44	96.78	93.00
8000	142.29	131.12	122.60	115.94	110.61	106.29
9000	160.08	147.51	137.93	130.43	124.44	119.57
10000	177.87	163.91	153.26	144.92	138.26	132.86
11000	195.65	180.30	168.58	159.41	152.09	146.15
12000	213.44	196.69	183.91	173.90	165.92	159.43
13000	231.23	213.08	199.23	188.40	179.74	172.72
14000	249.01	229.47	214.56	202.89	193.57	186.00
15000	266.80	245.86	229.88	217.38	207.39	199.29
16000	284.59	262.25	245.21	231.87	221.22	212.58
17000	302.37	278.64	260.53	246.36	235.05	225.86
18000	320.16	295.03	275.86	260.86	248.87	239.15
19000	337.95	311.42	291.19	275.35	262.70	252.43
20000	355.73	327.81	306.51	289.84	276.53	265.72
21000	373.52	344.20	321.84	304.33	290.35	279.01
22000	391.31	360.59	337.16	318.82	304.18	292.29
23000	409.09	376.98	352.49	333.32	318.00	305.58
24000	426.88	393.37	367.81	347.81	331.83	318.86
25000	444.67	409.76	383.14	362.30	345.66	332.15
30000	533.60	491.71	459.77	434.76	414.79	398.58
35000	622.53	573.67	536.39	507.22	483.92	465.01
40000	711.47	655.62	613.02	579.68	553.05	531.44
45000	800.40	737.57	689.65	652.14	622.18	597.87
50000	889.33	819.52	766.28	724.60	691.31	664.30
55000	978.27	901.48	842.90	797.06	760.44	730.73
60000	1067.20	983.43	919.53	869.52	829.57	797.16
65000	1156.13	1065.38	996.16	941.98	898.71	863.59
70000	1245.07	1147.33	1072.79	1014.44	967.84	930.02
75000	1334.00	1229.29	1149.41	1086.90	1036.97	996.45
80000	1422.93	1311.24	1226.04	1159.36	1106.10	1062.88
85000	1511.87	1393.19	1302.67	1231.82	1175.23	1129.30
90000	1600.80	1475.14	1379.30	1304.28	1244.36	1195.73
95000	1689.73	1557.09	1455.92	1376.74	1313.49	1262.16
100000	1778.67	1639.05	1532.55	1449.20	1382.62	1328.59
200000	3557.33	3278.09	3065.10	2898.39	2765.25	2657.19
300000	5336.00	4917.14	4597.65	4347.59	4147.87	3985.78
400000	7114.66	6556.19	6130.21	5796.78	5530.49	5314.38
500000	8893.33	8195.24	7662.76	7245.98	6913.12	6642.97

12 1/4%

MONTHLY PAYMENT
Necessary to amortize a loan

TERM / AMOUNT	13 YEARS	14 YEARS	15 YEARS	16 YEARS	17 YEARS	18 YEARS
500	6.42	6.24	6.08	5.95	5.84	5.74
600	7.71	7.48	7.30	7.14	7.01	6.89
700	8.99	8.73	8.51	8.33	8.18	8.04
800	10.27	9.98	9.73	9.52	9.34	9.19
900	11.56	11.23	10.95	10.71	10.51	10.34
1000	12.84	12.47	12.16	11.90	11.68	11.49
2000	25.68	24.95	24.33	23.80	23.36	22.98
3000	38.53	37.42	36.49	35.70	35.04	34.47
4000	51.37	49.89	48.65	47.61	46.72	45.96
5000	64.21	62.36	60.81	59.51	58.40	57.45
6000	77.05	74.84	72.98	71.41	70.08	68.94
7000	89.89	87.31	85.14	83.31	81.75	80.42
8000	102.73	99.78	97.30	95.21	93.43	91.91
9000	115.58	112.25	109.47	107.11	105.11	103.40
10000	128.42	124.73	121.63	119.02	116.79	114.89
11000	141.26	137.20	133.79	130.92	128.47	126.38
12000	154.10	149.67	145.96	142.82	140.15	137.87
13000	166.94	162.14	158.12	154.72	151.83	149.36
14000	179.78	174.62	170.28	166.62	163.51	160.85
15000	192.63	187.09	182.45	178.52	175.19	172.34
16000	205.47	199.56	194.61	190.42	186.87	183.83
17000	218.31	212.03	206.77	202.33	198.55	195.32
18000	231.15	224.51	218.93	214.23	210.23	206.81
19000	243.99	236.98	231.10	226.13	221.91	218.30
20000	256.83	249.45	243.26	238.03	233.58	229.79
21000	269.68	261.92	255.42	249.93	245.26	241.27
22000	282.52	274.40	267.59	261.83	256.94	252.76
23000	295.36	286.87	279.75	273.73	268.62	264.25
24000	308.20	299.34	291.91	285.64	280.30	275.74
25000	321.04	311.81	304.07	297.54	291.98	287.23
30000	385.25	374.18	364.89	357.05	350.38	344.68
35000	449.46	436.54	425.70	416.55	408.77	402.12
40000	513.67	498.90	486.52	476.06	467.17	459.57
45000	577.88	561.26	547.33	535.57	525.57	517.02
50000	642.09	623.63	608.15	595.07	583.96	574.46
55000	706.29	685.99	668.96	654.58	642.36	631.91
60000	770.50	748.35	729.78	714.09	700.75	689.36
65000	834.71	810.71	790.59	773.60	759.15	746.80
70000	898.92	873.08	851.41	833.10	817.55	804.25
75000	963.13	935.44	912.22	892.61	875.94	861.69
80000	1027.34	997.80	973.04	952.12	934.34	919.14
85000	1091.54	1060.16	1033.85	1011.63	992.73	976.59
90000	1155.75	1122.53	1094.67	1071.13	1051.13	1034.03
95000	1219.96	1184.89	1155.48	1130.64	1109.53	1091.48
100000	1284.17	1247.25	1216.30	1190.15	1167.92	1148.93
200000	2568.34	2494.50	2432.59	2380.30	2335.84	2297.85
300000	3852.51	3741.76	3648.89	3570.45	3503.76	3446.78
400000	5136.68	4989.01	4865.19	4760.59	4671.68	4595.70
500000	6420.85	6236.26	6081.48	5950.74	5839.61	5744.63

MONTHLY PAYMENT

Necessary to amortize a loan

12 1/4%

TERM / AMOUNT	19 YEARS	20 YEARS	25 YEARS	30 YEARS	35 YEARS	40 YEARS
500	5.66	5.59	5.36	5.24	5.18	5.14
600	6.80	6.71	6.43	6.29	6.21	6.17
700	7.93	7.83	7.50	7.34	7.25	7.20
800	9.06	8.95	8.57	8.38	8.28	8.23
900	10.19	10.07	9.65	9.43	9.32	9.26
1000	11.33	11.19	10.72	10.48	10.35	10.29
2000	22.65	22.37	21.43	20.96	20.71	20.57
3000	33.98	33.56	32.15	31.44	31.06	30.86
4000	45.30	44.74	42.87	41.92	41.41	41.15
5000	56.63	55.93	53.59	52.39	51.77	51.43
6000	67.96	67.11	64.30	62.87	62.12	61.72
7000	79.28	78.30	75.02	73.35	72.48	72.01
8000	90.61	89.49	85.74	83.83	82.83	82.29
9000	101.94	100.67	96.46	94.31	93.18	92.58
10000	113.26	111.86	107.17	104.79	103.54	102.87
11000	124.59	123.04	117.89	115.27	113.89	113.16
12000	135.91	134.23	128.61	125.75	124.25	123.44
13000	147.24	145.41	139.33	136.23	134.60	133.73
14000	158.57	156.60	150.04	146.71	144.95	144.02
15000	169.89	167.79	160.76	157.18	155.31	154.30
16000	181.22	178.97	171.48	167.66	165.66	164.59
17000	192.55	190.16	182.20	178.14	176.01	174.88
18000	203.87	201.34	192.91	188.62	186.37	185.16
19000	215.20	212.53	203.63	199.10	196.72	195.45
20000	226.52	223.71	214.35	209.58	207.07	205.74
21000	237.85	234.90	225.07	220.06	217.43	216.02
22000	249.18	246.08	235.78	230.54	227.78	226.31
23000	260.50	257.27	246.50	241.02	238.14	236.60
24000	271.83	268.46	257.22	251.50	248.49	246.89
25000	283.16	279.64	267.94	261.97	258.84	257.17
30000	339.79	335.57	321.52	314.37	310.61	308.61
35000	396.42	391.50	375.11	366.76	362.38	360.04
40000	453.05	447.43	428.70	419.16	414.15	411.47
45000	509.68	503.35	482.28	471.55	465.92	462.91
50000	566.31	559.28	535.87	523.95	517.69	514.34
55000	622.94	615.21	589.46	576.34	569.45	565.78
60000	679.57	671.14	643.05	628.74	621.22	617.21
65000	736.20	727.07	696.63	681.13	672.99	668.65
70000	792.83	783.00	750.22	733.53	724.76	720.08
75000	849.46	838.92	803.81	785.92	776.53	771.52
80000	906.10	894.85	857.39	838.32	828.30	822.95
85000	962.73	950.78	910.98	890.71	880.07	874.38
90000	1019.36	1006.71	964.57	943.11	931.83	925.82
95000	1075.99	1062.64	1018.16	995.50	983.60	977.25
100000	1132.62	1118.56	1071.74	1047.90	1035.37	1028.69
200000	2265.24	2237.13	2143.49	2095.79	2070.74	2057.37
300000	3397.85	3355.69	3215.23	3143.69	3106.11	3086.06
400000	4530.47	4474.25	4286.97	4191.58	4141.48	4114.74
500000	5663.09	5592.82	5358.71	5239.48	5176.85	5143.43

12 1/2%

MONTHLY PAYMENT
Necessary to amortize a loan

TERM / AMOUNT	1 YEAR	2 YEARS	3 YEARS	4 YEARS	5 YEARS	6 YEARS
500	44.54	23.65	16.73	13.29	11.25	9.91
600	53.45	28.38	20.07	15.95	13.50	11.89
700	62.36	33.12	23.42	18.61	15.75	13.87
800	71.27	37.85	26.76	21.26	18.00	15.85
900	80.18	42.58	30.11	23.92	20.25	17.83
1000	89.08	47.31	33.45	26.58	22.50	19.81
2000	178.17	94.62	66.91	53.16	45.00	39.62
3000	267.25	141.92	100.36	79.74	67.49	59.43
4000	356.33	189.23	133.82	106.32	89.99	79.25
5000	445.42	236.54	167.27	132.90	112.49	99.06
6000	534.50	283.85	200.72	159.48	134.99	118.87
7000	623.58	331.15	234.18	186.06	157.49	138.68
8000	712.67	378.46	267.63	212.64	179.98	158.49
9000	801.75	425.77	301.08	239.22	202.48	178.30
10000	890.83	473.08	334.54	265.80	224.98	198.11
11000	979.92	520.38	367.99	292.38	247.48	217.92
12000	1069.00	567.69	401.45	318.96	269.98	237.74
13000	1158.08	615.00	434.90	345.54	292.47	257.55
14000	1247.17	662.31	468.35	372.12	314.97	277.36
15000	1336.25	709.61	501.81	398.70	337.47	297.17
16000	1425.33	756.92	535.26	425.28	359.97	316.98
17000	1514.42	804.23	568.71	451.86	382.47	336.79
18000	1603.50	851.54	602.17	478.44	404.96	356.60
19000	1692.58	898.84	635.62	505.02	427.46	376.41
20000	1781.67	946.15	669.08	531.60	449.96	396.23
21000	1870.75	993.46	702.53	558.18	472.46	416.04
22000	1959.83	1040.77	735.98	584.76	494.96	435.85
23000	2048.92	1088.07	769.44	611.34	517.45	455.66
24000	2138.00	1135.38	802.89	637.92	539.95	475.47
25000	2227.08	1182.69	836.34	664.50	562.45	495.28
30000	2672.50	1419.23	1003.61	797.40	674.94	594.34
35000	3117.92	1655.76	1170.88	930.30	787.43	693.39
40000	3563.33	1892.30	1338.15	1063.20	899.92	792.45
45000	4008.75	2128.84	1505.42	1196.10	1012.41	891.51
50000	4454.17	2365.38	1672.69	1329.00	1124.90	990.56
55000	4899.58	2601.91	1839.96	1461.91	1237.39	1089.62
60000	5345.00	2838.45	2007.23	1594.81	1349.88	1188.67
65000	5790.42	3074.99	2174.49	1727.71	1462.37	1287.73
70000	6235.83	3311.53	2341.76	1860.61	1574.86	1386.79
75000	6681.25	3548.06	2509.03	1993.51	1687.35	1485.84
80000	7126.67	3784.60	2676.30	2126.41	1799.84	1584.90
85000	7572.08	4021.14	2843.57	2259.31	1912.33	1683.96
90000	8017.50	4257.68	3010.84	2392.21	2024.82	1783.01
95000	8462.92	4494.21	3178.11	2525.11	2137.31	1882.07
100000	8908.33	4730.75	3345.38	2658.01	2249.80	1981.12
200000	17816.70	9461.50	6690.75	5316.02	4499.60	3962.25
300000	26725.00	14192.30	10036.10	7974.03	6749.41	5943.37
400000	35633.30	18923.00	13381.50	10632.00	8999.21	7924.50
500000	44541.70	23653.80	16726.90	13290.00	11249.00	9905.62

MONTHLY PAYMENT

Necessary to amortize a loan

12 1/2%

TERM / AMOUNT	7 YEARS	8 YEARS	9 YEARS	10 YEARS	11 YEARS	12 YEARS
500	8.96	8.26	7.73	7.32	6.99	6.72
600	10.75	9.92	9.28	8.78	8.39	8.06
700	12.54	11.57	10.83	10.25	9.78	9.41
800	14.34	13.22	12.37	11.71	11.18	10.75
900	16.13	14.88	13.92	13.17	12.58	12.09
1000	17.92	16.53	15.47	14.64	13.98	13.44
2000	35.84	33.06	30.94	29.28	27.95	26.88
3000	53.76	49.59	46.40	43.91	41.93	40.32
4000	71.69	66.12	61.87	58.55	55.90	53.75
5000	89.61	82.64	77.34	73.19	69.88	67.19
6000	107.53	99.17	92.81	87.83	83.85	80.63
7000	125.45	115.70	108.27	102.46	97.83	94.07
8000	143.37	132.23	123.74	117.10	111.80	107.51
9000	161.29	148.76	139.21	131.74	125.78	120.95
10000	179.21	165.29	154.68	146.38	139.76	134.39
11000	197.13	181.82	170.14	161.01	153.73	147.83
12000	215.06	198.35	185.61	175.65	167.71	161.26
13000	232.98	214.88	201.08	190.29	181.68	174.70
14000	250.90	231.40	216.55	204.93	195.66	188.14
15000	268.82	247.93	232.01	219.57	209.63	201.58
16000	286.74	264.46	247.48	234.20	223.61	215.02
17000	304.66	280.99	262.95	248.84	237.58	228.46
18000	322.58	297.52	278.42	263.48	251.56	241.90
19000	340.51	314.05	293.88	278.12	265.53	255.33
20000	358.43	330.58	309.35	292.75	279.51	268.77
21000	376.35	347.11	324.82	307.39	293.49	282.21
22000	394.27	363.64	340.29	322.03	307.46	295.65
23000	412.19	380.16	355.76	336.67	321.44	309.09
24000	430.11	396.69	371.22	351.30	335.41	322.53
25000	448.03	413.22	386.69	365.94	349.39	335.97
30000	537.64	495.87	464.03	439.13	419.26	403.16
35000	627.25	578.51	541.37	512.32	489.14	470.35
40000	716.85	661.15	618.70	585.51	559.02	537.54
45000	806.46	743.80	696.04	658.69	628.90	604.74
50000	896.07	826.44	773.38	731.88	698.77	671.93
55000	985.67	909.09	850.72	805.07	768.65	739.12
60000	1075.28	991.73	928.06	878.26	838.53	806.32
65000	1164.88	1074.38	1005.39	951.45	908.41	873.51
70000	1254.49	1157.02	1082.73	1024.64	978.28	940.70
75000	1344.10	1239.66	1160.07	1097.82	1048.16	1007.90
80000	1433.70	1322.31	1237.41	1171.01	1118.04	1075.09
85000	1523.31	1404.95	1314.75	1244.20	1187.91	1142.28
90000	1612.92	1487.60	1392.08	1317.29	1257.79	1209.47
95000	1702.52	1570.24	1469.42	1390.58	1327.67	1276.67
100000	1792.13	1652.89	1546.76	1463.77	1397.55	1343.86
200000	3584.26	3305.77	3093.52	2927.53	2795.09	2687.72
300000	5376.39	4958.66	4640.28	4391.30	4192.64	4031.58
400000	7168.52	6611.54	6187.04	5855.06	5590.18	5375.44
500000	8960.65	8264.43	7733.80	7318.83	6987.73	6719.30

12 1/2% MONTHLY PAYMENT

Necessary to amortize a loan

TERM / AMOUNT	13 YEARS	14 YEARS	15 YEARS	16 YEARS	17 YEARS	18 YEARS
500	6.50	6.32	6.16	6.03	5.92	5.83
600	7.80	7.58	7.40	7.24	7.11	7.00
700	9.10	8.84	8.63	8.45	8.29	8.16
800	10.40	10.11	9.86	9.65	9.48	9.33
900	11.70	11.37	11.09	10.86	10.66	10.49
1000	13.00	12.63	12.33	12.07	11.85	11.66
2000	26.00	25.26	24.65	24.13	23.69	23.32
3000	38.99	37.90	36.98	36.20	35.54	34.98
4000	51.99	50.53	49.30	48.27	47.39	46.64
5000	64.99	63.16	61.63	60.33	59.24	58.30
6000	77.99	75.79	73.95	72.40	71.08	69.96
7000	90.98	88.42	86.28	84.47	82.93	81.62
8000	103.98	101.05	98.60	96.53	94.78	93.28
9000	116.98	113.69	110.93	108.60	106.63	104.94
10000	129.98	126.32	123.25	120.67	118.47	116.60
11000	142.98	138.95	135.58	132.73	130.32	128.26
12000	155.97	151.58	147.90	144.80	142.17	139.92
13000	168.97	164.21	160.23	156.87	154.02	151.58
14000	181.97	176.84	172.55	168.93	165.86	163.24
15000	194.97	189.48	184.88	181.00	177.71	174.90
16000	207.96	202.11	197.20	193.07	189.56	186.56
17000	220.96	214.74	209.53	205.13	201.40	198.22
18000	233.96	227.37	221.85	217.20	213.25	209.88
19000	246.96	240.00	234.18	229.27	225.10	221.54
20000	259.95	252.63	246.51	241.33	236.95	233.20
21000	272.95	265.27	258.83	253.40	248.79	244.86
22000	285.95	277.90	271.16	265.47	260.64	256.52
23000	298.95	290.53	283.48	277.53	272.49	268.18
24000	311.94	303.16	295.81	289.60	284.34	279.84
25000	324.94	315.79	308.13	301.67	296.18	291.50
30000	389.93	378.95	369.76	362.00	355.42	349.80
35000	454.92	442.11	431.38	422.34	414.66	408.10
40000	519.91	505.27	493.01	482.67	473.89	466.40
45000	584.90	568.43	554.64	543.00	533.13	524.70
50000	649.88	631.59	616.26	603.34	592.36	583.00
55000	714.87	694.74	677.89	663.67	651.60	641.30
60000	779.86	757.90	739.52	724.00	710.84	699.60
65000	844.85	821.06	801.14	784.34	770.07	757.90
70000	909.84	884.22	862.77	844.67	829.31	816.20
75000	974.83	947.38	924.39	905.00	888.55	874.50
80000	1039.81	1010.54	986.02	965.34	947.78	932.80
85000	1104.80	1073.70	1047.65	1025.67	1007.02	991.10
90000	1169.79	1136.85	1109.27	1086.00	1066.25	1049.40
95000	1234.78	1200.01	1170.90	1146.34	1125.49	1107.70
100000	1299.77	1263.17	1232.52	1206.67	1184.73	1166.00
200000	2599.54	2526.34	2465.05	2413.34	2369.46	2332.00
300000	3899.31	3789.51	3697.57	3620.02	3554.18	3498.01
400000	5199.07	5052.68	4930.10	4826.69	4738.91	4664.01
500000	6498.84	6315.85	6162.62	6033.36	5923.64	5830.01

MONTHLY PAYMENT

Necessary to amortize a loan

12 1/2%

TERM / AMOUNT	19 YEARS	20 YEARS	25 YEARS	30 YEARS	35 YEARS	40 YEARS
500	5.75	5.68	5.45	5.34	5.28	5.24
600	6.90	6.82	6.54	6.40	6.33	6.29
700	8.05	7.95	7.63	7.47	7.39	7.34
800	9.20	9.09	8.72	8.54	8.44	8.39
900	10.35	10.23	9.81	9.61	9.50	9.44
1000	11.50	11.36	10.90	10.67	10.55	10.49
2000	23.00	22.72	21.81	21.35	21.11	20.98
3000	34.50	34.08	32.71	32.02	31.66	31.47
4000	46.00	45.45	43.61	42.69	42.21	41.96
5000	57.50	56.81	54.52	53.36	52.76	52.45
6000	69.00	68.17	65.42	64.04	63.32	62.94
7000	80.50	79.53	76.32	74.71	73.87	73.42
8000	92.00	90.89	87.23	85.38	84.42	83.91
9000	103.50	102.25	98.13	96.05	94.97	94.40
10000	115.00	113.61	109.04	106.73	105.53	104.89
11000	126.50	124.98	119.94	117.40	116.08	115.38
12000	137.99	136.34	130.84	128.07	126.63	125.87
13000	149.49	147.70	141.75	138.74	137.18	136.36
14000	160.99	159.06	152.65	149.42	147.74	146.85
15000	172.49	170.42	163.55	160.09	158.29	157.34
16000	183.99	181.78	174.46	170.76	168.84	167.83
17000	195.49	193.14	185.36	181.43	179.39	178.32
18000	206.99	204.51	196.26	192.11	189.95	188.81
19000	218.49	215.87	207.17	202.78	200.50	199.30
20000	229.99	227.23	218.07	213.45	211.05	209.78
21000	241.49	238.59	228.97	224.12	221.60	220.27
22000	252.99	249.95	239.88	234.80	232.16	230.76
23000	264.49	261.31	250.78	245.47	242.71	241.25
24000	275.99	272.67	261.69	256.14	253.26	251.74
25000	287.49	284.04	272.59	266.82	263.81	262.23
30000	344.99	340.84	327.11	320.18	316.58	314.68
35000	402.48	397.65	381.62	373.54	369.34	367.12
40000	459.98	454.46	436.14	426.90	422.10	419.57
45000	517.48	511.26	490.66	480.27	474.87	472.01
50000	574.98	568.07	545.18	533.63	527.63	524.46
55000	632.47	624.88	599.70	586.99	580.39	576.91
60000	689.97	681.69	654.21	640.36	633.15	629.35
65000	747.47	738.49	708.73	693.72	685.92	681.80
70000	804.97	795.30	763.25	747.08	738.68	734.24
75000	862.46	852.11	817.77	800.44	791.44	786.69
80000	919.96	908.91	872.28	853.81	844.20	839.14
85000	977.46	965.72	926.80	907.17	896.97	891.58
90000	1034.96	1022.53	981.32	960.53	949.73	944.03
95000	1092.45	1079.33	1035.84	1013.90	1002.49	996.47
100000	1149.95	1136.14	1090.35	1067.26	1055.25	1048.92
200000	2299.90	2272.28	2180.71	2134.52	2110.51	2097.84
300000	3449.86	3408.43	3271.06	3201.77	3165.76	3146.76
400000	4599.81	4544.57	4361.42	4269.03	4221.02	4195.68
500000	5749.76	5680.71	5451.77	5336.29	5276.27	5244.60

12 3/4%

MONTHLY PAYMENT
Necessary to amortize a loan

TERM AMOUNT	1 YEAR	2 YEARS	3 YEARS	4 YEARS	5 YEARS	6 YEARS
500	44.60	23.71	16.79	13.35	11.31	9.97
600	53.52	28.45	20.14	16.02	13.58	11.97
700	62.44	33.20	23.50	18.69	15.84	13.96
800	71.36	37.94	26.86	21.36	18.10	15.95
900	80.28	42.68	30.22	24.03	20.36	17.95
1000	89.20	47.42	33.57	26.70	22.63	19.94
2000	178.40	94.85	67.15	53.41	45.25	39.88
3000	267.60	142.27	100.72	80.11	67.88	59.83
4000	356.80	189.70	134.30	106.81	90.50	79.77
5000	446.00	237.12	167.87	133.52	113.13	99.71
6000	535.20	284.55	201.44	160.22	135.75	119.65
7000	624.40	331.97	235.02	186.93	158.38	139.60
8000	713.60	379.40	268.59	213.63	181.00	159.54
9000	802.80	426.82	302.16	240.33	203.63	179.48
10000	892.00	474.25	335.74	267.04	226.25	199.42
11000	981.20	521.67	369.31	293.74	248.88	219.37
12000	1070.40	569.09	402.88	320.44	271.50	239.31
13000	1159.60	616.52	436.46	347.15	294.13	259.25
14000	1248.80	663.94	470.03	373.85	316.75	279.19
15000	1338.00	711.37	503.61	400.55	339.38	299.14
16000	1427.20	758.79	537.18	427.26	362.01	319.08
17000	1516.40	806.22	570.75	453.96	384.63	339.02
18000	1605.60	853.64	604.33	480.67	407.26	358.96
19000	1694.80	901.07	637.90	507.37	429.88	378.91
20000	1784.00	948.49	671.47	534.07	452.51	398.85
21000	1873.20	995.92	705.05	560.78	475.13	418.79
22000	1962.40	1043.34	738.62	587.48	497.76	438.73
23000	2051.60	1090.76	772.20	614.18	520.38	458.68
24000	2140.80	1138.19	805.77	640.89	543.01	478.62
25000	2230.00	1185.61	839.34	667.59	565.63	498.56
30000	2676.00	1422.74	1007.21	801.11	678.76	598.27
35000	3122.00	1659.86	1175.08	934.63	791.89	697.98
40000	3568.00	1896.98	1342.95	1068.14	905.01	797.70
45000	4014.00	2134.10	1510.82	1201.66	1018.14	897.41
50000	4460.00	2371.23	1678.68	1335.18	1131.27	997.12
55000	4906.00	2608.35	1846.55	1468.70	1244.39	1096.83
60000	5352.00	2845.47	2014.42	1602.22	1357.52	1196.54
65000	5798.00	3082.59	2182.29	1735.73	1470.65	1296.26
70000	6244.00	3319.72	2350.16	1869.25	1583.77	1395.97
75000	6690.00	3556.84	2518.03	2002.77	1696.90	1495.68
80000	7136.00	3793.96	2685.89	2136.29	1810.02	1595.39
85000	7582.00	4031.08	2853.76	2269.81	1923.15	1695.10
90000	8028.00	4268.21	3021.63	2403.32	2036.28	1794.82
95000	8474.00	4505.33	3189.50	2536.84	2149.40	1894.53
100000	8920.01	4742.45	3357.37	2670.36	2262.53	1994.24
200000	17840.00	9484.90	6714.74	5340.72	4525.06	3988.48
300000	26760.00	14227.40	10072.10	8011.08	6787.59	5982.72
400000	35680.00	18969.80	13429.50	10681.40	9050.12	7976.96
500000	44600.00	23712.30	16786.80	13351.80	11312.70	9971.21

MONTHLY PAYMENT

Necessary to amortize a loan

12 3/4%

TERM / AMOUNT	7 YEARS	8 YEARS	9 YEARS	10 YEARS	11 YEARS	12 YEARS
500	9.03	8.33	7.81	7.39	7.06	6.80
600	10.83	10.00	9.37	8.87	8.48	8.16
700	12.64	11.67	10.93	10.35	9.89	9.51
800	14.45	13.33	12.49	11.83	11.30	10.87
900	16.25	15.00	14.05	13.31	12.71	12.23
1000	18.06	16.67	15.61	14.78	14.13	13.59
2000	36.11	33.34	31.22	29.57	28.25	27.18
3000	54.17	50.00	46.83	44.35	42.38	40.78
4000	72.23	66.67	62.44	59.14	56.50	54.37
5000	90.28	83.34	78.05	73.92	70.63	67.96
6000	108.34	100.01	93.66	88.70	84.75	81.55
7000	126.39	116.67	109.27	103.49	98.88	95.14
8000	144.45	133.34	124.88	118.27	113.00	108.74
9000	162.51	150.01	140.49	133.06	127.13	122.33
10000	180.56	166.68	156.10	147.84	141.25	135.92
11000	198.62	183.35	171.71	162.62	155.38	149.51
12000	216.68	200.01	187.32	177.41	169.51	163.10
13000	234.73	216.68	202.93	192.19	183.63	176.70
14000	252.79	233.35	218.54	206.98	197.76	190.29
15000	270.85	250.02	234.15	221.76	211.88	203.88
16000	288.90	266.68	249.76	236.54	226.01	217.47
17000	306.96	283.35	265.37	251.33	240.13	231.06
18000	325.01	300.02	280.98	266.11	254.26	244.66
19000	343.07	316.69	296.60	280.90	268.38	258.25
20000	361.13	333.36	312.21	295.68	282.51	271.84
21000	379.18	350.02	327.82	310.46	296.63	285.43
22000	397.24	366.69	343.43	325.25	310.76	299.02
23000	415.30	383.36	359.04	340.03	324.88	312.62
24000	433.35	400.03	374.65	354.82	339.01	326.21
25000	451.41	416.69	390.26	369.60	353.14	339.80
30000	541.69	500.03	468.31	443.52	423.76	407.76
35000	631.97	583.37	546.36	517.44	494.39	475.72
40000	722.25	666.71	624.41	591.36	565.02	543.68
45000	812.54	750.05	702.46	665.28	635.64	611.64
50000	902.82	833.39	780.51	739.20	706.27	679.60
55000	993.10	916.73	858.56	813.12	776.90	747.56
60000	1083.38	1000.06	936.61	887.04	847.52	815.52
65000	1173.66	1083.40	1014.67	960.96	918.15	883.48
70000	1263.94	1166.74	1092.72	1034.88	988.78	951.44
75000	1354.22	1250.08	1170.77	1108.80	1059.40	1019.40
80000	1444.51	1333.42	1248.82	1182.72	1130.03	1087.36
85000	1534.79	1416.76	1326.87	1256.64	1200.66	1155.32
90000	1625.07	1500.10	1404.92	1330.56	1271.28	1223.28
95000	1715.35	1583.43	1482.97	1404.48	1341.91	1291.24
100000	1805.63	1666.77	1561.02	1478.40	1412.54	1359.20
200000	3611.27	3333.55	3122.05	2956.80	2825.08	2718.40
300000	5416.90	5000.32	4683.07	4435.20	4237.61	4077.60
400000	7222.53	6667.09	6244.10	5913.59	5650.15	5436.80
500000	9028.16	8333.86	7805.12	7391.99	7062.69	6796.00

12 3/4% MONTHLY PAYMENT

Necessary to amortize a loan

TERM / AMOUNT	13 YEARS	14 YEARS	15 YEARS	16 YEARS	17 YEARS	18 YEARS
500	6.58	6.40	6.24	6.12	6.01	5.92
600	7.89	7.68	7.49	7.34	7.21	7.10
700	9.21	8.95	8.74	8.56	8.41	8.28
800	10.52	10.23	9.99	9.79	9.61	9.47
900	11.84	11.51	11.24	11.01	10.81	10.65
1000	13.15	12.79	12.49	12.23	12.02	11.83
2000	26.31	25.58	24.98	24.47	24.03	23.66
3000	39.46	38.38	37.47	36.70	36.05	35.50
4000	52.62	51.17	49.95	48.93	48.06	47.33
5000	65.77	63.96	62.44	61.16	60.08	59.16
6000	78.93	76.75	74.93	73.40	72.10	70.99
7000	92.08	89.54	87.42	85.63	84.11	82.82
8000	105.24	102.33	99.91	97.86	96.13	94.65
9000	118.39	115.13	112.40	110.10	108.15	106.49
10000	131.55	127.92	124.88	122.33	120.16	118.32
11000	144.70	140.71	137.37	134.56	132.18	130.15
12000	157.85	153.50	149.86	146.79	144.20	141.98
13000	171.01	166.29	162.35	159.03	156.21	153.81
14000	184.16	179.08	174.84	171.26	168.23	165.64
15000	197.32	191.88	187.33	183.49	180.24	177.48
16000	210.47	204.67	199.81	195.73	192.26	189.31
17000	223.63	217.46	212.30	207.96	204.28	201.14
18000	236.78	230.25	224.79	220.19	216.29	212.97
19000	249.94	243.04	237.28	232.42	228.31	224.80
20000	263.09	255.83	249.77	244.66	240.33	236.63
21000	276.24	268.63	262.26	256.89	252.34	248.47
22000	289.40	281.42	274.74	269.12	264.36	260.30
23000	302.55	294.21	287.23	281.36	276.37	272.13
24000	315.71	307.00	299.72	293.59	288.39	283.96
25000	328.86	319.79	312.21	305.82	300.41	295.79
30000	394.63	383.75	374.65	366.99	360.49	354.95
35000	460.41	447.71	437.09	428.15	420.57	414.11
40000	526.18	511.67	499.54	489.31	480.65	473.27
45000	591.95	575.63	561.98	550.48	540.73	532.43
50000	657.72	639.59	624.42	611.64	600.81	591.59
55000	723.50	703.55	686.86	672.81	660.89	650.74
60000	789.27	767.50	749.30	733.97	720.97	709.90
65000	855.04	831.06	811.74	795.13	781.06	769.06
70000	920.81	895.42	874.19	856.30	841.14	828.22
75000	986.58	959.38	936.63	917.46	901.22	887.38
80000	1052.36	1023.34	999.07	978.63	961.30	946.54
85000	1118.13	1087.30	1061.51	1039.79	1021.28	1005.69
90000	1183.90	1151.26	1123.95	1100.95	1081.46	1064.85
95000	1249.67	1215.21	1186.40	1162.12	1141.54	1124.01
100000	1315.45	1279.17	1248.84	1223.28	1201.62	1183.17
200000	2630.89	2558.34	2497.67	2446.57	2403.25	2366.34
300000	3946.34	3837.52	3746.51	3669.85	3604.87	3549.51
400000	5261.78	5116.69	4995.35	4893.13	4806.50	4732.68
500000	6577.23	6395.86	6244.19	6116.42	6008.12	5915.85

MONTHLY PAYMENT
Necessary to amortize a loan

12 3/4%

TERM / AMOUNT	19 YEARS	20 YEARS	25 YEARS	30 YEARS	35 YEARS	40 YEARS
500	5.84	5.77	5.55	5.43	5.38	5.35
600	7.00	6.92	6.65	6.52	6.45	6.42
700	8.17	8.08	7.76	7.61	7.53	7.48
800	9.34	9.23	8.87	8.69	8.60	8.55
900	10.51	10.38	9.98	9.78	9.68	9.62
1000	11.67	11.54	11.09	10.87	10.75	10.69
2000	23.35	23.08	22.18	21.73	21.50	21.38
3000	35.02	34.61	33.27	32.60	32.26	32.08
4000	46.70	46.15	44.36	43.47	43.01	42.77
5000	58.37	57.69	55.45	54.33	53.76	53.46
6000	70.04	69.23	66.54	65.20	64.51	64.15
7000	81.72	80.77	77.63	76.07	75.26	74.84
8000	93.39	92.30	88.72	86.94	86.02	85.54
9000	105.06	103.84	99.81	97.80	96.77	96.23
10000	116.74	115.38	110.91	108.67	107.52	106.92
11000	128.41	126.92	122.00	119.54	118.27	117.61
12000	140.09	138.46	133.09	130.40	129.02	128.30
13000	151.76	150.00	144.18	141.27	139.78	139.00
14000	163.43	161.53	155.27	152.14	150.53	149.69
15000	175.11	173.07	166.36	163.00	161.28	160.38
16000	186.78	184.61	177.45	173.87	172.03	171.07
17000	198.45	196.15	188.54	184.74	182.78	181.76
18000	210.13	207.69	199.63	195.61	193.54	192.46
19000	221.80	219.22	210.72	206.47	204.29	203.15
20000	233.48	230.76	221.81	217.34	215.04	213.84
21000	245.15	242.30	232.90	228.21	225.79	224.53
22000	256.82	253.84	243.99	239.07	236.54	235.22
23000	268.50	265.38	255.08	249.94	247.30	245.92
24000	280.17	276.92	266.17	260.81	258.05	256.61
25000	291.84	288.45	277.26	271.67	268.80	267.30
30000	350.21	346.14	332.72	326.01	322.56	320.76
35000	408.58	403.83	388.17	380.34	376.32	374.22
40000	466.95	461.53	443.62	434.68	430.08	427.68
45000	525.32	519.22	499.07	489.01	483.84	481.14
50000	583.69	576.91	554.53	543.35	537.60	534.60
55000	642.06	634.60	609.98	597.68	591.36	588.06
60000	700.43	692.29	665.43	652.02	645.12	641.52
65000	758.80	749.98	720.88	706.35	698.88	694.98
70000	817.16	807.67	776.34	760.69	752.64	748.44
75000	875.53	865.36	831.79	815.02	806.40	801.90
80000	933.90	923.05	887.24	869.35	860.16	855.36
85000	992.27	980.74	942.69	923.69	913.92	908.82
90000	1050.64	1038.43	998.15	978.02	967.68	962.28
95000	1109.01	1096.12	1053.60	1032.36	1021.44	1015.74
100000	1167.38	1153.81	1109.05	1086.69	1075.20	1069.20
200000	2334.76	2307.62	2218.10	2173.39	2150.39	2138.39
300000	3502.13	3461.44	3327.16	3260.08	3225.59	3207.59
400000	4669.51	4615.25	4436.21	4346.77	4300.78	4276.79
500000	5836.89	5769.06	5545.26	5433.47	5375.98	5345.98

13%

MONTHLY PAYMENT

Necessary to amortize a loan

TERM / AMOUNT	1 YEAR	2 YEARS	3 YEARS	4 YEARS	5 YEARS	6 YEARS
500	44.66	23.77	16.85	13.41	11.38	10.04
600	53.59	28.53	20.22	16.10	13.65	12.04
700	62.52	33.28	23.59	18.78	15.93	14.05
800	71.45	38.03	26.96	21.46	18.20	16.06
900	80.39	42.79	30.32	24.14	20.48	18.07
1000	89.32	47.54	33.69	26.83	22.75	20.07
2000	178.63	95.08	67.39	53.65	45.51	40.15
3000	267.95	142.63	101.08	80.48	68.26	60.22
4000	357.27	190.17	134.78	107.31	91.01	80.30
5000	446.59	237.71	168.47	134.14	113.77	100.37
6000	535.90	285.25	202.16	160.97	136.52	120.44
7000	625.22	332.79	235.86	187.79	159.27	140.52
8000	714.54	380.33	269.55	214.62	182.02	160.59
9000	803.85	427.88	303.25	241.45	204.78	180.67
10000	893.17	475.42	336.94	268.27	227.53	200.74
11000	982.49	522.96	370.63	295.10	250.28	220.82
12000	1071.81	570.50	404.33	321.93	273.04	240.89
13000	1161.12	618.04	438.02	348.76	295.79	260.96
14000	1250.44	665.58	471.71	375.58	318.54	281.04
15000	1339.76	713.13	505.41	402.41	341.30	301.11
16000	1429.07	760.67	539.10	429.24	364.05	321.19
17000	1518.39	808.21	572.80	456.07	386.80	341.26
18000	1607.71	855.75	606.49	482.89	409.56	361.33
19000	1697.03	903.29	640.18	509.72	432.31	381.41
20000	1786.34	950.83	673.88	536.55	455.06	401.48
21000	1875.66	998.38	707.57	563.38	477.81	421.56
22000	1964.98	1045.92	741.27	590.20	500.57	441.63
23000	2054.29	1093.46	774.96	617.03	523.32	461.70
24000	2143.61	1141.00	808.65	643.86	546.07	481.78
25000	2232.93	1188.54	842.35	670.69	568.83	501.85
30000	2679.51	1426.25	1010.82	804.82	682.59	602.22
35000	3126.10	1663.96	1179.29	938.96	796.36	702.59
40000	3572.68	1901.67	1347.76	1073.10	910.12	802.96
45000	4019.27	2139.38	1516.22	1207.23	1023.89	903.33
50000	4465.86	2377.09	1684.69	1341.37	1137.65	1003.70
55000	4912.44	2614.79	1853.16	1475.51	1251.42	1104.07
60000	5359.03	2852.50	2021.63	1609.65	1365.18	1204.44
65000	5805.61	3090.21	2190.10	1743.78	1478.95	1304.81
70000	6252.20	3327.92	2358.57	1877.92	1592.71	1405.18
75000	6698.78	3565.63	2527.04	2012.06	1706.48	1505.56
80000	7145.37	3803.34	2695.51	2146.20	1820.24	1605.93
85000	7591.95	4041.05	2863.98	2280.33	1934.01	1706.30
90000	8038.54	4278.75	3032.45	2414.47	2047.77	1806.67
95000	8485.13	4516.46	3200.92	2548.61	2161.54	1907.04
100000	8931.71	4754.17	3369.39	2682.74	2275.30	2007.41
200000	17863.40	9508.34	6738.78	5365.49	4550.61	4014.81
300000	26795.10	14262.50	10108.20	8048.23	6825.91	6022.22
400000	35726.80	19016.70	13477.60	10731.00	9101.21	8029.63
500000	44658.60	23770.90	16846.90	13413.70	11376.50	10037.00

MONTHLY PAYMENT

Necessary to amortize a loan

13%

TERM AMOUNT	7 YEARS	8 YEARS	9 YEARS	10 YEARS	11 YEARS	12 YEARS
500	9.10	8.40	7.88	7.47	7.14	6.87
600	10.92	10.08	9.45	8.96	8.57	8.25
700	12.73	11.77	11.03	10.45	9.99	9.62
800	14.55	13.45	12.60	11.94	11.42	11.00
900	16.37	15.13	14.18	13.44	12.85	12.37
1000	18.19	16.81	15.75	14.93	14.28	13.75
2000	36.38	33.61	31.51	29.86	28.55	27.49
3000	54.58	50.42	47.26	44.79	42.83	41.24
4000	72.77	67.23	63.01	59.72	57.10	54.98
5000	90.96	84.04	78.77	74.66	71.38	68.73
6000	109.15	100.84	94.52	89.59	85.66	82.48
7000	127.34	117.65	110.28	104.52	99.93	96.22
8000	145.54	134.46	126.03	119.45	114.21	109.97
9000	163.73	151.27	141.78	134.38	128.49	123.72
10000	181.92	168.07	157.54	149.31	142.76	137.46
11000	200.11	184.88	173.29	164.24	157.04	151.21
12000	218.30	201.69	189.04	179.17	171.31	164.96
13000	236.50	218.49	204.80	194.10	185.59	178.70
14000	254.69	235.30	220.55	209.04	199.87	192.45
15000	272.88	252.11	236.30	223.97	214.14	206.19
16000	291.07	268.92	252.06	238.90	228.42	219.94
17000	309.26	285.72	267.81	253.83	242.69	233.69
18000	327.46	302.53	283.56	268.76	256.97	247.43
19000	345.65	319.34	299.32	283.69	271.25	261.18
20000	363.84	336.15	315.07	298.62	285.52	274.93
21000	382.03	352.95	330.83	313.55	299.80	288.67
22000	400.22	369.76	346.58	328.48	314.07	302.42
23000	418.41	386.57	362.33	343.41	328.35	316.16
24000	436.61	403.37	378.09	358.35	342.63	329.91
25000	454.80	420.18	393.84	373.28	356.90	343.66
30000	545.76	504.22	472.61	447.93	428.28	412.39
35000	636.72	588.25	551.38	522.59	499.66	481.12
40000	727.68	672.29	630.14	597.24	571.04	549.85
45000	818.64	756.33	708.91	671.90	642.42	618.58
50000	909.60	840.36	787.68	746.55	713.81	687.31
55000	1000.56	924.40	866.45	821.21	785.19	756.04
60000	1091.52	1008.43	945.21	895.21	856.57	824.77
65000	1182.48	1092.47	1023.98	970.52	927.95	893.51
70000	1273.44	1176.51	1102.75	1045.17	999.33	962.24
75000	1364.40	1260.54	1181.52	1119.83	1070.71	1030.97
80000	1455.35	1344.58	1260.29	1194.48	1142.09	1099.70
85000	1546.31	1428.61	1339.05	1269.14	1213.47	1168.43
90000	1637.27	1512.65	1417.82	1343.79	1284.85	1237.16
95000	1728.23	1596.69	1496.59	1418.45	1356.23	1305.89
100000	1819.19	1680.72	1575.36	1493.11	1427.61	1374.62
200000	3638.39	3361.45	3150.71	2986.21	2855.22	2749.25
300000	5457.58	5042.17	4726.07	4479.32	4282.83	4123.87
400000	7276.77	6722.89	6301.43	5972.42	5710.44	5498.49
500000	9095.97	8403.61	7876.78	7465.53	7138.05	6873.12

13% MONTHLY PAYMENT

Necessary to amortize a loan

TERM / AMOUNT	13 YEARS	14 YEARS	15 YEARS	16 YEARS	17 YEARS	18 YEARS
500	6.66	6.48	6.33	6.20	6.09	6.00
600	7.99	7.77	7.59	7.44	7.31	7.20
700	9.32	9.07	8.86	8.68	8.53	8.40
800	10.65	10.36	10.12	9.92	9.75	9.60
900	11.98	11.66	11.39	11.16	10.97	10.80
1000	13.31	12.95	12.65	12.40	12.19	12.00
2000	26.62	25.91	25.30	24.80	24.37	24.01
3000	39.94	38.86	37.96	37.20	36.56	36.01
4000	53.25	51.81	50.61	49.60	48.74	48.02
5000	66.56	64.76	63.26	62.00	60.93	60.02
6000	79.87	77.72	75.91	74.40	73.12	72.03
7000	93.18	90.67	88.57	86.80	85.30	84.03
8000	106.50	103.62	101.22	99.20	97.49	96.03
9000	119.81	116.57	113.87	111.60	109.68	108.04
10000	133.12	129.53	126.52	124.00	121.86	120.04
11000	146.43	142.48	139.18	136.40	134.05	132.05
12000	159.75	155.43	151.83	148.80	146.23	144.05
13000	173.06	168.38	164.48	161.20	158.42	156.06
14000	186.37	181.34	177.13	173.60	170.61	168.06
15000	199.68	194.29	189.79	186.00	182.79	180.07
16000	212.99	207.24	202.44	198.40	194.98	192.07
17000	226.31	220.20	215.09	210.80	207.16	204.07
18000	239.62	233.15	227.74	223.20	219.35	216.08
19000	252.93	246.10	240.40	235.60	231.54	228.08
20000	266.24	259.05	253.05	248.00	243.77	240.09
21000	279.55	272.01	265.70	260.40	255.91	252.09
22000	292.87	284.96	278.35	272.80	268.10	264.10
23000	306.18	297.91	291.01	285.20	280.28	276.10
24000	319.49	310.86	303.66	297.60	292.47	288.10
25000	332.80	323.82	316.31	310.00	304.65	300.11
30000	399.36	388.58	379.57	372.00	365.58	360.13
35000	465.92	453.34	442.83	434.00	426.52	420.15
40000	532.48	518.11	506.10	496.00	487.45	480.17
45000	599.04	582.87	569.36	557.99	548.38	540.19
50000	665.60	647.63	632.62	619.99	609.31	600.22
55000	732.17	712.39	695.88	681.99	670.24	660.24
60000	798.73	777.16	759.15	743.99	731.17	720.26
65000	865.29	841.92	822.41	805.99	792.10	780.28
70000	931.85	906.68	885.67	867.99	653.03	840.30
75000	998.41	971.45	948.93	929.99	913.96	900.32
80000	1064.97	1036.21	1012.19	991.99	974.89	960.35
85000	1131.53	1100.97	1075.45	1053.99	1035.82	1020.37
90000	1198.09	1165.74	1138.72	1115.99	1096.75	1080.39
95000	1264.65	1230.50	1201.98	1177.99	1157.68	1140.41
100000	1331.21	1295.26	1265.24	1239.99	1218.61	1200.43
200000	2662.42	2590.52	2530.48	2479.97	2437.23	2400.86
300000	3993.63	3885.79	3795.72	3719.96	3655.84	3601.29
400000	5324.84	5181.05	5060.96	4959.95	4874.45	4801.73
500000	6656.04	6476.31	6326.21	6199.93	6093.07	6002.16

MONTHLY PAYMENT

Necessary to amortize a loan

13%

TERM / AMOUNT	19 YEARS	20 YEARS	25 YEARS	30 YEARS	35 YEARS	40 YEARS
500	5.92	5.86	5.64	5.53	5.48	5.45
600	7.11	7.03	6.77	6.64	6.57	6.54
700	8.29	8.20	7.89	7.74	7.67	7.63
800	9.48	9.37	9.02	8.85	8.76	8.72
900	10.66	10.54	10.15	9.96	9.86	9.81
1000	11.85	11.72	11.28	11.06	10.95	10.90
2000	23.70	23.43	22.56	22.12	21.90	21.79
3000	35.55	35.15	33.84	33.19	32.86	32.69
4000	47.40	46.86	45.11	44.25	43.81	43.58
5000	59.24	58.58	56.39	55.31	54.76	54.48
6000	71.09	70.29	67.67	66.37	65.71	65.37
7000	82.94	82.01	78.95	77.43	76.66	76.27
8000	94.79	93.73	90.23	88.50	87.62	87.16
9000	106.64	105.44	101.51	99.56	98.57	98.06
10000	118.49	117.16	112.78	110.62	109.52	108.95
11000	130.34	128.87	124.06	121.68	120.47	119.85
12000	142.19	140.59	135.34	132.74	131.42	130.74
13000	154.04	152.31	146.62	143.81	142.38	141.64
14000	165.89	164.02	157.90	154.87	153.33	152.53
15000	177.74	175.74	169.18	165.93	164.28	163.43
16000	189.58	187.45	180.45	176.99	175.23	174.32
17000	201.43	199.17	191.73	188.05	186.18	185.22
18000	213.28	210.88	203.01	199.12	197.14	196.11
19000	225.13	222.60	214.29	210.18	208.09	207.01
20000	236.98	234.32	225.57	221.24	219.04	217.90
21000	248.83	246.03	236.85	232.30	229.99	228.80
22000	260.68	257.75	248.12	243.36	240.94	239.69
23000	272.53	269.46	259.40	254.43	251.89	150.59
24000	284.38	281.18	270.68	265.49	262.85	261.48
25000	296.22	292.89	281.96	276.55	273.80	272.38
30000	355.47	351.47	338.35	331.86	328.56	326.85
35000	414.71	410.05	394.74	387.17	383.32	381.33
40000	473.96	468.63	451.13	442.48	438.08	435.81
45000	533.20	527.21	507.53	497.79	492.84	490.28
50000	592.45	585.79	563.92	553.10	547.60	544.76
55000	651.69	644.37	620.31	608.41	602.36	599.23
60000	710.94	702.95	676.70	663.72	657.12	653.71
65000	770.18	761.52	733.09	719.03	711.88	708.18
70000	829.43	820.10	789.49	774.34	766.64	762.66
75000	888.67	878.68	845.88	829.65	821.40	817.14
80000	947.92	937.26	902.27	884.96	876.15	871.61
85000	1007.16	995.84	958.66	940.27	930.91	926.09
90000	1066.41	1054.42	1015.05	995.58	958.67	980.56
95000	1125.65	1113.00	1071.44	1050.89	1040.43	1035.04
100000	1184.90	1171.58	1127.84	1106.20	1095.19	1089.51
200000	2369.79	2343.15	2255.67	2212.40	2190.39	2179.03
300000	3554.69	3514.73	3383.51	3318.60	3285.58	3268.54
400000	4739.59	4686.30	4511.34	4424.80	4380.77	4358.06
500000	5924.49	5857.88	5639.18	5531.00	5475.97	5447.57

13 1/4% MONTHLY PAYMENT

Necessary to amortize a loan

TERM / AMOUNT	1 YEAR	2 YEARS	3 YEARS	4 YEARS	5 YEARS	6 YEARS
500	44.72	23.83	16.91	13.48	11.44	10.10
600	53.66	28.60	20.29	16.17	13.73	12.12
700	62.60	33.36	23.67	18.87	16.02	14.14
800	71.55	38.13	27.05	21.56	18.31	16.17
900	80.49	42.89	30.43	24.26	20.59	18.19
1000	89.43	47.66	33.81	26.95	22.88	20.21
2000	178.87	95.32	67.63	53.90	45.76	40.41
3000	268.30	142.98	101.44	80.86	68.64	60.62
4000	357.74	190.64	135.26	107.81	91.53	80.83
5000	447.17	238.30	169.07	134.76	114.41	101.03
6000	536.61	285.96	202.89	161.71	137.29	121.24
7000	626.04	333.62	236.70	188.66	160.17	141.44
8000	715.48	381.28	270.52	215.61	183.05	161.65
9000	804.91	428.93	304.33	242.57	205.93	181.86
10000	894.35	476.59	338.15	269.52	228.81	202.06
11000	983.78	524.25	371.96	296.47	251.69	222.27
12000	1073.22	571.91	405.77	323.42	274.58	242.48
13000	1162.65	619.57	439.59	350.37	297.46	262.68
14000	1252.09	667.23	473.40	377.33	320.34	282.89
15000	1341.52	714.89	507.22	404.28	343.22	303.10
16000	1430.96	762.55	541.03	431.23	366.10	323.30
17000	1520.39	810.21	574.85	458.18	388.98	343.51
18000	1609.82	857.87	608.66	485.13	411.86	363.71
19000	1699.26	905.53	642.48	512.08	434.74	383.92
20000	1788.69	953.19	676.29	539.04	457.63	404.13
21000	1878.13	1000.85	710.11	565.99	480.51	424.33
22000	1967.56	1048.51	743.92	592.94	503.39	444.54
23000	2057.00	1096.17	777.73	619.89	526.27	464.75
24000	2146.43	1143.83	811.55	646.84	549.15	484.95
25000	2235.87	1191.48	845.36	673.79	572.03	505.16
30000	2683.04	1429.78	1014.44	808.55	686.44	606.19
35000	3130.21	1668.08	1183.51	943.31	800.85	707.22
40000	3577.39	1906.38	1352.58	1078.07	915.25	808.25
45000	4024.56	2144.67	1521.65	1212.83	1029.66	909.28
50000	4471.73	2382.97	1690.73	1347.59	1144.06	1010.32
55000	4918.91	2621.27	1859.80	1482.35	1258.47	1111.35
60000	5366.08	2859.56	2028.87	1617.11	1372.88	1212.38
65000	5813.26	3097.86	2197.94	1751.86	1487.28	1313.41
70000	6260.43	3336.16	2367.02	1886.62	1601.69	1414.44
75000	6707.60	3574.45	2536.09	2021.38	1716.10	1515.47
80000	7154.78	3812.75	2705.16	2156.14	1830.50	1616.50
85000	7601.95	4051.05	2874.24	2290.90	1944.91	1717.54
90000	8049.12	4289.34	3043.31	2425.66	2059.31	1818.57
95000	8496.30	4527.64	3212.38	2560.42	2173.72	1919.60
100000	8943.47	4765.94	3381.45	2695.18	2288.13	2020.63
200000	17886.90	9531.88	6762.91	5390.35	4576.26	4041.26
300000	26830.40	14297.80	10144.40	8085.53	6864.38	6061.89
400000	35773.90	19063.80	13525.80	10780.70	9152.51	8082.52
500000	44717.40	23829.70	16907.30	13475.90	11440.60	10103.20

MONTHLY PAYMENT

Necessary to amortize a loan

13 1/4%

TERM AMOUNT	7 YEARS	8 YEARS	9 YEARS	10 YEARS	11 YEARS	12 YEARS
500	9.16	8.47	7.95	7.54	7.21	6.95
600	11.00	10.17	9.54	9.05	8.66	8.34
700	12.83	11.86	11.13	10.56	10.10	9.73
800	14.66	13.56	12.72	12.06	11.54	11.12
900	16.50	15.25	14.31	13.57	12.98	12.51
1000	18.33	16.95	15.90	15.08	14.43	13.90
2000	36.66	33.89	31.80	30.16	28.86	27.80
3000	54.98	50.84	47.69	45.24	43.28	41.70
4000	73.31	67.79	63.59	60.32	57.71	55.61
5000	91.64	84.74	79.49	75.39	72.14	69.51
6000	109.97	101.68	95.39	90.47	86.57	83.41
7000	128.30	118.63	111.28	105.55	100.99	97.31
8000	146.63	135.58	127.18	120.63	115.42	111.21
9000	164.95	152.53	143.08	135.71	129.85	125.11
10000	183.28	169.47	158.98	150.79	144.28	139.01
11000	201.61	186.42	174.87	165.87	158.70	152.92
12000	219.94	203.37	190.77	180.95	173.13	166.82
13000	238.27	220.32	206.67	196.03	187.56	180.72
14000	256.59	237.26	222.57	211.11	201.99	194.62
15000	274.92	254.21	238.46	226.18	216.41	208.52
16000	293.25	271.16	254.36	241.26	230.84	222.42
17000	311.58	288.11	270.26	256.34	245.27	236.32
18000	329.91	305.05	286.16	271.42	259.70	250.22
19000	348.24	322.00	302.06	286.50	274.13	264.13
20000	366.56	338.95	317.95	301.58	288.55	278.03
21000	384.89	355.90	333.85	316.66	302.98	291.93
22000	403.22	372.84	349.75	331.74	317.41	305.83
23000	421.55	389.79	365.65	346.82	331.84	319.73
24000	439.88	406.74	381.54	361.89	346.26	333.63
25000	458.20	423.69	397.44	376.97	360.69	347.53
30000	549.85	508.42	476.93	452.37	432.83	417.04
35000	641.49	593.16	556.42	527.76	504.97	486.55
40000	733.13	677.90	635.91	603.16	577.11	556.05
45000	824.77	762.63	715.39	678.55	649.24	625.56
50000	916.41	847.37	794.88	753.95	721.38	695.07
55000	1008.05	932.11	874.37	829.34	793.52	764.57
60000	1099.69	1016.84	953.86	904.73	865.66	834.08
65000	1191.33	1101.58	1033.35	980.13	937.80	903.59
70000	1282.97	1186.32	1112.83	1055.52	1009.93	973.09
75000	1374.61	1271.06	1192.32	1130.92	1082.07	1042.60
80000	1466.25	1355.79	1271.81	1206.31	1154.21	1112.11
85000	1557.89	1440.53	1351.30	1281.71	1226.35	1181.61
90000	1649.53	1525.27	1430.79	1357.10	1298.49	1251.12
95000	1741.18	1610.00	1510.27	1432.50	1370.62	1320.63
100000	1832.82	1694.74	1589.76	1507.89	1442.76	1390.13
200000	3665.63	3389.48	3179.53	3015.78	2885.52	2780.26
300000	5498.45	5084.22	4769.29	4523.67	4328.28	4170.40
400000	7331.27	6778.96	6359.05	6031.56	5771.05	5560.53
500000	9164.08	8473.71	7948.81	7539.45	7213.81	6950.66

13 1/4% MONTHLY PAYMENT

Necessary to amortize a loan

TERM / AMOUNT	13 YEARS	14 YEARS	15 YEARS	16 YEARS	17 YEARS	18 YEARS
500	6.74	6.56	6.41	6.28	6.18	6.09
600	8.08	7.87	7.69	7.54	7.41	7.31
700	9.43	9.18	8.97	8.80	8.65	8.52
800	10.78	10.49	10.25	10.05	9.89	9.74
900	12.12	11.80	11.54	11.31	11.12	10.96
1000	13.47	13.11	12.82	12.57	12.36	12.18
2000	26.94	26.23	25.63	25.14	24.71	24.36
3000	40.41	39.34	38.45	37.70	37.07	36.53
4000	53.88	52.46	51.27	50.27	49.43	48.71
5000	67.35	65.57	64.09	62.84	61.78	60.89
6000	80.82	78.69	76.90	75.41	74.14	73.07
7000	94.29	91.80	89.72	87.97	86.50	85.25
8000	107.77	104.92	102.54	100.54	98.86	97.42
9000	121.24	118.03	115.36	113.11	111.21	109.60
10000	134.71	131.14	128.17	125.68	123.57	121.78
11000	148.18	144.26	140.99	138.25	135.93	133.96
12000	161.65	157.37	153.81	150.81	148.28	146.13
13000	175.12	170.49	166.63	163.38	160.64	158.31
14000	188.59	183.60	179.44	175.95	173.00	170.49
15000	202.06	196.72	192.26	188.52	185.36	182.67
16000	215.53	209.83	205.08	201.09	197.71	194.85
17000	229.00	222.95	217.90	213.65	210.07	207.02
18000	242.47	236.06	230.71	226.22	222.43	219.20
19000	255.94	249.17	243.53	238.79	234.78	231.38
20000	269.41	262.29	256.35	251.36	247.14	243.56
21000	282.88	275.40	269.17	263.93	259.50	255.74
22000	296.35	288.52	281.98	276.49	271.85	267.91
23000	309.82	301.63	294.80	289.06	284.21	280.09
24000	323.29	314.75	307.62	301.63	296.57	292.27
25000	336.77	327.86	320.43	314.20	308.92	304.45
30000	404.12	393.43	384.52	377.04	370.71	365.34
35000	471.47	459.01	448.61	439.87	432.49	426.23
40000	538.82	524.58	512.70	502.71	494.28	487.12
45000	606.18	590.15	576.78	565.55	556.06	548.00
50000	673.53	655.72	640.87	628.39	617.85	608.89
55000	740.88	721.29	704.96	691.23	679.63	669.78
60000	808.24	786.87	769.04	754.07	741.42	730.67
65000	875.59	852.44	833.13	816.91	803.20	791.56
70000	942.94	918.01	897.22	879.75	864.99	852.45
75000	1010.29	983.58	961.30	942.59	926.77	913.34
80000	1077.65	1049.15	1025.39	1005.43	988.56	974.23
85000	1145.00	1114.73	1089.48	1068.27	1050.34	1035.12
90000	1212.35	1180.30	1153.56	1131.11	1112.13	1096.01
95000	1279.71	1245.87	1217.65	1193.94	1173.91	1156.90
100000	1347.06	1311.44	1281.74	1256.78	1235.70	1217.79
200000	2694.12	2622.89	2563.47	2513.57	2471.39	2435.57
300000	4041.18	3934.33	3845.21	3770.35	3707.09	3653.36
400000	5388.24	5245.77	5126.95	5027.13	4942.79	4871.15
500000	6735.30	6557.21	6408.68	6283.92	6178.48	6088.94

MONTHLY PAYMENT

Necessary to amortize a loan

13 1/4%

TERM / AMOUNT	19 YEARS	20 YEARS	25 YEARS	30 YEARS	35 YEARS	40 YEARS
500	6.01	5.95	5.73	5.63	5.58	5.55
600	7.22	7.14	6.88	6.75	6.69	6.66
700	8.42	8.33	8.03	7.88	7.81	7.77
800	9.62	9.52	9.17	9.01	8.92	8.88
900	10.82	10.70	10.32	10.13	10.04	9.99
1000	12.03	11.89	11.47	11.26	11.15	11.10
2000	24.05	23.79	22.93	22.52	22.30	22.20
3000	36.08	35.68	34.40	33.77	33.46	33.30
4000	48.10	47.58	45.87	45.03	44.61	44.39
5000	60.13	59.47	57.34	56.29	55.76	55.49
6000	72.15	71.37	68.80	67.55	66.91	66.59
7000	84.18	83.26	80.27	78.80	78.07	77.69
8000	96.20	95.15	91.74	90.06	89.22	88.79
9000	108.23	107.05	103.20	101.32	100.37	99.89
10000	120.25	118.94	114.67	112.58	111.52	110.99
11000	132.28	130.84	126.14	123.84	122.68	122.09
12000	144.30	142.73	137.60	135.09	133.83	133.18
13000	156.33	154.63	149.07	146.35	144.98	144.28
14000	168.35	166.52	160.54	157.61	156.13	155.38
15000	180.38	178.42	172.01	168.87	167.29	166.48
16000	192.40	190.31	183.47	180.12	178.44	177.58
17000	204.43	202.20	194.94	191.38	189.59	188.68
18000	216.45	214.10	206.41	202.64	200.74	199.78
19000	228.48	225.99	217.87	213.90	211.90	210.88
20000	240.50	237.89	229.34	225.16	223.05	221.97
21000	252.53	249.78	240.81	236.41	234.20	233.07
22000	264.55	261.68	252.27	247.67	245.35	244.17
23000	276.58	273.57	263.74	258.93	256.51	255.27
24000	288.60	285.46	275.21	270.19	267.66	266.37
25000	300.63	297.36	286.68	281.44	278.81	277.47
30000	360.75	356.83	344.01	337.73	334.57	332.96
35000	420.88	416.30	401.35	394.02	390.34	388.45
40000	481.00	475.77	458.68	450.31	446.10	443.95
45000	541.13	535.24	516.02	506.60	501.86	499.44
50000	601.26	594.77	573.35	562.89	557.62	554.94
55000	661.38	654.19	630.69	619.18	613.38	610.43
60000	721.51	713.66	688.02	675.46	669.15	665.92
65000	781.63	773.13	745.36	731.75	724.91	721.42
70000	841.76	832.60	802.69	788.04	780.67	776.91
75000	901.88	892.07	860.03	844.33	836.43	832.40
80000	962.01	951.55	917.36	900.62	892.19	887.90
85000	1022.13	1011.02	974.70	956.91	947.96	943.39
90000	1082.26	1070.49	1032.03	1013.20	1003.72	998.88
95000	1142.38	1129.96	1089.37	1069.48	1059.48	1054.38
100000	1202.51	1189.43	1146.70	1125.77	1115.24	1109.87
200000	2405.02	2378.86	2293.40	2251.55	2230.48	2219.74
300000	3607.53	3568.29	3440.10	3377.32	3345.73	3329.61
400000	4810.04	4757.72	4586.80	4503.09	4460.97	4439.48
500000	6012.55	5947.15	5733.50	5628.87	5576.21	5549.35

13 1/2%

MONTHLY PAYMENT

Necessary to amortize a loan

TERM AMOUNT	1 YEAR	2 YEARS	3 YEARS	4 YEARS	5 YEARS	6 YEARS
500	44.78	23.89	16.97	13.54	11.50	10.17
600	53.73	28.67	20.36	16.25	13.81	12.20
700	62.69	33.44	23.75	18.95	16.11	14.24
800	71.64	38.22	27.15	21.66	18.41	16.27
900	80.60	43.00	30.54	24.37	20.71	18.31
1000	89.55	47.78	33.94	27.08	23.01	20.34
2000	179.10	95.55	67.87	54.15	46.02	40.68
3000	268.66	143.33	101.81	81.23	69.03	61.02
4000	358.21	191.11	135.74	108.31	92.04	81.36
5000	447.76	238.88	169.68	135.38	115.05	101.69
6000	537.31	286.66	203.61	162.46	138.06	122.03
7000	626.86	334.44	237.55	189.53	161.07	142.37
8000	716.41	382.22	271.48	216.61	184.08	162.71
9000	805.97	429.99	305.42	243.69	207.09	183.05
10000	895.52	477.77	339.35	270.76	230.10	203.39
11000	985.07	525.55	373.29	297.84	253.11	223.73
12000	1074.62	573.32	407.22	324.92	276.12	244.07
13000	1164.17	621.10	441.16	351.99	299.13	264.41
14000	1253.72	668.88	475.09	379.07	322.14	284.75
15000	1343.28	716.65	509.03	406.14	345.15	305.08
16000	1432.83	764.43	542.96	433.22	368.16	325.42
17000	1522.38	812.21	576.90	460.30	391.17	345.76
18000	1611.93	859.98	610.83	487.37	414.18	366.10
19000	1701.48	907.76	644.77	514.45	437.19	386.44
20000	1791.03	955.54	678.70	541.53	460.20	406.78
21000	1880.59	1003.31	712.64	568.60	483.21	427.12
22000	1970.14	1051.09	746.57	595.68	506.22	447.46
23000	2059.69	1098.87	780.51	622.75	529.23	467.80
24000	2149.24	1146.64	814.44	649.83	552.24	488.13
25000	2238.79	1194.42	848.38	676.91	575.24	508.47
30000	2686.55	1433.30	1018.05	812.29	690.29	610.17
35000	3134.31	1672.19	1187.73	947.67	805.34	711.86
40000	3582.07	1911.07	1357.41	1083.05	920.39	813.56
45000	4029.83	2149.96	1527.08	1218.43	1035.44	915.25
50000	4477.58	2388.84	1696.76	1353.81	1150.49	1016.94
55000	4925.34	2627.72	1866.43	1489.19	1265.54	1118.64
60000	5373.10	2866.61	2036.11	1624.57	1380.59	1220.33
65000	5820.86	3105.49	2205.79	1759.95	1495.64	1322.03
70000	6268.62	3344.38	2375.46	1895.34	1610.68	1423.72
75000	6716.38	3583.26	2545.14	2030.72	1725.73	1525.42
80000	7164.13	3822.15	2714.81	2166.10	1840.78	1627.11
85000	7611.89	4061.03	2884.49	2301.48	1955.83	1728.81
90000	8059.65	4299.91	3054.16	2436.86	2070.88	1830.50
95000	8507.41	4538.80	3223.84	2572.24	2185.93	1932.20
100000	8955.17	4777.68	3393.52	2707.62	2300.98	2033.89
200000	17910.30	9555.36	6787.03	5415.25	4601.95	4067.78
300000	26865.60	14333.00	10180.50	8122.87	6902.93	6101.67
400000	35820.70	19110.70	13574.10	10830.50	9203.91	8135.56
500000	44775.80	23888.40	16967.60	13538.10	11504.90	10169.40

MONTHLY PAYMENT
Necessary to amortize a loan

13 1/2%

TERM / AMOUNT	7 YEARS	8 YEARS	9 YEARS	10 YEARS	11 YEARS	12 YEARS
500	9.23	8.54	8.02	7.61	7.29	7.03
600	11.08	10.25	9.63	9.14	8.75	8.43
700	12.93	11.96	11.23	10.66	10.21	9.84
800	14.77	13.67	12.83	12.18	11.66	11.25
900	16.62	15.38	14.44	13.70	13.12	12.65
1000	18.46	17.09	16.04	15.23	14.58	14.06
2000	36.93	34.18	32.08	30.45	29.16	28.11
3000	55.39	51.26	48.13	45.68	43.74	42.17
4000	73.86	68.35	64.17	60.91	58.32	56.23
5000	92.32	85.44	80.21	76.14	72.90	70.29
6000	110.79	102.53	96.25	91.36	87.48	84.34
7000	129.25	119.62	112.30	106.59	102.06	98.40
8000	147.72	136.71	128.34	121.82	116.64	112.46
9000	166.18	153.79	144.38	137.05	131.22	126.51
10000	184.65	170.88	160.42	152.27	145.80	140.57
11000	203.11	187.97	176.47	167.50	160.38	154.63
12000	221.58	205.06	192.51	182.73	174.96	168.69
13000	240.04	222.15	208.55	197.96	189.54	182.74
14000	258.51	239.23	224.59	213.18	204.12	196.80
15000	276.97	256.32	240.63	228.41	218.70	210.86
16000	295.44	273.41	256.68	243.64	233.28	224.91
17000	313.90	290.50	272.72	258.87	247.86	238.97
18000	332.37	307.59	288.76	274.09	262.44	253.03
19000	350.83	324.67	304.80	289.32	277.02	267.09
20000	369.30	341.76	320.85	304.55	291.60	281.14
21000	387.76	358.85	336.89	319.78	306.18	295.20
22000	406.23	375.94	352.93	335.00	320.76	309.26
23000	424.69	393.03	368.97	350.23	335.34	323.31
24000	443.16	410.12	385.02	365.46	349.92	337.37
25000	461.62	427.20	401.06	380.69	364.50	351.43
30000	553.95	512.64	481.27	456.82	437.40	421.71
35000	646.27	598.08	561.48	532.96	510.29	492.00
40000	738.59	683.53	641.69	609.10	583.19	562.29
45000	830.92	768.97	721.90	685.23	656.09	632.57
50000	923.24	854.41	802.11	761.37	728.99	702.86
55000	1015.57	939.85	882.33	837.51	801.89	773.14
60000	1107.89	1025.29	962.54	913.64	874.79	843.43
65000	1200.21	1110.73	1042.75	989.78	947.69	913.71
70000	1292.54	1196.17	1122.96	1065.92	1020.59	984.00
75000	1384.86	1281.61	1203.17	1142.05	1093.49	1054.29
80000	1477.19	1367.05	1283.38	1218.19	1166.39	1124.57
85000	1569.51	1452.49	1363.59	1294.33	1239.29	1194.86
90000	1661.84	1537.93	1443.80	1370.47	1312.19	1265.14
95000	1754.16	1623.37	1524.02	1446.60	1385.08	1335.43
100000	1846.48	1708.81	1604.23	1522.74	1457.98	1405.71
200000	3692.97	3417.62	3208.46	3045.48	2915.97	2811.43
300000	5539.45	5126.43	4812.68	4568.22	4373.95	4217.14
400000	7385.94	6835.25	6416.91	6090.96	5831.93	5622.86
500000	9232.42	8544.06	8021.14	7613.70	7289.92	7028.57

13 1/2%

MONTHLY PAYMENT

Necessary to amortize a loan

TERM / AMOUNT	13 YEARS	14 YEARS	15 YEARS	16 YEARS	17 YEARS	18 YEARS
500	6.81	6.64	6.49	6.37	6.26	6.18
600	8.18	7.97	7.79	7.64	7.52	7.41
700	9.54	9.29	9.09	8.92	8.77	8.65
800	10.90	10.62	10.39	10.19	10.02	9.88
900	12.27	11.95	11.68	11.46	11.28	11.12
1000	13.63	13.28	12.98	12.74	12.53	12.35
2000	27.26	26.55	25.97	25.47	25.06	24.70
3000	40.89	39.83	38.95	38.21	37.59	37.06
4000	54.52	53.11	51.93	50.95	50.11	49.41
5000	68.15	66.39	64.92	63.68	62.64	61.76
6000	81.78	79.66	77.90	76.42	75.17	74.11
7000	95.41	92.94	90.88	89.16	87.70	86.47
8000	109.04	106.22	103.87	101.89	100.23	98.82
9000	122.67	119.49	116.85	114.63	112.76	111.17
10000	136.30	132.77	129.83	127.37	125.29	123.52
11000	149.93	146.05	142.82	140.10	137.82	135.88
12000	163.56	159.33	155.80	152.84	150.34	148.23
13000	177.19	172.60	168.78	165.58	162.87	160.58
14000	190.82	185.88	181.76	178.31	175.40	172.93
15000	204.45	199.16	194.75	191.05	187.93	185.28
16000	218.08	212.43	207.73	203.79	200.46	197.64
17000	231.71	225.71	220.71	216.52	212.99	209.99
18000	245.34	238.99	233.70	229.26	225.52	222.34
19000	258.97	252.26	246.68	242.00	238.05	234.69
20000	272.60	265.54	259.66	254.73	250.57	247.05
21000	286.23	278.82	272.65	267.47	263.10	259.40
22000	299.86	292.10	285.63	280.21	275.63	271.75
23000	313.49	305.37	298.61	292.94	288.16	284.10
24000	327.12	318.65	311.60	305.68	300.69	296.46
25000	340.75	331.93	324.58	318.42	313.22	308.81
30000	408.90	398.31	389.50	382.10	375.86	370.57
35000	477.05	464.70	454.41	445.78	438.50	432.33
40000	545.20	531.08	519.33	509.47	501.15	494.09
45000	613.35	597.47	584.24	573.15	563.79	555.85
50000	681.50	663.85	649.16	636.83	626.43	617.62
55000	749.64	730.24	714.07	700.52	689.08	679.38
60000	817.79	796.62	778.99	764.20	751.72	741.14
65000	885.94	863.01	843.91	827.88	814.36	802.90
70000	954.09	929.39	908.82	891.57	877.01	864.66
75000	1022.24	995.78	973.74	955.25	939.65	926.42
80000	1090.39	1062.16	1038.65	1018.93	1002.29	988.18
85000	1158.54	1128.55	1103.57	1082.62	1064.94	1049.95
90000	1226.69	1194.93	1168.49	1146.30	1127.58	1111.71
95000	1294.84	1261.32	1233.40	1209.98	1190.22	1173.47
100000	1362.99	1327.70	1298.32	1273.67	1252.87	1235.23
200000	2725.98	2655.41	2596.63	2547.33	2505.73	2470.46
300000	4088.97	3983.11	3894.95	3821.00	3758.60	3705.69
400000	5451.96	5310.82	5193.27	5094.67	5011.47	4940.92
500000	6814.95	6638.52	6491.58	6368.33	6264.34	6176.15

MONTHLY PAYMENT

Necessary to amortize a loan

13 1/2%

TERM / AMOUNT	19 YEARS	20 YEARS	25 YEARS	30 YEARS	35 YEARS	40 YEARS
500	6.10	6.04	5.83	5.73	5.68	5.65
600	7.32	7.24	6.99	6.87	6.81	6.78
700	8.54	8.45	8.16	8.02	7.95	7.91
800	9.76	9.66	9.33	9.16	9.08	9.04
900	10.98	10.87	10.49	10.31	10.22	10.17
1000	12.20	12.07	11.66	11.45	11.35	11.30
2000	24.40	24.15	23.31	22.91	22.71	22.61
3000	36.61	36.22	34.97	34.36	34.06	33.91
4000	48.81	48.29	46.63	45.82	45.41	45.21
5000	61.01	60.37	58.28	57.27	56.77	56.51
6000	73.21	72.44	69.94	68.72	68.12	67.82
7000	85.41	84.52	81.60	80.18	79.47	79.12
8000	97.62	96.59	93.25	91.63	90.83	90.42
9000	109.82	108.66	104.91	103.09	102.18	101.72
10000	122.02	120.74	116.56	114.54	113.53	113.03
11000	134.22	132.81	128.22	126.00	124.89	124.33
12000	146.43	144.89	139.88	137.45	136.24	135.63
13000	158.63	156.96	151.53	148.90	147.59	146.93
14000	170.83	169.03	163.19	160.36	158.95	158.24
15000	183.03	181.11	174.85	171.81	170.30	169.54
16000	195.23	193.18	186.50	183.27	181.65	180.84
17000	207.44	205.25	198.16	194.72	193.01	192.14
18000	219.64	217.33	209.82	206.17	204.36	203.45
19000	231.84	229.40	221.47	217.63	215.72	214.75
20000	244.04	241.48	233.13	229.08	227.07	226.05
21000	256.24	253.55	244.79	240.54	238.42	237.36
22000	268.45	265.62	256.44	251.99	249.78	248.66
23000	280.65	277.70	268.10	263.45	261.13	259.96
24000	292.85	289.77	279.76	274.90	272.48	271.26
25000	305.05	301.84	291.41	286.35	283.84	282.57
30000	366.06	362.21	349.69	343.62	340.60	339.08
35000	427.07	422.58	407.98	400.89	397.37	395.59
40000	488.08	482.95	466.26	458.17	454.14	452.10
45000	549.10	543.32	524.54	515.44	510.90	508.62
50000	610.11	603.69	582.82	572.71	567.67	565.13
55000	671.12	664.06	641.10	629.98	624.44	621.64
60000	732.13	724.42	699.39	687.25	681.20	678.16
65000	793.14	784.79	757.67	744.52	737.97	734.67
70000	854.15	845.16	815.95	801.79	794.74	791.18
75000	915.16	905.53	874.23	859.06	851.51	847.70
80000	976.17	965.90	932.52	916.33	908.27	904.21
85000	1037.18	1026.27	990.80	973.60	965.04	960.72
90000	1098.19	1086.64	1049.08	1030.87	1021.81	1017.23
95000	1159.20	1147.00	1107.36	1088.14	1078.57	1073.75
100000	1220.21	1207.37	1165.64	1145.41	1135.34	1130.26
200000	2440.42	2414.75	2331.29	2290.82	2270.68	2260.52
300000	3660.63	3622.12	3496.93	3436.24	3406.02	3390.78
400000	4880.84	4829.49	4662.58	4581.65	4541.36	4521.04
500000	6101.05	6036.87	5828.22	5727.06	5676.70	5651.31

13 3/4% MONTHLY PAYMENT

Necessary to amortize a loan

TERM / AMOUNT	1 YEAR	2 YEARS	3 YEARS	4 YEARS	5 YEARS	6 YEARS
500	44.84	23.95	17.03	13.60	11.57	10.24
600	53.80	28.74	20.43	16.32	13.88	12.28
700	62.77	33.53	23.84	19.04	16.20	14.33
800	71.74	38.32	27.25	21.76	18.51	16.38
900	80.70	43.11	30.65	24.48	20.83	18.43
1000	89.67	47.90	34.06	27.20	23.14	20.47
2000	179.34	95.79	68.11	54.40	46.28	40.94
3000	269.01	143.69	102.17	81.60	69.42	61.42
4000	358.68	191.58	136.23	108.81	92.56	81.89
5000	448.35	239.48	170.28	136.01	115.70	102.36
6000	538.02	287.37	204.34	163.21	138.83	122.83
7000	627.69	335.27	238.40	190.41	161.97	143.31
8000	717.36	383.16	272.45	217.61	185.11	163.78
9000	807.03	431.06	306.51	244.81	208.25	184.25
10000	896.70	478.95	340.57	272.01	231.39	204.72
11000	986.37	526.85	374.62	299.22	254.53	225.19
12000	1076.04	574.74	408.68	326.42	277.67	245.67
13000	1165.71	622.64	442.74	353.62	300.81	266.14
14000	1255.38	670.53	476.79	380.82	323.95	286.61
15000	1345.05	718.43	510.85	408.02	347.08	307.08
16000	1434.72	766.32	544.90	435.22	370.22	327.56
17000	1524.39	814.22	578.96	462.42	393.36	348.03
18000	1614.06	862.11	613.02	489.63	416.50	368.50
19000	1703.73	910.01	647.07	516.83	439.64	388.97
20000	1793.40	957.90	681.13	544.03	462.78	409.44
21000	1883.07	1005.80	715.19	571.23	485.92	429.92
22000	1972.74	1053.69	749.24	598.43	509.06	450.39
23000	2062.41	1101.59	783.30	625.63	532.20	470.86
24000	2152.08	1149.48	817.36	652.83	555.34	491.33
25000	2241.75	1197.38	851.41	680.03	578.47	511.81
30000	2690.10	1436.86	1021.70	816.04	694.17	614.17
35000	3138.45	1676.33	1191.98	952.05	809.86	716.53
40000	3586.80	1915.81	1362.26	1088.06	925.56	818.89
45000	4035.16	2155.28	1532.54	1224.06	1041.25	921.25
50000	4483.51	2394.76	1702.83	1360.07	1156.95	1023.61
55000	4931.86	2634.23	1873.11	1496.08	1272.64	1125.97
60000	5380.21	2873.71	2043.39	1632.08	1388.34	1228.33
65000	5828.56	3113.19	2213.67	1768.09	1504.03	1330.69
70000	6276.91	3352.66	2383.96	1904.10	1619.73	1433.05
75000	6725.26	3592.14	2554.24	2040.10	1735.42	1535.42
80000	7173.61	3831.61	2724.52	2176.11	1851.12	1637.78
85000	7621.96	4071.09	2894.81	2312.12	1966.81	1740.14
90000	8070.31	4310.56	3065.09	2448.12	2082.51	1842.50
95000	8518.66	4550.04	3235.37	2584.13	2198.20	1944.86
100000	8967.01	4789.52	3405.65	2720.14	2313.90	2047.22
200000	17934.00	9579.03	6811.31	5440.28	4627.79	4094.44
300000	26901.00	14368.60	10217.00	8160.41	6941.69	6141.66
400000	35868.10	19158.10	13622.60	10880.60	9255.58	8188.88
500000	44835.10	23947.60	17028.30	13600.70	11569.50	10236.10

MONTHLY PAYMENT
Necessary to amortize a loan

13 3/4%

TERM / AMOUNT	7 YEARS	8 YEARS	9 YEARS	10 YEARS	11 YEARS	12 YEARS
500	9.30	8.61	8.09	7.69	7.37	7.11
600	11.16	10.34	9.71	9.23	8.84	8.53
700	13.02	12.06	11.33	10.76	10.31	9.95
800	14.88	13.78	12.95	12.30	11.79	11.37
900	16.74	15.51	14.57	13.84	13.26	12.79
1000	18.60	17.23	16.19	15.38	14.73	14.21
2000	37.20	34.46	32.38	30.75	29.47	28.43
3000	55.81	51.69	48.56	46.13	44.20	42.64
4000	74.41	68.92	64.75	61.51	58.93	56.86
5000	93.01	86.15	80.94	76.88	73.66	71.07
6000	111.61	103.38	97.13	92.26	88.40	85.28
7000	130.22	120.61	113.31	107.64	103.13	99.50
8000	148.82	137.84	129.50	123.01	117.86	113.71
9000	167.42	155.07	145.69	138.39	132.60	127.93
10000	186.02	172.30	161.88	153.77	147.33	142.14
11000	204.63	189.53	178.07	169.14	162.06	156.35
12000	223.23	206.76	194.25	184.52	176.80	170.57
13000	241.83	223.99	210.44	199.90	191.53	184.78
14000	260.43	241.21	226.63	215.27	206.26	198.99
15000	279.03	258.44	242.82	230.65	220.99	213.21
16000	297.64	275.67	259.00	246.03	235.73	227.42
17000	316.24	292.90	275.19	261.40	250.46	241.64
18000	334.84	310.13	291.38	276.78	265.19	255.85
19000	353.44	327.36	307.57	292.16	279.93	270.06
20000	372.05	344.59	323.76	307.54	294.66	284.28
21000	390.65	361.82	339.94	322.91	309.39	298.49
22000	409.25	379.05	356.13	338.29	324.13	312.71
23000	427.85	396.28	372.32	353.67	338.86	326.92
24000	446.45	413.51	388.51	369.04	353.59	341.13
25000	465.06	430.74	404.69	384.42	368.32	355.35
30000	558.07	516.89	485.63	461.30	441.99	426.42
35000	651.08	603.04	566.57	538.19	515.65	497.49
40000	744.09	689.18	647.51	615.07	589.32	568.56
45000	837.10	775.33	728.45	691.95	662.98	639.62
50000	930.11	861.48	809.39	768.84	736.65	710.69
55000	1023.12	947.63	890.33	845.72	810.31	781.76
60000	1116.14	1033.78	971.26	922.60	883.98	852.83
65000	1209.15	1119.92	1052.20	999.49	957.64	923.90
70000	1302.16	1206.07	1133.14	1076.37	1031.31	994.97
75000	1395.17	1292.22	1214.08	1153.26	1104.97	1066.04
80000	1488.18	1378.37	1295.02	1230.14	1178.63	1137.11
85000	1581.19	1464.52	1375.96	1307.02	1252.30	1208.18
90000	1674.20	1550.66	1456.90	1383.91	1325.96	1279.25
95000	1767.21	1636.81	1537.84	1460.79	1399.63	1350.32
100000	1860.23	1722.96	1618.77	1537.67	1473.29	1421.39
200000	3720.45	3445.92	3237.55	3075.35	2946.59	2842.77
300000	5580.68	5168.88	4856.32	4613.02	4419.88	4264.16
400000	7440.90	6891.84	6475.09	6150.69	5893.17	5685.55
500000	9301.13	8614.80	8093.87	7688.37	7366.47	7106.93

13 3/4% MONTHLY PAYMENT

Necessary to amortize a loan

TERM / AMOUNT	13 YEARS	14 YEARS	15 YEARS	16 YEARS	17 YEARS	18 YEARS
500	6.90	6.72	6.57	6.45	6.35	6.26
600	8.27	8.06	7.89	7.74	7.62	7.52
700	9.65	9.41	9.20	9.03	8.89	8.77
800	11.03	10.75	10.52	10.33	10.16	10.02
900	12.41	12.10	11.83	11.62	11.43	11.27
1000	13.79	13.44	13.15	12.91	12.70	12.53
2000	27.58	26.88	26.30	25.81	25.40	25.06
3000	41.37	40.32	39.45	38.72	38.10	37.58
4000	55.16	53.76	52.60	51.63	50.81	50.11
5000	68.95	67.20	65.75	64.53	63.51	62.64
6000	82.74	80.64	78.90	77.44	76.21	75.17
7000	96.53	94.08	92.05	90.35	88.91	87.69
8000	110.32	107.53	105.20	103.25	101.61	100.22
9000	124.11	120.97	118.35	116.16	114.31	112.75
10000	137.90	134.41	131.50	129.06	127.01	125.28
11000	151.69	147.85	144.65	141.97	139.71	137.80
12000	165.48	161.29	157.80	154.88	152.42	150.33
13000	179.27	174.73	170.95	167.78	165.12	162.86
14000	193.06	188.17	184.10	180.69	177.82	175.39
15000	206.85	201.61	197.25	193.60	190.52	187.92
16000	220.64	215.05	210.40	206.50	203.22	200.44
17000	234.43	228.49	223.55	219.41	215.92	212.97
18000	248.22	241.93	236.70	232.32	228.62	225.50
19000	262.01	255.37	249.85	245.22	241.33	238.03
20000	275.80	268.81	263.00	258.13	254.03	250.55
21000	289.59	282.25	276.15	271.04	266.73	263.08
22000	303.38	295.69	289.30	283.94	279.43	275.61
23000	317.17	309.13	302.45	296.85	292.13	288.14
24000	330.96	322.57	315.60	309.75	304.83	300.66
25000	344.75	336.02	328.75	322.66	317.53	313.19
30000	413.70	403.22	394.50	387.19	381.04	375.83
35000	482.65	470.42	460.25	451.73	444.55	438.37
40000	551.60	537.62	526.00	516.26	508.05	501.11
45000	620.56	604.83	591.75	580.79	571.56	563.75
50000	689.51	672.03	657.50	645.32	635.07	626.38
55000	758.46	739.23	723.25	709.85	698.57	689.02
60000	827.41	806.44	788.99	774.39	762.08	751.66
65000	896.36	873.64	854.74	838.92	825.59	814.30
70000	965.31	940.84	920.49	903.45	889.09	876.94
75000	1034.26	1008.04	986.24	967.98	952.60	939.57
80000	1103.21	1075.25	1051.99	1032.51	1016.11	1002.21
85000	1172.16	1142.45	1117.74	1097.05	1079.61	1064.85
90000	1241.11	1209.65	1183.49	1161.58	1143.12	1127.49
95000	1310.06	1276.86	1249.24	1226.11	1206.62	1190.13
100000	1379.01	1344.06	1314.99	1290.64	1270.13	1252.77
200000	2758.02	2688.12	2629.98	2581.29	2540.26	2505.53
300000	4137.03	4032.18	3944.97	3871.93	3810.39	3758.30
400000	5516.04	5376.24	5259.96	5162.57	5080.53	5011.06
500000	6895.05	6720.30	6574.95	6453.21	6350.66	6263.83

MONTHLY PAYMENT

Necessary to amortize a loan

13 3/4%

TERM / AMOUNT	19 YEARS	20 YEARS	25 YEARS	30 YEARS	35 YEARS	40 YEARS
500	6.19	6.13	5.92	5.83	5.78	5.75
600	7.43	7.35	7.11	6.99	6.93	6.90
700	8.67	8.58	8.29	8.16	8.09	8.05
800	9.90	9.80	9.48	9.32	9.24	9.21
900	11.14	11.03	10.66	10.49	10.40	10.36
1000	12.38	12.25	11.85	11.65	11.55	11.51
2000	24.76	24.51	23.69	23.30	23.11	23.01
3000	37.14	36.76	35.54	34.95	34.66	34.52
4000	49.52	49.02	47.39	46.60	46.22	46.03
5000	61.90	61.27	59.23	58.26	57.77	57.53
6000	74.28	73.52	71.08	69.91	69.33	69.04
7000	86.66	85.78	82.93	81.56	80.88	80.55
8000	99.04	98.03	94.77	93.21	92.44	92.05
9000	111.42	110.29	106.62	104.86	103.99	103.56
10000	123.80	122.54	118.47	116.51	115.55	115.07
11000	136.18	134.80	130.31	128.16	127.10	126.58
12000	148.56	147.05	142.16	139.81	138.66	138.08
13000	160.94	159.30	154.01	151.47	150.21	149.59
14000	173.32	171.56	165.85	163.12	161.77	161.10
15000	185.70	183.81	177.70	174.77	173.32	172.60
16000	198.08	196.07	189.55	186.42	184.88	184.11
17000	210.46	208.32	201.39	198.07	196.43	195.62
18000	222.84	220.57	213.24	209.72	207.99	207.12
19000	235.22	232.83	225.09	221.37	219.54	218.63
20000	247.60	245.08	236.93	233.02	231.10	230.14
21000	259.98	257.34	248.78	244.67	242.65	241.64
22000	272.36	269.59	260.63	256.33	254.21	253.15
23000	284.74	281.84	272.47	267.98	265.76	264.66
24000	297.12	294.10	284.32	279.63	277.32	276.16
25000	309.50	306.35	296.17	291.28	288.87	287.67
30000	371.40	367.62	355.40	349.53	346.65	345.21
35000	433.30	428.89	414.63	407.79	404.42	402.74
40000	495.20	490.16	473.87	466.05	462.19	460.27
45000	557.10	551.43	533.10	524.30	519.97	517.81
50000	619.00	612.70	592.33	582.56	577.74	575.34
55000	680.90	673.97	651.57	640.81	635.52	632.88
60000	742.80	735.24	710.80	699.07	693.29	690.41
65000	804.70	796.52	770.03	757.32	751.07	747.95
70000	866.60	857.79	829.27	815.58	808.84	805.48
75000	928.50	919.06	888.50	873.84	866.61	863.01
80000	990.40	980.33	947.73	932.09	924.39	920.55
85000	1052.30	1041.60	1006.97	990.35	982.16	978.08
90000	1114.20	1102.87	1066.20	1048.60	1039.94	1035.62
95000	1176.10	1164.14	1125.43	1106.86	1097.71	1093.15
100000	1238.00	1225.41	1184.67	1165.11	1155.49	1150.69
200000	2476.01	2450.81	2369.33	2330.23	2310.97	2301.37
300000	3714.01	3676.22	3554.00	3495.34	3466.46	3452.06
400000	4952.01	4901.63	4738.67	4660.45	4621.94	4602.74
500000	6190.01	6127.04	5923.33	5825.56	5777.43	5753.43

14%

MONTHLY PAYMENT

Necessary to amortize a loan

TERM / AMOUNT	1 YEAR	2 YEARS	3 YEARS	4 YEARS	5 YEARS	6 YEARS
500	44.89	24.01	17.09	13.66	11.63	10.30
600	53.87	28.81	20.51	16.40	13.96	12.36
700	62.85	33.61	23.92	19.13	16.29	14.42
800	71.83	38.41	27.34	21.86	18.61	16.48
900	80.81	43.21	30.76	24.59	20.94	18.55
1000	89.79	48.01	34.18	27.33	23.27	20.61
2000	179.57	96.03	68.36	54.65	46.54	41.21
3000	269.36	144.04	102.53	81.98	69.80	61.82
4000	359.15	192.05	136.71	109.31	93.07	82.42
5000	448.94	240.06	170.89	136.63	116.34	103.03
6000	538.72	288.08	205.07	163.96	139.61	123.63
7000	628.51	336.09	239.24	191.29	162.88	144.24
8000	718.30	384.10	273.42	218.61	186.15	164.85
9000	808.08	432.12	307.60	245.94	209.41	185.45
10000	897.87	480.13	341.78	273.26	232.68	206.06
11000	987.66	528.14	375.95	300.59	255.95	226.66
12000	1077.44	576.15	410.13	327.92	279.22	247.27
13000	1167.23	624.17	444.31	355.24	302.49	267.87
14000	1257.02	672.18	478.49	382.57	325.76	288.48
15000	1346.80	720.19	512.66	409.90	349.02	309.09
16000	1436.59	768.21	546.84	437.22	372.29	329.69
17000	1526.38	816.22	581.02	464.55	395.56	350.30
18000	1616.17	864.23	615.20	491.88	418.83	370.90
19000	1705.95	912.24	649.37	519.20	442.10	391.51
20000	1795.74	960.26	683.55	546.53	465.37	412.11
21000	1885.53	1008.27	717.73	573.86	488.63	432.72
22000	1975.31	1056.28	751.91	601.18	511.90	453.33
23000	2065.10	1104.29	786.08	628.51	535.17	473.93
24000	2154.89	1152.31	820.26	655.84	558.44	494.54
25000	2244.67	1200.32	854.44	683.16	581.71	515.14
30000	2693.61	1440.38	1025.33	819.79	698.05	618.17
35000	3142.54	1680.45	1196.22	956.43	814.39	721.20
40000	3591.48	1920.51	1367.10	1093.06	930.73	824.23
45000	4040.41	2160.58	1537.99	1229.69	1047.07	927.26
50000	4489.35	2400.64	1708.88	1366.32	1163.41	1030.29
55000	4938.28	2640.70	1879.77	1502.95	1279.75	1133.31
60000	5387.22	2880.77	2050.66	1639.59	1396.09	1236.34
65000	5836.15	3120.83	2221.54	1776.22	1512.43	1339.37
70000	6285.09	3360.90	2392.43	1912.85	1628.78	1442.40
75000	6734.02	3600.96	2563.32	2049.48	1745.12	1545.43
80000	7182.96	3841.03	2734.21	2186.12	1861.46	1648.46
85000	7631.89	4081.09	2905.09	2322.75	1977.80	1751.49
90000	8080.83	4321.15	3075.98	2459.38	2094.14	1854.51
95000	8529.76	4561.22	3246.87	2596.01	2210.48	1957.54
100000	8978.70	4801.28	3417.76	2732.64	2326.82	2060.57
200000	17957.40	9602.56	6835.52	5465.29	4653.65	4121.14
300000	26936.10	14403.80	10253.30	8197.93	6980.47	6181.72
400000	35914.80	19205.10	13671.00	10930.60	9307.29	8242.29
500000	44893.50	24006.40	17088.80	13663.20	11634.10	10302.90

MONTHLY PAYMENT

Necessary to amortize a loan

14%

TERM / AMOUNT	7 YEARS	8 YEARS	9 YEARS	10 YEARS	11 YEARS	12 YEARS
500	9.37	8.69	8.17	7.76	7.44	7.19
600	11.24	10.42	9.80	9.32	8.93	8.62
700	13.12	12.16	11.43	10.87	10.42	10.06
800	14.99	13.90	13.07	12.42	11.91	11.50
900	16.87	15.63	14.70	13.97	13.40	12.93
1000	18.74	17.37	16.33	15.53	14.89	14.37
2000	37.48	34.74	32.67	31.05	29.77	28.74
3000	56.22	52.11	49.00	46.58	44.66	43.11
4000	74.96	69.49	65.33	62.11	59.55	57.49
5000	93.70	86.86	81.67	77.63	74.43	71.86
6000	112.44	104.23	98.00	93.16	89.32	86.23
7000	131.18	121.60	114.34	108.69	104.21	100.60
8000	149.92	138.97	130.67	124.21	119.09	114.97
9000	168.66	156.34	147.00	139.74	133.98	129.34
10000	187.40	173.72	163.34	155.27	148.87	143.71
11000	206.14	191.09	179.67	170.79	163.75	158.08
12000	224.88	208.46	196.00	186.32	178.64	172.46
13000	243.62	225.83	212.34	201.85	193.53	186.83
14000	262.36	243.20	228.67	217.37	208.41	201.20
15000	281.10	260.57	245.01	232.90	223.30	215.57
16000	299.84	277.94	261.34	248.43	238.19	229.94
17000	318.58	295.32	277.67	263.95	253.07	244.31
18000	337.32	312.69	294.01	279.48	267.96	258.68
19000	356.06	330.06	310.34	295.01	282.85	273.05
20000	374.80	347.43	326.67	310.53	297.73	287.43
21000	393.54	364.80	343.01	326.06	312.62	301.80
22000	412.28	382.17	359.34	341.59	327.51	316.17
23000	431.02	399.54	375.68	357.11	342.39	330.54
24000	449.76	416.92	392.01	372.64	357.28	344.91
25000	468.50	434.29	408.34	388.17	372.17	359.28
30000	562.20	521.15	490.01	465.80	446.60	431.14
35000	655.90	608.00	571.68	543.43	521.03	502.99
40000	749.60	694.86	653.35	621.07	595.47	574.85
45000	843.30	781.72	735.02	698.70	669.90	646.71
50000	937.00	868.57	816.68	776.33	744.33	718.56
55000	1030.70	955.43	898.35	853.97	818.77	790.42
60000	1124.40	1042.29	980.02	931.60	893.20	862.28
65000	1218.10	1129.15	1061.69	1009.23	967.63	934.13
70000	1311.80	1216.00	1143.36	1086.86	1042.07	1005.99
75000	1405.50	1302.86	1225.03	1164.50	1116.50	1077.84
80000	1499.20	1389.72	1306.70	1242.13	1190.93	1149.70
85000	1592.90	1476.58	1388.36	1319.76	1265.37	1221.56
90000	1686.60	1563.43	1470.03	1397.40	1339.80	1293.41
95000	1780.30	1650.29	1551.70	1475.03	1414.23	1365.27
100000	1874.00	1737.15	1633.37	1552.66	1488.67	1437.13
200000	3748.00	3474.30	3266.74	3105.33	2977.33	2874.25
300000	5622.00	5122.45	4900.11	4657.99	4466.00	4311.38
400000	7496.00	6948.60	6533.48	6210.65	5954.66	5748.50
500000	9370.00	8685.74	8166.84	7763.32	7443.33	7185.63

14%

MONTHLY PAYMENT

Necessary to amortize a loan

TERM / AMOUNT	13 YEARS	14 YEARS	15 YEARS	16 YEARS	17 YEARS	18 YEARS
500	6.98	6.80	6.66	6.54	6.44	6.35
600	8.37	8.16	7.99	7.85	7.72	7.62
700	9.77	9.52	9.32	9.15	9.01	8.89
800	11.16	10.88	10.65	10.46	10.30	10.16
900	12.56	12.24	11.99	11.77	11.59	11.43
1000	13.95	13.60	13.32	13.08	12.87	12.70
2000	27.90	27.21	26.63	26.15	25.75	25.41
3000	41.85	40.81	39.95	39.23	38.62	38.11
4000	55.80	54.42	53.27	52.31	51.50	50.82
5000	69.76	68.02	66.59	65.38	64.37	63.52
6000	83.71	81.63	79.90	78.46	77.25	76.22
7000	97.66	95.23	93.22	91.54	90.12	88.93
8000	111.61	108.84	106.54	104.62	103.00	101.63
9000	125.56	122.44	119.86	117.69	115.87	114.33
10000	139.51	136.05	133.17	130.77	128.75	127.04
11000	153.46	149.65	146.49	143.85	141.62	139.74
12000	167.41	163.26	159.81	156.92	154.50	152.45
13000	181.36	176.86	173.13	170.00	167.37	165.15
14000	195.31	190.47	186.44	183.08	180.25	177.85
15000	209.27	204.07	199.76	196.16	193.12	190.56
16000	223.22	217.68	213.08	209.23	206.00	203.26
17000	237.17	231.28	226.40	222.31	218.87	215.97
18000	251.12	244.89	239.71	235.39	231.75	228.67
19000	265.07	258.49	253.03	248.46	244.62	241.37
20000	279.02	272.10	266.35	261.54	257.50	254.08
21000	292.97	285.70	279.67	274.62	270.37	266.78
22000	306.92	299.31	292.98	287.69	283.25	279.48
23000	320.87	312.91	306.30	300.77	296.12	292.19
24000	334.83	326.52	319.62	313.85	308.99	304.89
25000	348.78	340.12	332.94	326.93	321.87	317.60
30000	418.53	408.15	399.52	392.31	386.24	381.12
35000	488.29	476.17	466.11	457.70	450.62	444.63
40000	558.04	544.20	532.70	523.08	514.99	508.15
45000	627.80	612.22	599.28	588.46	579.36	571.67
50000	697.55	680.24	665.87	653.85	643.74	635.19
55000	767.31	748.27	732.46	719.23	708.11	698.71
60000	837.06	816.29	799.04	784.62	772.49	762.23
65000	906.82	884.32	865.63	850.00	836.86	825.75
70000	976.57	952.34	932.22	915.39	901.23	889.27
75000	1046.33	1020.37	998.81	980.77	965.61	952.79
80000	1116.08	1088.39	1065.39	1046.16	1029.98	1016.31
85000	1185.84	1156.42	1131.98	1111.54	1094.35	1079.83
90000	1255.59	1224.44	1198.57	1176.93	1158.73	1143.34
95000	1325.35	1292.46	1265.15	1242.31	1223.10	1206.86
100000	1395.10	1360.49	1331.74	1307.70	1287.48	1270.38
200000	2790.21	2720.98	2663.48	2615.40	2574.95	2540.77
300000	4185.31	4081.47	3995.22	3923.10	3862.43	3811.15
400000	5580.41	5441.96	5326.96	5230.79	5149.90	5081.53
500000	6975.51	6802.44	6658.70	6538.49	6437.38	6351.91

MONTHLY PAYMENT

Necessary to amortize a loan

14%

TERM / AMOUNT	19 YEARS	20 YEARS	25 YEARS	30 YEARS	35 YEARS	40 YEARS
500	6.28	6.22	6.02	5.92	5.88	5.86
600	7.54	7.46	7.22	7.11	7.05	7.03
700	8.79	8.70	8.43	8.29	8.23	8.20
800	10.05	9.95	9.63	9.48	9.41	9.37
900	11.30	11.19	10.83	10.66	10.58	10.54
1000	12.56	12.44	12.04	11.85	11.76	11.71
2000	25.12	24.87	24.08	23.70	23.51	23.42
3000	37.68	37.31	36.11	35.55	35.27	35.13
4000	50.24	49.74	48.15	47.39	47.03	46.85
5000	62.79	62.18	60.19	59.24	58.78	58.56
6000	75.35	74.61	72.23	71.09	70.54	70.27
7000	87.91	87.05	84.26	82.94	82.30	81.98
8000	100.47	99.48	96.30	94.79	94.05	93.69
9000	113.03	111.92	108.34	106.64	105.81	105.40
10000	125.59	124.35	120.38	118.49	117.57	117.11
11000	138.15	136.79	132.41	130.34	129.32	128.83
12000	150.71	149.22	144.45	142.19	141.08	140.54
13000	163.26	161.66	156.49	154.03	152.84	152.25
14000	175.82	174.09	168.53	165.88	164.59	163.96
15000	188.38	186.53	180.56	177.73	176.35	175.67
16000	200.94	198.96	192.60	189.58	188.11	187.38
17000	213.50	211.40	204.64	201.43	199.86	199.09
18000	226.06	223.83	216.68	213.28	211.62	210.81
19000	238.62	236.27	228.72	225.13	223.38	222.52
20000	251.18	248.70	240.75	236.97	235.14	234.23
21000	263.73	261.14	252.79	248.82	246.89	245.94
22000	276.29	273.57	264.83	260.67	258.65	257.65
23000	288.85	286.01	276.87	272.52	270.41	269.36
24000	301.41	298.45	288.90	284.37	282.16	281.07
25000	313.97	310.88	300.94	296.22	293.92	292.79
30000	376.76	373.06	361.13	355.46	352.70	351.34
35000	439.56	435.23	421.32	414.71	411.49	409.90
40000	502.35	497.41	481.50	473.95	470.27	468.46
45000	565.14	559.58	541.69	533.19	529.05	527.01
50000	627.94	621.76	601.88	592.44	587.84	585.57
55000	690.73	683.94	662.07	651.68	646.62	644.13
60000	753.53	746.11	722.26	710.92	705.40	702.68
65000	816.32	808.29	782.45	770.17	764.19	761.24
70000	879.11	870.46	842.63	829.41	822.97	819.80
75000	941.91	932.64	902.82	888.65	881.76	878.36
80000	1004.70	994.82	963.01	947.90	940.54	936.91
85000	1067.49	1056.99	1023.20	1007.14	999.32	995.47
90000	1130.29	1119.17	1083.39	1066.38	1058.11	1054.03
95000	1193.08	1181.34	1143.57	1125.63	1116.89	1112.58
100000	1255.88	1243.52	1203.76	1184.87	1175.67	1171.14
200000	2511.75	2487.04	2407.52	2369.74	2351.35	2342.28
300000	3767.63	3730.56	3611.28	3554.62	3527.02	3513.42
400000	5023.50	4974.08	4815.04	4739.49	4702.69	4684.56
500000	6279.38	6217.60	6018.81	5924.36	5878.37	5855.70

14 1/4%

MONTHLY PAYMENT
Necessary to amortize a loan

TERM / AMOUNT	1 YEAR	2 YEARS	3 YEARS	4 YEARS	5 YEARS	6 YEARS
500	44.95	24.07	17.15	13.73	11.70	10.37
600	53.94	28.88	20.58	16.47	14.04	12.44
700	62.93	33.69	24.01	19.22	16.38	14.52
800	71.92	38.50	27.44	21.96	18.72	16.59
900	80.91	43.32	30.87	24.71	21.06	18.67
1000	89.90	48.13	34.30	27.45	23.40	20.74
2000	179.81	96.26	68.60	54.90	46.80	41.48
3000	269.71	144.39	102.90	82.36	70.19	62.22
4000	359.62	192.52	137.20	109.81	93.59	82.96
5000	449.52	240.66	171.50	137.26	116.99	103.70
6000	539.43	288.79	205.79	164.71	140.39	124.44
7000	629.33	336.92	240.09	192.16	163.79	145.18
8000	719.24	385.05	274.39	219.62	187.18	165.92
9000	809.14	433.18	308.69	247.07	210.58	186.66
10000	899.05	481.31	342.99	274.52	233.98	207.40
11000	988.95	529.44	377.29	301.97	257.38	228.14
12000	1078.85	577.57	411.59	329.42	280.78	248.88
13000	1168.76	625.70	445.89	356.88	304.17	269.62
14000	1258.66	673.83	480.19	384.33	327.57	290.36
15000	1348.57	721.96	514.49	411.78	350.97	311.10
16000	1438.47	770.10	548.79	439.23	374.37	331.84
17000	1528.38	818.23	583.08	466.68	397.77	352.58
18000	1618.28	866.36	617.38	494.14	421.16	373.32
19000	1708.19	914.49	651.68	521.59	444.56	394.06
20000	1798.09	962.62	685.98	549.04	467.96	414.80
21000	1887.99	1010.75	720.28	576.49	491.36	435.54
22000	1977.90	1058.88	754.58	603.94	514.76	456.28
23000	2067.80	1107.01	788.88	631.40	538.15	477.02
24000	2157.71	1155.14	823.88	658.85	561.55	497.76
25000	2247.61	1203.27	857.48	686.30	584.95	518.50
30000	2697.13	1443.93	1028.97	823.56	701.94	622.19
35000	3146.66	1684.58	1200.47	960.82	818.93	725.89
40000	3596.18	1925.24	1371.96	1098.08	935.92	829.59
45000	4045.70	2165.89	1543.46	1235.34	1052.91	933.29
50000	4495.22	2406.55	1714.95	1372.60	1169.90	1036.99
55000	4944.75	2647.20	1886.45	1509.86	1286.89	1140.69
60000	5394.27	2887.86	2057.94	1647.12	1403.88	1244.39
65000	5843.79	3128.51	2229.44	1784.38	1520.87	1348.09
70000	6293.31	3369.16	2400.94	1921.64	1637.86	1451.79
75000	6742.84	3609.82	2572.43	2058.90	1754.85	1555.48
80000	7192.36	3850.47	2743.93	2196.16	1871.84	1659.18
85000	7641.88	4091.13	2915.42	2333.42	1988.83	1762.88
90000	8091.40	4331.78	3086.92	2470.68	2105.82	1866.58
95000	8540.93	4572.44	3258.41	2607.94	2222.81	1970.28
100000	8990.45	4813.09	3429.91	2745.20	2339.80	2073.98
200000	17980.90	9626.18	6859.82	5490.40	4679.60	4147.96
300000	26971.30	14439.30	10289.70	8235.59	7019.40	6221.94
400000	35961.80	19252.40	13719.60	10980.80	9359.20	8295.92
500000	44952.20	24065.50	17149.50	13726.00	11699.00	10369.90

MONTHLY PAYMENT

Necessary to amortize a loan

14 1/4%

TERM / AMOUNT	7 YEARS	8 YEARS	9 YEARS	10 YEARS	11 YEARS	12 YEARS
500	9.44	8.76	8.24	7.84	7.52	7.26
600	11.33	10.51	9.89	9.41	9.02	8.72
700	13.21	12.26	11.54	10.97	10.53	10.17
800	15.10	14.01	13.18	12.54	12.03	11.62
900	16.99	15.76	14.83	14.11	13.54	13.08
1000	18.88	17.51	16.48	15.68	15.04	14.53
2000	37.76	35.03	32.96	31.35	30.08	29.06
3000	56.64	52.54	49.44	47.03	45.12	43.59
4000	75.51	70.06	65.92	62.71	60.16	58.12
5000	94.39	87.57	82.40	78.39	75.21	72.65
6000	113.27	105.08	98.88	94.06	90.25	87.18
7000	132.15	122.60	115.36	109.74	105.29	101.71
8000	151.03	140.11	131.84	125.42	120.33	116.24
9000	169.91	157.63	148.32	141.10	135.37	130.77
10000	188.78	175.14	164.80	156.77	150.41	145.30
11000	207.66	192.66	181.28	172.45	165.45	159.82
12000	226.54	210.17	197.76	188.13	180.49	174.35
13000	245.42	227.68	214.25	203.81	195.54	188.88
14000	264.30	245.20	230.73	219.48	210.58	203.41
15000	283.18	262.71	247.21	235.16	225.62	217.94
16000	302.05	280.23	263.69	250.84	240.66	232.47
17000	320.93	297.74	280.17	266.51	255.70	247.00
18000	339.81	315.25	296.65	282.19	270.74	261.53
19000	358.69	332.77	313.13	297.87	285.78	276.06
20000	377.57	350.28	329.61	313.55	300.82	290.59
21000	396.45	367.80	346.09	329.22	315.86	305.12
22000	415.32	385.31	362.57	344.90	330.91	319.65
23000	434.20	402.82	379.05	360.58	345.95	334.18
24000	453.08	420.34	395.53	376.26	360.99	348.71
25000	471.96	437.85	412.01	391.93	376.03	363.24
30000	566.35	525.42	494.41	470.32	451.24	435.88
35000	660.74	612.99	576.81	548.71	526.44	508.53
40000	755.13	700.56	659.21	627.09	601.65	581.18
45000	849.53	788.13	741.62	705.48	676.85	653.83
50000	943.92	875.70	824.02	783.86	752.06	726.47
55000	1038.31	963.27	906.42	862.25	827.26	799.12
60000	1132.70	1050.84	988.82	940.64	902.47	871.77
65000	1227.09	1138.41	1071.22	1019.02	977.68	944.42
70000	1321.48	1225.98	1153.62	1097.41	1052.88	1017.06
75000	1415.88	1313.55	1236.03	1175.80	1128.09	1089.71
80000	1510.27	1401.12	1318.43	1254.18	1203.29	1162.36
85000	1604.66	1488.69	1400.83	1332.57	1278.50	1235.01
90000	1699.05	1576.26	1483.23	1410.96	1353.70	1307.65
95000	1793.44	1663.83	1565.63	1489.34	1428.91	1380.30
100000	1887.83	1751.40	1648.04	1567.73	1504.12	1452.95
200000	3775.67	3502.81	3296.07	3135.46	3008.23	2905.89
300000	5663.50	5254.21	4944.11	4703.19	4512.35	4358.84
400000	7551.34	7005.62	6592.14	6270.91	6016.46	5811.79
500000	9439.17	8757.02	8240.18	7838.64	7520.58	7264.74

14 1/4%

MONTHLY PAYMENT
Necessary to amortize a loan

TERM / AMOUNT	13 YEARS	14 YEARS	15 YEARS	16 YEARS	17 YEARS	18 YEARS
500	7.06	6.89	6.74	6.62	6.52	6.44
600	8.47	8.26	8.09	7.95	7.83	7.73
700	9.88	9.64	9.44	9.27	9.13	9.02
800	11.29	11.02	10.79	10.60	10.44	10.30
900	12.70	12.39	12.14	11.92	11.74	11.59
1000	14.11	13.77	13.49	13.25	13.05	12.88
2000	28.23	27.54	26.97	26.50	26.10	25.76
3000	42.34	41.31	40.46	39.75	39.15	38.64
4000	56.45	55.08	53.94	52.99	52.20	51.52
5000	70.56	68.85	67.43	66.24	65.25	64.40
6000	84.68	82.62	80.91	79.49	78.29	77.29
7000	98.79	96.39	94.40	92.74	91.34	90.17
8000	112.90	110.16	107.89	105.99	104.39	103.05
9000	127.02	123.93	121.37	119.24	117.44	115.93
10000	141.13	137.70	134.86	132.48	130.49	128.81
11000	155.24	151.47	148.34	145.73	143.54	141.69
12000	169.35	165.24	161.83	158.98	156.59	154.57
13000	183.47	179.01	175.32	172.23	169.64	167.45
14000	197.58	192.78	188.80	185.48	182.69	180.33
15000	211.69	206.55	202.29	198.73	195.74	193.21
16000	225.81	220.32	215.77	211.98	208.79	206.09
17000	239.92	234.09	229.26	225.22	221.83	218.98
18000	254.03	247.86	242.74	238.47	234.88	231.86
19000	268.14	261.63	256.23	251.72	247.93	244.74
20000	282.26	275.40	269.72	264.97	260.98	257.62
21000	296.37	289.17	283.20	278.22	274.03	270.50
22000	310.48	302.94	296.69	291.47	287.08	283.38
23000	324.59	316.71	310.17	304.71	300.13	296.26
24000	338.71	330.48	323.66	317.96	313.18	309.14
25000	352.82	344.25	337.15	331.21	326.23	322.02
30000	423.38	413.10	404.57	397.45	391.47	386.43
35000	493.95	481.95	472.00	463.70	456.72	450.83
40000	564.51	550.80	539.43	529.94	521.96	515.23
45000	635.08	619.65	606.86	596.18	587.21	579.64
50000	705.64	688.50	674.29	662.42	652.45	644.04
55000	776.20	757.35	741.72	728.66	717.70	708.45
60000	846.77	826.20	809.15	794.91	782.94	772.85
65000	917.33	895.05	876.58	861.15	848.19	837.26
70000	987.90	963.90	944.01	927.39	913.44	901.66
75000	1058.46	1032.75	1011.43	993.63	978.68	966.07
80000	1129.02	1101.60	1078.86	1059.87	1043.93	1030.47
85000	1199.59	1170.45	1146.29	1126.12	1109.17	1094.87
90000	1270.15	1239.30	1213.72	1192.36	1174.42	1159.28
95000	1340.71	1308.15	1281.15	1258.60	1239.66	1223.68
100000	1411.28	1377.00	1348.58	1324.84	1304.91	1288.09
200000	2822.56	2754.01	2697.16	2649.68	2609.81	2576.17
300000	4233.84	4131.01	4045.73	3974.52	3914.72	3864.26
400000	5645.11	5508.02	5394.31	5299.37	5219.63	5152.34
500000	7056.39	6885.02	6742.89	6624.21	6524.54	6440.43

MONTHLY PAYMENT
Necessary to amortize a loan

14 1/4%

TERM / AMOUNT	19 YEARS	20 YEARS	25 YEARS	30 YEARS	35 YEARS	40 YEARS
500	6.37	6.31	6.11	6.02	5.98	5.96
600	7.64	7.57	7.34	7.23	7.18	7.15
700	8.92	8.83	8.56	8.43	8.37	8.34
800	10.19	10.09	9.78	9.64	9.57	9.53
900	11.46	11.36	11.01	10.84	10.76	10.72
1000	12.74	12.62	12.23	12.05	11.96	11.92
2000	25.48	25.23	24.46	24.09	23.92	23.83
3000	38.22	37.85	36.69	36.14	35.88	35.75
4000	50.95	50.47	48.92	48.19	47.84	47.66
5000	63.69	63.09	61.15	60.23	59.80	59.58
6000	76.43	75.70	73.38	72.28	71.75	71.50
7000	89.17	88.32	85.60	84.33	83.71	83.41
8000	101.91	100.94	97.83	96.38	95.67	95.33
9000	114.65	113.56	110.06	108.42	107.63	107.25
10000	127.38	126.17	122.29	120.47	119.59	119.16
11000	140.12	138.79	134.52	132.52	131.55	131.08
12000	152.86	151.41	146.75	144.56	143.51	143.00
13000	165.60	164.02	158.98	156.61	155.47	154.91
14000	178.34	176.64	171.21	168.66	167.43	166.83
15000	191.08	189.26	183.44	180.70	179.39	178.74
16000	203.81	201.88	195.67	192.75	191.34	190.66
17000	216.55	214.49	207.90	204.80	203.30	202.58
18000	229.29	227.11	220.13	216.84	215.26	214.49
19000	242.03	239.73	232.36	228.89	227.22	226.41
20000	254.77	252.34	244.59	240.94	239.18	238.33
21000	267.51	264.96	256.82	252.98	252.14	250.24
22000	280.24	277.58	269.04	265.03	263.10	262.16
23000	292.98	290.20	281.27	277.08	275.06	274.07
24000	305.72	302.81	293.50	289.13	287.02	285.99
25000	318.46	315.43	305.73	301.17	298.98	297.91
30000	382.15	378.52	366.88	361.41	358.77	357.49
35000	445.84	441.60	428.03	421.64	418.57	417.07
40000	509.53	504.69	489.17	481.88	478.36	476.65
45000	573.23	567.77	550.32	542.11	538.16	536.23
50000	636.92	630.86	611.46	602.34	597.95	595.81
55000	700.61	693.95	672.61	662.58	657.75	655.39
60000	764.30	757.03	733.76	722.81	717.54	714.97
65000	827.99	820.12	794.90	783.05	777.34	774.56
70000	891.68	883.20	856.05	843.28	837.13	834.14
75000	955.38	946.29	917.20	903.52	896.93	893.72
80000	1019.07	1009.37	978.34	963.75	956.72	953.30
85000	1082.76	1072.46	1039.49	1023.98	1016.52	1012.88
90000	1146.45	1135.55	1100.63	1084.22	1076.31	1072.46
95000	1210.14	1198.63	1161.78	1144.45	1136.11	1132.04
100000	1273.83	1261.72	1222.93	1204.69	1195.90	1191.62
200000	2547.67	2523.44	2445.85	2409.37	2391.80	2383.25
300000	3821.50	3785.15	3668.78	3614.06	3587.71	3574.87
400000	5095.34	5046.87	4891.71	4818.75	4783.61	4766.49
500000	6369.17	6308.59	6114.64	6023.43	5979.51	5958.12

14 1/2%

MONTHLY PAYMENT

Necessary to amortize a loan

TERM / AMOUNT	1 YEAR	2 YEARS	3 YEARS	4 YEARS	5 YEARS	6 YEARS
500	45.01	24.12	17.21	13.79	11.76	10.44
600	54.01	28.95	20.65	16.55	14.12	12.52
700	63.02	33.77	24.09	19.30	16.47	14.61
800	72.02	38.60	27.54	22.06	18.82	16.70
900	81.02	43.42	30.98	24.82	21.18	18.79
1000	90.02	48.25	34.42	27.58	23.53	20.87
2000	180.05	96.50	68.84	55.16	47.06	41.75
3000	270.07	144.75	103.26	82.73	70.58	62.62
4000	360.09	193.00	137.68	110.31	94.11	83.50
5000	450.11	241.25	172.11	137.89	117.64	104.37
6000	540.14	289.50	206.53	165.47	141.17	125.25
7000	630.16	337.75	240.95	193.05	164.70	146.12
8000	720.18	386.00	275.37	220.62	188.23	167.00
9000	810.20	434.25	309.79	248.20	211.76	187.87
10000	900.23	482.50	344.21	275.78	235.28	208.74
11000	990.25	530.74	378.63	303.36	258.81	229.62
12000	1080.27	578.99	413.05	330.94	282.34	250.49
13000	1170.29	627.24	447.47	358.51	305.87	271.37
14000	1260.32	675.49	481.89	386.09	329.40	292.24
15000	1350.34	723.74	516.32	413.67	352.93	313.12
16000	1440.36	771.99	550.74	441.25	376.45	333.99
17000	1530.38	820.24	585.16	468.83	399.98	354.87
18000	1620.41	868.49	619.58	496.40	423.51	375.74
19000	1710.43	916.74	654.00	523.98	447.04	396.61
20000	1800.45	964.99	688.42	551.56	470.57	417.49
21000	1890.48	1013.24	722.84	579.14	494.09	438.36
22000	1980.50	1061.49	757.26	606.72	517.62	459.24
23000	2070.52	1109.74	791.68	634.29	541.15	480.11
24000	2160.54	1157.99	826.10	661.87	564.68	500.99
25000	2250.57	1206.24	860.53	689.45	588.21	521.86
30000	2700.68	1447.48	1032.63	827.34	705.85	626.23
35000	3150.79	1688.73	1204.74	965.23	823.49	730.61
40000	3600.91	1929.98	1376.84	1103.12	941.13	834.98
45000	4051.02	2171.23	1548.95	1241.01	1058.77	939.35
50000	4501.13	2412.47	1721.05	1378.90	1176.42	1043.72
55000	4951.25	2653.72	1893.16	1516.79	1294.06	1148.09
60000	5401.36	2894.97	2065.26	1654.68	1411.70	1252.47
65000	5851.47	3136.22	2237.37	1792.57	1529.34	1356.84
70000	6301.58	3377.46	2409.47	1930.46	1646.98	1461.21
75000	6751.70	3618.71	2581.58	2068.35	1764.62	1565.58
80000	7201.81	3859.96	2753.68	2206.24	1882.26	1669.96
85000	7651.92	4101.21	2925.79	2344.13	1999.91	1774.33
90000	8102.04	4342.45	3097.89	2482.02	2117.55	1878.70
95000	8552.15	4583.70	3270.00	2619.91	2235.19	1983.07
100000	9002.26	4824.95	3442.10	2757.80	2352.83	2087.44
200000	18004.50	9649.90	6884.20	5515.60	4705.66	4174.89
300000	27006.80	14474.80	10326.30	8273.40	7058.49	6262.33
400000	36009.10	19299.80	13768.40	11031.20	9411.32	8349.78
500000	45011.30	24124.70	17210.50	13789.00	11764.20	10437.20

MONTHLY PAYMENT

Necessary to amortize a loan

14 1/2%

TERM / AMOUNT	7 YEARS	8 YEARS	9 YEARS	10 YEARS	11 YEARS	12 YEARS
500	9.51	8.83	8.31	7.91	7.60	7.34
600	11.41	10.59	9.98	9.50	9.12	8.81
700	13.31	12.36	11.64	11.08	10.64	10.28
800	15.21	14.13	13.30	12.66	12.16	11.75
900	17.12	15.89	14.97	14.25	13.68	13.22
1000	19.02	17.66	16.63	15.83	15.20	14.69
2000	38.03	35.31	33.26	31.66	30.39	29.38
3000	57.05	52.97	49.88	47.49	45.59	44.07
4000	76.07	70.63	66.51	63.31	60.79	58.75
5000	95.09	88.29	83.14	79.14	75.98	73.44
6000	114.10	105.94	99.77	94.97	91.18	88.13
7000	133.12	123.60	116.39	110.80	106.38	102.82
8000	152.14	141.26	133.02	126.63	121.57	117.51
9000	171.16	158.92	149.65	142.46	136.77	132.20
10000	190.17	176.57	166.28	158.29	151.96	146.89
11000	209.19	194.23	182.91	174.12	167.16	161.57
12000	228.21	211.89	199.53	189.94	182.36	176.26
13000	247.23	229.55	216.16	205.77	197.55	190.95
14000	266.24	247.20	232.79	221.60	212.75	205.64
15000	285.26	264.86	249.42	237.43	227.95	220.33
16000	304.28	282.52	266.04	253.26	243.14	235.02
17000	323.29	300.17	282.67	269.09	258.34	249.70
18000	342.31	317.83	299.30	284.92	273.54	264.39
19000	361.33	335.49	315.93	300.75	288.73	279.08
20000	380.35	353.15	332.56	316.57	303.93	293.77
21000	399.36	370.80	349.18	332.40	319.13	308.46
22000	418.38	388.46	365.81	348.23	334.32	323.15
23000	437.40	406.12	382.44	364.06	349.52	337.84
24000	456.42	423.77	399.07	379.89	364.72	352.52
25000	475.43	441.43	415.69	395.72	379.91	367.21
30000	570.52	529.72	498.83	474.86	455.89	440.66
35000	665.61	618.00	581.97	554.00	531.88	514.10
40000	760.69	706.29	665.11	633.15	607.86	587.54
45000	855.78	794.58	748.25	712.29	683.84	660.98
50000	950.87	882.86	831.39	791.43	759.82	734.43
55000	1045.95	971.15	914.53	870.58	835.81	807.87
60000	1141.04	1059.44	997.66	949.72	911.79	881.31
65000	1236.13	1147.72	1080.80	1028.86	987.77	954.75
70000	1331.21	1236.01	1163.94	1108.01	1063.75	1028.19
75000	1426.30	1324.30	1247.08	1187.15	1139.73	1101.64
80000	1521.39	1412.58	1330.22	1266.30	1215.72	1175.08
85000	1616.47	1500.87	1413.36	1345.44	1291.70	1248.52
90000	1711.56	1589.15	1496.50	1424.58	1367.68	1321.96
95000	1806.65	1677.44	1579.63	1503.73	1443.66	1395.41
100000	1901.73	1765.73	1662.77	1582.87	1519.64	1468.85
200000	3803.46	3531.45	3325.55	3165.74	3039.29	2937.70
300000	5705.20	5297.18	4988.32	4748.61	4558.93	4406.55
400000	7606.93	7062.91	6651.09	6331.48	6078.58	5875.40
500000	9508.66	8828.63	8313.87	7914.34	7598.22	7344.25

14 1/2% MONTHLY PAYMENT

Necessary to amortize a loan

TERM / AMOUNT	13 YEARS	14 YEARS	15 YEARS	16 YEARS	17 YEARS	18 YEARS
500	7.14	6.97	6.83	6.71	6.61	6.53
600	8.57	8.36	8.19	8.05	7.93	7.84
700	9.99	9.76	9.56	9.39	9.26	9.14
800	11.42	11.15	10.92	10.74	10.58	10.45
900	12.85	12.54	12.29	12.08	11.90	11.75
1000	14.28	13.94	13.66	13.42	13.22	13.06
2000	28.55	27.87	27.31	26.84	26.45	26.12
3000	42.83	41.81	40.97	40.26	39.67	39.18
4000	57.10	55.74	54.62	53.68	52.90	52.24
5000	71.38	69.68	68.28	67.10	66.12	65.29
6000	85.65	83.62	81.93	80.52	79.35	78.35
7000	99.93	97.55	95.59	93.94	92.57	91.41
8000	114.20	111.49	109.24	107.37	105.79	104.47
9000	128.48	125.42	122.90	120.79	119.02	117.53
10000	142.75	139.36	136.55	134.21	132.24	130.59
11000	157.03	153.30	150.21	147.63	145.47	143.65
12000	171.31	167.23	163.86	161.05	158.69	156.71
13000	185.58	181.17	177.52	174.47	171.92	169.76
14000	199.86	195.11	191.17	187.89	185.14	182.82
15000	214.13	209.04	204.83	201.31	198.36	195.88
16000	228.41	222.98	218.48	214.73	211.59	208.94
17000	242.68	236.91	232.14	228.15	224.81	222.00
18000	256.96	250.85	245.79	241.57	238.04	235.06
19000	271.23	264.79	259.45	254.99	251.26	248.12
20000	285.51	278.72	273.10	268.41	264.49	261.18
21000	299.78	292.66	286.76	281.84	277.71	274.23
22000	314.06	306.59	300.41	295.26	290.93	287.29
23000	328.33	320.53	314.07	308.68	304.16	300.35
24000	342.61	334.47	327.72	322.10	317.38	313.41
25000	356.89	348.40	341.38	335.52	330.61	326.47
30000	428.26	418.08	409.65	402.62	396.73	391.76
35000	499.64	487.76	477.93	469.73	462.85	457.06
40000	571.02	557.44	546.20	536.83	528.97	522.35
45000	642.39	627.12	614.48	603.93	595.09	587.64
50000	713.77	696.80	682.75	671.04	661.21	652.94
55000	785.15	766.48	751.03	738.14	727.33	718.23
60000	856.52	836.16	819.30	805.24	793.46	783.53
65000	927.90	905.84	887.58	872.35	859.58	848.82
70000	999.28	975.52	955.85	939.45	925.70	914.11
75000	1070.65	1045.20	1024.13	1006.55	991.82	979.41
80000	1142.03	1114.88	1092.40	1073.66	1057.94	1044.70
85000	1213.41	1184.56	1160.68	1140.76	1124.06	1109.99
90000	1284.78	1254.24	1228.95	1207.86	1190.18	1175.29
95000	1356.16	1323.92	1297.23	1274.97	1256.30	1240.58
100000	1427.54	1393.60	1365.50	1342.07	1322.42	1305.87
200000	2855.08	2787.21	2731.00	2684.14	2644.85	2611.75
300000	4282.61	4180.81	4096.50	4026.21	3967.27	3917.62
400000	5710.15	5574.42	5462.01	5368.28	5289.70	5223.50
500000	7137.69	6968.02	6827.51	6710.35	6612.12	6529.37

MONTHLY PAYMENT

Necessary to amortize a loan

14 1/2%

TERM AMOUNT	19 YEARS	20 YEARS	25 YEARS	30 YEARS	35 YEARS	40 YEARS
500	6.46	6.40	6.21	6.12	6.08	6.06
600	7.75	7.68	7.45	7.35	7.30	7.27
700	9.04	8.96	8.70	8.57	8.51	8.48
800	10.34	10.24	9.94	9.80	9.73	9.70
900	11.63	11.52	11.18	11.02	10.95	10.91
1000	12.92	12.80	12.42	12.25	12.16	12.12
2000	25.84	25.60	24.84	24.49	24.32	24.24
3000	38.76	38.40	37.26	36.74	36.49	36.36
4000	51.68	51.20	49.69	48.98	48.65	48.49
5000	64.59	64.00	62.11	61.23	60.81	60.61
6000	77.51	76.80	74.53	73.47	72.97	72.73
7000	90.43	89.60	86.95	85.72	85.13	84.85
8000	103.35	102.40	99.37	97.96	97.29	96.97
9000	116.27	115.20	111.80	110.21	109.46	109.09
10000	129.19	128.00	124.22	122.46	121.62	121.21
11000	142.11	140.80	136.64	134.70	133.78	133.34
12000	155.03	153.60	149.06	146.95	145.94	145.46
13000	167.94	166.40	161.48	159.19	158.10	157.58
14000	180.86	179.20	173.90	171.44	170.26	169.70
15000	193.78	192.00	186.32	183.68	182.43	181.82
16000	206.70	204.80	198.75	195.93	194.59	193.94
17000	219.62	217.60	211.17	208.18	206.75	206.06
18000	232.54	230.40	223.59	220.42	218.91	218.18
19000	245.46	243.20	236.01	232.67	231.07	230.31
20000	258.38	256.00	248.43	244.91	243.23	242.43
21000	271.29	268.80	260.85	257.16	255.40	254.55
22000	284.21	281.60	273.28	269.40	267.56	266.67
23000	297.13	294.40	285.70	281.65	279.72	278.79
24000	310.05	307.20	298.12	293.89	291.88	290.91
25000	322.97	320.00	310.54	306.14	304.04	303.03
30000	387.56	384.00	372.65	367.37	364.85	363.64
35000	452.16	448.00	434.76	428.60	425.66	424.25
40000	516.75	512.00	496.87	489.82	486.47	484.85
45000	581.35	576.00	558.97	551.05	547.28	545.46
50000	645.94	640.00	621.08	612.28	608.09	606.07
55000	710.53	704.00	683.19	673.51	668.89	666.67
60000	775.13	768.00	745.30	734.73	729.70	727.28
65000	839.72	832.00	807.41	795.96	790.51	787.89
70000	904.31	896.00	869.51	857.19	851.32	848.49
75000	968.91	960.00	931.62	918.42	912.13	909.10
80000	1033.50	1024.00	993.73	979.65	972.94	969.71
85000	1098.10	1088.00	1055.84	1040.87	1033.75	1030.31
90000	1162.69	1152.00	1117.95	1102.10	1094.55	1090.92
95000	1227.28	1216.00	1180.06	1163.33	1155.36	1151.53
100000	1291.88	1280.00	1242.16	1224.56	1216.17	1212.13
200000	2583.75	2560.00	2484.33	2449.11	2432.34	2424.27
300000	3875.63	3839.99	3726.49	3673.67	3648.51	3636.40
400000	5167.51	5119.99	4968.65	4898.22	4864.68	4848.53
500000	6459.38	6399.99	6210.82	6122.78	6080.85	6060.67

14 3/4%

MONTHLY PAYMENT

Necessary to amortize a loan

TERM AMOUNT	1 YEAR	2 YEARS	3 YEARS	4 YEARS	5 YEARS	6 YEARS
500	45.07	24.18	17.27	13.85	11.83	10.50
600	54.08	29.02	20.73	16.62	14.20	12.61
700	63.10	33.86	24.18	19.39	16.56	14.71
800	72.11	38.69	27.63	22.16	18.93	16.81
900	81.13	43.53	31.09	24.93	21.29	18.91
1000	90.14	48.37	34.54	27.70	23.66	21.01
2000	180.28	96.74	69.09	55.41	47.32	42.02
3000	270.42	145.10	103.63	83.11	70.98	63.03
4000	360.56	193.47	138.47	110.82	94.64	84.04
5000	450.70	241.84	172.72	138.52	118.30	105.05
6000	540.84	290.21	207.26	166.23	141.95	126.06
7000	630.98	338.58	241.80	193.93	165.61	147.07
8000	721.12	386.94	276.35	221.63	189.27	168.08
9000	811.27	435.31	310.89	249.34	212.93	189.09
10000	901.41	483.68	345.43	277.04	236.59	210.10
11000	991.55	532.05	379.97	304.75	260.25	231.11
12000	1081.69	580.42	414.52	332.45	283.91	252.11
13000	1171.83	628.78	449.06	360.16	307.57	273.12
14000	1261.97	677.15	483.60	387.86	331.23	294.13
15000	1352.11	725.52	518.15	415.56	354.88	315.14
16000	1442.25	773.89	552.69	443.27	378.54	336.15
17000	1532.39	822.26	587.23	470.97	402.20	357.16
18000	1622.53	870.63	621.78	498.68	425.86	378.17
19000	1712.67	918.99	656.32	526.38	449.52	399.18
20000	1802.81	967.36	690.86	554.08	473.18	420.19
21000	1892.95	1015.73	725.41	581.79	496.84	441.20
22000	1983.09	1064.10	759.95	609.49	520.50	462.21
23000	2073.23	1112.46	794.49	637.20	544.16	483.22
24000	2163.37	1160.83	829.03	664.90	567.81	504.23
25000	2253.51	1209.20	863.58	692.61	591.47	525.24
30000	2704.22	1451.04	1036.29	831.13	709.77	630.29
35000	3154.92	1692.88	1209.01	969.65	828.06	735.33
40000	3605.62	1934.72	1381.72	1108.17	946.36	840.38
45000	4056.32	2176.56	1554.44	1246.69	1064.65	945.43
50000	4507.03	2418.40	1727.15	1385.21	1182.95	1050.48
55000	4957.73	2660.24	1899.87	1523.73	1301.24	1155.52
60000	5408.43	2902.08	2072.58	1662.25	1419.54	1260.57
65000	5859.14	3143.92	2245.30	1800.77	1537.83	1365.62
70000	6309.84	3385.76	2418.02	1939.30	1656.13	1470.67
75000	6760.54	3627.60	2590.73	2077.82	1774.42	1575.71
80000	7211.24	3869.44	2763.45	2216.34	1892.71	1680.76
85000	7661.95	4111.28	2936.16	2354.86	2011.01	1785.81
90000	8112.65	4353.12	3108.88	2493.38	2129.30	1890.86
95000	8563.35	4594.96	3281.59	2631.90	2247.60	1995.90
100000	9014.05	4836.80	3454.31	2770.42	2365.89	2100.95
200000	18028.10	9673.61	6908.62	5540.84	4731.79	4201.90
300000	27042.20	14510.40	10362.90	8311.27	7097.68	6302.85
400000	36056.20	19347.20	13817.20	11081.70	9463.57	8403.80
500000	45070.30	24184.00	17271.50	13852.10	11829.50	10504.80

MONTHLY PAYMENT

Necessary to amortize a loan

14 3/4%

TERM / AMOUNT	7 YEARS	8 YEARS	9 YEARS	10 YEARS	11 YEARS	12 YEARS
500	9.58	8.90	8.39	7.99	7.68	7.42
600	11.49	10.68	10.07	9.59	9.21	8.91
700	13.41	12.46	11.74	11.19	10.75	10.39
800	15.33	14.24	13.42	12.78	12.28	11.88
900	17.24	16.02	15.10	14.38	13.82	13.36
1000	19.16	17.80	16.78	15.98	15.35	14.85
2000	38.31	35.60	33.55	31.96	30.70	29.70
3000	57.47	53.40	50.33	47.94	46.06	44.54
4000	76.63	71.20	67.10	63.92	61.41	59.39
5000	95.78	89.01	83.88	79.90	76.76	74.24
6000	114.94	106.81	100.65	95.88	92.11	89.09
7000	134.10	124.61	117.43	111.87	107.47	103.94
8000	153.25	142.41	134.21	127.85	122.82	118.79
9000	172.41	160.21	150.98	143.83	138.17	133.63
10000	191.57	178.01	167.76	159.81	153.52	148.48
11000	210.73	195.81	184.53	175.79	168.88	163.33
12000	229.88	213.61	201.31	191.77	184.23	178.18
13000	249.04	231.41	218.08	207.75	199.58	193.03
14000	268.20	249.22	234.86	223.73	214.93	207.88
15000	287.35	267.02	251.64	239.71	230.29	222.72
16000	306.51	284.82	268.41	255.69	245.64	237.57
17000	325.67	302.62	285.19	271.67	260.99	252.42
18000	344.82	320.42	301.96	287.65	276.34	267.27
19000	363.98	338.22	318.74	303.63	291.70	282.12
20000	383.14	356.02	335.51	319.62	307.05	296.97
21000	402.29	373.82	352.29	335.60	322.40	311.81
22000	421.45	391.62	369.07	351.58	337.75	326.66
23000	440.61	409.42	385.84	367.56	353.11	341.51
24000	459.76	427.23	402.62	383.54	368.46	356.36
25000	478.92	445.03	419.39	399.52	383.81	371.21
30000	574.70	534.03	503.27	479.42	460.57	445.45
35000	670.49	623.04	587.15	559.33	537.34	519.69
40000	766.27	712.04	671.03	639.23	614.10	593.93
45000	862.06	801.05	754.91	719.13	690.86	668.17
50000	957.84	890.05	838.79	799.04	767.62	742.41
55000	1053.62	979.06	922.67	878.94	844.38	816.65
60000	1149.41	1068.06	1006.54	958.85	921.15	890.90
65000	1245.19	1157.07	1090.42	1038.75	997.91	965.14
70000	1340.97	1246.07	1174.30	1118.65	1074.67	1039.38
75000	1436.76	1335.08	1258.18	1198.56	1151.43	1113.62
80000	1532.54	1424.08	1342.06	1278.46	1228.20	1187.86
85000	1628.33	1513.09	1425.94	1358.36	1304.96	1262.10
90000	1724.11	1602.09	1509.81	1438.27	1381.72	1336.34
95000	1819.89	1691.10	1593.69	1518.17	1458.48	1410.58
100000	1915.68	1780.11	1677.57	1598.08	1535.24	1484.83
200000	3831.36	3560.21	3355.14	3196.15	3070.49	2969.65
300000	5747.03	5340.31	5032.72	4794.23	4605.73	4454.48
400000	7662.71	7120.42	6710.29	6392.30	6140.98	5939.30
500000	9578.39	8900.53	8387.86	7990.38	7676.22	7424.13

14 3/4%

MONTHLY PAYMENT
Necessary to amortize a loan

TERM / AMOUNT	13 YEARS	14 YEARS	15 YEARS	16 YEARS	17 YEARS	18 YEARS
500	7.22	7.05	6.91	6.80	6.70	6.62
600	8.66	8.46	8.30	8.16	8.04	7.94
700	10.11	9.87	9.68	9.52	9.38	9.27
800	11.55	11.28	11.06	10.88	10.72	10.59
900	12.99	12.69	12.44	12.23	12.06	11.91
1000	14.44	14.10	13.83	13.59	13.40	13.24
2000	28.88	28.21	27.65	27.19	26.80	26.47
3000	43.32	42.31	41.48	40.78	40.20	39.71
4000	57.76	56.41	55.30	54.38	53.60	52.95
5000	72.19	70.51	69.13	67.97	67.00	66.19
6000	86.63	84.62	82.95	81.56	80.40	79.42
7000	101.07	98.72	96.78	95.16	93.80	92.66
8000	115.51	112.82	110.60	108.75	107.20	105.90
9000	129.95	126.93	124.43	122.34	120.60	119.14
10000	144.39	141.03	138.25	135.94	134.00	132.37
11000	158.83	155.13	152.08	149.53	147.40	145.61
12000	173.27	169.23	165.90	163.13	160.80	158.85
13000	187.70	183.34	179.73	176.72	174.20	172.09
14000	202.14	197.44	193.55	190.31	187.60	185.32
15000	216.58	211.54	207.38	203.91	201.00	198.56
16000	231.02	225.65	221.20	217.50	214.40	211.80
17000	245.46	239.75	235.03	231.10	227.80	225.04
18000	259.90	253.85	248.85	244.69	241.20	238.27
19000	274.34	267.95	262.68	258.28	254.60	251.51
20000	288.78	282.06	276.50	271.88	268.01	264.75
21000	303.21	296.16	290.33	285.47	281.41	277.99
22000	317.65	310.26	304.15	299.06	294.81	291.22
23000	332.09	324.37	317.98	312.66	308.21	304.46
24000	346.53	338.47	331.80	326.25	321.61	317.70
25000	360.97	352.57	345.63	339.85	335.01	330.94
30000	433.16	423.09	414.75	407.81	402.01	397.12
35000	505.36	493.60	483.88	475.78	469.01	463.31
40000	577.55	564.11	553.00	543.75	536.01	529.50
45000	649.74	634.63	622.13	611.72	603.01	595.68
50000	721.94	705.14	691.25	679.69	670.01	661.87
55000	794.13	775.66	760.38	747.66	737.01	728.06
60000	866.33	846.17	829.50	815.63	804.01	794.25
65000	938.52	916.68	898.63	883.60	871.02	860.43
70000	1010.71	987.20	967.75	951.57	938.02	926.62
75000	1082.91	1057.71	1036.88	1019.54	1005.02	992.81
80000	1155.10	1128.23	1106.00	1087.50	1072.02	1058.99
85000	1227.29	1198.74	1175.13	1155.47	1139.02	1125.18
90000	1299.49	1269.25	1244.25	1223.44	1206.02	1191.37
95000	1371.68	1339.77	1313.38	1291.41	1273.02	1257.56
100000	1443.87	1410.28	1382.50	1359.38	1340.02	1323.74
200000	2887.75	2820.56	2765.01	2718.76	2680.05	2647.49
300000	4331.62	4230.85	4147.51	4078.14	4020.07	3971.23
400000	5775.50	5641.13	5530.02	5437.52	5360.09	5294.97
500000	7219.37	7051.41	6912.52	6796.90	6700.11	6618.71

MONTHLY PAYMENT

Necessary to amortize a loan

14 3/4%

TERM / AMOUNT	19 YEARS	20 YEARS	25 YEARS	30 YEARS	35 YEARS	40 YEARS
500	6.55	6.49	6.31	6.22	6.18	6.16
600	7.86	7.79	7.57	7.47	7.42	7.40
700	9.17	9.09	8.83	8.71	8.66	8.63
800	10.48	10.39	10.09	9.96	9.89	9.86
900	11.79	11.69	11.35	11.20	11.13	11.09
1000	13.10	12.98	12.61	12.44	12.36	12.33
2000	26.20	25.97	25.23	24.89	24.73	24.65
3000	39.30	38.95	37.84	37.33	37.09	36.98
4000	52.40	51.93	50.46	49.78	49.46	49.31
5000	65.50	64.92	63.07	62.22	61.82	61.63
6000	78.60	77.90	75.69	74.67	74.19	73.96
7000	91.70	90.88	88.30	87.11	86.55	86.29
8000	104.80	103.87	100.92	99.56	98.92	98.61
9000	117.90	116.85	113.53	112.00	111.28	110.94
10000	131.00	129.84	126.15	124.45	123.65	123.27
11000	144.10	142.82	138.76	136.89	136.01	135.59
12000	157.20	155.80	151.38	149.34	148.38	147.92
13000	170.30	168.79	163.99	161.78	160.74	160.25
14000	183.40	181.77	176.61	174.23	173.11	172.57
15000	196.50	194.75	189.22	186.67	185.47	184.90
16000	209.60	207.74	201.83	199.12	197.84	197.23
17000	222.70	220.72	214.45	211.56	210.20	209.55
18000	235.80	233.70	227.06	224.01	222.57	221.88
19000	248.90	246.69	239.68	236.45	234.93	234.21
20000	262.00	259.67	252.29	248.90	247.30	246.53
21000	275.10	272.66	264.91	261.34	259.66	258.86
22000	288.20	285.64	277.52	273.79	272.02	271.19
23000	301.30	298.62	290.14	286.23	284.39	283.51
24000	314.40	311.61	302.75	298.67	296.75	295.84
25000	327.50	324.59	315.37	311.12	309.12	308.17
30000	393.00	389.51	378.44	373.34	370.94	369.80
35000	458.50	454.42	441.51	435.57	432.77	431.43
40000	524.00	519.34	504.59	497.79	494.59	493.07
45000	589.50	584.26	567.66	560.01	556.41	554.70
50000	655.00	649.18	630.73	622.24	618.24	616.33
55000	720.50	714.10	693.81	684.46	680.06	677.97
60000	786.00	779.01	756.88	746.69	741.89	739.60
65000	851.50	843.93	819.95	808.91	803.71	801.23
70000	917.00	908.85	883.03	871.13	865.53	862.87
75000	982.50	973.77	946.10	933.36	927.36	924.50
80000	1048.00	1038.68	1009.17	995.58	989.18	986.13
85000	1113.50	1103.60	1072.24	1057.80	1051.00	1047.77
90000	1179.00	1168.52	1135.32	1120.03	1112.83	1109.40
95000	1244.50	1233.44	1198.39	1182.25	1174.65	1171.03
100000	1310.00	1298.36	1261.46	1244.48	1236.47	1232.67
200000	2620.00	2596.71	2522.93	2488.95	2472.95	2465.33
300000	3929.99	3895.07	3784.39	3733.43	3709.42	3698.00
400000	5239.99	5193.42	5045.86	4977.90	4945.90	4930.67
500000	6549.99	6491.78	6307.32	6222.38	6182.37	6163.34

15%

MONTHLY PAYMENT
Necessary to amortize a loan

TERM / AMOUNT	1 YEAR	2 YEARS	3 YEARS	4 YEARS	5 YEARS	6 YEARS
500	45.13	24.24	17.33	13.92	11.89	10.57
600	54.15	29.09	20.80	16.70	14.27	12.69
700	63.18	33.94	24.27	19.48	16.65	14.80
800	72.21	38.79	27.73	22.26	19.03	16.92
900	81.23	43.64	31.20	25.05	21.41	19.03
1000	90.26	48.49	34.67	27.83	23.79	21.14
2000	180.52	96.97	69.33	55.66	47.58	42.29
3000	270.77	145.46	104.00	83.49	71.37	63.43
4000	361.03	193.95	138.66	111.32	95.16	84.58
5000	451.29	242.43	173.33	139.15	118.95	105.73
6000	541.55	290.92	207.99	166.98	142.74	126.87
7000	631.81	339.41	242.66	194.81	166.53	148.02
8000	722.06	387.89	277.32	222.65	190.32	169.16
9000	812.32	436.38	311.99	250.48	214.11	190.30
10000	902.58	484.86	346.65	278.31	237.90	211.45
11000	992.84	533.35	381.32	306.14	261.69	232.59
12000	1083.09	581.84	415.98	333.97	285.48	253.74
13000	1173.35	630.32	450.65	361.80	309.27	274.88
14000	1263.61	678.81	485.31	389.63	333.06	296.03
15000	1353.87	727.30	519.98	417.46	356.85	317.17
16000	1444.13	775.78	554.64	445.29	380.64	338.32
17000	1534.38	824.27	589.31	473.12	404.43	359.46
18000	1624.64	872.76	623.97	500.95	428.22	380.61
19000	1714.90	921.24	658.64	528.78	452.01	401.75
20000	1805.16	969.73	693.30	556.61	475.80	422.90
21000	1895.41	1018.21	727.97	584.44	499.59	444.04
22000	1985.67	1066.70	762.63	612.27	523.38	465.19
23000	2075.93	1115.19	797.30	640.11	547.17	486.33
24000	2166.19	1163.67	831.96	667.94	570.96	507.48
25000	2256.45	1212.16	866.63	695.77	594.75	528.62
30000	2707.73	1454.59	1039.96	834.92	713.70	634.35
35000	3159.02	1697.02	1213.28	974.07	832.65	740.07
40000	3610.31	1939.46	1386.61	1113.23	951.59	845.80
45000	4061.60	2181.89	1559.93	1252.38	1070.54	951.52
50000	4512.89	2424.32	1733.26	1391.53	1189.49	1057.25
55000	4964.18	2666.75	1906.59	1530.69	1308.44	1162.97
60000	5415.47	2909.19	2079.91	1669.84	1427.39	1268.70
65000	5866.76	3151.62	2253.24	1808.99	1546.34	1374.42
70000	6318.05	3394.05	2426.56	1948.14	1665.29	1480.15
75000	6769.34	3636.48	2599.89	2087.30	1784.24	1585.87
80000	7220.62	3878.91	2773.21	2226.45	1903.19	1691.60
85000	7671.91	4121.35	2946.54	2365.60	2022.14	1797.32
90000	8123.20	4363.78	3119.87	2504.76	2141.09	1903.04
95000	8574.49	4606.21	3293.19	2643.91	2260.04	2008.77
100000	9025.78	4848.64	3466.52	2783.06	2378.98	2114.49
200000	18051.60	9697.28	6933.04	5566.13	4757.97	4228.99
300000	27077.30	14545.90	10399.60	8349.19	7136.95	6343.48
400000	36103.10	19394.60	13866.10	11132.30	9515.94	8457.98
500000	45128.90	24243.20	17332.60	13915.30	11894.90	10572.50

MONTHLY PAYMENT

Necessary to amortize a loan

15%

TERM / AMOUNT	7 YEARS	8 YEARS	9 YEARS	10 YEARS	11 YEARS	12 YEARS
500	9.65	8.97	8.46	8.07	7.75	7.50
600	11.58	10.77	10.15	9.68	9.31	9.01
700	13.51	12.56	11.85	11.29	10.86	10.51
800	15.44	14.36	13.54	12.91	12.41	12.01
900	17.37	16.15	15.23	14.52	13.96	13.51
1000	19.30	17.95	16.92	16.13	15.51	15.01
2000	38.59	35.89	33.85	32.27	31.02	30.02
3000	57.89	53.84	50.77	48.40	46.53	45.03
4000	77.19	71.78	67.70	64.53	62.04	60.04
5000	96.48	89.73	84.62	80.67	77.55	75.04
6000	115.78	107.67	101.55	96.80	93.05	90.05
7000	135.08	125.62	118.47	112.93	108.56	105.06
8000	154.37	143.56	135.39	129.07	124.07	120.07
9000	173.67	161.51	152.32	145.20	139.58	135.08
10000	192.97	179.45	169.24	161.34	155.09	150.09
11000	212.26	197.40	186.17	177.47	170.60	165.10
12000	231.56	215.34	203.09	193.60	186.11	180.11
13000	250.86	233.29	220.02	209.74	201.62	195.11
14000	270.15	251.24	236.94	225.87	217.13	210.12
15000	289.45	269.18	253.86	242.00	232.64	225.13
16000	308.75	287.13	270.79	258.14	248.15	240.14
17000	328.04	305.07	287.71	274.27	263.66	255.15
18000	347.34	323.02	304.64	290.40	279.16	270.16
19000	366.64	340.96	321.56	306.54	294.67	285.17
20000	385.93	358.91	338.49	322.67	310.18	300.18
21000	405.23	376.85	355.41	338.80	325.69	315.18
22000	424.53	394.80	372.33	354.94	341.20	330.19
23000	443.82	412.74	389.26	371.07	356.71	345.20
24000	463.12	430.69	406.18	387.20	372.22	360.21
25000	482.42	448.63	423.11	403.34	387.73	375.22
30000	578.90	538.36	507.73	484.00	465.27	450.26
35000	675.38	628.09	592.35	564.67	542.82	525.31
40000	771.87	717.81	676.97	645.34	620.37	600.35
45000	868.35	807.54	761.59	726.01	697.91	675.39
50000	964.84	897.27	846.22	806.67	775.46	750.44
55000	1061.32	987.00	930.84	887.34	853.00	825.48
60000	1157.80	1076.72	1015.46	968.01	930.55	900.52
65000	1254.29	1166.45	1100.08	1048.67	1008.09	975.57
70000	1350.77	1256.17	1184.70	1129.34	1085.64	1050.61
75000	1447.25	1345.90	1269.32	1210.01	1163.18	1125.66
80000	1543.74	1435.63	1353.94	1290.68	1240.73	1200.70
85000	1640.22	1525.36	1438.56	1371.34	1318.27	1275.74
90000	1736.70	1615.08	1523.19	1452.01	1395.82	1350.79
95000	1833.19	1704.81	1607.81	1532.68	1473.37	1425.83
100000	1929.67	1794.54	1692.43	1613.35	1550.91	1500.87
200000	3859.34	3589.07	3384.86	3226.69	3101.82	3001.75
300000	5789.01	5383.61	5077.29	4840.04	4652.74	4502.62
400000	7718.68	7178.14	6769.72	6453.38	6203.65	6003.50
500000	9648.35	8972.68	8462.15	8066.73	7754.56	7504.37

15%

MONTHLY PAYMENT

Necessary to amortize a loan

TERM / AMOUNT	13 YEARS	14 YEARS	15 YEARS	16 YEARS	17 YEARS	18 YEARS
500	7.30	7.14	7.00	6.88	6.79	6.71
600	8.76	8.56	8.40	8.26	8.15	8.05
700	10.22	9.99	9.80	9.64	9.50	9.39
800	11.68	11.42	11.20	11.01	10.86	10.73
900	13.14	12.84	12.60	12.39	12.22	12.08
1000	14.60	14.27	14.00	13.77	13.58	13.42
2000	29.21	28.54	27.99	27.54	27.15	26.83
3000	43.81	42.81	41.99	41.30	40.73	40.25
4000	58.41	57.08	55.98	55.07	54.31	53.67
5000	73.01	71.35	69.98	68.84	67.88	67.08
6000	87.62	85.62	83.98	82.61	81.46	80.50
7000	102.22	99.89	97.97	96.37	95.04	93.92
8000	116.82	114.16	111.97	110.14	108.62	107.34
9000	131.43	128.43	125.96	123.91	122.19	120.75
10000	146.03	142.70	139.96	137.68	135.77	134.17
11000	160.63	156.97	153.95	151.44	149.35	147.59
12000	175.23	171.24	167.95	165.21	162.92	161.00
13000	189.84	185.52	181.95	178.98	176.50	174.42
14000	204.44	199.79	195.94	192.75	190.08	187.84
15000	219.04	214.06	209.94	206.52	203.66	201.25
16000	233.65	228.33	223.93	220.28	217.23	214.67
17000	248.25	242.60	237.93	234.05	230.81	228.09
18000	262.85	256.87	251.93	247.82	244.39	241.50
19000	277.45	271.14	265.92	261.59	257.96	254.92
20000	292.06	285.41	279.92	275.35	271.54	268.34
21000	306.66	299.68	293.91	289.12	285.12	281.76
22000	321.26	313.95	307.91	302.89	298.69	295.17
23000	335.87	328.22	321.91	316.66	312.27	308.59
24000	350.47	342.49	335.90	330.42	325.85	322.01
25000	365.07	356.76	349.90	344.19	339.43	335.42
30000	438.09	428.11	419.88	413.03	407.31	402.51
35000	511.10	499.46	489.86	481.87	475.20	469.59
40000	584.11	570.82	559.83	550.71	543.08	536.68
45000	657.13	642.17	629.81	619.55	610.96	603.76
50000	730.14	713.52	699.79	688.38	678.85	670.85
55000	803.16	784.87	769.77	757.22	746.73	737.93
60000	876.17	856.22	839.75	826.06	814.62	805.01
65000	949.19	927.57	909.73	894.90	882.50	872.10
70000	1022.20	998.93	979.71	963.74	950.39	939.18
75000	1095.21	1070.28	1049.69	1032.58	1018.27	1006.27
80000	1168.23	1141.63	1119.67	1101.41	1086.16	1073.35
85000	1241.24	1212.98	1189.65	1170.25	1154.04	1140.44
90000	1314.26	1284.33	1259.63	1239.09	1221.93	1207.52
95000	1387.27	1355.69	1329.61	1307.93	1289.81	1274.60
100000	1460.28	1427.04	1399.59	1376.77	1357.70	1341.69
200000	2920.57	2854.07	2799.17	2753.54	2715.40	2683.38
300000	4380.85	4281.11	4198.76	4130.30	4073.10	4025.07
400000	5841.14	5708.15	5598.34	5507.07	5430.80	5366.76
500000	7301.42	7135.19	6997.93	6883.84	6788.49	6708.45

MONTHLY PAYMENT
Necessary to amortize a loan

15%

TERM / AMOUNT	19 YEARS	20 YEARS	25 YEARS	30 YEARS	35 YEARS	40 YEARS
500	6.64	6.58	6.40	6.32	6.28	6.27
600	7.97	7.90	7.68	7.59	7.54	7.52
700	9.30	9.22	8.97	8.85	8.80	8.77
800	10.63	10.53	10.25	10.12	10.05	10.03
900	11.95	11.85	11.53	11.38	11.31	11.28
1000	13.28	13.17	12.81	12.64	12.57	12.53
2000	26.56	26.34	25.62	25.29	25.14	25.06
3000	39.85	39.50	38.42	37.93	37.70	37.60
4000	53.13	52.67	51.23	50.58	50.27	50.13
5000	66.41	65.84	64.04	63.22	62.84	62.66
6000	79.69	79.01	76.85	75.87	75.41	75.19
7000	92.97	92.18	89.66	88.51	87.98	87.73
8000	106.26	105.34	102.47	101.16	100.55	100.26
9000	119.54	118.51	115.28	113.80	113.11	112.79
10000	132.82	131.68	128.08	126.44	125.68	125.32
11000	146.10	144.85	140.89	139.09	138.25	137.86
12000	159.38	158.02	153.70	151.73	150.82	150.39
13000	172.67	171.18	166.51	164.38	163.39	162.92
14000	185.95	184.35	179.32	177.02	175.95	175.45
15000	199.23	197.52	192.12	189.67	188.52	187.98
16000	212.51	210.69	204.93	202.31	201.09	200.52
17000	225.79	223.85	217.74	214.96	213.66	213.05
18000	239.08	237.02	230.55	227.60	226.23	225.58
19000	252.36	250.19	243.36	240.24	238.79	238.11
20000	265.64	263.36	256.17	252.89	251.36	250.65
21000	278.92	276.53	268.97	265.53	263.93	263.18
22000	292.20	289.69	281.78	278.18	276.50	275.71
23000	305.49	302.86	294.59	290.82	289.07	288.24
24000	318.77	316.03	307.40	303.47	301.64	300.77
25000	332.05	329.20	320.21	316.11	314.20	313.31
30000	398.46	395.04	384.25	379.33	377.04	375.97
35000	464.87	460.88	448.29	442.56	439.89	438.63
40000	531.28	526.72	512.33	505.78	502.73	501.29
45000	597.69	592.56	576.37	569.00	565.57	563.95
50000	664.10	658.39	640.42	632.22	628.41	626.61
55000	730.51	724.23	704.46	695.44	691.25	689.27
60000	796.92	790.07	768.50	758.67	754.09	751.93
65000	863.33	855.91	832.54	821.89	816.93	814.60
70000	929.74	921.75	896.58	885.11	879.77	877.26
75000	996.15	987.59	960.62	948.33	942.61	939.92
80000	1062.56	1053.43	1024.66	1011.55	1005.45	1002.58
85000	1128.97	1119.27	1088.71	1074.78	1068.29	1065.24
90000	1195.38	1185.11	1152.75	1138.00	1131.13	1127.90
95000	1261.79	1250.95	1216.79	1201.22	1193.97	1190.56
100000	1328.20	1316.79	1280.83	1264.44	1256.81	1253.22
200000	2656.39	2633.58	2561.66	2528.89	2513.63	2506.45
300000	3984.59	3950.37	3842.49	3793.33	3770.44	3759.67
400000	5312.79	5267.15	5123.32	5057.77	5027.25	5012.90
500000	6640.98	6583.94	6404.15	6322.22	6284.06	6266.12

15 1/4% MONTHLY PAYMENT

Necessary to amortize a loan

TERM / AMOUNT	1 YEAR	2 YEARS	3 YEARS	4 YEARS	5 YEARS	6 YEARS
500	45.19	24.30	17.39	13.98	11.96	10.64
600	54.23	29.16	20.87	16.77	14.35	12.77
700	63.26	34.02	24.35	19.57	16.75	14.90
800	72.30	38.88	27.83	22.37	19.14	17.02
900	81.34	43.75	31.31	25.16	21.53	19.15
1000	90.38	48.61	34.79	27.96	23.92	21.28
2000	180.75	97.21	69.58	55.92	47.84	42.56
3000	271.13	145.82	104.36	83.87	71.76	63.84
4000	361.51	194.42	139.15	111.83	95.69	85.12
5000	451.88	243.03	173.94	139.79	119.61	106.41
6000	542.26	291.63	208.73	167.75	143.53	127.69
7000	632.64	340.24	243.52	195.70	167.45	148.97
8000	723.01	388.85	278.30	223.66	191.37	170.25
9000	813.39	437.45	313.09	251.62	215.29	191.53
10000	903.77	486.06	347.88	279.58	239.21	212.81
11000	994.14	534.66	382.67	307.53	263.14	234.09
12000	1084.52	583.27	417.46	335.49	287.06	255.37
13000	1174.89	631.87	452.24	363.45	310.98	276.65
14000	1265.27	680.48	487.03	391.41	334.90	297.93
15000	1355.65	729.08	521.82	419.37	358.82	319.22
16000	1446.02	777.69	556.61	447.32	382.74	340.50
17000	1536.40	826.30	591.40	475.28	406.66	361.78
18000	1626.78	874.90	626.18	503.24	430.59	383.06
19000	1717.15	923.51	660.97	531.20	454.51	404.34
20000	1807.53	972.11	695.76	559.15	478.43	425.62
21000	1897.91	1020.72	730.55	587.11	502.35	446.90
22000	1988.28	1069.32	765.33	615.07	526.27	468.18
23000	2078.66	1117.93	800.12	643.03	550.19	489.46
24000	2169.04	1166.53	834.91	670.98	574.11	510.75
25000	2259.41	1215.14	869.70	698.94	598.03	532.03
30000	2711.29	1458.17	1043.64	838.73	717.64	638.43
35000	3163.18	1701.19	1217.58	978.52	837.25	744.84
40000	3615.06	1944.22	1391.52	1118.31	956.86	851.24
45000	4066.94	2187.25	1565.46	1258.10	1076.46	957.65
50000	4518.82	2430.28	1739.40	1397.88	1196.07	1064.05
55000	4970.71	2673.31	1913.34	1537.67	1315.68	1170.46
60000	5422.59	2916.33	2087.27	1677.46	1435.28	1276.86
65000	5874.47	3159.36	2261.21	1817.25	1554.89	1383.27
70000	6326.35	3402.39	2435.15	1957.04	1674.50	1489.67
75000	6778.23	3645.42	2609.09	2096.83	1794.10	1596.08
80000	7230.12	3888.45	2783.03	2236.61	1913.71	1702.48
85000	7682.00	4131.47	2956.97	2376.40	2033.32	1808.89
90000	8133.88	4374.50	3130.91	2516.19	2152.92	1915.29
95000	8585.76	4617.53	3304.85	2655.98	2272.53	2021.70
100000	9037.65	4860.56	3478.79	2795.77	2392.14	2128.10
200000	18075.30	9721.11	6957.58	5591.53	4784.28	4256.21
300000	27112.90	14581.70	10436.40	8387.30	7176.41	6384.31
400000	36150.60	19442.20	13915.20	11183.10	9568.55	8512.41
500000	45188.20	24302.80	17394.00	13978.80	11960.70	10640.50

MONTHLY PAYMENT

Necessary to amortize a loan

15 1/4%

TERM / AMOUNT	7 YEARS	8 YEARS	9 YEARS	10 YEARS	11 YEARS	12 YEARS
500	9.72	9.05	8.54	8.14	7.83	7.59
600	11.66	10.85	10.24	9.77	9.40	9.10
700	13.61	12.66	11.95	11.40	10.97	10.62
800	15.55	14.47	13.66	13.03	12.53	12.14
900	17.49	16.28	15.37	14.66	14.10	13.65
1000	19.44	18.09	17.07	16.29	15.67	15.17
2000	38.87	36.18	34.15	32.57	31.33	30.34
3000	58.31	54.27	51.22	48.86	47.00	45.51
4000	77.75	72.36	68.29	65.15	62.67	60.68
5000	97.19	90.45	85.37	81.43	78.33	75.85
6000	116.62	108.54	102.44	97.72	94.00	91.02
7000	136.06	126.63	119.52	114.01	109.67	106.19
8000	155.50	144.72	136.59	130.30	125.33	121.36
9000	174.94	162.81	153.66	146.58	141.00	136.53
10000	194.37	180.90	170.74	162.87	156.67	151.70
11000	213.81	198.99	187.81	179.16	172.33	166.87
12000	233.25	217.09	204.88	195.44	188.00	182.04
13000	252.69	235.18	221.96	211.73	203.67	197.21
14000	272.12	253.27	239.03	228.02	219.33	212.38
15000	291.56	271.36	256.10	244.30	235.00	227.55
16000	311.00	289.45	273.18	260.59	250.67	242.72
17000	330.43	307.54	290.25	276.88	266.33	257.89
18000	349.87	325.63	307.33	293.17	282.00	273.06
19000	369.31	343.72	324.40	309.45	297.67	288.23
20000	388.75	361.81	341.47	325.74	313.33	303.40
21000	408.18	379.90	358.55	342.03	329.00	318.57
22000	427.62	397.99	375.62	358.31	344.67	333.74
23000	447.06	416.08	392.69	374.60	360.33	348.91
24000	466.50	434.17	409.77	390.89	376.00	364.08
25000	485.93	452.26	426.84	407.17	391.67	379.25
30000	583.12	542.71	512.21	488.61	470.00	455.10
35000	680.31	633.16	597.58	570.04	548.33	530.95
40000	777.49	723.62	682.95	651.48	626.66	606.80
45000	874.68	814.07	768.31	732.91	705.00	682.65
50000	971.87	904.52	853.68	814.35	783.33	758.50
55000	1069.05	994.97	939.05	895.78	861.66	834.35
60000	1166.24	1085.42	1024.42	977.22	940.00	910.20
65000	1263.42	1175.87	1109.79	1058.65	1018.33	986.05
70000	1360.61	1266.33	1195.15	1140.09	1096.66	1061.90
75000	1457.80	1356.78	1280.52	1221.52	1174.99	1137.75
80000	1554.98	1447.23	1365.89	1302.96	1253.33	1213.60
85000	1652.17	1537.68	1451.26	1384.39	1331.66	1289.45
90000	1749.36	1628.13	1536.63	1465.82	1409.99	1365.30
95000	1846.54	1718.59	1621.99	1547.26	1488.33	1441.15
100000	1943.73	1809.04	1707.36	1628.69	1566.66	1517.00
200000	3887.46	3618.08	3414.72	3257.39	3133.32	3034.01
300000	5831.19	5427.11	5122.09	4886.08	4699.98	4551.01
400000	7774.92	7236.15	6829.45	6514.78	6266.64	6068.02
500000	9718.65	9045.19	8536.81	8143.47	7833.30	7585.02

15 1/4%

MONTHLY PAYMENT

Necessary to amortize a loan

TERM / AMOUNT	13 YEARS	14 YEARS	15 YEARS	16 YEARS	17 YEARS	18 YEARS
500	7.38	7.22	7.08	6.97	6.88	6.80
600	8.86	8.66	8.50	8.37	8.25	8.16
700	10.34	10.11	9.92	9.76	9.63	9.52
800	11.81	11.55	11.33	11.15	11.00	10.88
900	13.29	12.99	12.75	12.55	12.38	12.24
1000	14.77	14.44	14.17	13.94	13.75	13.60
2000	29.54	28.88	28.34	27.88	27.51	27.19
3000	44.30	43.32	42.50	41.83	41.26	40.79
4000	59.07	57.76	56.67	55.77	55.02	54.39
5000	73.84	72.19	70.84	69.71	68.77	67.99
6000	88.61	86.63	85.01	83.65	82.53	81.58
7000	103.38	101.07	99.17	97.60	96.28	95.18
8000	118.14	115.51	113.34	111.54	110.04	108.78
9000	132.91	129.95	127.51	125.48	123.79	122.38
10000	147.68	144.39	141.68	139.42	137.55	135.97
11000	162.45	158.83	155.84	153.37	151.30	149.57
12000	177.21	173.27	170.01	167.31	165.06	163.17
13000	191.98	187.70	184.18	181.25	178.81	176.76
14000	206.75	202.14	198.35	195.19	192.56	190.36
15000	221.52	216.58	212.51	209.14	206.32	203.96
16000	236.29	231.02	226.68	223.08	220.07	217.56
17000	251.05	245.46	240.85	237.02	233.83	231.15
18000	265.82	259.90	255.02	250.96	247.58	244.75
19000	280.59	274.34	269.18	264.91	261.34	258.35
20000	295.36	288.78	283.35	278.85	275.09	271.94
21000	310.12	303.21	297.52	292.79	288.85	285.54
22000	324.89	317.65	311.69	306.73	302.60	299.14
23000	339.66	332.09	325.85	320.68	316.36	312.74
24000	354.43	346.53	340.02	334.62	330.11	326.33
25000	369.20	360.97	354.19	348.56	343.87	339.93
30000	443.03	433.16	425.03	418.27	412.64	407.92
35000	516.87	505.36	495.86	487.98	481.41	475.90
40000	590.71	577.55	566.70	557.70	550.18	543.89
45000	664.55	649.74	637.54	627.41	618.96	611.87
50000	738.39	721.94	708.38	697.12	687.73	679.86
55000	812.23	794.13	779.21	766.83	756.50	747.84
60000	886.07	866.33	850.05	836.54	825.28	815.83
65000	959.91	938.52	920.89	906.26	894.05	883.82
70000	1033.75	1010.71	991.73	975.97	962.82	951.80
75000	1107.58	1082.91	1062.56	1045.68	1031.59	1019.79
80000	1181.42	1155.10	1133.40	1115.39	1100.37	1087.77
85000	1255.26	1227.30	1204.24	1185.10	1169.14	1155.76
90000	1329.10	1299.49	1275.08	1254.82	1237.91	1223.75
95000	1402.94	1371.68	1345.91	1324.53	1306.69	1291.73
100000	1476.78	1443.88	1416.75	1394.24	1375.46	1359.72
200000	2953.56	2887.75	2833.50	2788.48	2750.92	2719.43
300000	4430.34	4331.63	4250.25	4182.72	4126.37	4079.15
400000	5907.12	5775.51	5667.00	5576.96	5501.83	5438.87
500000	7383.90	7219.38	7083.75	6971.20	6877.29	6798.59

MONTHLY PAYMENT

Necessary to amortize a loan

15 1/4%

TERM / AMOUNT	19 YEARS	20 YEARS	25 YEARS	30 YEARS	35 YEARS	40 YEARS
500	6.73	6.68	6.50	6.42	6.39	6.37
600	8.08	8.01	7.80	7.71	7.66	7.64
700	9.43	9.35	9.10	8.99	8.94	8.92
800	10.77	10.68	10.40	10.28	10.22	10.19
900	12.12	12.02	11.70	11.56	11.49	11.46
1000	13.46	13.35	13.00	12.84	12.77	12.74
2000	26.93	26.71	26.01	25.69	25.54	25.48
3000	40.39	40.06	39.01	38.53	38.32	38.21
4000	53.86	53.41	52.01	51.38	51.09	50.95
5000	67.32	66.76	65.01	64.22	63.86	63.69
6000	80.79	80.12	78.02	77.07	76.63	76.43
7000	94.25	93.47	91.02	89.91	89.40	89.17
8000	107.72	106.82	104.02	102.76	102.18	101.90
9000	121.18	120.18	117.02	115.60	114.95	114.64
10000	134.65	133.53	130.03	128.45	127.72	127.38
11000	148.11	146.88	143.03	141.29	140.49	140.12
12000	161.58	160.24	156.03	154.14	153.26	152.86
13000	175.04	173.59	169.03	166.98	166.03	165.59
14000	188.51	186.94	182.04	179.82	178.81	178.33
15000	201.97	200.30	195.04	192.67	191.58	191.07
16000	215.44	213.65	208.04	205.51	204.35	203.81
17000	228.90	227.00	221.04	218.36	217.12	216.55
18000	242.37	240.35	234.05	231.20	229.89	229.28
19000	255.83	253.71	247.05	244.05	242.67	242.02
20000	269.30	267.06	260.05	256.89	255.44	254.76
21000	282.76	280.41	273.05	269.74	268.21	267.50
22000	296.22	293.77	286.06	282.58	280.98	280.24
23000	309.69	307.12	299.06	295.43	293.75	292.97
24000	323.15	320.47	312.06	308.27	306.52	305.71
25000	336.62	333.83	325.07	321.12	319.30	318.45
30000	403.94	400.59	390.08	385.34	383.16	382.14
35000	471.27	467.36	455.09	449.56	447.01	445.83
40000	538.59	534.12	520.10	513.78	510.87	509.52
45000	605.91	600.89	585.12	578.01	574.73	573.21
50000	673.24	667.65	650.13	642.23	638.59	636.90
55000	740.56	734.41	715.14	706.45	702.45	700.59
60000	807.89	801.18	780.16	770.68	766.31	764.28
65000	875.21	867.94	845.17	834.90	830.17	827.97
70000	942.53	934.71	910.18	899.12	894.03	891.66
75000	1009.86	1001.47	975.19	963.34	957.89	955.35
80000	1077.18	1068.24	1040.21	1027.57	1021.75	1019.04
85000	1144.50	1135.00	1105.22	1091.79	1085.61	1082.73
90000	1211.83	1201.77	1170.23	1156.01	1149.47	1146.42
95000	1279.15	1268.53	1235.25	1220.24	1213.32	1210.11
100000	1346.47	1335.30	1300.26	1284.46	1277.18	1273.80
200000	2692.95	2670.60	2600.52	2568.92	2554.37	2547.60
300000	4039.42	4005.90	3900.77	3853.38	3831.55	3821.41
400000	5385.90	5341.20	5201.03	5137.83	5108.74	5095.21
500000	6732.37	6676.50	6501.29	6422.29	6385.92	6369.01

15 1/2%

MONTHLY PAYMENT
Necessary to amortize a loan

TERM / AMOUNT	1 YEAR	2 YEARS	3 YEARS	4 YEARS	5 YEARS	6 YEARS
500	45.25	24.36	17.46	14.04	12.03	10.71
600	54.30	29.23	20.95	16.85	14.43	12.85
700	63.35	34.11	24.44	19.66	16.84	14.99
800	72.40	38.98	27.93	22.47	19.24	17.13
900	81.44	43.85	31.42	25.28	21.65	19.28
1000	90.49	48.72	34.91	28.08	24.05	21.42
2000	180.99	97.45	69.82	56.17	48.11	42.83
3000	271.48	146.17	104.73	84.25	72.16	64.25
4000	361.98	194.90	139.64	112.34	96.21	85.67
5000	452.47	243.62	174.55	140.42	120.27	107.09
6000	542.96	292.35	209.46	168.51	144.32	128.51
7000	633.46	341.07	244.37	196.59	168.37	149.92
8000	723.95	389.80	279.29	224.68	192.43	171.34
9000	814.45	438.52	314.20	252.76	216.48	192.76
10000	904.94	487.24	349.11	280.85	240.53	214.17
11000	995.44	535.97	384.02	308.93	264.58	235.59
12000	1085.93	584.69	418.93	337.02	288.64	257.01
13000	1176.42	633.42	453.84	365.10	312.69	278.43
14000	1266.92	682.14	488.75	393.19	336.74	299.84
15000	1357.41	730.87	523.66	421.27	360.80	321.26
16000	1447.91	779.59	558.57	449.36	384.85	342.68
17000	1538.40	828.31	593.48	477.44	408.90	364.10
18000	1628.89	877.04	628.39	505.53	432.96	385.51
19000	1719.39	925.76	663.30	533.61	457.01	406.93
20000	1809.88	974.49	698.21	561.70	481.06	428.35
21000	1900.38	1023.21	733.12	589.78	505.12	449.77
22000	1990.87	1071.94	768.03	617.87	529.17	471.18
23000	2081.36	1120.66	802.94	645.95	553.22	492.60
24000	2171.86	1169.39	837.85	674.04	577.28	514.02
25000	2262.35	1218.11	872.76	702.12	601.33	535.44
30000	2714.82	1461.73	1047.32	842.54	721.59	642.52
35000	3167.29	1705.35	1221.87	982.97	841.86	749.61
40000	3619.76	1948.98	1396.42	1123.39	962.13	856.70
45000	4072.23	2192.60	1570.98	1263.81	1082.39	963.79
50000	4524.70	2436.22	1745.53	1404.24	1202.66	1070.87
55000	4977.17	2679.84	1920.08	1544.66	1322.92	1177.96
60000	5429.64	2923.46	2094.63	1685.09	1443.19	1285.05
65000	5882.11	3167.08	2269.19	1825.51	1563.45	1392.13
70000	6334.59	3410.71	2443.74	1965.93	1683.72	1499.22
75000	6787.06	3654.33	2618.29	2106.36	1803.98	1606.31
80000	7239.53	3897.95	2792.85	2246.78	1924.25	1713.39
85000	7692.00	4141.57	2967.40	2387.21	2044.52	1820.48
90000	8144.47	4385.19	3141.95	2527.63	2164.78	1927.57
95000	8596.94	4628.82	3316.50	2668.05	2285.05	2034.66
100000	9049.41	4872.44	3491.06	2808.48	2405.31	2141.74
200000	18098.80	9744.88	6982.11	5616.96	4810.63	4283.49
300000	27148.20	14617.30	10473.20	8425.43	7215.94	6425.23
400000	36197.60	19489.80	13964.20	11233.90	9621.25	8566.97
500000	45247.00	24362.20	17455.30	14042.40	12026.60	10708.70

MONTHLY PAYMENT

Necessary to amortize a loan

15 1/2%

TERM / AMOUNT	7 YEARS	8 YEARS	9 YEARS	10 YEARS	11 YEARS	12 YEARS
500	9.79	9.12	8.61	8.22	7.91	7.67
600	11.75	10.94	10.33	9.86	9.49	9.20
700	13.70	12.77	12.06	11.51	11.08	10.73
800	15.66	14.59	13.78	13.15	12.66	12.27
900	17.62	16.41	15.50	14.80	14.24	13.80
1000	19.58	18.24	17.22	16.44	15.82	15.33
2000	39.16	36.47	34.45	32.88	31.65	30.66
3000	58.73	54.71	51.67	49.32	47.47	46.00
4000	78.31	72.94	68.89	65.76	63.30	61.33
5000	97.89	91.18	86.12	82.21	79.12	76.66
6000	117.47	109.42	103.34	98.65	94.95	91.99
7000	137.05	127.65	120.56	115.09	110.77	107.32
8000	156.63	145.89	137.79	131.53	126.60	122.66
9000	176.21	164.12	155.01	147.97	142.42	137.99
10000	195.78	182.36	172.24	164.41	158.25	153.32
11000	215.36	200.60	189.46	180.85	174.07	168.65
12000	234.94	218.83	206.68	197.29	189.90	183.98
13000	254.52	237.07	223.91	213.73	205.72	199.32
14000	274.10	255.30	241.13	230.17	221.55	214.65
15000	293.68	273.54	258.35	246.62	237.37	229.98
16000	313.25	291.77	275.58	263.06	253.20	245.31
17000	332.83	310.01	292.80	279.50	269.02	260.64
18000	352.41	328.25	310.02	295.94	284.85	275.98
19000	371.99	346.48	327.25	312.38	300.67	291.31
20000	391.57	364.72	344.47	328.82	316.49	306.64
21000	411.14	382.95	361.69	345.26	332.32	321.97
22000	430.72	401.19	378.92	361.70	348.14	337.30
23000	450.30	419.43	396.14	378.14	363.97	352.64
24000	469.88	437.66	413.36	394.59	379.79	367.97
25000	489.46	455.90	430.59	411.03	395.62	383.30
30000	587.35	547.08	516.71	493.23	474.74	459.96
35000	685.24	638.26	602.82	575.44	553.87	536.62
40000	783.13	729.44	688.94	657.64	632.99	613.28
45000	881.02	820.62	775.06	739.85	712.11	689.94
50000	978.92	911.79	861.18	822.05	791.24	766.60
55000	1076.81	1002.97	947.29	904.26	870.36	843.26
60000	1174.70	1094.15	1033.41	986.46	949.48	919.92
65000	1272.59	1185.33	1119.53	1068.67	1028.61	996.58
70000	1370.48	1276.51	1205.64	1150.87	1107.73	1073.24
75000	1468.37	1367.69	1291.76	1233.08	1186.85	1149.90
80000	1566.26	1458.87	1377.88	1315.28	1265.98	1226.56
85000	1664.16	1550.05	1464.00	1397.49	1345.10	1303.22
90000	1762.05	1641.23	1550.11	1479.69	1424.22	1379.88
95000	1859.94	1732.41	1636.23	1561.90	1503.35	1456.54
100000	1957.83	1823.59	1722.35	1644.10	1582.47	1533.20
200000	3915.66	3647.18	3444.70	3288.21	3164.94	3066.40
300000	5873.49	5470.77	5167.05	4932.31	4747.42	4599.61
400000	7831.32	7294.35	6889.40	6576.41	6329.89	6132.81
500000	9789.15	9117.94	8611.75	8220.51	7912.36	7666.01

15 1/2%

MONTHLY PAYMENT

Necessary to amortize a loan

TERM / AMOUNT	13 YEARS	14 YEARS	15 YEARS	16 YEARS	17 YEARS	18 YEARS
500	7.47	7.30	7.17	7.06	6.97	6.89
600	8.96	8.76	8.60	8.47	8.36	8.27
700	10.45	10.23	10.04	9.88	9.75	9.64
800	11.95	11.69	11.47	11.29	11.15	11.02
900	13.44	13.15	12.91	12.71	12.54	12.40
1000	14.93	14.61	14.34	14.12	13.93	13.78
2000	29.87	29.22	28.68	28.24	27.87	27.56
3000	44.80	43.82	43.02	42.35	41.80	41.33
4000	59.73	58.43	57.36	56.47	55.73	55.11
5000	74.67	73.04	71.70	70.59	69.66	68.89
6000	89.60	87.65	86.04	84.71	83.60	82.67
7000	104.53	102.26	100.38	98.83	97.53	96.45
8000	119.47	116.86	114.72	112.94	111.46	110.23
9000	134.40	131.47	129.06	127.06	125.40	124.00
10000	149.33	146.08	143.40	141.18	139.33	137.78
11000	164.27	160.69	157.74	155.30	153.26	151.56
12000	179.20	175.30	172.08	169.41	167.20	165.34
13000	194.14	189.90	186.42	183.53	181.13	179.12
14000	209.07	204.51	200.76	197.65	195.06	192.90
15000	224.00	219.12	215.10	211.77	208.99	206.67
16000	238.94	233.73	229.44	225.89	222.93	220.45
17000	253.87	248.33	243.78	240.00	236.86	234.23
18000	268.80	262.94	258.12	254.12	250.79	248.01
19000	283.74	277.55	272.46	268.24	264.73	261.79
20000	298.67	292.16	286.80	282.36	278.66	275.56
21000	313.60	306.77	301.14	296.48	292.59	289.34
22000	328.54	321.37	315.48	310.59	306.52	303.12
23000	343.47	335.98	329.82	324.71	320.46	316.90
24000	358.40	350.59	344.16	338.83	334.39	330.68
25000	373.34	365.20	358.50	352.95	348.32	344.46
30000	448.00	438.24	430.20	423.54	417.99	413.35
35000	522.67	511.28	501.90	494.13	487.65	482.24
40000	597.34	485.32	573.60	564.71	557.32	551.13
45000	672.01	657.36	645.30	635.30	626.98	620.02
50000	746.67	730.39	716.99	705.89	696.65	688.91
55000	821.34	803.43	788.69	776.48	766.31	757.80
60000	896.01	876.47	860.39	847.07	835.98	826.69
65000	970.67	949.51	932.09	917.66	905.64	895.58
70000	1045.34	1022.55	1003.79	988.25	975.30	964.47
75000	1120.01	1095.59	1075.49	1058.84	1044.97	1033.36
80000	1194.67	1168.63	1147.19	1129.43	1114.63	1102.25
85000	1269.34	1241.67	1218.89	1200.02	1184.30	1171.15
90000	1344.01	1314.71	1290.59	1270.61	1253.96	1240.04
95000	1418.68	1387.75	1362.29	1341.20	1323.63	1308.93
100000	1493.34	1460.79	1433.99	1411.79	1393.29	1377.82
200000	2986.69	2921.58	2867.98	2823.57	2786.58	2755.64
300000	4480.03	4382.36	4301.97	4235.36	4179.87	4133.46
400000	5973.37	5843.15	5735.96	5647.14	5573.16	5511.27
500000	7466.72	7303.94	7169.94	7058.93	6966.46	6889.09

MONTHLY PAYMENT

Necessary to amortize a loan

15 1/2%

TERM / AMOUNT	19 YEARS	20 YEARS	25 YEARS	30 YEARS	35 YEARS	40 YEARS
500	6.82	6.77	6.60	6.52	6.49	6.47
600	8.19	8.12	7.92	7.83	7.79	7.77
700	9.55	9.48	9.24	9.13	9.08	9.06
800	10.92	10.83	10.56	10.44	10.38	10.36
900	12.28	12.18	11.88	11.74	11.68	11.65
1000	13.65	13.54	13.20	13.05	12.98	12.94
2000	27.30	27.08	26.39	26.09	25.95	25.89
3000	40.94	40.62	39.59	39.14	38.93	38.83
4000	54.59	54.16	52.79	52.18	51.90	51.78
5000	68.24	67.69	65.99	65.23	64.88	64.72
6000	81.89	81.23	79.18	78.27	77.86	77.66
7000	95.54	94.77	92.38	91.32	90.83	90.61
8000	109.19	108.31	105.58	104.36	103.81	103.55
9000	122.83	121.85	118.78	117.41	116.78	116.50
10000	136.48	135.39	131.98	130.45	129.76	129.44
11000	150.13	148.93	145.17	143.50	142.73	142.38
12000	163.78	162.47	158.37	156.54	155.71	155.33
13000	177.43	176.00	171.57	169.59	168.69	168.27
14000	191.08	189.54	184.76	182.63	181.66	181.22
15000	204.72	203.08	197.96	195.68	194.64	194.16
16000	218.37	216.62	211.16	208.72	207.61	207.10
17000	232.02	230.16	224.36	221.77	220.59	220.05
18000	245.67	243.70	237.55	234.81	233.57	232.99
19000	259.32	257.24	250.75	247.86	246.54	245.94
20000	272.97	270.78	263.95	260.90	259.52	258.88
21000	286.61	284.32	277.15	273.95	272.49	271.82
22000	300.26	297.85	290.34	286.99	285.47	284.77
23000	313.91	311.39	303.54	300.04	298.44	297.71
24000	327.56	324.93	316.74	313.08	311.42	310.66
25000	341.21	338.47	329.94	326.13	324.40	323.60
30000	409.45	406.16	395.92	391.36	389.28	388.32
35000	477.69	473.86	461.91	456.58	454.16	453.04
40000	545.93	541.55	527.90	521.81	519.03	517.76
45000	614.17	609.25	593.89	587.03	583.91	582.48
50000	682.41	676.94	659.87	652.26	648.79	647.20
55000	750.65	744.63	725.86	717.48	713.67	711.92
60000	818.90	812.33	791.85	782.71	778.55	776.64
65000	887.14	880.02	857.83	847.94	843.43	841.36
70000	955.38	947.72	923.82	913.16	908.31	906.08
75000	1023.62	1015.41	989.81	978.39	973.19	970.80
80000	1091.86	1083.10	1055.80	1043.61	1038.07	1035.52
85000	1160.10	1150.80	1121.78	1108.84	1102.95	1100.24
90000	1228.34	1218.49	1187.77	1174.07	1167.83	1164.96
95000	1296.58	1286.19	1253.76	1239.29	1232.71	1229.68
100000	1364.83	1353.88	1319.75	1304.52	1297.58	1294.40
200000	2729.65	2707.76	2639.49	2609.03	2595.17	2588.80
300000	4094.48	4061.64	3959.24	3913.55	3892.75	3883.20
400000	5459.30	5415.52	5278.98	5218.07	5190.34	5177.60
500000	6824.13	6769.40	6598.73	6522.58	6487.92	6472.00

15 3/4% MONTHLY PAYMENT

Necessary to amortize a loan

TERM / AMOUNT	1 YEAR	2 YEARS	3 YEARS	4 YEARS	5 YEARS	6 YEARS
500	45.31	24.42	17.52	14.11	12.09	10.78
600	54.37	29.31	21.02	16.93	14.51	12.93
700	63.43	34.19	24.52	19.75	16.93	15.09
800	72.49	39.08	28.03	22.57	19.35	17.24
900	81.55	43.96	31.53	25.39	21.77	19.40
1000	90.61	48.84	35.03	28.21	24.19	21.55
2000	181.23	97.69	70.07	56.43	48.37	43.11
3000	271.84	146.53	105.10	84.64	72.56	64.66
4000	362.45	195.38	140.14	112.85	96.74	86.22
5000	453.07	244.22	175.17	141.06	120.93	107.77
6000	543.68	293.06	210.20	169.28	145.11	129.33
7000	634.29	341.91	245.24	197.49	169.30	150.88
8000	724.90	390.75	280.27	225.70	193.48	172.44
9000	815.52	439.60	315.31	253.91	217.67	193.99
10000	906.13	488.44	350.34	282.13	241.86	215.55
11000	996.74	537.28	385.37	310.34	266.04	237.10
12000	1087.36	586.13	420.41	338.55	290.23	258.65
13000	1177.97	634.97	455.44	366.76	314.41	280.21
14000	1268.58	683.82	490.47	394.98	338.60	301.76
15000	1359.20	732.66	525.51	423.19	362.78	323.32
16000	1449.81	781.50	560.54	451.40	386.97	344.87
17000	1540.42	830.35	595.58	479.61	411.15	366.43
18000	1631.04	879.19	630.61	507.83	435.34	387.98
19000	1721.65	928.04	665.64	536.04	459.53	409.54
20000	1812.26	976.88	700.68	564.25	483.71	431.09
21000	1902.87	1025.72	735.71	592.46	507.90	452.65
22000	1993.49	1074.57	770.75	620.68	532.08	474.20
23000	2084.10	1123.41	805.78	648.89	556.27	495.75
24000	2174.71	1172.26	840.81	677.10	580.45	517.31
25000	2265.33	1221.10	875.85	705.31	604.64	538.86
30000	2718.39	1465.32	1051.02	846.38	725.57	646.64
35000	3171.46	1709.54	1226.19	987.44	846.49	754.41
40000	3624.52	1953.76	1401.36	1128.50	967.42	862.18
45000	4077.59	2197.98	1576.52	1269.56	1088.35	969.95
50000	4530.65	2442.20	1751.69	1410.63	1209.28	1077.73
55000	4983.72	2686.42	1926.86	1551.69	1330.20	1185.50
60000	5436.78	2930.64	2102.03	1692.75	1451.13	1293.27
65000	5889.85	3174.86	2277.20	1833.81	1572.06	1401.04
70000	6342.91	3419.08	2452.37	1974.88	1692.99	1508.82
75000	6795.98	3663.30	2627.54	2115.94	1813.91	1616.59
80000	7249.04	3907.52	2802.71	2257.00	1934.84	1724.36
85000	7702.11	4151.74	2977.88	2398.06	2055.77	1832.13
90000	8155.17	4395.96	3153.05	2539.13	2176.70	1939.91
95000	8608.24	4640.18	3328.22	2680.19	2297.62	2047.68
100000	9061.31	4884.40	3503.39	2821.25	2418.55	2155.45
200000	18122.60	9768.79	7006.78	5642.50	4837.10	4310.90
300000	27183.90	14653.20	10510.20	8463.75	7255.65	6466.35
400000	36245.20	19537.60	14013.60	11285.00	9674.20	8621.80
500000	45306.50	24422.00	17516.90	14106.30	12092.80	10777.30

MONTHLY PAYMENT

Necessary to amortize a loan

15 3/4%

TERM / AMOUNT	7 YEARS	8 YEARS	9 YEARS	10 YEARS	11 YEARS	12 YEARS
500	9.86	9.19	8.69	8.30	7.99	7.75
600	11.83	11.03	10.42	9.96	9.59	9.30
700	13.80	12.87	12.16	11.62	11.19	10.85
800	15.78	14.71	13.90	13.28	12.79	12.40
900	17.75	16.54	15.64	14.94	14.39	13.95
1000	19.72	18.38	17.37	16.60	15.98	15.49
2000	39.44	36.76	34.75	33.19	31.97	30.99
3000	59.16	55.15	52.12	49.79	47.95	46.48
4000	78.88	73.53	69.50	66.38	63.93	61.98
5000	98.60	91.91	86.87	82.98	79.92	77.47
6000	118.32	110.29	104.25	99.58	95.90	92.97
7000	138.04	128.68	121.62	116.17	111.89	108.46
8000	157.76	147.06	138.99	132.77	127.87	123.96
9000	177.48	165.44	156.37	149.36	143.85	139.45
10000	197.20	183.82	173.74	165.96	159.84	154.95
11000	216.92	202.20	191.12	182.56	175.82	170.44
12000	236.64	220.59	208.49	199.15	191.80	185.94
13000	256.36	238.97	225.86	215.75	207.79	201.43
14000	276.08	257.35	243.24	232.34	223.77	216.93
15000	295.80	275.73	260.61	248.94	239.76	232.42
16000	315.52	294.11	277.99	265.53	255.74	247.92
17000	335.24	312.50	295.36	282.13	271.72	263.41
18000	354.96	330.88	312.73	298.73	287.71	278.91
19000	374.68	349.26	330.11	315.32	303.69	294.40
20000	394.40	367.64	347.48	331.92	319.67	309.90
21000	414.12	386.02	364.86	348.51	335.66	325.39
22000	433.84	404.41	382.23	365.11	351.64	340.89
23000	453.56	422.79	399.61	381.71	367.62	356.38
24000	473.28	441.17	416.98	398.30	383.61	371.88
25000	493.00	459.55	434.35	414.90	399.59	387.37
30000	591.60	551.46	521.22	497.88	479.51	464.84
35000	690.20	643.37	608.09	580.86	559.43	542.32
40000	788.80	735.28	694.97	663.84	639.35	619.79
45000	887.40	827.20	781.84	746.82	719.26	697.27
50000	986.00	919.11	868.71	829.79	799.18	774.74
55000	1084.60	1011.02	955.58	912.77	879.10	852.22
60000	1183.20	1102.93	1042.45	995.75	959.02	929.69
65000	1281.80	1194.84	1129.32	1078.73	1038.94	1007.16
70000	1380.40	1286.75	1216.19	1161.71	1118.85	1084.64
75000	1479.00	1378.66	1303.06	1244.69	1198.77	1162.11
80000	1577.60	1470.57	1389.93	1327.67	1278.69	1239.59
85000	1676.20	1562.48	1476.80	1410.54	1358.61	1317.06
90000	1774.80	1654.39	1563.67	1493.63	1438.53	1394.53
95000	1873.40	1746.30	1650.54	1576.61	1518.45	1472.01
100000	1972.00	1838.21	1737.41	1659.59	1598.36	1549.48
200000	3944.00	3676.42	3474.82	3319.18	3196.73	3098.96
300000	5916.00	5514.63	5212.23	4978.77	4795.09	4648.44
400000	7888.00	7352.84	6949.65	6638.35	6393.46	6197.93
500000	9860.00	9191.06	8687.06	8297.94	7991.82	7747.41

15 3/4%

MONTHLY PAYMENT

Necessary to amortize a loan

TERM / AMOUNT	13 YEARS	14 YEARS	15 YEARS	16 YEARS	17 YEARS	18 YEARS
500	7.55	7.39	7.26	7.15	7.06	6.98
600	9.06	8.87	8.71	8.58	8.47	8.38
700	10.57	10.34	10.16	10.01	9.88	9.77
800	12.08	11.82	11.61	11.44	11.29	11.17
900	13.59	13.30	13.06	12.86	12.70	12.56
1000	15.10	14.78	14.51	14.29	14.11	13.96
2000	30.20	29.56	29.03	28.59	28.22	27.92
3000	45.30	44.33	43.54	42.88	42.34	41.88
4000	60.40	59.11	58.05	57.18	56.45	55.84
5000	75.50	73.89	72.57	71.47	70.56	69.80
6000	90.60	88.67	87.08	85.76	84.67	83.76
7000	105.70	103.45	101.59	100.06	98.78	97.72
8000	120.80	118.22	116.11	114.35	112.90	111.68
9000	135.90	133.00	130.62	128.65	127.01	125.64
10000	151.00	147.78	145.13	142.94	141.12	139.60
11000	166.10	162.56	159.64	157.24	155.23	153.56
12000	181.20	177.33	174.16	171.53	169.35	167.52
13000	196.30	192.11	188.67	185.82	183.46	181.48
14000	211.40	206.89	203.18	200.12	197.57	195.44
15000	226.50	221.67	217.70	214.41	211.68	209.40
16000	241.60	236.45	232.21	228.71	225.79	223.36
17000	256.70	251.22	246.72	243.00	239.91	237.32
18000	271.80	266.00	261.24	257.29	254.02	251.28
19000	286.90	280.78	275.75	271.59	268.13	265.24
20000	302.00	295.56	290.26	285.88	282.24	279.20
21000	317.10	310.33	304.78	300.18	296.35	293.16
22000	332.20	325.11	319.29	314.47	310.47	307.12
23000	347.30	339.89	333.80	328.77	324.58	321.08
24000	362.40	354.67	348.31	343.06	338.69	335.04
25000	377.50	369.45	362.83	357.35	352.80	349.00
30000	453.00	443.34	435.39	428.82	423.36	418.80
35000	528.50	517.22	507.96	500.29	493.92	488.60
40000	604.00	591.11	580.52	571.77	564.48	558.40
45000	679.50	665.00	653.09	643.24	635.04	628.20
50000	755.00	738.89	725.66	714.71	705.60	698.00
55000	830.50	812.78	798.22	786.18	776.16	767.80
60000	905.99	886.67	870 79	857.65	846.72	837.60
65000	981.49	960.56	943.35	929.12	917.28	907.40
70000	1056.99	1034.45	1015.92	1000.59	987.84	977.20
75000	1132.49	1108.34	1088.48	1072.06	1058.40	1047.00
80000	1207.99	1182.23	1161.05	1143.53	1128.96	1116.80
85000	1283.49	1256.11	1233.61	1215.00	1199.52	1186.60
90000	1358.99	1330.00	1306.18	1286.47	1270.08	1256.40
95000	1434.49	1403.89	1378.74	1357.94	1340.64	1326.20
100000	1509.99	1477.78	1451.31	1429.41	1411.20	1396.00
200000	3019.98	2955.56	2902.62	2858.83	2822.41	2792.00
300000	4529.97	4433.35	4353.93	4288.24	4233.61	4187.99
400000	6039.96	5911.13	5805.24	5717.65	5644.82	5583.99
500000	7549.95	7388.91	7256.55	7147.06	7056.02	6979.99

MONTHLY PAYMENT

Necessary to amortize a loan

15 3/4%

TERM / AMOUNT	19 YEARS	20 YEARS	25 YEARS	30 YEARS	35 YEARS	40 YEARS
500	6.92	6.86	6.70	6.62	6.59	6.58
600	8.30	8.24	8.04	7.95	7.91	7.89
700	9.68	9.61	9.38	9.27	9.23	9.21
800	11.07	10.98	10.71	10.60	10.54	10.52
900	12.45	12.35	12.05	11.92	11.86	11.84
1000	13.83	13.73	13.39	13.25	13.18	13.15
2000	27.67	27.45	26.79	26.49	26.36	26.30
3000	41.50	41.18	40.18	39.74	39.54	39.45
4000	55.33	54.90	53.57	52.98	52.72	52.60
5000	69.16	68.63	66.96	66.23	65.90	65.75
6000	83.00	82.35	80.36	79.48	79.08	78.90
7000	96.83	96.08	93.75	92.72	92.26	92.05
8000	110.66	109.80	107.14	105.97	105.44	105.20
9000	124.49	123.53	120.54	119.22	118.62	118.35
10000	138.33	137.25	133.93	132.46	131.80	131.50
11000	152.16	150.98	147.32	145.71	144.98	144.65
12000	165.99	164.70	160.72	158.95	158.16	157.80
13000	179.82	178.43	174.11	172.20	171.34	170.95
14000	193.66	192.16	187.50	185.45	184.52	184.10
15000	207.49	205.88	200.89	198.69	197.70	197.25
16000	221.32	219.61	214.29	211.94	210.88	210.40
17000	235.15	233.33	227.68	225.19	224.06	223.55
18000	248.99	247.06	241.07	238.43	237.24	236.70
19000	262.82	260.78	254.47	251.68	250.42	249.85
20000	276.65	274.51	267.86	264.92	263.60	263.00
21000	290.48	288.23	281.25	278.17	276.78	276.15
22000	304.32	301.96	294.64	291.42	289.96	289.30
23000	318.15	315.68	308.04	304.66	303.14	302.45
24000	331.98	329.41	321.43	317.91	316.32	315.60
25000	345.81	343.13	334.82	331.15	329.50	328.75
30000	414.98	411.76	401.79	397.39	395.40	394.51
35000	484.14	480.39	468.75	463.62	461.31	460.26
40000	553.30	549.01	535.72	529.85	527.21	526.01
45000	622.46	617.64	602.68	596.08	593.11	591.76
50000	691.63	686.27	669.65	662.31	659.01	657.51
55000	760.79	754.89	736.61	728.54	724.91	723.26
60000	829.95	823.52	803.57	794.77	790.81	789.01
65000	899.11	892.15	870.54	861.00	856.71	854.76
70000	968.28	960.77	937.50	927.23	922.61	920.51
75000	1037.44	1029.40	1004.47	993.46	988.51	986.26
80000	1106.60	1098.03	1071.43	1059.69	1054.41	1052.01
85000	1175.76	1166.65	1138.40	1125.92	1120.31	1117.76
90000	1244.93	1235.28	1205.36	1192.16	1186.21	1183.51
95000	1314.09	1303.91	1272.33	1258.39	1252.11	1249.27
100000	1383.25	1372.53	1339.29	1324.62	1318.01	1315.02
200000	2766.50	2745.07	2678.58	2649.23	2636.03	2630.03
300000	4149.75	4117.60	4017.87	3973.85	3954.04	3945.05
400000	5533.01	5490.14	5357.16	5298.47	5272.06	5260.06
500000	6916.26	6862.67	6696.45	6623.09	6590.07	6575.08

16% MONTHLY PAYMENT
Necessary to amortize a loan

TERM / AMOUNT	1 YEAR	2 YEARS	3 YEARS	4 YEARS	5 YEARS	6 YEARS
500	45.37	24.48	17.58	14.17	12.16	10.85
600	54.44	29.38	21.09	17.00	14.59	13.02
700	63.51	34.27	24.61	19.84	17.02	15.18
800	72.58	39.17	28.13	22.67	19.45	17.35
900	81.66	44.07	31.64	25.51	21.89	19.52
1000	90.73	48.96	35.16	28.34	24.32	21.69
2000	181.46	97.93	70.31	56.68	48.64	43.38
3000	272.19	146.89	105.47	85.02	72.95	65.08
4000	362.92	195.85	140.63	113.36	97.27	86.77
5000	453.66	244.82	175.79	141.70	121.59	100.40
6000	544.39	293.78	210.94	170.04	145.91	130.15
7000	635.12	342.74	246.10	198.38	170.23	151.84
8000	725.85	391.71	281.26	226.72	194.55	173.54
9000	816.58	440.67	316.41	255.06	218.86	195.23
10000	907.31	489.63	351.57	283.40	243.18	216.92
11000	998.04	538.60	386.73	311.74	267.50	238.61
12000	1088.77	587.56	421.89	340.08	291.82	260.30
13000	1179.50	636.52	457.04	368.42	316.14	281.99
14000	1270.24	685.49	492.20	396.77	340.45	303.69
15000	1360.97	734.45	527.36	425.11	364.77	325.38
16000	1451.70	783.41	562.51	453.45	389.09	347.07
17000	1542.43	832.38	597.67	481.79	413.41	368.76
18000	1633.16	881.34	632.83	510.13	437.73	390.45
19000	1723.89	930.30	667.99	538.47	462.04	412.15
20000	1814.62	979.26	703.14	566.81	486.36	433.84
21000	1905.35	1028.23	738.30	595.15	510.68	455.53
22000	1996.08	1077.19	773.46	623.49	535.00	477.22
23000	2086.81	1126.15	808.61	651.83	559.32	498.91
24000	2177.55	1175.12	843.77	680.17	583.63	520.61
25000	2268.28	1224.08	878.93	708.51	607.95	542.30
30000	2721.93	1468.90	1054.71	850.21	729.54	650.76
35000	3175.59	1713.71	1230.50	991.91	851.13	759.22
40000	3629.24	1958.53	1406.28	1133.61	972.72	867.68
45000	4082.90	2203.34	1582.07	1275.32	1094.31	976.13
50000	4536.55	2448.16	1757.86	1417.02	1215.90	1084.59
55000	4990.21	2692.98	1933.64	1558.72	1337.50	1193.05
60000	5443.86	2937.79	2109.43	1700.42	1459.09	1301.51
65000	5897.52	3182.61	2285.21	1842.12	1580.68	1409.97
70000	6351.18	3427.43	2461.00	1983.82	1702.27	1518.43
75000	6804.83	3672.24	2636.78	2125.52	1823.86	1626.89
80000	7258.49	3917.06	2812.57	2267.23	1945.45	1735.35
85000	7712.14	4161.87	2988.35	2408.93	2067.04	1843.81
90000	8165.80	4406.69	3164.14	2550.63	2188.63	1952.27
95000	8619.45	4651.51	3339.93	2692.33	2310.22	2060.73
100000	9073.11	4896.32	3515.71	2834.03	2431.81	2169.19
200000	18146.20	9792.64	7031.42	5668.07	4863.62	4338.38
300000	27219.30	14689.00	10547.10	8502.10	7295.43	6507.56
400000	36292.40	19585.30	14062.80	11336.10	9727.24	8676.75
500000	45365.50	24481.60	17578.60	14170.20	12159.10	10845.90

MONTHLY PAYMENT

Necessary to amortize a loan

16%

TERM / AMOUNT	7 YEARS	8 YEARS	9 YEARS	10 YEARS	11 YEARS	12 YEARS
500	9.93	9.26	8.76	8.38	8.07	7.83
600	11.92	11.12	10.52	10.05	9.69	9.39
700	13.90	12.97	12.27	11.73	11.30	10.96
800	15.89	14.82	14.02	13.40	12.91	12.53
900	17.88	16.68	15.77	15.08	14.53	14.09
1000	19.86	18.53	17.53	16.75	16.14	15.66
2000	39.72	37.06	35.05	33.50	32.29	31.32
3000	59.59	55.59	52.58	50.25	48.43	46.97
4000	79.45	74.12	70.10	67.01	64.57	62.63
5000	99.31	92.64	87.63	83.76	80.72	78.29
6000	119.17	111.17	105.15	100.51	96.86	93.95
7000	139.04	129.70	122.68	117.26	113.00	109.61
8000	158.90	148.23	140.20	134.01	129.15	125.27
9000	178.76	166.76	157.73	150.76	145.29	140.92
10000	198.62	185.29	175.25	167.51	161.43	156.58
11000	218.48	203.82	192.78	184.27	177.58	172.24
12000	238.35	222.35	210.30	201.02	193.72	187.90
13000	258.21	240.88	227.83	217.77	209.86	203.56
14000	278.07	259.40	245.35	234.52	226.01	219.22
15000	297.93	277.93	262.88	251.27	242.15	234.87
16000	317.79	296.46	280.40	268.02	258.29	250.53
17000	337.66	314.99	297.93	284.77	274.43	266.19
18000	357.52	333.52	315.46	301.52	290.58	281.85
19000	377.38	352.05	332.98	318.28	306.72	297.51
20000	397.24	370.58	350.51	335.03	322.86	313.17
21000	417.10	389.11	368.03	351.78	339.01	328.82
22000	436.97	407.63	385.56	368.53	355.15	344.48
23000	456.83	426.16	403.08	385.28	371.29	360.14
24000	476.69	444.69	420.61	402.03	387.44	375.80
25000	496.55	463.22	438.13	418.78	403.58	391.46
30000	595.86	555.86	525.76	502.54	484.30	469.75
35000	695.17	648.51	613.38	586.30	565.01	548.04
40000	794.48	741.15	701.01	670.05	645.73	626.33
45000	893.79	833.80	788.64	753.81	726.44	704.62
50000	993.11	926.44	876.26	837.57	807.16	782.91
55000	1092.42	1019.08	963.89	921.32	887.88	861.21
60000	1191.73	1111.73	1051.52	1005.08	968.59	939.50
65000	1291.04	1204.37	1139.14	1088.84	1049.31	1017.79
70000	1390.35	1297.02	1226.77	1172.59	1130.02	1096.08
75000	1489.66	1389.66	1314.40	1256.35	1210.74	1174.37
80000	1588.97	1482.30	1402.02	1340.11	1291.46	1252.66
85000	1688.28	1574.95	1489.65	1423.86	1372.17	1330.95
90000	1787.59	1667.59	1577.27	1507.62	1452.89	1409.24
95000	1886.90	1760.24	1664.90	1591.38	1533.60	1487.54
100000	1986.21	1852.88	1752.53	1675.13	1614.32	1565.83
200000	3972.42	3705.76	3505.05	3350.27	3228.64	3131.65
300000	5958.63	5558.64	5257.58	5025.40	4842.96	4697.48
400000	7944.84	7411.52	7010.11	6700.53	6457.28	6263.31
500000	9931.05	9264.41	8762.64	8375.67	8071.59	7829.13

16%

MONTHLY PAYMENT

Necessary to amortize a loan

TERM / AMOUNT	13 YEARS	14 YEARS	15 YEARS	16 YEARS	17 YEARS	18 YEARS
500	7.63	7.47	7.34	7.24	7.15	7.07
600	9.16	8.97	8.81	8.68	8.58	8.49
700	10.69	10.46	10.28	10.13	10.00	9.90
800	12.21	11.96	11.75	11.58	11.43	11.31
900	13.74	13.45	13.22	13.02	12.86	12.73
1000	15.27	14.95	14.69	14.47	14.29	14.14
2000	30.53	29.90	29.37	28.94	28.58	28.29
3000	45.80	44.85	44.06	43.41	42.88	42.43
4000	61.07	59.79	58.75	57.88	57.17	56.57
5000	76.34	74.74	73.44	72.36	71.46	70.71
6000	91.60	89.69	88.12	86.83	85.75	84.85
7000	106.87	104.64	102.81	101.30	100.04	99.00
8000	122.14	119.59	117.50	115.77	114.34	113.14
9000	137.40	134.54	132.18	130.24	128.63	127.28
10000	152.67	149.49	146.87	144.71	142.92	141.43
11000	167.94	164.43	161.56	159.18	157.21	155.57
12000	183.21	179.38	176.24	173.65	171.50	169.71
13000	198.47	194.33	190.93	188.12	185.80	183.85
14000	213.74	209.28	205.62	202.60	200.09	198.00
15000	229.01	224.23	220.31	217.07	214.38	212.14
16000	244.27	239.18	234.99	231.54	228.67	226.28
17000	259.54	254.12	249.68	246.01	242.96	240.42
18000	274.81	269.07	264.37	260.48	257.25	254.57
19000	290.07	284.02	279.05	274.95	271.55	268.71
20000	305.34	298.97	293.74	289.42	285.84	282.85
21000	320.61	313.92	308.43	303.89	300.13	296.99
22000	335.88	328.87	323.11	318.36	314.42	311.13
23000	351.14	343.82	337.80	332.84	328.71	325.28
24000	366.41	358.76	352.49	347.31	343.01	339.42
25000	381.68	373.71	367.18	361.78	357.30	353.56
30000	458.01	448.45	440.61	434.13	428.76	424.27
35000	534.35	523.20	514.05	506.49	500.22	494.99
40000	610.68	597.94	587.48	578.84	571.68	565.70
45000	687.02	672.68	660.92	651.20	643.14	636.41
50000	763.35	747.42	734.35	723.56	714.59	707.12
55000	839.69	822.17	807.79	795.91	786.05	777.84
60000	916.02	896.91	881.22	868.27	857.51	848.55
65000	992.36	971.65	954.66	940.62	928.97	919.26
70000	1068.69	1046.39	1028.09	1012.98	1000.43	989.97
75000	1145.03	1121.13	1101.53	1085.33	1071.89	1060.69
80000	1221.36	1195.88	1174.96	1157.69	1143.35	1131.40
85000	1297.70	1270.62	1248.40	1230.04	1214.81	1202.11
90000	1374.04	1345.36	1321.83	1302.40	1286.27	1272.82
95000	1450.37	1420.10	1395.27	1374.76	1357.73	1343.54
100000	1526.71	1494.85	1468.70	1447.11	1429.19	1414.25
200000	3053.41	2989.69	2937.40	2894.22	2858.38	2828.50
300000	4580.12	4484.54	4406.10	4341.33	4287.57	4242.74
400000	6106.82	5979.39	5874.81	5788.44	5716.76	5656.99
500000	7633.53	7474.23	7343.51	7235.56	7145.94	7071.24

MONTHLY PAYMENT

Necessary to amortize a loan

16%

TERM / AMOUNT	19 YEARS	20 YEARS	25 YEARS	30 YEARS	35 YEARS	40 YEARS
500	7.01	6.96	6.79	6.72	6.69	6.68
600	8.41	8.35	8.15	8.07	8.03	8.01
700	9.81	9.74	9.51	9.41	9.37	9.35
800	11.21	11.13	10.87	10.76	10.71	10.69
900	12.62	12.52	12.23	12.10	12.05	12.02
1000	14.02	13.91	13.59	13.45	13.38	13.36
2000	28.03	27.83	27.18	26.90	26.77	26.71
3000	42.05	41.74	40.77	40.34	40.15	40.07
4000	56.07	55.65	54.36	53.79	53.54	53.43
5000	70.09	69.56	67.94	67.24	66.92	66.78
6000	84.10	83.48	81.53	80.69	80.31	80.14
7000	98.12	97.39	95.12	94.13	93.69	93.50
8000	112.14	111.30	108.71	107.58	107.08	106.85
9000	126.16	125.21	122.30	121.03	120.46	120.21
10000	140.18	139.13	135.89	134.48	133.85	133.57
11000	154.19	153.04	149.48	147.92	147.23	146.92
12000	168.21	166.95	163.07	161.37	160.62	160.28
13000	182.23	180.86	176.66	174.82	174.00	173.63
14000	196.25	194.78	190.24	188.27	187.39	186.99
15000	210.26	208.69	203.83	201.71	200.77	200.35
16000	224.28	222.60	217.42	215.16	214.16	213.70
17000	238.30	236.51	231.01	228.61	227.54	227.06
18000	252.31	250.43	244.60	242.06	240.92	240.42
19000	266.33	264.34	258.19	255.50	254.31	253.77
20000	280.35	278.25	271.78	268.95	267.69	267.13
21000	294.37	292.16	285.37	282.40	281.08	280.49
22000	308.38	306.08	298.96	295.85	294.46	293.84
23000	322.40	319.99	312.54	309.29	307.85	307.20
24000	336.42	333.90	326.13	322.74	321.23	320.56
25000	350.44	347.81	339.72	336.19	334.62	333.91
30000	420.52	417.38	407.67	403.43	401.54	400.70
35000	490.61	486.94	475.61	470.67	468.46	467.48
40000	560.70	556.50	543.56	537.90	535.39	534.26
45000	630.79	626.07	611.50	605.14	602.31	601.04
50000	700.87	695.63	679.44	672.38	669.24	667.82
55000	770.96	765.19	747.39	739.62	736.16	734.61
60000	841.05	834.75	815.33	806.85	803.08	801.39
65000	911.14	904.32	883.28	874.09	870.01	868.17
70000	981.22	973.88	951.22	941.33	936.93	934.95
75000	1051.31	1043.44	1019.17	1008.57	1003.85	1001.74
80000	1121.40	1113.01	1087.11	1075.81	1070.78	1068.52
85000	1191.48	1182.57	1155.06	1143.04	1137.70	1135.30
90000	1261.57	1252.13	1223.00	1210.28	1204.62	1202.08
95000	1331.66	1321.69	1290.94	1277.52	1271.55	1268.87
100000	1401.75	1391.26	1358.89	1344.76	1338.47	1335.65
200000	2803.49	2782.51	2717.78	2689.51	2676.94	2671.30
300000	4205.24	4173.77	4076.67	4034.27	4015.41	4006.95
400000	5606.99	5565.03	5435.56	5379.03	5353.88	5342.59
500000	7008.73	6956.28	6794.44	6723.78	6692.35	6678.24

16 1/4%

MONTHLY PAYMENT

Necessary to amortize a loan

TERM / AMOUNT	1 YEAR	2 YEARS	3 YEARS	4 YEARS	5 YEARS	6 YEARS
500	45.42	24.54	17.64	14.23	12.23	10.91
600	54.51	29.45	21.17	17.08	14.67	13.10
700	63.59	34.36	24.70	19.93	17.12	15.28
800	72.68	39.27	28.22	22.77	19.56	17.46
900	81.76	44.17	31.75	25.62	22.01	19.65
1000	90.85	49.08	35.28	28.47	24.45	21.83
2000	181.70	98.17	70.56	56.94	48.90	43.66
3000	272.55	147.25	105.84	85.41	73.35	65.49
4000	363.40	196.33	141.12	113.87	97.80	87.32
5000	454.25	245.41	176.40	142.34	122.26	109.15
6000	545.09	294.50	211.68	170.81	146.71	130.98
7000	635.94	343.58	246.96	199.28	171.16	152.81
8000	726.79	392.66	282.24	227.75	195.61	174.64
9000	817.64	441.74	317.53	256.22	220.06	196.47
10000	908.49	490.83	352.81	284.68	244.51	218.30
11000	999.34	539.91	388.09	313.15	268.96	240.13
12000	1090.19	588.99	423.37	341.62	293.41	261.96
13000	1181.04	638.07	458.65	370.09	317.86	283.79
14000	1271.89	687.16	493.93	398.56	342.32	305.62
15000	1362.74	736.24	529.21	427.03	366.77	327.45
16000	1453.59	785.32	564.49	455.50	391.22	349.28
17000	1544.43	834.40	599.77	483.96	415.67	371.11
18000	1635.28	883.49	635.05	512.43	440.12	392.93
19000	1726.13	932.57	670.33	540.90	464.57	414.76
20000	1816.98	981.65	705.61	569.37	489.02	436.59
21000	1907.83	1030.73	740.89	597.84	513.47	458.42
22000	1998.68	1079.82	776.17	626.31	537.92	480.25
23000	2089.53	1128.90	811.45	654.77	562.37	502.08
24000	2180.38	1177.98	846.73	683.24	586.83	523.91
25000	2271.23	1227.06	882.01	711.71	611.28	545.74
30000	2725.47	1472.48	1058.42	854.05	733.53	654.89
35000	3179.72	1717.89	1234.82	996.40	855.79	764.04
40000	3633.96	1963.30	1411.22	1138.74	978.04	873.19
45000	4088.21	2208.72	1587.62	1281.08	1100.30	982.34
50000	4542.45	2454.13	1764.03	1423.42	1222.55	1091.48
55000	4996.70	2699.54	1940.43	1565.76	1344.81	1200.63
60000	5450.94	2944.95	2116.83	1708.11	1467.06	1309.78
65000	5905.19	3190.37	2293.23	1850.45	1589.32	1418.93
70000	6359.44	3435.78	2469.64	1992.79	1711.57	1528.08
75000	6813.68	3681.19	2646.04	2135.13	1833.83	1637.23
80000	7267.93	3926.61	2822.44	2277.48	1956.08	1746.38
85000	7722.17	4172.02	2998.84	2419.82	2078.34	1855.52
90000	8176.42	4417.43	3175.25	2562.16	2200.60	1964.67
95000	8630.66	4662.84	3351.65	2704.50	2322.85	2073.82
100000	9084.91	4908.26	3528.05	2846.84	2445.11	2182.97
200000	18169.80	9816.51	7056.11	5693.69	4890.21	4365.94
300000	27254.70	14724.80	10584.20	8540.53	7335.32	6548.91
400000	36339.60	19633.00	14112.20	11387.40	9780.42	8731.88
500000	45424.50	24541.30	17640.30	14234.20	12225.50	10914.80

MONTHLY PAYMENT

Necessary to amortize a loan

16 1/4%

TERM / AMOUNT	7 YEARS	8 YEARS	9 YEARS	10 YEARS	11 YEARS	12 YEARS
500	10.00	9.34	8.84	8.45	8.15	7.91
600	12.00	11.21	10.61	10.14	9.78	9.49
700	14.00	13.07	12.37	11.84	11.41	11.08
800	16.00	14.94	14.14	13.53	13.04	12.66
900	18.00	16.81	15.91	15.22	14.67	14.24
1000	20.00	18.68	17.68	16.91	16.30	15.82
2000	40.01	37.35	35.35	33.81	32.61	31.64
3000	60.01	56.03	53.03	50.72	48.91	47.47
4000	80.02	74.70	70.71	67.63	65.21	63.29
5000	100.02	93.38	88.39	84.54	81.52	79.11
6000	120.03	112.06	106.06	101.45	97.82	94.93
7000	140.03	130.73	123.74	118.35	114.12	110.76
8000	160.04	149.41	141.42	135.26	130.43	126.58
9000	180.04	168.09	159.09	152.17	146.73	142.40
10000	200.05	186.76	176.77	169.07	163.03	158.22
11000	220.05	205.44	194.45	185.98	179.34	174.05
12000	240.06	224.11	212.12	202.89	195.64	189.87
13000	260.06	242.79	229.80	219.80	211.94	205.69
14000	280.07	261.47	247.48	236.70	228.25	221.51
15000	300.07	280.14	265.16	253.61	244.55	237.34
16000	320.08	298.82	282.83	270.52	260.86	253.16
17000	340.08	317.49	300.51	287.43	277.16	268.98
18000	360.08	336.17	318.19	304.33	293.46	284.80
19000	380.09	354.85	335.86	321.24	309.77	300.63
20000	400.09	373.52	353.54	338.15	326.07	316.45
21000	420.10	392.20	371.22	355.06	342.37	332.27
22000	440.10	410.87	388.90	371.96	358.68	348.09
23000	460.11	429.55	406.57	388.87	374.98	363.92
24000	480.11	448.23	424.25	405.78	391.28	379.74
25000	500.12	466.90	441.93	422.69	407.59	395.56
30000	600.14	560.28	530.31	507.22	489.10	474.67
35000	700.16	653.66	618.70	591.76	570.62	553.79
40000	800.19	747.04	707.08	676.30	652.14	632.90
45000	900.21	840.42	795.47	760.83	733.65	712.01
50000	1000.23	933.80	883.85	845.37	815.17	791.12
55000	1100.26	1027.18	972.24	929.91	896.69	870.23
60000	1200.28	1120.56	1060.62	1014.45	978.21	949.35
65000	1300.30	1213.94	1149.01	1098.98	1059.72	1028.46
70000	1400.33	1307.32	1237.39	1183.52	1141.24	1107.57
75000	1500.35	1400.71	1325.78	1268.06	1222.76	1186.68
80000	1600.38	1494.09	1414.16	1352.59	1304.27	1265.79
85000	1700.40	1587.47	1502.55	1437.13	1385.79	1344.91
90000	1800.42	1680.85	1590.93	1521.67	1467.31	1424.02
95000	1900.45	1774.23	1679.32	1606.21	1548.83	1503.13
100000	2000.47	1867.61	1767.70	1690.74	1630.34	1582.24
200000	4000.94	3735.21	3535.41	3381.49	3260.68	3164.49
300000	6001.41	5602.82	5303.11	5072.23	4891.03	4746.73
400000	8001.88	7470.43	7070.82	6762.97	6521.37	6328.97
500000	10002.30	9338.04	8838.52	8453.71	8151.71	7911.21

16 1/4%

MONTHLY PAYMENT

Necessary to amortize a loan

TERM / AMOUNT	13 YEARS	14 YEARS	15 YEARS	16 YEARS	17 YEARS	18 YEARS
500	7.72	7.56	7.43	7.32	7.24	7.16
600	9.26	9.07	8.92	8.79	8.68	8.60
700	10.80	10.58	10.40	10.25	10.13	10.03
800	12.35	12.10	11.89	11.72	11.58	11.46
900	13.89	13.61	13.38	13.18	13.03	12.89
1000	15.43	15.12	14.86	14.65	14.47	14.33
2000	30.87	30.24	29.72	29.30	28.94	28.65
3000	46.30	45.36	44.59	43.95	43.42	42.98
4000	61.74	60.48	59.45	58.60	57.89	57.30
5000	77.17	75.60	74.31	73.24	72.36	71.63
6000	92.61	90.72	89.17	87.89	86.83	85.95
7000	108.05	105.84	104.03	102.54	101.31	100.28
8000	123.48	120.96	118.89	117.19	115.78	114.61
9000	138.91	136.08	133.76	131.84	130.25	128.93
10000	154.35	151.20	148.62	146.49	144.73	143.26
11000	169.78	166.32	163.48	161.14	159.20	157.58
12000	185.22	181.44	178.34	175.79	173.67	171.91
13000	200.65	196.56	193.20	190.44	188.14	186.23
14000	216.09	211.68	208.06	205.08	202.61	200.56
15000	231.52	226.80	222.93	219.73	217.09	214.89
16000	246.96	241.92	237.79	234.38	231.56	229.21
17000	262.39	257.04	252.65	249.03	246.03	243.54
18000	277.83	272.16	267.51	263.68	260.50	257.86
19000	293.26	287.28	282.37	278.33	274.98	272.19
20000	308.70	302.40	297.23	292.98	289.45	286.51
21000	324.13	317.52	312.10	307.63	303.92	300.84
22000	339.57	332.64	326.96	322.27	318.39	315.17
23000	355.00	347.76	341.82	336.92	332.87	329.49
24000	370.44	362.88	356.68	351.57	347.34	343.82
25000	385.87	378.00	371.54	366.22	361.81	358.14
30000	463.05	453.60	445.85	439.47	434.17	429.77
35000	540.22	529.19	520.16	512.71	506.54	501.40
40000	617.40	604.79	594.47	585.95	578.90	573.03
45000	694.57	680.39	668.78	659.20	651.26	644.66
50000	771.75	755.99	743.08	732.44	723.62	716.28
55000	848.92	831.59	817.39	805.69	795.99	787.91
60000	926.10	907.19	891.70	878.93	868.35	859.54
65000	1003.27	982.79	966.01	952.17	940.71	931.17
70000	1080.45	1058.39	1040.32	1025.42	1013.07	1002.80
75000	1157.62	1133.99	1114.63	1098.66	1085.43	1074.43
80000	1234.79	1209.59	1188.93	1171.91	1157.80	1146.05
85000	1311.97	1285.19	1263.24	1245.15	1230.16	1217.68
90000	1389.14	1360.79	1337.55	1318.39	1302.52	1289.31
95000	1466.32	1436.38	1411.86	1391.64	1374.88	1360.94
100000	1543.49	1511.98	1486.17	1464.88	1447.25	1432.57
200000	3086.99	3023.97	2972.33	2929.77	2894.49	2865.14
300000	4630.48	4535.95	4458.50	4394.65	4341.74	4297.70
400000	6173.97	6047.94	5944.67	5859.53	5788.98	5730.27
500000	7717.47	7559.92	7430.84	7324.42	7236.23	7162.84

MONTHLY PAYMENT

Necessary to amortize a loan

16 1/4%

TERM / AMOUNT	19 YEARS	20 YEARS	25 YEARS	30 YEARS	35 YEARS	40 YEARS
500	7.10	7.05	6.89	6.82	6.79	6.78
600	8.52	8.46	8.27	8.19	8.15	8.14
700	9.94	9.87	9.65	9.55	9.51	9.49
800	11.36	11.28	11.03	10.92	10.87	10.85
900	12.78	12.69	12.41	12.28	12.23	12.21
1000	14.20	14.10	13.79	13.65	13.59	13.56
2000	28.41	28.20	27.57	27.30	27.18	27.13
3000	42.61	42.30	41.36	40.95	40.77	40.69
4000	56.81	56.40	55.14	54.60	54.36	54.25
5000	71.02	70.50	68.93	68.25	67.95	67.81
6000	85.22	84.60	82.71	81.90	81.54	81.38
7000	99.42	98.70	96.50	95.55	95.13	94.94
8000	113.63	112.80	110.28	109.20	108.72	108.50
9000	127.83	126.90	124.07	122.84	122.31	122.07
10000	142.03	141.01	137.85	136.49	135.90	135.63
11000	156.23	155.11	151.64	150.14	149.48	149.19
12000	170.44	169.21	165.43	163.79	163.07	162.76
13000	184.64	183.31	179.21	177.44	176.66	176.32
14000	198.84	197.41	193.00	191.09	190.25	189.88
15000	213.05	211.51	206.78	204.74	203.84	203.44
16000	227.25	225.61	220.57	218.39	217.43	217.01
17000	241.45	239.71	234.35	232.04	231.02	230.57
18000	255.66	253.81	248.14	245.69	244.61	244.13
19000	269.86	267.91	261.92	259.34	258.20	257.70
20000	284.06	282.01	275.71	272.99	271.79	271.26
21000	298.27	296.11	289.49	286.64	285.38	284.82
22000	312.47	310.21	303.28	300.29	298.97	298.39
23000	326.67	324.31	317.06	313.94	312.56	311.95
24000	340.88	338.41	330.85	327.58	326.15	325.51
25000	355.08	352.51	344.64	341.23	339.74	339.07
30000	426.09	423.01	413.56	409.48	407.69	406.89
35000	497.11	493.52	482.49	477.73	475.63	474.70
40000	568.13	564.02	551.42	545.97	543.58	542.52
45000	639.14	634.52	620.34	614.22	611.53	610.33
50000	710.16	705.02	689.27	682.47	679.48	678.15
55000	781.17	775.53	758.20	750.71	747.42	745.96
60000	852.19	846.03	827.12	818.96	815.37	813.78
65000	923.20	916.53	896.05	887.21	883.32	881.59
70000	994.22	987.03	964.98	955.45	951.27	949.41
75000	1065.23	1057.53	1033.91	1023.70	1019.21	1017.22
80000	1136.25	1128.04	1102.83	1091.95	1087.16	1085.04
85000	1207.26	1198.54	1171.76	1160.19	1155.11	1152.85
90000	1278.28	1269.04	1240.69	1228.44	1223.05	1220.67
95000	1349.30	1339.54	1309.61	1296.69	1291.00	1288.48
100000	1420.31	1410.04	1378.54	1364.93	1358.95	1356.30
200000	2840.62	2820.09	2757.08	2729.87	2717.90	2712.59
300000	4260.93	4230.13	4135.62	4094.80	4076.85	4068.89
400000	5681.24	5640.18	5514.16	5459.74	5435.80	5425.19
500000	7101.56	7050.23	6892.70	6824.67	6794.75	6781.48

16 1/2%

MONTHLY PAYMENT
Necessary to amortize a loan

TERM AMOUNT	1 YEAR	2 YEARS	3 YEARS	4 YEARS	5 YEARS	6 YEARS
500	45.48	24.60	17.70	14.30	12.29	10.98
600	54.58	29.52	21.24	17.16	14.75	13.18
700	63.68	34.44	24.78	20.02	17.21	15.38
800	72.77	39.36	28.32	22.88	19.67	17.57
900	81.87	44.28	31.86	25.74	22.13	19.77
1000	90.97	49.20	35.40	28.60	24.58	21.97
2000	181.94	98.41	70.81	57.19	49.17	43.94
3000	272.90	147.61	106.21	85.79	73.75	65.90
4000	363.87	196.81	141.62	114.39	98.34	87.87
5000	454.84	246.01	177.02	142.99	122.92	109.84
6000	545.81	295.22	212.43	171.58	147.51	131.81
7000	636.78	344.42	247.83	200.18	172.09	153.78
8000	727.74	393.62	283.24	228.78	196.68	175.75
9000	818.71	442.82	318.64	257.37	221.26	197.71
10000	909.68	492.03	354.05	285.97	245.85	219.68
11000	1000.65	541.23	389.45	314.57	270.43	241.65
12000	1091.62	590.43	424.85	343.17	295.02	263.62
13000	1182.58	639.63	460.26	371.76	319.60	285.59
14000	1273.55	688.84	495.66	400.36	344.18	307.55
15000	1364.52	738.04	531.07	428.96	368.77	329.52
16000	1455.49	787.24	566.47	457.55	393.35	351.49
17000	1546.45	836.44	601.88	486.15	417.94	373.46
18000	1637.42	885.65	637.28	514.75	442.52	395.43
19000	1728.39	934.85	672.69	543.34	467.11	417.39
20000	1819.36	984.05	708.09	571.94	491.69	439.36
21000	1910.33	1033.25	743.49	600.54	516.28	461.33
22000	2001.29	1082.45	778.90	629.14	540.86	483.30
23000	2092.26	1131.66	814.30	657.73	565.45	505.27
24000	2183.23	1180.86	849.71	686.33	590.03	527.23
25000	2274.20	1230.06	885.11	714.93	614.61	549.20
30000	2729.04	1476.07	1062.13	857.91	737.54	659.04
35000	3183.88	1722.09	1239.16	1000.90	860.46	768.88
40000	3638.72	1968.10	1416.18	1143.88	983.38	878.72
45000	4093.56	2214.11	1593.20	1286.87	1106.31	988.57
50000	4548.40	2460.12	1770.22	1429.85	1229.23	1098.41
55000	5003.24	2706.14	1947.25	1572.84	1352.15	1208.25
60000	5458.08	2952.15	2124.27	1715.82	1475.07	1318.09
65000	5912.91	3198.16	2301.29	1858.81	1598.00	1427.93
70000	6367.75	3444.17	2478.31	2001.80	1720.92	1537.77
75000	6822.59	3690.19	2655.34	2144.78	1843.84	1647.61
80000	7277.43	3936.20	2832.36	2287.77	1966.77	1757.45
85000	7732.27	4182.21	3009.38	2430.75	2089.69	1867.29
90000	8187.11	4428.22	3186.40	2573.74	2212.61	1977.13
95000	8641.95	4674.24	3363.43	2716.72	2335.53	2086.97
100000	9096.79	4920.25	3540.45	2859.71	2458.46	2196.81
200000	18193.60	9840.50	7080.90	5719.42	4916.92	4393.62
300000	27290.40	14760.70	10621.30	8579.12	7375.37	6590.43
400000	36387.20	19681.00	14161.80	11438.80	9833.83	8787.24
500000	45484.00	24601.20	17702.20	14298.50	12292.30	10984.10

MONTHLY PAYMENT

Necessary to amortize a loan

16 1/2%

TERM / AMOUNT	7 YEARS	8 YEARS	9 YEARS	10 YEARS	11 YEARS	12 YEARS
500	10.07	9.41	8.91	8.53	8.23	7.99
600	12.09	11.29	10.70	10.24	9.88	9.59
700	14.10	13.18	12.48	11.95	11.53	11.19
800	16.12	15.06	14.26	13.65	13.17	12.79
900	18.13	16.94	16.05	15.36	14.82	14.39
1000	20.15	18.82	17.83	17.06	16.46	15.99
2000	40.30	37.65	35.66	34.13	32.93	31.97
3000	60.44	56.47	53.49	51.19	49.39	47.96
4000	80.59	75.30	71.32	68.26	65.86	63.95
5000	100.74	94.12	89.15	85.32	82.32	79.94
6000	120.89	112.94	106.98	102.39	98.79	95.92
7000	141.04	131.77	124.81	119.45	115.25	111.91
8000	161.18	150.59	142.64	136.51	131.72	127.90
9000	181.33	169.42	160.47	153.58	148.18	143.89
10000	201.48	188.24	178.30	170.64	164.64	159.87
11000	221.63	207.06	196.13	187.71	181.11	175.86
12000	241.78	225.89	213.95	204.77	197.57	191.85
13000	261.92	244.71	231.78	221.84	214.04	207.84
14000	282.07	263.54	249.61	238.90	230.50	223.82
15000	302.22	282.36	267.44	255.96	246.97	239.81
16000	322.37	301.18	285.27	273.03	263.43	255.80
17000	342.52	320.01	303.10	290.09	279.90	271.79
18000	362.66	338.83	320.93	307.16	296.36	287.77
19000	382.81	357.66	338.76	324.22	312.82	303.76
20000	402.96	376.48	356.59	341.29	329.29	319.75
21000	423.11	395.30	374.42	358.35	345.75	335.73
22000	443.25	414.13	392.25	375.41	362.22	351.72
23000	463.40	432.95	410.08	392.48	378.68	367.71
24000	483.55	451.78	427.91	409.54	395.15	383.70
25000	503.70	470.60	445.74	426.61	411.61	399.68
30000	604.44	564.72	534.89	511.93	493.93	479.62
35000	705.18	658.84	624.03	597.25	576.25	559.56
40000	805.92	752.96	713.18	682.57	658.58	639.49
45000	906.66	847.08	802.33	767.89	740.90	719.43
50000	1007.40	941.20	891.48	853.21	823.22	799.37
55000	1108.14	1035.32	980.62	938.53	905.54	879.30
60000	1208.88	1129.44	1069.77	1023.86	987.86	959.24
65000	1309.62	1223.56	1158.92	1109.18	1070.19	1039.18
70000	1410.35	1317.68	1248.07	1194.50	1152.51	1119.11
75000	1511.09	1411.80	1337.21	1279.82	1234.83	1199.05
80000	1611.83	1505.92	1426.36	1365.14	1317.15	1278.99
85000	1712.57	1600.04	1515.51	1450.46	1399.47	1358.93
90000	1813.31	1694.16	1604.66	1535.78	1481.80	1438.86
95000	1914.05	1788.28	1693.80	1621.10	1564.12	1518.80
100000	2014.79	1882.40	1782.95	1706.43	1646.44	1598.74
200000	4029.59	3764.80	3565.90	3412.85	3292.88	3197.47
300000	6044.38	5647.20	5348.85	5119.28	4939.32	4796.21
400000	8059.17	7529.60	7131.80	6825.70	6585.76	6394.94
500000	10074.00	9412.00	8914.75	8532.13	8232.20	7993.68

16 1/2%

MONTHLY PAYMENT

Necessary to amortize a loan

TERM AMOUNT	13 YEARS	14 YEARS	15 YEARS	16 YEARS	17 YEARS	18 YEARS
500	7.80	7.65	7.52	7.41	7.33	7.25
600	9.36	9.18	9.02	8.90	8.79	8.71
700	10.92	10.70	10.53	10.38	10.26	10.16
800	12.48	12.23	12.03	11.86	11.72	11.61
900	14.04	13.76	13.53	13.34	13.19	13.06
1000	15.60	15.29	15.04	14.83	14.65	14.51
2000	31.21	30.58	30.07	29.65	29.31	29.02
3000	46.81	45.88	45.11	44.48	43.96	43.53
4000	62.41	61.17	60.15	59.31	58.62	58.04
5000	78.02	76.46	75.19	74.14	73.27	72.55
6000	93.62	91.75	90.22	88.96	87.92	87.06
7000	109.23	107.04	105.26	103.79	102.58	101.57
8000	124.83	122.34	120.30	118.62	117.23	116.08
9000	140.43	137.63	135.33	133.45	131.88	130.59
10000	156.04	152.92	150.37	148.27	146.54	145.10
11000	171.64	168.21	165.41	163.10	161.19	159.61
12000	187.24	183.50	180.45	177.93	175.85	174.12
13000	202.85	198.80	195.48	192.76	190.50	188.63
14000	218.45	214.09	210.52	207.58	205.15	203.14
15000	234.05	229.38	225.56	222.41	219.81	217.64
16000	249.66	244.67	240.59	237.24	234.46	232.15
17000	265.26	259.96	255.63	252.06	249.11	246.66
18000	280.87	275.26	270.67	266.89	263.77	261.17
19000	296.47	290.55	285.71	281.72	278.42	275.68
20000	312.07	305.84	300.74	296.55	293.08	290.19
21000	327.68	321.13	315.78	311.37	307.73	304.70
22000	343.28	336.42	330.82	326.20	322.38	319.21
23000	358.88	351.72	345.85	341.03	337.04	333.72
24000	374.49	367.01	360.89	355.86	351.69	348.23
25000	390.09	382.30	375.93	370.68	366.34	362.74
30000	468.11	458.76	451.11	444.82	439.61	435.29
35000	546.13	535.22	526.30	518.96	512.88	507.84
40000	624.14	611.68	601.48	593.09	586.15	580.39
45000	702.16	688.14	676.67	667.23	659.42	652.93
50000	780.18	764.60	751.86	741.37	732.69	725.48
55000	858.20	841.06	827.04	815.50	805.96	798.03
60000	936.22	917.52	902.23	889.64	879.23	870.58
65000	1014.23	993.98	977.41	963.78	952.50	943.13
70000	1092.25	1070.44	1052.60	1037.91	1025.76	1015.67
75000	1170.27	1146.90	1127.78	1112.05	1099.03	1088.22
80000	1248.29	1223.36	1202.97	1186.18	1172.30	1160.77
85000	1326.30	1299.82	1278.15	1260.32	1245.57	1233.32
90000	1404.32	1376.28	1353.34	1334.46	1318.84	1305.87
95000	1482.34	1452.74	1428.52	1408.59	1392.11	1378.41
100000	1560.36	1529.20	1503.71	1482.73	1465.38	1450.96
200000	3120.72	3058.40	3007.42	2965.46	2930.75	2901.92
300000	4681.07	4587.60	4511.13	4448.19	4396.13	4352.88
400000	6241.43	6116.80	6014.84	5930.92	5861.51	5803.85
500000	7801.79	7646.00	7518.55	7413.65	7326.88	7254.81

MONTHLY PAYMENT

Necessary to amortize a loan

16 1/2%

TERM / AMOUNT	19 YEARS	20 YEARS	25 YEARS	30 YEARS	35 YEARS	40 YEARS
500	7.19	7.14	6.99	6.93	6.90	6.88
600	8.63	8.57	8.39	8.31	8.28	8.26
700	10.07	10.00	9.79	9.70	9.66	9.64
800	11.51	11.43	11.19	11.08	11.04	11.02
900	12.95	12.86	12.58	12.47	12.42	12.39
1000	14.39	14.29	13.98	13.85	13.79	13.77
2000	28.78	28.58	27.96	27.70	27.59	27.54
3000	43.17	42.87	41.95	41.55	41.38	41.31
4000	57.56	57.16	55.93	55.41	55.18	55.08
5000	71.95	71.45	69.91	69.26	68.97	68.85
6000	86.34	85.73	83.89	83.11	82.77	82.62
7000	100.73	100.02	97.88	96.96	96.56	96.39
8000	115.12	114.31	111.86	110.81	110.36	110.16
9000	129.51	128.60	125.84	124.66	124.15	123.93
10000	143.90	142.89	139.83	138.52	137.95	137.70
11000	158.28	157.18	153.81	152.37	151.74	151.47
12000	172.67	171.47	167.79	166.22	165.53	165.24
13000	187.06	185.76	181.77	180.07	179.33	179.01
14000	201.45	200.05	195.75	193.92	193.12	192.77
15000	215.84	214.34	209.74	207.77	206.92	206.54
16000	230.23	228.62	223.72	221.62	220.71	220.31
17000	244.62	242.91	237.70	235.48	234.51	234.08
18000	259.01	257.20	251.68	249.33	248.30	247.85
19000	273.40	271.49	265.67	263.18	262.10	261.62
20000	287.79	285.78	279.65	277.03	275.89	275.39
21000	302.18	300.07	293.63	290.88	289.69	289.16
22000	316.57	314.36	307.61	304.73	303.48	302.93
23000	330.96	328.65	321.60	318.58	317.27	316.70
24000	345.35	342.94	335.58	332.44	331.07	330.47
25000	359.74	357.23	349.56	346.29	344.86	344.24
30000	431.68	428.67	419.47	415.54	413.84	413.09
35000	503.63	500.12	489.39	484.80	482.81	481.94
40000	575.58	571.56	559.30	554.06	551.78	550.78
45000	647.53	643.01	629.21	623.32	620.75	619.63
50000	719.47	714.45	699.12	692.57	689.73	688.48
55000	791.42	785.90	769.04	761.83	758.70	757.33
60000	863.37	857.34	838.95	831.09	827.67	826.18
65000	935.32	928.79	908.86	900.35	896.65	895.02
70000	1007.26	1000.23	978.77	969.60	965.62	963.87
75000	1079.21	1071.68	1048.68	1038.86	1034.59	1032.72
80000	1151.16	1143.12	1118.60	1108.12	1103.56	1101.57
85000	1223.10	1214.57	1188.51	1177.38	1172.54	1170.42
90000	1295.05	1286.01	1258.42	1246.63	1241.51	1239.26
95000	1367.00	1357.46	1328.33	1315.89	1310.48	1308.11
100000	1438.95	1428.90	1398.25	1385.15	1379.45	1376.96
200000	2877.89	2857.80	2796.49	2770.30	2758.91	2753.92
300000	4316.84	4286.70	4194.74	4155.44	4138.36	4130.88
400000	5755.78	5715.61	5592.98	5540.59	5517.82	5507.84
500000	7194.73	7144.51	6991.23	6925.74	6897.27	6884.80

16 3/4% MONTHLY PAYMENT

Necessary to amortize a loan

TERM / AMOUNT	1 YEAR	2 YEARS	3 YEARS	4 YEARS	5 YEARS	6 YEARS
500	45.54	24.66	17.76	14.36	12.36	11.05
600	54.65	29.59	21.32	17.24	14.83	13.26
700	63.76	34.53	24.87	20.11	17.30	15.47
800	72.87	39.46	28.42	22.98	19.77	17.69
900	81.98	44.39	31.98	25.85	22.25	19.90
1000	91.09	49.32	35.53	28.73	24.72	22.11
2000	182.17	98.64	71.06	57.45	49.44	44.21
3000	273.26	147.97	106.59	86.18	74.16	66.32
4000	364.35	197.29	142.11	114.90	98.87	88.43
5000	455.43	246.61	177.64	143.63	123.59	110.53
6000	546.52	295.93	213.17	172.36	148.31	132.64
7000	637.60	345.26	248.70	201.08	173.03	154.75
8000	728.69	394.58	284.23	229.81	197.75	176.86
9000	819.78	443.90	319.76	258.53	222.47	198.96
10000	910.86	493.22	355.29	287.26	247.18	221.07
11000	1001.95	542.55	390.81	315.99	271.90	243.18
12000	1093.04	591.87	426.34	344.71	296.62	265.28
13000	1184.12	641.19	461.87	373.44	321.34	287.39
14000	1275.21	690.51	497.40	402.16	346.06	309.50
15000	1366.29	739.84	532.93	430.89	370.78	331.60
16000	1457.38	789.16	568.46	459.61	395.49	353.71
17000	1548.47	838.48	603.98	488.34	420.21	375.82
18000	1639.55	887.80	639.51	517.07	444.93	397.92
19000	1730.64	937.12	675.04	545.79	469.65	420.03
20000	1821.73	986.45	710.57	574.52	494.37	442.14
21000	1912.81	1035.77	746.10	603.24	519.09	464.25
22000	2003.90	1085.09	781.63	631.97	543.80	486.35
23000	2094.99	1134.41	817.16	660.70	568.52	508.46
24000	2186.70	1183.74	852.68	689.42	593.24	530.57
25000	2277.16	1233.06	888.21	718.15	617.96	552.67
30000	2732.59	1479.67	1065.85	861.78	741.55	663.21
35000	3188.02	1726.28	1243.50	1005.41	865.14	773.74
40000	3643.45	1972.89	1421.14	1149.04	988.74	884.28
45000	4098.88	2219.50	1598.78	1292.67	1112.33	994.81
50000	4554.32	2466.12	1776.42	1436.29	1235.92	1105.34
55000	5009.75	2712.73	1954.07	1579.92	1359.51	1215.88
60000	5465.18	2959.34	2131.71	1723.55	1483.10	1326.41
65000	5920.61	3205.95	2309.35	1867.18	1606.69	1436.95
70000	6376.04	3452.56	2486.99	2010.81	1730.29	1547.48
75000	6831.47	3699.17	2664.64	2154.44	1853.88	1658.02
80000	7286.90	3945.78	2842.28	2298.07	1977.47	1768.55
85000	7742.34	4192.40	3019.92	2441.70	2101.06	1879.09
90000	8197.77	4439.01	3197.56	2585.33	2224.65	1989.62
95000	8653.20	4685.62	3375.21	2728.96	2348.25	2100.15
100000	9108.63	4932.23	3552.85	2872.59	2471.84	2210.69
200000	18217.30	9864.46	7105.70	5745.18	4943.68	4421.38
300000	27325.90	14796.70	10658.50	8617.77	7415.51	6632.07
400000	36434.50	19728.90	14211.40	11490.40	9887.35	8842.76
500000	45543.20	24661.20	17764.20	14363.00	12359.20	11053.40

MONTHLY PAYMENT

Necessary to amortize a loan

16 3/4%

TERM / AMOUNT	7 YEARS	8 YEARS	9 YEARS	10 YEARS	11 YEARS	12 YEARS
500	10.15	9.49	8.99	8.61	8.31	8.08
600	12.18	11.38	10.79	10.33	9.98	9.69
700	14.20	13.28	12.59	12.06	11.64	11.31
800	16.23	15.18	14.39	13.78	13.30	12.92
900	18.26	17.08	16.18	15.50	14.96	14.54
1000	20.29	18.97	17.98	17.22	16.63	16.15
2000	40.58	37.94	35.97	34.44	33.25	32.31
3000	60.87	56.92	53.95	51.67	49.88	48.46
4000	81.17	75.89	71.93	68.89	66.50	64.61
5000	101.46	94.86	89.91	86.11	83.13	80.76
6000	121.75	113.84	107.90	103.33	99.76	96.92
7000	142.04	132.81	125.88	120.55	116.38	113.07
8000	162.33	151.78	143.86	137.77	133.01	129.22
9000	182.62	170.75	161.84	155.00	149.63	145.38
10000	202.92	189.72	179.83	172.22	166.26	161.53
11000	223.21	208.70	197.81	189.44	182.89	177.68
12000	243.50	227.67	215.79	206.66	199.51	193.84
13000	263.79	246.64	233.77	223.88	216.14	209.99
14000	284.08	265.61	251.76	241.10	232.76	226.14
15000	304.37	284.59	269.74	258.33	249.39	242.29
16000	324.67	303.56	287.72	275.55	266.02	258.45
17000	344.96	322.53	305.70	292.77	282.64	274.60
18000	365.25	341.50	323.69	309.99	299.27	290.75
19000	385.54	360.48	341.67	327.21	315.89	306.91
20000	405.83	379.45	359.65	344.43	332.52	323.06
21000	426.12	398.42	377.63	361.66	349.15	339.21
22000	446.42	417.39	395.62	378.88	365.77	355.37
23000	466.71	436.37	413.60	396.10	382.40	371.52
24000	487.00	455.34	431.58	413.32	399.03	387.67
25000	507.29	474.31	449.56	430.54	415.65	403.82
30000	608.75	569.17	539.48	516.65	498.78	484.59
35000	710.21	664.04	629.39	602.76	581.91	565.35
40000	811.66	758.90	719.30	688.87	665.04	646.12
45000	913.12	853.76	809.21	774.98	748.17	726.88
50000	1014.58	948.62	899.13	861.08	831.30	807.65
55000	1116.04	1043.48	989.04	947.19	914.43	888.41
60000	1217.50	1138.35	1078.95	1033.30	997.56	969.18
65000	1318.95	1233.21	1168.87	1119.41	1080.69	1049.94
70000	1420.41	1328.07	1258.78	1205.52	1163.82	1130.71
75000	1521.87	1422.93	1348.69	1291.63	1246.95	1211.47
80000	1623.33	1517.80	1438.60	1377.73	1330.08	1292.24
85000	1724.79	1612.66	1528.52	1463.84	1413.21	1373.00
90000	1826.24	1707.52	1618.43	1549.95	1496.34	1453.77
95000	1927.70	1802.38	1708.34	1636.06	1579.47	1534.53
100000	2029.16	1897.24	1798.25	1722.17	1662.60	1615.29
200000	4058.32	3794.49	3596.51	3444.34	3325.20	3230.59
300000	6087.48	5691.73	5394.76	5166.51	4987.81	4845.88
400000	8116.64	7588.98	7193.02	6888.67	6650.41	6461.18
500000	10145.80	9486.22	8991.27	8610.84	8313.01	8076.47

16 3/4%

MONTHLY PAYMENT

Necessary to amortize a loan

TERM / AMOUNT	13 YEARS	14 YEARS	15 YEARS	16 YEARS	17 YEARS	18 YEARS
500	7.89	7.73	7.61	7.50	7.42	7.35
600	9.46	9.28	9.13	9.00	8.90	8.82
700	11.04	10.83	10.65	10.50	10.39	10.29
800	12.62	12.37	12.17	12.01	11.87	11.76
900	14.20	13.92	13.69	13.51	13.35	13.22
1000	15.77	15.46	15.21	15.01	14.84	14.69
2000	31.55	30.93	30.43	30.01	29.67	29.39
3000	47.32	46.39	45.64	45.02	44.51	44.08
4000	63.09	61.86	60.85	60.03	59.34	58.78
5000	78.86	77.32	76.07	75.03	74.18	73.47
6000	94.64	92.79	91.28	90.04	89.01	88.17
7000	110.41	108.25	106.49	105.05	103.85	102.86
8000	126.18	123.72	121.71	120.05	118.69	117.55
9000	141.96	139.18	136.92	135.06	133.52	132.25
10000	157.73	154.65	152.13	150.07	148.36	146.94
11000	173.50	170.11	167.35	165.07	163.19	161.64
12000	189.28	185.58	182.56	180.08	178.03	176.33
13000	205.05	201.04	197.77	195.08	192.87	191.03
14000	220.82	216.51	212.99	210.09	207.70	205.72
15000	236.59	231.97	228.20	225.10	222.54	220.41
16000	252.37	247.44	243.41	240.10	237.37	235.11
17000	268.14	262.90	258.63	255.11	252.21	249.80
18000	283.91	278.37	273.84	270.12	267.04	264.50
19000	299.69	293.83	289.05	285.12	281.88	279.19
20000	315.46	309.30	304.26	300.13	296.72	293.88
21000	331.23	324.76	319.48	315.14	311.55	308.58
22000	347.00	340.23	334.69	330.14	326.39	323.27
23000	362.78	355.69	349.90	345.15	341.22	337.97
24000	378.55	371.16	365.12	360.16	356.06	352.66
25000	394.32	386.62	380.33	375.16	370.89	367.36
30000	473.19	463.95	456.40	450.19	445.07	440.83
35000	552.05	541.27	532.46	525.23	519.25	514.30
40000	630.92	618.59	608.53	600.26	593.43	587.77
45000	709.78	695.92	684.60	675.29	667.61	661.24
50000	788.65	773.24	760.66	750.32	741.79	734.71
55000	867.51	850.57	836.73	825.36	815.97	808.18
60000	946.38	927.89	912.79	900.39	890.15	881.65
65000	1025.24	1005.21	988.86	975.42	964.32	955.12
70000	1104.10	1082.54	1064.93	1050.45	1038.50	1028.59
75000	1182.97	1159.86	1140.99	1125.49	1112.68	1102.07
80000	1261.83	1237.19	1217.06	1200.52	1186.86	1175.54
85000	1340.70	1314.51	1293.12	1275.55	1261.04	1249.01
90000	1419.56	1391.84	1369.19	1350.58	1335.22	1322.48
95000	1498.43	1469.16	1445.26	1425.62	1409.40	1395.95
100000	1577.29	1546.48	1521.32	1500.65	1483.58	1469.42
200000	3154.58	3092.97	3042.64	3001.29	2967.15	2938.84
300000	4731.87	4639.45	4563.97	4501.94	4450.73	4408.26
400000	6309.17	6185.93	6085.29	6002.59	5934.30	5877.68
500000	7886.46	7732.42	7606.61	7503.24	7417.88	7347.10

MONTHLY PAYMENT

Necessary to amortize a loan

16 3/4%

TERM / AMOUNT	19 YEARS	20 YEARS	25 YEARS	30 YEARS	35 YEARS	40 YEARS
500	7.29	7.24	7.09	7.03	7.00	6.99
600	8.75	8.69	8.51	8.43	8.40	8.39
700	10.20	10.13	9.93	9.84	9.80	9.78
800	11.66	11.58	11.34	11.24	11.20	11.18
900	13.12	13.03	12.76	12.65	12.60	12.58
1000	14.58	14.48	14.18	14.05	14.00	13.98
2000	29.15	28.96	28.36	28.11	28.00	27.95
3000	43.73	43.43	42.54	42.16	42.00	41.93
4000	58.31	57.91	56.72	56.22	56.00	55.91
5000	72.88	72.39	70.90	70.27	70.00	69.88
6000	87.46	86.87	85.08	84.32	84.00	83.86
7000	102.04	101.35	99.26	98.38	98.00	97.83
8000	116.61	115.83	113.44	112.43	112.00	111.81
9000	131.19	130.30	127.62	126.49	126.00	125.79
10000	145.76	144.78	141.80	140.54	140.00	139.76
11000	160.34	159.26	155.98	154.59	154.00	153.74
12000	174.92	173.74	170.16	168.65	168.00	167.72
13000	189.49	188.22	184.34	182.70	182.00	181.69
14000	204.07	202.70	198.52	196.76	196.00	195.67
15000	218.65	217.17	212.70	210.81	210.00	209.65
16000	233.22	231.65	226.88	224.86	224.00	223.62
17000	247.80	246.13	241.06	238.92	238.00	237.60
18000	262.38	260.61	255.24	252.97	252.00	251.57
19000	276.95	275.09	269.42	267.03	266.00	265.55
20000	291.53	289.56	283.60	281.08	280.00	279.53
21000	306.11	304.04	297.78	295.13	294.00	293.50
22000	320.68	318.52	311.96	309.19	308.00	307.48
23000	335.26	333.00	326.14	323.24	322.00	321.46
24000	349.84	347.48	340.32	337.30	336.00	335.43
25000	364.41	361.96	354.50	351.35	350.00	349.41
30000	437.29	434.35	425.40	421.62	419.99	419.29
35000	510.18	506.74	496.30	491.89	489.99	489.17
40000	583.06	579.13	567.20	562.16	559.99	559.05
45000	655.94	651.52	638.10	632.43	629.99	628.94
50000	728.82	723.91	709.00	702.70	699.99	698.82
55000	801.71	796.30	779.90	772.97	769.99	768.70
60000	874.59	868.69	850.80	843.24	839.99	838.58
65000	947.47	941.08	921.70	913.51	909.99	908.46
70000	1020.35	1013.47	992.60	983.78	979.99	978.35
75000	1093.23	1085.86	1063.50	1054.05	1049.99	1048.23
80000	1166.12	1158.26	1134.40	1124.32	1119.98	1118.11
85000	1239.00	1230.65	1205.30	1194.59	1189.98	1187.99
90000	1311.88	1303.04	1276.20	1264.86	1259.98	1257.87
95000	1384.76	1375.43	1347.10	1335.13	1329.98	1327.75
100000	1457.64	1447.82	1418.00	1405.40	1399.98	1397.64
200000	2915.29	2895.64	2835.99	2810.79	2799.96	2795.27
300000	4372.93	4343.46	4253.99	4216.19	4199.94	4192.91
400000	5830.58	5791.28	5671.99	5621.58	5599.92	5590.54
500000	7288.22	7239.10	7089.99	7026.98	6999.90	6988.18

17% MONTHLY PAYMENT

Necessary to amortize a loan

TERM / AMOUNT	1 YEAR	2 YEARS	3 YEARS	4 YEARS	5 YEARS	6 YEARS
500	45.60	24.72	17.83	14.43	12.43	11.12
600	54.72	29.67	21.39	17.31	14.91	13.35
700	63.84	34.61	24.96	20.20	17.40	15.57
800	72.96	39.55	28.52	23.08	19.88	17.80
900	82.08	44.50	32.09	25.97	22.37	20.02
1000	91.20	49.44	35.65	28.85	24.85	22.25
2000	182.41	98.88	71.31	57.71	49.71	44.49
3000	273.61	148.33	106.96	86.56	74.56	66.74
4000	364.82	197.77	142.61	115.42	99.41	88.98
5000	456.02	247.21	178.26	144.28	124.26	111.23
6000	547.23	296.65	213.92	173.13	149.12	133.48
7000	638.43	346.09	249.57	201.99	173.97	155.72
8000	729.64	395.54	285.22	230.84	198.82	177.97
9000	820.84	444.98	320.87	259.69	223.67	200.22
10000	912.04	494.42	356.53	288.55	248.53	222.46
11000	1003.25	543.86	392.18	317.40	273.38	244.71
12000	1094.45	593.31	427.83	346.26	298.23	266.95
13000	1185.66	642.75	463.48	375.11	323.08	289.20
14000	1276.86	692.19	499.14	403.97	347.94	311.45
15000	1368.07	741.63	534.79	432.82	372.82	333.69
16000	1459.27	791.07	570.44	461.68	397.64	355.94
17000	1550.47	840.52	606.09	490.53	422.49	378.18
18000	1641.68	889.96	641.75	519.39	447.35	400.43
19000	1732.88	939.40	677.40	548.24	472.20	422.68
20000	1824.09	988.84	713.05	577.10	497.05	444.92
21000	1915.29	1038.28	748.70	605.95	521.90	467.17
22000	2006.50	1087.73	784.36	634.81	546.76	489.41
23000	2097.70	1137.17	820.01	663.66	571.61	511.66
24000	2188.90	1186.61	855.66	692.52	596.46	533.91
25000	2280.11	1236.05	891.32	721.37	621.31	556.15
30000	2736.13	1483.26	1069.58	865.65	745.58	667.38
35000	3192.15	1730.47	1247.84	1009.92	869.84	778.61
40000	3648.17	1977.68	1426.10	1154.20	994.10	889.84
45000	4104.20	2224.89	1604.37	1298.47	1118.36	1001.07
50000	4560.22	2472.10	1782.63	1442.75	1242.62	1112.30
55000	5016.24	2719.31	1960.89	1587.02	1366.89	1223.53
60000	5472.26	2966.52	2139.16	1731.30	1491.15	1334.76
65000	5928.28	3213.73	2317.42	1875.57	1615.41	1445.99
70000	6384.30	3460.94	2495.68	2019.85	1739.67	1557.22
75000	6840.33	3708.15	2673.94	2164.12	1863.94	1668.46
80000	7296.35	3955.36	2852.21	2308.40	1988.20	1779.69
85000	7752.37	4202.57	3030.47	2452.67	2112.46	1890.92
90000	8208.39	4449.78	3208.73	2596.94	2236.72	2002.15
95000	8664.41	4696.99	3387.00	2741.22	2360.99	2113.38
100000	9120.43	4944.21	3565.26	2885.49	2485.25	2224.61
200000	18240.90	9888.41	7130.52	5770.99	4970.50	4449.21
300000	27361.30	14832.60	10695.80	8656.48	7455.75	6673.82
400000	36481.70	19776.80	14261.00	11542.00	9941.00	8898.43
500000	45602.20	24721.00	17826.30	14427.50	12426.20	11123.00

MONTHLY PAYMENT

Necessary to amortize a loan

17%

TERM / AMOUNT	7 YEARS	8 YEARS	9 YEARS	10 YEARS	11 YEARS	12 YEARS
500	10.22	9.56	9.07	8.69	8.39	8.16
600	12.26	11.47	10.88	10.43	10.07	9.79
700	14.31	13.39	12.70	12.17	11.75	11.42
800	16.35	15.30	14.51	13.90	13.43	13.06
900	18.39	17.21	16.32	15.64	15.11	14.69
1000	20.44	19.12	18.14	17.38	16.79	16.32
2000	40.87	38.24	36.27	34.76	33.58	32.64
3000	61.31	57.36	54.41	52.14	50.36	48.96
4000	81.74	76.49	72.54	69.52	67.15	65.28
5000	102.18	95.61	90.68	86.90	83.94	81.60
6000	122.62	114.73	108.82	104.28	100.73	97.92
7000	143.05	133.85	126.95	121.66	117.52	114.23
8000	163.49	152.97	145.09	139.04	134.31	130.55
9000	183.92	172.09	163.23	156.42	151.10	146.87
10000	204.36	191.21	181.36	173.80	167.88	163.19
11000	224.79	210.34	199.50	191.18	184.67	179.51
12000	245.23	229.46	217.63	208.56	201.46	195.83
13000	265.67	248.58	235.77	225.94	218.25	212.15
14000	286.10	267.70	253.91	243.32	235.04	228.47
15000	306.54	286.82	272.04	260.70	251.82	244.79
16000	326.97	305.94	290.18	278.08	268.61	261.11
17000	347.41	325.06	308.32	295.46	285.40	277.43
18000	367.84	344.19	326.45	312.84	302.19	293.75
19000	388.28	363.31	344.59	330.22	318.98	310.07
20000	408.72	382.43	362.72	347.60	335.77	326.38
21000	429.15	401.55	380.86	364.97	352.55	342.70
22000	449.59	420.67	399.00	382.35	369.34	359.02
23000	470.02	439.79	417.13	399.73	386.13	375.34
24000	490.46	458.91	435.27	417.11	402.92	391.66
25000	510.89	478.04	453.40	434.49	419.71	407.98
30000	613.07	573.64	544.08	521.39	503.65	489.58
35000	715.25	669.25	634.77	608.29	587.59	571.17
40000	817.43	764.86	725.45	695.19	671.53	652.77
45000	919.61	860.46	816.13	782.09	755.47	734.36
50000	1021.79	956.07	906.81	868.99	839.42	815.96
55000	1123.97	1051.68	997.49	955.89	923.36	897.56
60000	1226.15	1147.28	1088.17	1042.78	1007.30	979.15
65000	1328.32	1242.89	1178.85	1129.68	1091.24	1060.75
70000	1430.50	1338.50	1269.53	1216.58	1175.18	1142.34
75000	1532.68	1434.11	1360.21	1303.48	1259.12	1223.94
80000	1634.86	1529.71	1450.89	1390.38	1343.06	1305.54
85000	1737.04	1625.32	1541.57	1477.28	1427.00	1387.13
90000	1839.22	1720.93	1632.25	1564.18	1510.95	1468.73
95000	1941.40	1816.53	1722.93	1651.07	1594.89	1550.32
100000	2043.58	1912.14	1813.61	1737.97	1678.83	1631.92
200000	4087.15	3824.28	3627.23	3475.95	3357.66	3263.84
300000	6130.73	5736.42	5440.84	5213.92	5036.49	4895.76
400000	8174.30	7648.56	7254.46	6951.89	6715.32	6527.68
500000	10217.90	9560.70	9068.07	8689.87	8394.15	8159.60

17% MONTHLY PAYMENT

Necessary to amortize a loan

TERM AMOUNT	13 YEARS	14 YEARS	15 YEARS	16 YEARS	17 YEARS	18 YEARS
500	7.97	7.82	7.70	7.59	7.51	7.44
600	9.57	9.38	9.23	9.11	9.01	8.93
700	11.16	10.95	10.77	10.63	10.51	10.42
800	12.75	12.51	12.31	12.15	12.01	11.90
900	14.35	14.07	13.85	13.67	13.52	13.39
1000	15.94	15.64	15.39	15.19	15.02	14.88
2000	31.89	31.28	30.78	30.37	30.04	29.76
3000	47.83	46.92	46.17	45.56	45.06	44.64
4000	63.77	62.55	61.56	60.75	60.07	59.52
5000	79.71	78.19	76.95	75.93	75.09	74.40
6000	95.66	93.83	92.34	91.12	90.11	89.28
7000	111.60	109.47	107.73	106.30	105.13	104.16
8000	127.54	125.11	123.12	121.49	120.15	119.04
9000	143.49	140.75	138.51	136.68	135.17	133.92
10000	159.43	156.38	153.90	151.86	150.18	148.80
11000	175.37	172.02	169.29	167.05	165.20	163.67
12000	191.32	187.66	184.68	182.24	180.22	178.55
13000	207.26	203.30	200.07	197.42	195.24	193.43
14000	223.20	218.94	215.46	212.61	210.26	208.31
15000	239.14	234.58	230.85	227.80	225.28	223.19
16000	255.09	250.21	246.24	242.98	240.30	238.07
17000	271.03	265.85	261.63	258.17	255.31	252.95
18000	286.97	281.49	277.02	273.35	270.33	267.83
19000	302.92	297.13	292.41	288.54	285.35	282.71
20000	318.86	312.77	307.80	303.73	300.37	297.59
21000	334.80	328.41	323.19	318.91	315.39	312.47
22000	350.74	344.04	338.58	334.10	330.41	327.35
23000	366.69	359.68	353.97	349.29	345.42	342.23
24000	382.63	375.32	369.36	364.47	360.44	357.11
25000	398.57	390.96	384.75	379.66	375.46	371.99
30000	478.29	469.15	461.70	455.59	450.55	446.38
35000	558.00	547.34	538.65	531.52	525.65	520.78
40000	637.72	625.53	615.60	607.45	600.74	595.18
45000	717.43	703.73	692.55	683.39	675.83	669.58
50000	797.15	781.92	769.50	759.32	750.92	743.97
55000	876.86	860.11	846.45	835.25	826.01	818.37
60000	956.58	938.30	923.40	911.18	901.11	892.77
65000	1036.29	1016.49	1000.35	987.11	976.20	967.17
70000	1116.01	1094.69	1077.30	1063.04	1051.29	1041.56
75000	1195.72	1172.88	1154.25	1138.97	1126.38	1115.96
80000	1275.43	1251.07	1231.20	1214.91	1201.47	1190.36
85000	1355.15	1329.26	1308.15	1290.84	1276.57	1264.75
90000	1434.86	1407.45	1385.10	1366.77	1351.66	1339.15
95000	1514.58	1485.64	1462.05	1442.70	1426.75	1413.55
100000	1594.29	1563.84	1539.00	1518.63	1501.84	1487.95
200000	3188.59	3127.67	3078.01	3037.26	3003.68	2975.89
300000	4782.88	4691.51	4617.01	4555.90	4505.53	4463.84
400000	6377.17	6255.35	6156.01	6074.53	6007.37	5951.78
500000	7971.46	7819.18	7695.01	7593.16	7509.21	7439.73

MONTHLY PAYMENT

Necessary to amortize a loan

17%

TERM / AMOUNT	19 YEARS	20 YEARS	25 YEARS	30 YEARS	35 YEARS	40 YEARS
500	7.38	7.33	7.19	7.13	7.10	7.09
600	8.86	8.80	8.63	8.55	8.52	8.51
700	10.33	10.27	10.06	9.98	9.94	9.93
800	11.81	11.73	11.50	11.41	11.36	11.35
900	13.29	13.20	12.94	12.83	12.78	12.76
1000	14.76	14.67	14.38	14.26	14.21	14.18
2000	29.53	29.34	28.76	28.51	28.41	28.37
3000	44.29	44.00	43.13	42.77	42.62	42.55
4000	59.06	58.67	57.51	57.03	56.82	56.73
5000	73.82	73.34	71.89	71.28	71.03	70.92
6000	88.58	88.01	86.27	85.54	85.23	85.10
7000	103.35	102.68	100.65	99.80	99.44	99.28
8000	118.11	117.34	115.02	114.05	113.64	113.47
9000	132.88	132.01	129.40	128.31	127.85	127.65
10000	147.64	146.68	143.78	142.57	142.05	141.83
11000	162.41	161.35	158.16	156.82	156.26	156.02
12000	177.17	176.02	172.54	171.08	170.46	170.20
13000	191.93	190.68	186.91	185.34	184.67	184.38
14000	206.70	205.35	201.29	199.60	198.87	198.57
15000	221.46	220.02	215.67	213.85	213.08	212.75
16000	236.23	234.69	230.05	228.11	227.28	226.93
17000	250.99	249.36	244.43	242.37	241.49	241.12
18000	265.75	264.02	258.80	256.62	255.70	255.30
19000	280.52	278.69	273.18	270.88	269.90	269.48
20000	295.28	293.36	287.56	285.14	284.11	283.67
21000	310.05	308.03	301.94	299.39	298.31	297.85
22000	324.81	322.70	316.32	313.65	312.52	312.03
23000	339.57	337.36	330.69	327.91	326.72	326.21
24000	354.34	352.03	345.07	342.16	340.93	340.40
25000	369.10	366.70	359.45	356.42	355.13	354.58
30000	442.92	440.04	431.34	427.70	426.16	425.50
35000	516.74	513.38	503.23	498.99	497.18	496.41
40000	590.56	586.72	575.12	570.27	568.21	567.33
45000	664.38	660.06	647.01	641.55	639.24	638.25
50000	738.20	733.40	718.90	712.84	710.26	709.16
55000	812.02	806.74	790.79	784.12	781.29	780.08
60000	885.84	880.08	862.68	855.41	852.32	850.99
65000	959.67	953.42	934.57	926.69	923.34	921.01
70000	1033.49	1026.76	1006.46	997.97	994.37	992.83
75000	1107.31	1100.10	1078.35	1069.26	1065.39	1063.74
80000	1181.13	1173.44	1150.24	1140.54	1136.42	1134.66
85000	1254.95	1246.78	1222.13	1211.82	1207.45	1205.58
90000	1328.77	1320.12	1294.02	1283.11	1278.47	1276.49
95000	1402.59	1393.46	1365.91	1354.39	1349.50	1347.41
100000	1476.41	1466.80	1437.80	1425.68	1420.53	1418.32
200000	2952.82	2933.60	2875.59	2851.35	2841.05	2836.65
300000	4429.22	4400.40	4313.39	4277.03	4261.58	4254.97
400000	5905.63	5867.20	5751.19	5702.70	5682.10	5673.29
500000	7382.04	7334.00	7188.98	7128.38	7102.63	7091.62

17 1/4%

MONTHLY PAYMENT

Necessary to amortize a loan

TERM / AMOUNT	1 YEAR	2 YEARS	3 YEARS	4 YEARS	5 YEARS	6 YEARS
500	45.66	24.78	17.89	14.49	12.49	11.19
600	54.79	29.74	21.47	17.39	14.99	13.43
700	63.93	34.69	25.04	20.29	17.49	15.67
800	73.06	39.65	28.62	23.19	19.99	17.91
900	82.19	44.61	32.20	26.09	22.49	20.15
1000	91.32	49.56	35.78	28.98	24.99	22.39
2000	182.65	99.13	71.55	57.97	49.97	44.77
3000	273.97	148.69	107.33	86.95	74.96	67.16
4000	305.00	108.25	143.11	115.94	99.95	89.54
5000	456.62	247.81	178.89	144.92	124.94	111.03
6000	547.94	297.38	214.66	173.91	149.92	134.32
7000	639.27	346.94	250.44	202.89	174.91	156.70
8000	730.59	396.50	286.22	231.88	199.90	179.09
9000	821.91	446.06	322.00	260.86	224.89	201.47
10000	913.24	495.63	357.77	289.85	249.87	223.86
11000	1004.56	545.19	393.55	318.83	274.86	246.25
12000	1095.88	594.75	429.33	347.82	299.85	268.63
13000	1187.21	644.31	465.11	376.80	324.83	291.02
14000	1278.53	693.88	500.88	405.79	349.82	313.40
15000	1369.86	743.44	536.66	434.77	374.81	335.79
16000	1461.18	793.00	572.44	463.75	399.80	358.17
17000	1552.50	842.57	608.22	492.74	424.78	380.56
18000	1643.83	892.13	643.99	521.72	449.77	402.95
19000	1735.15	941.69	679.77	550.71	474.76	425.33
20000	1826.47	991.25	715.55	579.69	499.75	447.72
21000	1917.80	1040.81	751.33	608.68	524.73	470.10
22000	2009.12	1090.38	787.10	637.66	549.72	492.49
23000	2100.45	1139.94	822.88	666.65	574.71	514.88
24000	2191.77	1189.50	858.66	695.63	599.69	537.26
25000	2283.09	1239.07	894.43	724.62	624.68	559.65
30000	2739.71	1486.88	1073.32	869.54	749.62	671.58
35000	3196.33	1734.69	1252.21	1014.46	874.55	783.51
40000	3652.95	1982.50	1431.09	1159.38	999.49	895.44
45000	4109.57	2230.32	1609.98	1304.31	1124.43	1007.37
50000	4566.19	2478.13	1788.87	1449.23	1249.36	1119.30
55000	5022.80	2725.94	1967.76	1594.15	1374.30	1231.22
60000	5479.42	2973.76	2146.64	1739.08	1499.24	1343.15
65000	5936.04	3221.57	2325.53	1884.00	1624.17	1455.08
70000	6392.66	3469.38	2504.42	2028.92	1749.11	1567.01
75000	6849.28	3717.20	2683.30	2173.85	1874.04	1678.94
80000	7305.90	3965.01	2862.19	2318.77	1998.98	1790.87
85000	7762.52	4212.82	3041.08	2463.69	2123.92	1902.80
90000	8219.13	4460.64	3219.96	2608.62	2248.85	2014.73
95000	8675.75	4708.45	3398.85	2753.54	2373.79	2126.66
100000	9132.37	4956.26	3577.74	2898.46	2498.72	2238.59
200000	18264.70	9912.52	7155.47	5796.92	4997.45	4477.18
300000	27397.10	14868.80	10733.20	8695.38	7496.17	6715.77
400000	36529.50	19825.00	14310.90	11593.80	9994.90	8954.36
500000	45661.90	24781.30	17888.70	14492.30	12493.60	11193.00

MONTHLY PAYMENT

Necessary to amortize a loan

17 1/4%

TERM / AMOUNT	7 YEARS	8 YEARS	9 YEARS	10 YEARS	11 YEARS	12 YEARS
500	10.29	9.64	9.15	8.77	8.48	8.24
600	12.35	11.56	10.97	10.52	10.17	9.89
700	14.41	13.49	12.80	12.28	11.87	11.54
800	16.46	15.42	14.63	14.03	13.56	13.19
900	18.52	17.34	16.46	15.78	15.26	14.84
1000	20.58	19.27	18.29	17.54	16.95	16.49
2000	41.16	38.54	36.58	35.08	33.90	32.97
3000	61.74	57.81	54.87	52.62	50.85	49.46
4000	82.32	77.08	73.16	70.15	67.81	65.94
5000	102.90	96.36	91.45	87.69	84.76	82.43
6000	123.48	115.63	109.74	105.23	101.71	98.92
7000	144.06	134.90	128.03	122.77	118.66	115.40
8000	164.65	154.17	146.32	140.31	135.61	131.89
9000	185.23	173.44	164.61	157.85	152.56	148.38
10000	205.81	192.71	182.91	175.39	169.51	164.86
11000	226.39	211.98	201.20	192.92	186.46	181.35
12000	246.97	231.25	219.49	210.46	203.42	197.84
13000	267.55	250.52	237.78	228.00	220.37	214.32
14000	288.13	269.80	256.07	245.54	237.32	230.81
15000	308.71	289.07	274.36	263.08	254.27	247.29
16000	329.29	308.34	292.65	280.62	271.22	263.78
17000	349.87	327.61	310.94	298.16	288.17	280.27
18000	370.45	346.88	329.23	315.69	305.12	296.75
19000	391.03	366.15	347.52	333.23	322.08	313.24
20000	411.61	385.42	365.81	350.77	339.03	329.73
21000	432.19	404.69	384.10	368.31	355.98	346.21
22000	452.77	423.96	402.39	385.85	372.93	362.70
23000	473.35	443.24	420.68	403.39	389.88	379.18
24000	493.93	462.51	438.97	420.93	406.83	395.67
25000	514.51	481.78	457.26	438.46	423.78	412.16
30000	617.42	578.13	548.71	526.16	508.54	494.59
35000	720.32	674.49	640.17	613.85	593.30	577.02
40000	823.22	770.84	731.62	701.54	678.05	659.45
45000	926.13	867.20	823.07	789.23	762.81	741.88
50000	1029.03	963.55	914.52	876.93	847.57	824.31
55000	1131.93	1059.91	1005.98	964.62	932.32	906.74
60000	1234.83	1156.26	1097.43	1052.31	1017.08	989.17
65000	1337.74	1252.62	1188.88	1140.00	1101.84	1071.60
70000	1440.64	1340.98	1280.33	1227.70	1186.59	1154.04
75000	1543.54	1445.33	1371.79	1315.39	1271.35	1236.47
80000	1646.45	1541.69	1463.24	1403.08	1356.11	1318.90
85000	1749.35	1638.04	1554.69	1490.77	1440.86	1401.33
90000	1852.25	1734.40	1646.14	1578.47	1525.62	1483.76
95000	1955.15	1830.75	1737.60	1666.16	1610.38	1566.19
100000	2058.06	1927.11	1829.05	1753.85	1695.13	1648.62
200000	4116.12	3854.22	3658.10	3507.70	3390.26	3297.25
300000	6174.17	5781.32	5487.15	5261.56	5085.40	4945.87
400000	8232.23	7708.43	7316.19	7015.41	6780.53	6594.49
500000	10290.30	9635.54	9145.24	8769.26	8475.66	8243.11

17 1/4% MONTHLY PAYMENT

Necessary to amortize a loan

TERM AMOUNT	13 YEARS	14 YEARS	15 YEARS	16 YEARS	17 YEARS	18 YEARS
500	8.06	7.91	7.78	7.68	7.60	7.53
600	9.67	9.49	9.34	9.22	9.12	9.04
700	11.28	11.07	10.90	10.76	10.64	10.55
800	12.89	12.65	12.45	12.29	12.16	12.05
900	14.50	14.23	14.01	13.83	13.68	13.56
1000	16.11	15.82	15.57	15.37	15.20	15.07
2000	32.23	31.63	31.14	30.73	30.40	30.13
3000	48.34	47.44	46.70	46.10	45.61	45.20
4000	64.45	63.25	62.27	61.47	60.81	60.26
5000	80.57	79.06	77.84	76.83	76.01	75.33
6000	96.68	94.88	93.41	92.20	91.21	90.39
7000	112.80	110.69	108.97	107.57	106.41	105.46
8000	128.91	126.50	124.54	122.94	121.61	120.52
9000	145.02	142.31	140.11	138.30	136.82	135.59
10000	161.14	158.13	155.68	153.67	152.02	150.65
11000	177.25	173.94	171.24	169.04	167.22	165.72
12000	193.37	189.75	186.81	184.40	182.42	180.79
13000	209.48	205.56	202.38	199.77	197.62	195.85
14000	225.59	221.38	217.95	215.14	212.83	210.92
15000	241.71	237.19	233.51	230.50	228.03	225.98
16000	257.82	253.00	249.08	245.87	243.23	241.05
17000	273.93	268.82	264.65	261.24	258.43	256.11
18000	290.05	284.63	280.22	276.60	273.63	271.18
19000	306.16	300.44	295.78	291.97	288.83	286.24
20000	322.27	316.25	311.35	307.34	304.04	301.31
21000	338.39	332.07	326.92	322.71	319.24	316.37
22000	354.50	347.88	342.49	338.07	334.44	331.44
23000	370.62	363.69	358.05	353.44	349.64	346.50
24000	386.73	379.50	373.62	368.81	364.84	361.57
25000	402.84	395.32	389.19	384.17	380.05	376.64
30000	483.41	474.38	467.03	461.01	456.05	451.96
35000	563.98	553.44	544.87	537.84	532.06	527.29
40000	644.55	632.51	622.70	614.68	608.07	602.62
45000	725.12	711.57	700.54	691.51	684.08	677.94
50000	805.69	790.63	778.38	768.35	760.09	753.27
55000	886.25	869.70	856.22	845.18	836.10	828.60
60000	966.82	948.76	934.06	922.02	912.11	903.92
65000	1047.39	1027.82	1011.89	998.85	988.12	979.25
70000	1127.96	1106.89	1089.73	1075.68	1064.13	1054.58
75000	1208.53	1185.95	1167.57	1152.52	1140.13	1129.91
80000	1289.10	1265.01	1245.41	1229.35	1216.14	1205.23
85000	1369.67	1344.08	1323.24	1306.19	1292.15	1280.56
90000	1450.23	1423.14	1401.08	1383.02	1368.16	1355.89
95000	1530.80	1502.20	1478.92	1459.86	1444.17	1431.21
100000	1611.37	1581.27	1556.76	1536.69	1520.18	1506.54
200000	3222.74	3162.53	3113.52	3073.38	3040.36	3013.08
300000	4834.11	4743.80	4670.27	4610.07	4560.54	4519.62
400000	6445.48	6325.06	6227.03	6146.76	6080.72	6026.16
500000	8056.86	7906.33	7783.79	7683.45	7600.90	7532.70

MONTHLY PAYMENT

Necessary to amortize a loan

17 1/4%

TERM / AMOUNT	19 YEARS	20 YEARS	25 YEARS	30 YEARS	35 YEARS	40 YEARS
500	7.48	7.43	7.29	7.23	7.21	7.20
600	8.97	8.92	8.75	8.68	8.65	8.63
700	10.47	10.40	10.20	10.12	10.09	10.07
800	11.96	11.89	11.66	11.57	11.53	11.51
900	13.46	13.37	13.12	13.01	12.97	12.95
1000	14.95	14.86	14.58	14.46	14.41	13.39
2000	29.90	29.72	29.15	28.92	28.82	28.78
3000	44.86	44.58	43.73	43.38	43.23	43.17
4000	59.81	59.43	58.31	57.84	57.64	57.56
5000	74.76	74.29	72.88	72.30	72.05	71.95
6000	89.71	89.15	87.46	86.76	86.47	86.34
7000	104.67	104.01	102.04	101.22	100.88	100.73
8000	119.62	118.87	116.61	115.68	115.29	115.12
9000	134.57	133.73	131.19	130.14	129.70	129.51
10000	149.52	148.58	145.76	144.60	144.11	143.90
11000	164.48	163.44	160.34	159.06	158.52	158.29
12000	179.43	178.30	174.92	173.52	172.93	172.68
13000	194.38	193.16	189.49	187.98	187.34	187.07
14000	209.33	208.02	204.07	202.44	201.75	201.46
15000	224.29	222.88	218.65	216.90	216.16	215.85
16000	239.24	237.74	233.22	231.36	230.58	230.24
17000	254.19	252.59	247.80	245.82	244.99	244.63
18000	269.14	267.45	262.38	260.28	259.40	259.02
19000	284.10	282.31	276.95	274.74	273.81	273.41
20000	299.05	297.17	291.53	289.20	288.22	287.81
21000	314.00	312.03	306.11	303.66	302.63	302.20
22000	328.95	326.89	320.68	318.12	317.04	316.59
23000	343.90	341.74	335.26	332.58	331.45	330.98
24000	358.86	356.60	349.83	347.04	345.86	345.37
25000	373.81	371.46	364.41	361.50	360.27	359.76
30000	448.57	445.75	437.29	433.80	432.33	431.71
35000	523.33	520.05	510.18	506.10	504.38	503.66
40000	598.09	594.34	583.06	578.39	576.44	575.61
45000	672.86	668.63	655.94	650.69	648.49	647.56
50000	747.62	742.92	728.82	722.99	720.55	719.51
55000	822.38	817.21	801.70	795.29	792.60	791.46
60000	897.14	891.51	874.59	867.59	864.66	863.41
65000	971.90	965.80	947.47	939.89	936.71	935.37
70000	1046.67	1040.09	1020.35	1012.19	1008.76	1007.32
75000	1121.43	1114.38	1093.23	1084.49	1080.82	1079.27
80000	1196.19	1188.67	1166.11	1156.79	1152.87	1151.22
85000	1270.95	1262.97	1239.00	1229.09	1224.93	1223.17
90000	1345.71	1337.26	1311.88	1301.39	1296.98	1295.12
95000	1420.47	1411.55	1384.76	1373.69	1369.04	1367.07
100000	1495.24	1485.84	1457.64	1445.99	1441.09	1439.02
200000	2990.47	2971.68	2915.28	2891.97	2882.18	2878.05
300000	4485.71	4457.53	4372.92	4337.96	4323.28	4317.07
400000	5980.94	5943.37	5830.57	5783.94	5764.37	5756.09
500000	7476.18	7429.21	7288.21	7229.93	7205.46	7195.12

17 1/2%

MONTHLY PAYMENT
Necessary to amortize a loan

TERM / AMOUNT	1 YEAR	2 YEARS	3 YEARS	4 YEARS	5 YEARS	6 YEARS
500	45.72	24.84	17.95	14.56	12.56	11.26
600	54.87	29.81	21.54	17.47	15.07	13.52
700	64.01	34.78	25.13	20.38	17.59	15.77
800	73.15	39.75	28.72	23.29	20.10	18.02
900	82.30	44.71	32.31	26.20	22.61	20.27
1000	91.44	49.68	35.90	29.11	25.12	22.53
2000	182.88	99.37	71.80	58.23	50.24	45.05
3000	274.33	149.05	107.71	87.34	75.37	67.58
4000	366.77	198.73	143.61	116.46	100.49	90.10
5000	457.21	248.41	179.51	145.57	125.61	112.03
6000	548.65	298.10	215.41	174.69	150.73	135.16
7000	640.09	347.78	251.31	203.80	175.86	157.68
8000	731.54	397.46	287.22	232.92	200.98	180.21
9000	822.98	447.15	323.12	262.03	226.10	202.73
10000	914.42	496.83	359.02	291.14	251.22	225.26
11000	1005.86	546.51	394.92	320.26	276.34	247.79
12000	1097.30	596.19	430.82	349.37	301.47	270.31
13000	1188.75	645.88	466.73	378.49	326.59	292.84
14000	1280.19	695.56	502.63	407.60	351.71	315.36
15000	1371.63	745.24	538.53	436.72	376.83	337.89
16000	1463.07	794.92	574.43	465.83	401.96	360.42
17000	1554.51	844.61	610.33	494.94	427.08	382.94
18000	1645.96	894.29	646.24	524.06	452.20	405.47
19000	1737.40	943.97	682.14	553.17	477.32	427.99
20000	1828.84	993.66	718.04	582.29	502.44	450.52
21000	1920.28	1043.34	753.94	611.40	527.57	473.05
22000	2011.73	1093.02	789.84	640.52	552.69	495.57
23000	2103.17	1142.70	825.75	669.63	577.81	518.10
24000	2194.61	1192.39	861.65	698.74	602.93	540.63
25000	2286.05	1242.07	897.55	727.86	628.06	563.15
30000	2743.26	1490.48	1077.06	873.43	753.67	675.78
35000	3200.47	1738.90	1256.57	1019.00	879.28	788.41
40000	3657.68	1987.31	1436.08	1164.57	1004.89	901.04
45000	4114.89	2235.72	1615.59	1310.15	1130.50	1013.67
50000	4572.10	2484.14	1795.10	1455.72	1256.11	1126.30
55000	5029.31	2732.55	1974.61	1601.29	1381.72	1238.93
60000	5486.52	2980.97	2154.12	1746.86	1507.33	1351.56
65000	5943.73	3229.38	2333.63	1892.43	1632.94	1464.19
70000	6400.94	3477.79	2513.14	2038.00	1758.55	1576.82
75000	6858.15	3726.21	2692.65	2183.57	1884.16	1689.45
80000	7315.36	3974.62	2872.16	2329.15	2009.77	1802.08
85000	7772.57	4223.04	3051.67	2474.72	2135.39	1914.71
90000	8229.78	4471.45	3231.18	2620.29	2261.00	2027.34
95000	8686.99	4719.86	3410.69	2765.86	2386.61	2139.97
100000	9144.21	4968.28	3590.20	2911.43	2512.22	2252.60
200000	18288.40	9936.55	7180.40	5822.87	5024.44	4505.20
300000	27432.60	14904.80	10770.60	8734.30	7536.65	6757.81
400000	36576.80	19873.10	14360.80	11645.70	10048.90	9010.41
500000	45721.00	24841.40	17951.00	14557.20	12561.10	11263.00

MONTHLY PAYMENT

Necessary to amortize a loan

17 1/2%

TERM AMOUNT	7 YEARS	8 YEARS	9 YEARS	10 YEARS	11 YEARS	12 YEARS
500	10.36	9.71	9.22	8.85	8.56	8.33
600	12.44	11.65	11.07	10.62	10.27	9.99
700	14.51	13.59	12.91	12.39	11.98	11.66
800	16.58	15.54	14.76	14.16	13.69	13.32
900	18.65	17.48	16.60	15.93	15.40	14.99
1000	20.73	19.42	18.45	17.70	17.11	16.65
2000	41.45	38.84	36.89	35.40	34.23	33.31
3000	62.18	58.26	55.34	53.09	51.34	49.96
4000	82.90	77.68	73.78	70.79	68.46	66.62
5000	103.63	97.11	92.23	88.49	85.57	83.27
6000	124.36	116.53	110.67	106.19	102.69	99.92
7000	145.08	135.95	129.12	123.89	119.80	116.58
8000	165.81	155.37	147.56	141.58	136.92	133.23
9000	186.53	174.79	166.01	159.28	154.03	149.89
10000	207.26	194.21	184.45	176.98	171.15	166.54
11000	227.98	213.63	202.90	194.68	188.26	183.19
12000	248.71	233.05	221.34	212.37	205.38	199.85
13000	269.44	252.48	239.79	230.07	222.49	216.50
14000	290.16	271.90	258.23	247.77	239.61	233.15
15000	310.89	291.32	276.68	265.47	256.72	249.81
16000	331.61	310.74	295.13	283.17	273.84	266.46
17000	352.34	330.16	313.57	300.86	290.95	283.12
18000	373.06	349.58	332.02	318.56	308.07	299.77
19000	393.79	369.00	350.46	336.26	325.18	316.42
20000	414.52	388.42	368.91	353.96	342.30	333.08
21000	435.24	407.85	387.35	371.66	359.41	349.73
22000	455.97	427.27	405.80	389.35	376.53	366.39
23000	476.69	446.69	424.24	407.05	393.64	383.04
24000	497.42	466.11	442.69	424.75	410.76	399.69
25000	518.14	485.53	461.13	442.45	427.87	416.35
30000	621.77	582.64	553.36	530.94	513.45	499.62
35000	725.40	679.74	645.59	619.43	599.02	582.89
40000	829.03	776.85	737.81	707.91	684.60	666.15
45000	932.66	873.95	830.04	796.40	770.17	749.42
50000	1036.29	971.06	922.27	884.89	855.75	832.69
55000	1139.92	1068.17	1014.49	973.38	941.32	915.96
60000	1243.55	1165.27	1106.72	1061.87	1026.90	999.23
65000	1347.18	1262.38	1198.95	1150.36	1112.47	1082.50
70000	1450.80	1359.48	1291.17	1238.85	1198.04	1165.77
75000	1554.43	1456.59	1383.40	1327.34	1283.62	1249.04
80000	1658.06	1553.70	1475.63	1415.83	1369.19	1332.31
85000	1761.69	1650.80	1567.85	1504.32	1454.77	1415.58
90000	1865.32	1747.91	1660.08	1592.81	1540.34	1498.85
95000	1968.95	1845.01	1752.31	1681.30	1625.92	1582.12
100000	2072.58	1942.12	1844.53	1769.79	1711.49	1665.39
200000	4145.15	3884.24	3689.06	3539.57	3422.99	3330.77
300000	6217.73	5826.36	5533.60	5309.36	5134.48	4996.16
400000	8290.31	7768.48	7378.13	7079.15	6845.97	6661.54
500000	10362.90	9710.60	9222.66	8848.93	8557.46	8326.93

17 1/2% MONTHLY PAYMENT

Necessary to amortize a loan

TERM / AMOUNT	13 YEARS	14 YEARS	15 YEARS	16 YEARS	17 YEARS	18 YEARS
500	8.14	7.99	7.87	7.77	7.69	7.63
600	9.77	9.59	9.45	9.33	9.23	9.15
700	11.40	11.19	11.02	10.88	10.77	10.68
800	13.03	12.79	12.60	12.44	12.31	12.20
900	14.66	14.39	14.17	13.99	13.85	13.73
1000	16.29	15.99	15.75	15.55	15.39	15.25
2000	32.57	31.98	31.49	31.10	30.77	30.50
3000	48.86	47.96	47.24	46.64	46.16	45.76
4000	65.14	63.95	62.98	62.19	61.54	61.01
5000	81.43	79.94	78.73	77.74	76.93	76.26
6000	97.71	95.93	94.47	93.29	92.31	91.51
7000	114.00	111.91	110.22	108.84	107.70	106.76
8000	130.28	127.90	125.97	124.39	123.09	122.02
9000	146.57	143.89	141.71	139.93	138.47	137.27
10000	162.85	159.88	157.46	155.48	153.86	152.52
11000	179.14	175.86	173.20	171.03	169.24	167.77
12000	195.42	191.85	188.95	186.58	184.63	183.02
13000	211.71	207.84	204.70	202.13	200.02	198.28
14000	227.99	223.83	220.44	217.67	215.40	213.53
15000	244.28	239.81	236.19	233.22	230.79	228.78
16000	260.56	255.80	251.93	248.77	246.17	244.03
17000	276.85	271.79	267.68	264.32	261.56	259.28
18000	293.13	287.78	283.42	279.87	276.94	274.54
19000	309.42	303.76	299.17	295.41	292.33	289.79
20000	325.70	319.75	314.92	310.96	307.72	305.04
21000	341.99	335.74	330.66	326.51	323.10	320.29
22000	358.27	351.73	346.41	342.06	338.49	335.54
23000	374.56	367.71	362.15	357.61	353.87	350.80
24000	390.84	383.70	377.90	373.16	369.26	366.05
25000	407.13	399.69	393.64	388.70	384.65	381.30
30000	488.55	479.63	472.37	466.44	461.57	457.56
35000	569.98	559.57	551.10	544.18	538.50	533.82
40000	651.41	639.50	629.83	621.93	615.43	610.08
45000	732.83	719.44	708.56	699.67	692.36	686.34
50000	814.26	799.38	787.29	777.41	769.29	762.60
55000	895.68	879.32	866.02	855.15	846.22	838.86
60000	977.11	959.26	944.75	932.89	923.15	915.12
65000	1058.53	1039.19	1023.48	1010.63	1000.08	991.38
70000	1139.96	1119.13	1102.20	1088.37	1077.01	1067.64
75000	1221.38	1199.07	1180.93	1166.11	1153.93	1143.90
80000	1302.81	1279.01	1259.66	1243.85	1230.86	1220.16
85000	1384.23	1358.94	1338.39	1321.59	1307.79	1296.42
90000	1465.66	1438.88	1417.12	1399.33	1384.72	1372.68
95000	1547.09	1518.82	1495.85	1477.07	1461.65	1448.93
100000	1628.51	1598.76	1574.58	1554.81	1538.58	1525.19
200000	3257.02	3197.52	3149.16	3109.62	3077.16	3050.39
300000	4885.53	4796.27	4723.73	4664.44	4615.74	4575.58
400000	6514.05	6395.03	6298.31	6219.25	6154.32	6100.78
500000	8142.56	7993.79	7872.89	7774.06	7692.89	7625.97

MONTHLY PAYMENT

Necessary to amortize a loan

17 1/2%

TERM / AMOUNT	19 YEARS	20 YEARS	25 YEARS	30 YEARS	35 YEARS	40 YEARS
500	7.57	7.52	7.39	7.33	7.31	7.30
600	9.08	9.03	8.87	8.80	8.77	8.76
700	10.60	10.53	10.34	10.26	10.23	10.22
800	12.11	12.04	11.82	11.73	11.69	11.68
900	13.63	13.54	13.30	13.20	13.16	13.14
1000	15.14	15.05	14.78	14.66	14.62	14.60
2000	30.28	30.10	29.55	29.33	29.23	29.19
3000	45.42	45.15	44.33	43.99	43.85	43.79
4000	60.56	60.20	59.10	58.65	58.47	58.39
5000	75.71	75.25	73.88	73.32	73.08	72.99
6000	90.85	90.30	88.65	87.98	87.70	87.58
7000	105.99	105.35	103.43	102.64	102.32	102.18
8000	121.13	120.40	118.20	117.31	116.93	116.78
9000	136.27	135.45	132.98	131.97	131.55	131.38
10000	151.41	150.49	147.75	146.63	146.17	145.97
11000	166.55	165.54	162.53	161.30	160.78	160.57
12000	181.70	180.59	177.30	175.96	175.40	175.17
13000	196.84	195.64	192.08	190.62	190.02	189.77
14000	211.98	210.69	206.85	205.29	204.64	204.36
15000	227.12	225.74	221.63	219.95	219.25	218.96
16000	242.26	240.79	236.41	234.61	233.87	233.56
17000	257.40	255.84	251.18	249.28	248.49	248.16
18000	272.54	270.89	265.96	263.94	263.10	262.75
19000	287.68	285.94	280.73	278.60	277.72	277.35
20000	302.83	300.99	295.51	293.27	292.34	291.95
21000	317.97	316.04	310.28	307.93	306.95	306.54
22000	333.11	331.09	325.06	322.59	321.57	321.14
23000	348.25	346.14	339.83	337.26	336.19	335.74
24000	363.39	361.19	354.61	351.92	350.80	350.34
25000	378.53	376.24	369.38	366.58	365.42	364.93
30000	454.24	451.48	443.26	439.90	438.50	437.92
35000	529.94	526.73	517.14	513.21	511.59	510.91
40000	605.65	601.98	591.01	586.53	584.67	583.89
45000	681.36	677.22	664.89	659.85	657.75	656.88
50000	757.06	752.47	738.77	733.16	730.84	729.87
55000	832.77	827.72	812.64	806.48	803.92	802.85
60000	908.47	902.97	886.52	879.80	877.01	875.84
65000	984.18	978.21	960.39	953.11	950.09	948.83
70000	1059.89	1053.46	1034.27	1026.43	1023.17	1021.81
75000	1135.59	1128.71	1108.15	1099.74	1096.26	1094.80
80000	1211.30	1203.95	1182.02	1173.06	1169.34	1167.79
85000	1287.00	1279.20	1255.90	1246.38	1242.42	1240.77
90000	1362.71	1354.45	1329.78	1319.69	1315.51	1313.76
95000	1438.42	1429.69	1403.65	1393.01	1388.59	1386.75
100000	1514.12	1504.94	1477.53	1466.33	1461.68	1459.73
200000	3028.25	3009.88	2955.06	2932.65	2923.35	2919.47
300000	4542.37	4514.82	4432.59	4398.97	4385.03	4379.20
400000	6056.49	6019.77	5910.12	5865.30	5846.70	5838.93
500000	7570.62	7524.71	7387.65	7331.62	7308.38	7298.67

17 3/4% MONTHLY PAYMENT

Necessary to amortize a loan

TERM / AMOUNT	1 YEAR	2 YEARS	3 YEARS	4 YEARS	5 YEARS	6 YEARS
500	45.78	24.90	18.01	14.62	12.63	11.33
600	54.94	29.88	21.62	17.55	15.15	13.60
700	64.09	34.86	25.22	20.47	17.68	15.87
800	73.25	39.84	28.82	23.40	20.21	18.13
900	82.41	44.82	32.42	26.32	22.73	20.40
1000	91.56	49.80	36.03	29.24	25.26	22.67
2000	183.12	99.61	72.05	58.49	50.52	45.33
3000	274.69	149.41	108.08	87.73	75.77	68.00
4000	366.25	199.22	144.11	116.98	101.03	90.67
5000	457.81	249.02	180.14	146.22	126.29	113.33
6000	549.37	298.82	216.16	175.47	151.55	136.00
7000	640.93	348.63	252.19	204.71	176.80	158.67
8000	732.49	398.43	288.22	233.96	202.06	181.33
9000	824.05	448.23	324.25	263.20	227.32	204.00
10000	915.62	498.04	360.27	292.45	252.58	226.67
11000	1007.18	547.84	396.30	321.69	277.84	249.33
12000	1098.74	597.64	432.33	350.94	303.09	272.00
13000	1190.30	647.45	468.36	380.18	328.35	294.67
14000	1281.86	697.25	504.38	409.43	353.61	317.34
15000	1373.42	747.06	540.41	438.67	378.87	340.00
16000	1464.99	796.86	576.44	467.91	404.12	362.67
17000	1556.55	846.66	612.46	497.16	429.38	385.34
18000	1648.11	896.47	648.49	526.40	454.64	408.00
19000	1739.67	946.27	684.52	555.65	479.90	430.67
20000	1831.23	996.07	720.55	584.89	505.15	453.34
21000	1922.79	1045.88	756.57	614.14	530.41	476.00
22000	2014.35	1095.68	792.60	643.38	555.67	498.67
23000	2105.92	1145.48	828.63	672.63	580.93	521.34
24000	2197.48	1195.29	864.66	701.87	606.19	544.00
25000	2289.04	1245.09	900.68	731.12	631.44	566.67
30000	2746.85	1494.11	1080.82	877.34	757.73	680.00
35000	3204.66	1743.13	1260.95	1023.56	884.02	793.34
40000	3662.46	1992.15	1441.09	1169.79	1010.31	906.67
45000	4120.27	2241.16	1621.23	1316.01	1136.60	1020.00
50000	4578.08	2490.18	1801.36	1462.23	1262.89	1133.34
55000	5035.89	2739.20	1981.50	1608.46	1389.17	1246.67
60000	5493.69	2988.22	2161.64	1754.68	1515.46	1360.01
65000	5951.50	3237.24	2341.77	1900.90	1641.75	1473.34
70000	6409.31	3486.26	2521.91	2047.13	1768.04	1586.67
75000	6867.12	3735.27	2702.05	2193.35	1894.33	1700.01
80000	7324.93	3984.29	2882.18	2339.57	2020.62	1813.34
85000	7782.73	4233.31	3062.32	2485.80	2146.91	1926.68
90000	8240.54	4482.33	3242.46	2632.02	2273.20	2040.01
95000	8698.35	4731.35	3422.59	2778.24	2399.48	2153.34
100000	9156.16	4980.37	3602.73	2924.47	2525.77	2266.68
200000	18312.30	9960.73	7205.46	5848.93	5051.54	4533.35
300000	27468.50	14941.10	10808.20	8773.40	7577.32	6800.03
400000	36624.60	19921.50	14410.90	11697.90	10103.10	9066.71
500000	45780.80	24901.80	18013.60	14622.30	12628.90	11333.40

MONTHLY PAYMENT

Necessary to amortize a loan

17 3/4%

TERM / AMOUNT	7 YEARS	8 YEARS	9 YEARS	10 YEARS	11 YEARS	12 YEARS
500	10.44	9.79	9.30	8.93	8.64	8.41
600	12.52	11.74	11.16	10.71	10.37	10.09
700	14.61	13.70	13.02	12.50	12.10	11.78
800	16.70	15.66	14.88	14.29	13.82	13.46
900	18.78	17.61	16.74	16.07	15.55	15.14
1000	20.87	19.57	18.60	17.86	17.28	16.82
2000	41.74	39.14	37.20	35.72	34.56	33.64
3000	62.61	58.72	55.80	53.57	51.84	50.47
4000	83.49	78.29	74.40	71.43	69.12	67.29
5000	104.36	97.86	93.00	89.29	86.40	84.11
6000	125.23	117.43	111.61	107.15	103.68	100.93
7000	146.10	137.00	130.21	125.01	120.96	117.76
8000	166.97	156.58	148.81	142.86	138.23	134.58
9000	187.85	176.15	167.41	160.72	155.51	151.40
10000	208.72	195.72	186.01	178.58	172.79	168.22
11000	229.59	215.29	204.61	196.44	190.07	185.05
12000	250.46	234.86	223.21	214.30	207.35	201.87
13000	271.33	254.44	241.81	232.15	224.63	218.69
14000	292.20	274.01	260.41	250.01	241.91	235.51
15000	313.07	293.58	279.01	267.87	259.19	252.33
16000	333.95	313.15	297.61	285.73	276.47	269.16
17000	354.82	332.72	316.22	303.59	293.75	285.98
18000	375.69	352.30	334.82	321.44	311.03	302.80
19000	396.56	371.87	353.42	339.30	328.31	319.62
20000	417.43	391.44	372.02	357.16	345.59	336.45
21000	438.30	411.01	390.62	375.02	362.87	353.27
22000	459.18	430.58	409.22	392.87	380.14	370.09
23000	480.05	450.16	427.82	410.73	397.42	386.91
24000	500.92	469.73	446.42	428.59	414.70	403.73
25000	521.79	489.30	465.02	446.45	431.98	420.56
30000	626.15	587.16	558.03	535.74	518.38	504.67
35000	730.51	685.02	651.03	625.03	604.77	588.78
40000	834.87	782.88	744.03	714.32	691.17	672.89
45000	939.22	880.74	837.04	803.61	777.57	757.00
50000	1043.58	978.60	930.04	892.90	863.96	841.11
55000	1147.94	1076.46	1023.05	982.19	950.36	925.22
60000	1252.30	1174.32	1116.05	1071.48	1036.76	1009.33
65000	1356.66	1272.18	1209.06	1160.77	1123.15	1093.45
70000	1461.01	1370.04	1302.06	1250.05	1209.55	1177.56
75000	1565.37	1467.90	1395.06	1339.34	1295.95	1261.67
80000	1669.73	1565.76	1488.07	1428.63	1382.34	1345.78
85000	1774.09	1663.62	1581.07	1517.92	1468.74	1429.89
90000	1878.45	1761.48	1674.08	1607.21	1555.13	1514.00
95000	1982.80	1859.34	1767.08	1696.50	1641.53	1598.11
100000	2087.16	1957.20	1860.09	1785.79	1727.93	1682.22
200000	4174.33	3914.40	3720.17	3571.59	3455.85	3364.45
300000	6261.49	5871.60	5580.26	5357.38	5183.78	5046.67
400000	8348.65	7818.80	7440.34	7143.17	6911.71	6728.89
500000	10435.80	9785.99	9300.43	8928.96	8639.63	8411.12

17 3/4%

MONTHLY PAYMENT

Necessary to amortize a loan

TERM / AMOUNT	13 YEARS	14 YEARS	15 YEARS	16 YEARS	17 YEARS	18 YEARS
500	8.23	8.08	7.96	7.87	7.79	7.72
600	9.87	9.70	9.55	9.44	9.34	9.26
700	11.52	11.31	11.15	11.01	10.90	10.81
800	13.17	12.93	12.74	12.58	12.46	12.35
900	14.81	14.55	14.33	14.16	14.01	13.90
1000	16.46	16.16	15.92	15.73	15.57	15.44
2000	32.91	32.33	31.85	31.46	31.14	30.88
3000	49.37	48.49	47.77	47.19	46.71	46.32
4000	65.83	64.65	63.70	62.92	62.28	61.76
5000	82.29	80.82	79.62	78.65	77.85	77.20
6000	98.74	96.98	95.55	94.38	93.42	92.63
7000	115.20	113.14	111.47	110.11	108.99	108.07
8000	131.66	129.31	127.40	125.84	124.56	123.51
9000	148.12	145.47	143.32	141.57	140.13	138.95
10000	164.57	161.63	159.25	157.30	155.71	154.39
11000	181.03	177.80	175.17	173.03	171.28	169.83
12000	197.49	193.96	191.10	188.76	186.85	185.27
13000	213.94	210.12	207.02	204.49	202.42	200.71
14000	230.40	226.29	222.95	220.22	217.99	216.15
15000	246.86	242.45	238.87	235.95	233.56	231.59
16000	263.32	258.61	254.80	251.68	249.13	247.03
17000	279.77	274.78	270.72	267.41	264.70	262.47
18000	296.23	290.94	286.64	283.14	280.27	277.91
19000	312.69	307.10	302.57	298.87	295.84	293.34
20000	329.15	323.27	318.49	314.60	311.41	308.78
21000	345.60	339.43	334.42	330.33	326.98	324.22
22000	362.06	355.59	350.34	346.06	342.55	339.66
23000	378.52	371.75	366.27	361.79	358.12	355.10
24000	394.97	387.92	382.19	377.52	373.69	370.54
25000	411.43	404.08	398.12	393.25	389.26	385.98
30000	493.72	484.90	477.74	471.90	467.11	463.17
35000	576.00	565.71	557.36	550.55	544.97	540.37
40000	658.29	646.53	636.99	629.20	622.82	617.57
45000	740.58	727.35	716.61	707.85	700.67	694.76
50000	822.86	808.16	796.23	786.50	778.52	771.96
55000	905.15	888.98	875.86	865.15	856.38	849.15
60000	987.44	969.79	955.48	943.80	934.23	926.35
65000	1069.72	1050.61	1035.10	1022.45	1012.08	1003.54
70000	1152.01	1131.43	1114.73	1101.10	1089.93	1080.74
75000	1234.29	1212.24	1194.35	1179.75	1167.78	1157.94
80000	1316.58	1293.06	1273.97	1258.40	1245.64	1235.13
85000	1398.87	1373.87	1353.60	1337.05	1323.49	1312.33
90000	1481.15	1454.69	1433.22	1415.70	1401.34	1389.52
95000	1563.44	1535.51	1512.85	1494.35	1479.19	1466.72
100000	1645.73	1616.32	1592.47	1573.00	1557.05	1543.91
200000	3291.45	3232.65	3184.94	3146.01	3114.09	3087.83
300000	4937.18	4848.97	4777.41	4719.01	4671.14	4631.74
400000	6582.90	6465.29	6369.87	6292.01	6228.18	6175.66
500000	8228.63	8081.62	7962.34	7865.02	7785.23	7719.57

MONTHLY PAYMENT

Necessary to amortize a loan

17 3/4%

TERM AMOUNT	19 YEARS	20 YEARS	25 YEARS	30 YEARS	35 YEARS	40 YEARS
500	7.67	7.62	7.49	7.43	7.41	7.40
600	9.20	9.14	8.98	8.92	8.89	8.88
700	10.73	10.67	10.48	10.41	10.38	10.36
800	12.26	12.19	11.98	11.89	11.86	11.84
900	13.80	13.72	13.48	13.38	13.34	13.32
1000	15.33	15.24	14.97	14.87	14.82	14.80
2000	30.66	30.48	29.95	29.73	29.65	29.61
3000	45.99	45.72	44.92	44.60	44.47	44.41
4000	61.32	60.96	59.90	59.47	59.29	59.22
5000	76.65	76.21	74.87	74.33	74.11	74.02
6000	91.98	91.45	89.85	89.20	88.94	88.83
7000	107.32	106.69	104.82	104.07	103.76	103.63
8000	122.65	121.93	119.80	118.94	118.58	118.44
9000	137.98	137.17	134.77	133.80	133.41	133.24
10000	153.31	152.41	149.75	148.67	148.23	148.05
11000	168.64	167.65	164.72	163.54	163.05	162.85
12000	183.97	182.89	179.70	178.40	177.87	177.65
13000	199.30	198.13	194.67	193.27	192.70	192.46
14000	214.63	213.37	209.64	208.14	207.52	207.26
15000	229.96	228.62	224.62	223.00	222.34	222.07
16000	245.29	243.86	239.59	237.87	237.16	236.87
17000	260.62	259.10	254.57	252.74	251.99	251.68
18000	275.95	274.34	269.54	267.61	266.81	266.48
19000	291.28	289.58	284.52	282.47	281.63	281.29
20000	306.62	304.82	299.49	297.34	296.46	296.09
21000	321.95	320.06	314.47	312.21	311.28	310.90
22000	337.28	335.30	329.44	327.07	326.10	325.70
23000	352.61	350.54	344.42	341.94	340.92	340.50
24000	367.94	365.78	359.39	356.81	355.75	355.31
25000	383.27	381.03	374.37	371.67	370.57	370.11
30000	459.92	457.23	449.24	446.01	444.68	444.14
35000	536.58	533.44	524.11	520.34	518.80	518.16
40000	613.23	609.64	598.98	594.68	592.91	592.18
45000	689.88	685.85	673.86	669.01	667.02	666.20
50000	766.54	762.05	748.73	743.35	741.14	740.23
55000	843.19	838.26	823.60	817.68	815.25	814.25
60000	919.84	914.46	898.48	892.02	889.37	888.27
65000	996.50	990.67	973.35	966.35	963.48	962.30
70000	1073.15	1066.87	1048.22	1040.68	1037.59	1036.32
75000	1149.80	1143.08	1123.09	1115.02	1111.71	1110.34
80000	1226.46	1219.28	1197.97	1189.35	1185.82	1104.30
85000	1303.11	1295.49	1272.84	1263.69	1259.93	1258.39
90000	1379.77	1371.69	1347.71	1338.02	1334.05	1332.41
95000	1456.42	1447.89	1422.59	1412.36	1408.16	1406.43
100000	1533.07	1524.10	1497.46	1486.69	1482.28	1480.45
200000	3066.15	3048.20	2994.92	2973.38	2964.55	2960.91
300000	4599.22	4572.30	4492.38	4460.08	4446.83	4441.36
400000	6132.29	6096.40	5989.84	5946.77	5929.10	5921.81
500000	7665.37	7620.50	7487.30	7433.46	7411.38	7402.27

18%

MONTHLY PAYMENT

Necessary to amortize a loan

TERM / AMOUNT	1 YEAR	2 YEARS	3 YEARS	4 YEARS	5 YEARS	6 YEARS
500	45.84	24.96	18.08	14.69	12.70	11.40
600	55.01	29.95	21.69	17.63	15.24	13.68
700	64.18	34.95	25.31	20.56	17.78	15.97
800	73.34	39.94	28.92	23.50	20.31	18.25
900	82.51	44.93	32.54	26.44	22.85	20.53
1000	91.68	49.92	36.15	29.38	25.39	22.81
2000	183.36	99.85	72.31	58.75	50.79	45.62
3000	275.04	149.77	108.46	88.13	76.18	68.42
4000	366.72	199.70	144.61	117.50	101.57	91.23
5000	458.40	249.62	180.76	146.88	126.97	114.04
6000	550.08	299.55	216.92	176.25	152.36	136.85
7000	641.76	349.47	253.07	205.63	177.75	159.66
8000	733.44	399.39	289.22	235.00	203.15	182.46
9000	825.12	449.32	325.37	264.38	228.54	205.27
10000	916.80	499.24	361.53	293.75	253.94	228.08
11000	1008.48	549.17	397.68	323.13	279.33	250.89
12000	1100.16	599.09	433.83	352.50	304.72	273.69
13000	1191.84	649.02	469.98	381.88	330.12	296.50
14000	1283.52	698.94	506.14	411.25	355.51	319.31
15000	1375.20	748.86	542.29	440.63	380.90	342.12
16000	1466.88	798.79	578.44	470.00	406.30	364.93
17000	1558.56	848.71	614.59	499.38	431.69	387.73
18000	1650.25	898.64	650.75	528.75	457.08	410.54
19000	1741.93	948.56	686.90	558.13	482.48	433.35
20000	1833.61	998.49	723.05	587.50	507.87	456.16
21000	1925.29	1048.41	759.20	616.88	533.26	478.97
22000	2016.97	1098.33	795.36	646.25	558.66	501.77
23000	2108.65	1148.26	831.51	675.63	584.05	524.58
24000	2200.33	1198.18	867.66	705.00	609.44	547.39
25000	2292.01	1248.11	903.81	734.38	634.84	570.20
30000	2750.41	1497.73	1084.57	881.25	761.80	684.24
35000	3208.81	1747.35	1265.34	1028.13	888.77	798.27
40000	3667.21	1996.97	1446.10	1175.00	1015.74	912.31
45000	4125.61	2246.59	1626.86	1321.88	1142.71	1026.35
50000	4584.01	2496.21	1807.62	1468.75	1269.67	1140.39
55000	5042.42	2745.83	1988.39	1615.63	1396.64	1254.43
60000	5500.82	2995.45	2169.15	1762.50	1523.61	1368.47
65000	5959.22	3245.08	2349.91	1909.38	1650.58	1482.51
70000	6417.62	3494.70	2530.67	2056.25	1777.54	1596.55
75000	6876.02	3744.32	2711.44	2203.13	1904.51	1710.59
80000	7334.42	3993.94	2892.20	2350.01	2031.48	1824.63
85000	7792.82	4243.56	3072.96	2496.88	2158.45	1938.67
90000	8251.23	4493.18	3253.72	2643.76	2285.41	2052.71
95000	8709.63	4742.80	3434.49	2790.63	2412.38	2166.74
100000	9168.03	4992.42	3615.25	2937.51	2539.35	2280.78
200000	18336.10	9984.85	7230.50	5875.01	5078.70	4561.57
300000	27504.10	14977.30	10845.70	8812.52	7618.04	6842.35
400000	36672.10	19969.70	14461.00	11750.00	10157.40	9123.13
500000	45840.10	24962.10	18076.20	14687.50	12696.70	11403.90

MONTHLY PAYMENT

Necessary to amortize a loan

18%

TERM / AMOUNT	7 YEARS	8 YEARS	9 YEARS	10 YEARS	11 YEARS	12 YEARS
500	10.51	9.86	9.38	9.01	8.72	8.50
600	12.61	11.83	11.25	10.81	10.47	10.19
700	14.71	13.81	13.13	12.61	12.21	11.89
800	16.81	15.78	15.01	14.41	13.96	13.59
900	18.92	17.75	16.88	16.22	15.70	15.29
1000	21.02	19.72	18.76	18.02	17.44	16.99
2000	42.04	39.45	37.51	36.04	34.89	33.98
3000	63.05	59.17	56.27	54.06	52.33	50.97
4000	84.07	78.89	75.03	72.07	69.78	67.96
5000	105.09	98.62	93.78	90.09	87.22	84.96
6000	126.11	118.34	112.54	108.11	104.67	101.95
7000	147.13	138.06	131.30	126.13	122.11	118.94
8000	168.14	157.79	150.06	144.15	139.55	135.93
9000	189.16	177.51	168.81	162.17	157.00	152.92
10000	210.18	197.23	187.57	180.19	174.44	169.91
11000	231.20	216.96	206.33	198.20	191.89	186.90
12000	252.21	236.68	225.08	216.22	209.33	203.90
13000	273.23	256.40	243.84	234.24	226.78	220.89
14000	294.25	276.13	262.60	252.26	244.22	237.88
15000	315.27	295.85	281.35	270.28	261.66	254.87
16000	335.29	315.57	300.11	288.30	279.11	271.86
17000	357.30	335.30	318.87	306.32	296.55	288.85
18000	378.32	355.02	337.62	324.33	314.00	305.84
19000	399.34	374.74	356.38	342.35	331.44	322.83
20000	420.36	394.47	375.14	360.37	348.88	339.82
21000	441.38	414.19	393.90	378.39	366.33	356.82
22000	462.39	433.91	412.65	396.41	383.77	373.81
23000	483.41	453.64	431.41	414.43	401.22	390.80
24000	504.43	473.36	450.17	432.45	418.66	407.79
25000	525.45	493.08	468.92	450.46	436.11	424.78
30000	630.54	591.70	562.71	540.56	523.33	509.74
35000	735.63	690.31	656.49	630.65	610.55	594.69
40000	840.72	788.93	750.28	720.74	697.77	679.65
45000	945.80	887.55	844.06	810.83	784.99	764.61
50000	1050.89	986.16	937.85	900.93	872.21	849.56
55000	1155.98	1084.78	1031.63	991.02	959.43	934.52
60000	1261.07	1183.39	1125.41	1081.11	1046.65	1019.47
65000	1366.16	1282.01	1219.20	1171.21	1133.87	1104.43
70000	1471.25	1380.63	1312.98	1261.30	1221.09	1189.38
75000	1576.34	1479.24	1406.77	1351.39	1308.31	1274.34
80000	1681.43	1577.86	1500.55	1441.48	1395.54	1359.30
85000	1786.52	1676.48	1594.34	1531.58	1482.76	1444.25
90000	1891.61	1775.09	1688.12	1621.67	1569.98	1529.21
95000	1996.70	1873.71	1781.91	1711.76	1657.20	1614.17
100000	2101.79	1972.32	1875.69	1801.85	1744.42	1699.12
200000	4203.57	3944.65	3751.38	3603.71	3488.84	3398.24
300000	6305.36	5916.97	5627.07	5405.56	5233.26	5097.36
400000	8407.15	7889.30	7502.77	7207.42	6977.68	6796.48
500000	10508.90	9861.62	9378.46	9009.27	8722.10	8495.61

18%

MONTHLY PAYMENT

Necessary to amortize a loan

TERM / AMOUNT	13 YEARS	14 YEARS	15 YEARS	16 YEARS	17 YEARS	18 YEARS
500	8.32	8.17	8.05	7.96	7.88	7.81
600	9.98	9.80	9.66	9.55	9.45	9.38
700	11.64	11.44	11.27	11.14	11.03	10.94
800	13.30	13.07	12.88	12.73	12.60	12.50
900	14.97	14.71	14.49	14.32	14.18	14.06
1000	16.63	16.34	16.10	15.91	15.76	15.63
2000	33.26	32.68	32.21	31.83	31.51	31.25
3000	49.89	49.02	48.31	47.74	47.27	46.88
4000	66.52	65.36	64.42	63.65	63.02	62.51
5000	83.15	81.70	80.52	79.56	78.78	78.13
6000	99.78	98.04	96.63	95.48	94.53	93.76
7000	116.41	114.38	112.73	111.39	110.29	109.39
8000	133.04	130.72	128.83	127.30	126.05	125.02
9000	149.67	147.06	144.94	143.21	141.80	140.64
10000	166.30	163.40	161.04	159.13	157.56	156.27
11000	182.93	179.74	177.15	175.04	173.31	171.90
12000	199.56	196.07	193.25	190.95	189.07	187.52
13000	216.19	212.41	209.36	206.86	204.83	203.15
14000	232.82	228.75	225.46	222.78	220.58	218.78
15000	249.45	245.09	241.56	238.69	236.34	234.40
16000	266.08	261.43	257.67	254.60	252.09	250.03
17000	282.71	277.77	273.77	270.51	267.85	265.66
18000	299.34	294.11	289.88	286.43	283.60	281.29
19000	315.97	310.45	305.98	302.34	299.36	296.91
20000	332.60	326.79	322.08	318.25	315.12	312.54
21000	349.23	343.13	338.19	334.16	330.87	328.17
22000	365.86	359.47	354.29	350.08	346.63	343.79
23000	382.49	375.81	370.40	365.99	362.38	359.42
24000	399.12	392.15	386.50	381.90	378.14	375.05
25000	415.75	408.49	402.61	397.81	393.89	390.67
30000	498.90	490.19	483.13	477.38	472.67	468.81
35000	582.05	571.88	563.65	556.94	551.45	546.94
40000	665.20	653.58	644.17	636.50	630.23	625.08
45000	748.35	735.28	724.69	716.07	709.01	703.21
50000	831.50	816.98	805.21	795.63	787.79	781.35
55000	914.65	898.67	885.73	875.19	866.57	859.48
60000	997.80	980.37	966.25	954.75	945.34	937.62
65000	1080.95	1062.07	1046.77	1034.32	1024.12	1015.75
70000	1164.10	1143.77	1127.30	1113.88	1102.90	1093.88
75000	1247.25	1225.46	1207.82	1193.44	1181.68	1172.02
80000	1330.40	1307.16	1288.34	1273.01	1260.46	1250.15
85000	1413.55	1388.86	1368.86	1352.57	1339.24	1328.29
90000	1496.70	1470.56	1449.38	1432.13	1418.02	1406.42
95000	1579.85	1552.25	1529.90	1511.69	1496.79	1484.56
100000	1663.00	1633.95	1610.42	1591.26	1575.57	1562.69
200000	3326.00	3267.90	3220.84	3182.51	3151.15	3125.38
300000	4989.01	4901.85	4831.27	4773.77	4726.72	4688.08
400000	6652.01	6535.81	6441.69	6365.03	6302.29	6250.77
500000	8315.01	8169.76	8052.11	7956.28	7877.87	7813.46

MONTHLY PAYMENT

Necessary to amortize a loan

18%

TERM / AMOUNT	19 YEARS	20 YEARS	25 YEARS	30 YEARS	35 YEARS	40 YEARS
500	7.76	7.72	7.59	7.54	7.51	7.51
600	9.31	9.26	9.10	9.04	9.02	9.01
700	10.86	10.80	10.62	10.55	10.52	10.51
800	12.42	12.35	12.14	12.06	12.02	12.01
900	13.97	13.89	13.66	13.56	13.53	13.51
1000	15.52	15.43	15.17	15.07	15.03	15.01
2000	31.04	30.87	30.35	30.14	30.06	30.02
3000	46.56	46.30	45.52	45.21	45.09	45.04
4000	62.08	61.73	60.70	60.28	60.12	60.05
5000	77.60	77.17	75.87	75.35	75.14	75.06
6000	93.12	92.60	91.05	90.43	90.17	90.07
7000	108.65	108.03	106.22	105.50	105.20	105.08
8000	124.17	123.47	121.39	120.57	120.23	120.10
9000	139.69	138.90	136.57	135.64	135.26	135.11
10000	155.21	154.33	151.74	150.71	150.29	150.12
11000	170.73	169.76	166.92	165.78	165.32	165.13
12000	186.25	185.20	182.09	180.85	180.35	180.14
13000	201.77	200.63	197.27	195.92	195.38	195.15
14000	217.29	216.06	212.44	210.99	210.41	210.17
15000	232.81	231.50	227.62	226.06	225.43	225.18
16000	248.33	246.93	242.79	241.13	240.46	240.19
17000	263.85	262.36	257.96	256.21	255.49	255.20
18000	279.37	277.80	273.14	271.28	270.52	270.21
19000	294.90	293.23	288.31	286.35	285.55	285.23
20000	310.42	308.66	303.49	301.42	300.58	300.24
21000	325.94	324.10	318.66	316.49	315.61	315.25
22000	341.46	339.53	333.84	331.56	330.64	330.26
23000	356.98	354.96	349.01	346.63	345.67	345.27
24000	372.50	370.40	364.18	361.70	360.69	360.28
25000	388.02	385.83	379.36	376.77	375.72	375.30
30000	465.62	462.99	455.23	452.13	450.87	450.36
35000	543.23	540.16	531.10	527.48	526.01	525.41
40000	620.83	617.33	606.97	602.83	601.16	600.47
45000	698.44	694.49	682.84	678.19	676.30	675.53
50000	776.04	771.66	758.72	753.54	751.45	750.59
55000	853.64	848.82	834.59	828.90	826.59	825.65
60000	931.25	925.99	910.46	904.25	901.74	900.71
65000	1008.85	1003.15	986.33	979.61	976.88	975.77
70000	1086.46	1080.32	1062.20	1054.96	1052.02	1050.83
75000	1164.06	1157.48	1138.07	1130.31	1127.17	1125.89
80000	1241.66	1234.65	1213.94	1205.67	1202.31	1200.95
85000	1319.27	1311.82	1289.82	1281.02	1277.46	1276.01
90000	1396.87	1388.98	1365.69	1356.38	1352.60	1351.06
95000	1474.47	1466.15	1441.56	1431.73	1427.75	1426.12
100000	1552.08	1543.31	1517.43	1507.09	1502.89	1501.18
200000	3104.16	3086.62	3034.86	3014.17	3005.78	3002.36
300000	4656.24	4629.94	4552.29	4521.26	4508.68	4503.55
400000	6208.32	6173.25	6069.72	6028.34	6011.57	6004.73
500000	7760.39	7716.56	7587.15	7535.43	7514.46	7505.91

18 1/4%

MONTHLY PAYMENT

Necessary to amortize a loan

TERM / AMOUNT	1 YEAR	2 YEARS	3 YEARS	4 YEARS	5 YEARS	6 YEARS
500	45.90	25.02	18.14	14.75	12.76	11.47
600	55.08	30.03	21.77	17.70	15.32	13.77
700	64.26	35.03	25.39	20.65	17.87	16.06
800	73.44	40.04	29.02	23.60	20.42	18.36
900	82.62	45.04	32.65	26.56	22.98	20.65
1000	91.80	50.05	36.28	29.51	25.53	22.95
2000	183.60	100.09	72.56	59.01	51.06	45.90
3000	275.40	150.14	108.83	88.52	76.59	68.85
4000	367.20	200.18	145.11	118.02	102.12	91.80
5000	459.00	250.23	181.39	147.53	127.65	114.75
6000	550.79	300.27	217.67	177.04	153.18	137.70
7000	642.59	350.32	253.95	206.54	178.71	160.65
8000	734.39	400.36	290.22	236.06	204.24	183.60
9000	826.19	450.41	326.50	265.55	229.77	206.54
10000	917.99	500.45	362.78	295.06	255.30	229.45
11000	1009.79	550.50	399.06	324.56	280.83	252.44
12000	1101.59	600.54	435.34	354.07	306.36	275.39
13000	1193.39	650.59	471.61	383.58	331.89	298.34
14000	1285.19	700.63	507.89	413.08	357.42	321.29
15000	1376.99	750.68	544.17	442.59	382.94	344.24
16000	1468.78	800.72	580.45	472.09	408.47	367.19
17000	1560.58	850.77	616.73	501.60	434.00	390.14
18000	1652.38	900.81	653.00	531.10	459.53	413.09
19000	1744.18	950.85	689.28	560.61	485.06	436.04
20000	1835.98	1000.90	725.56	590.12	510.59	458.99
21000	1927.78	1050.94	761.84	619.62	536.12	481.94
22000	2019.58	1100.99	798.11	649.13	561.65	504.89
23000	2111.38	1151.03	834.39	678.63	587.18	527.84
24000	2203.18	1201.08	870.67	708.14	612.71	550.78
25000	2294.98	1251.12	906.95	737.65	638.24	573.73
30000	2753.97	1501.35	1088.34	885.17	765.89	688.48
35000	3212.97	1751.57	1269.73	1032.70	893.54	803.23
40000	3671.96	2001.80	1451.12	1180.23	1021.18	917.97
45000	4130.96	2252.02	1632.51	1327.76	1148.83	1032.72
50000	4589.95	2502.25	1813.90	1475.29	1276.48	1147.47
55000	5048.95	2752.47	1995.29	1622.82	1404.13	1262.21
60000	5507.94	3002.70	2176.68	1770.35	1531.78	1376.96
65000	5966.94	3252.92	2358.07	1917.88	1659.43	1491.71
70000	6425.93	3503.15	2539.45	2065.41	1787.07	1606.45
75000	6884.93	3753.37	2720.84	2212.93	1914.72	1721.20
80000	7343.92	4003.60	2902.23	2360.46	2042.37	1835.95
85000	7802.92	4253.82	3083.62	2507.99	2170.02	1950.69
90000	8261.91	4504.05	3265.01	2655.52	2297.67	2065.44
95000	8720.91	4754.27	3446.40	2803.05	2425.31	2180.19
100000	9179.90	5004.50	3627.79	2950.58	2552.96	2294.93
200000	18359.80	10009.00	7255.58	5901.16	5105.92	4589.87
300000	27539.70	15013.50	10883.40	8851.74	7658.89	6884.80
400000	36719.60	20018.00	14511.20	11802.30	10211.80	9179.74
500000	45899.50	25022.50	18139.00	14752.90	12764.80	11474.70

MONTHLY PAYMENT
Necessary to amortize a loan

18 1/4%

TERM / AMOUNT	7 YEARS	8 YEARS	9 YEARS	10 YEARS	11 YEARS	12 YEARS
500	10.58	9.94	9.46	9.09	8.80	8.58
600	12.70	11.93	11.35	10.91	10.57	10.30
700	14.82	13.91	13.24	12.73	12.33	12.01
800	16.93	15.90	15.13	14.54	14.09	13.73
900	19.05	17.89	17.02	16.36	15.85	15.44
1000	21.16	19.88	18.91	18.18	17.61	17.16
2000	42.33	39.75	37.83	36.36	35.22	34.32
3000	63.49	59.63	56.74	54.54	52.83	51.48
4000	84.66	79.50	75.65	72.72	70.44	68.64
5000	105.82	99.38	94.57	90.90	88.05	85.80
6000	126.99	119.25	113.48	109.08	105.66	102.97
7000	148.15	139.13	132.40	127.26	123.27	120.13
8000	169.32	159.00	151.31	145.44	140.88	137.29
9000	190.48	178.88	170.22	163.62	158.49	154.45
10000	211.65	198.75	189.14	181.80	176.10	171.61
11000	232.81	218.63	208.05	199.98	193.71	188.77
12000	253.98	238.50	226.96	218.16	211.32	205.93
13000	275.14	258.38	245.88	236.34	228.93	223.09
14000	296.31	278.25	264.79	254.52	246.54	240.25
15000	317.47	298.13	283.70	272.70	264.15	257.41
16000	338.63	318.00	302.62	290.88	281.76	274.57
17000	359.80	337.88	321.53	309.06	299.37	291.73
18000	380.96	357.75	340.44	327.24	316.98	308.90
19000	402.13	377.63	359.36	345.42	334.59	326.06
20000	423.29	397.50	378.27	363.60	352.20	343.22
21000	444.46	417.38	397.19	381.78	369.81	360.38
22000	465.62	437.25	416.10	399.96	387.42	377.54
23000	486.79	457.13	435.01	418.14	405.03	394.70
24000	507.95	477.00	453.93	436.32	422.63	411.86
25000	529.12	496.88	472.84	454.49	440.24	429.02
30000	634.94	596.25	567.41	545.39	528.29	514.83
35000	740.76	695.63	661.97	636.29	616.34	600.63
40000	846.59	795.00	756.54	727.19	704.39	686.43
45000	952.41	894.38	851.11	818.09	792.44	772.24
50000	1058.23	993.75	945.68	908.99	880.49	858.04
55000	1164.05	1093.13	1040.25	999.89	968.54	943.85
60000	1269.88	1192.50	1134.81	1090.79	1056.59	1029.65
65000	1375.70	1291.88	1229.38	1181.69	1144.63	1115.45
70000	1481.52	1391.25	1323.95	1272.58	1232.68	1201.26
75000	1587.35	1490.63	1418.52	1363.48	1320.73	1287.06
80000	1693.17	1590.00	1513.08	1454.38	1408.78	1372.87
85000	1798.99	1689.38	1607.65	1545.28	1496.83	1458.67
90000	1904.82	1788.75	1702.22	1636.18	1584.88	1544.48
95000	2010.64	1888.13	1796.79	1727.08	1672.93	1630.28
100000	2116.46	1987.51	1891.36	1817.98	1760.98	1716.08
200000	4232.92	3975.01	3782.01	3635.96	3521.95	3432.17
300000	6349.39	5962.52	5674.07	5453.93	5282.93	5148.25
400000	8465.85	7950.02	7565.42	7271.91	7043.91	6864.34
500000	10582.30	9937.53	9456.78	9089.89	8804.88	8580.42

18 1/4%

MONTHLY PAYMENT

Necessary to amortize a loan

TERM / AMOUNT	13 YEARS	14 YEARS	15 YEARS	16 YEARS	17 YEARS	18 YEARS
500	8.40	8.26	8.14	8.05	7.97	7.91
600	10.08	9.91	9.77	9.66	9.56	9.49
700	11.76	11.56	11.40	11.27	11.16	11.07
800	13.44	13.21	13.03	12.88	12.75	12.65
900	15.12	14.86	14.66	14.49	14.35	14.23
1000	16.80	16.52	16.28	16.10	15.94	15.82
2000	33.61	33.03	32.57	32.19	31.88	31.63
3000	50.41	49.55	48.85	48.29	47.82	47.45
4000	67.21	66.07	65.14	64.38	63.77	63.26
5000	84.02	82.58	81.42	80.48	79.71	79.08
6000	100.82	99.10	97.71	96.57	95.65	94.89
7000	117.62	115.62	113.99	112.67	111.59	110.71
8000	134.43	132.13	130.28	128.77	127.53	126.52
9000	151.23	148.65	146.56	144.86	143.48	142.34
10000	168.03	165.17	162.84	160.96	159.42	158.15
11000	184.84	181.68	179.13	177.05	175.36	173.97
12000	201.64	198.20	195.41	193.15	191.30	189.78
13000	218.45	214.71	211.70	209.24	207.24	205.60
14000	235.25	231.23	227.98	225.34	223.18	221.41
15000	252.05	247.75	244.27	241.44	239.12	237.23
16000	268.86	264.26	260.55	257.53	255.07	253.05
17000	285.66	280.78	276.84	273.63	271.01	268.86
18000	302.46	297.30	293.12	289.72	286.95	284.68
19000	319.27	313.81	309.40	305.82	302.89	300.49
20000	336.07	330.33	325.69	321.92	318.83	316.31
21000	352.87	346.85	341.97	338.01	334.77	332.12
22000	369.68	363.36	358.26	354.11	350.72	347.94
23000	386.48	379.88	374.54	370.20	366.66	363.75
24000	403.28	396.40	390.83	386.30	382.60	379.57
25000	420.09	412.91	407.11	402.39	398.54	395.38
30000	504.10	495.49	488.53	482.87	478.25	474.46
35000	588.12	578.08	569.95	563.35	557.96	553.54
40000	672.14	660.66	651.38	643.83	637.67	632.61
45000	756.16	743.24	732.80	724.31	717.37	711.69
50000	840.17	825.82	814.22	804.79	797.08	790.77
55000	924.19	908.41	895.64	885.27	876.79	869.84
60000	1008.21	990.99	977.06	965.74	956.50	948.92
65000	1092.22	1073.57	1058.49	1046.22	1036.21	1027.99
70000	1176.24	1156.15	1139.91	1126.70	1115.91	1107.07
75000	1260.26	1238.73	1221.33	1207.18	1195.62	1186.15
80000	1344.28	1321.32	1302.75	1287.66	1275.33	1265.22
85000	1428.29	1403.90	1384.17	1368.14	1355.04	1344.30
90000	1512.31	1486.48	1465.60	1448.62	1434.75	1423.38
95000	1596.33	1569.06	1547.02	1529.09	1514.45	1502.45
100000	1680.34	1651.65	1628.44	1609.57	1594.16	1581.53
200000	3360.69	3303.29	3256.88	3219.15	3188.32	3163.06
300000	5041.03	4954.94	4885.32	4828.72	4782.49	4744.59
400000	6721.38	6606.58	6513.76	6438.29	6376.65	6326.12
500000	8401.72	8258.23	8142.20	8047.86	7970.81	7907.65

MONTHLY PAYMENT

Necessary to amortize a loan

18 1/4%

TERM / AMOUNT	19 YEARS	20 YEARS	25 YEARS	30 YEARS	35 YEARS	40 YEARS
500	7.86	7.81	7.69	7.64	7.62	7.61
600	9.43	9.38	9.22	9.17	9.14	9.13
700	11.00	10.94	10.76	10.69	10.66	10.65
800	12.57	12.50	12.30	12.22	12.19	12.18
900	14.14	14.06	13.84	13.75	13.71	13.70
1000	15.71	15.63	15.37	15.28	15.24	15.22
2000	31.42	31.25	30.75	30.55	30.47	30.44
3000	47.13	46.88	46.12	45.83	45.71	45.66
4000	62.85	62.50	61.50	61.10	60.94	60.88
5000	78.56	78.13	76.87	76.38	76.18	76.10
6000	94.27	93.75	92.25	91.65	91.41	91.32
7000	109.98	109.38	107.62	106.93	106.65	106.53
8000	125.69	125.01	123.00	122.20	121.88	121.75
9000	141.40	140.63	138.37	137.48	137.12	136.97
10000	157.11	156.26	153.74	152.75	152.35	152.19
11000	172.83	171.88	169.12	168.03	167.59	167.41
12000	188.54	187.51	184.49	183.30	182.82	182.63
13000	204.25	203.14	199.87	198.58	198.06	197.85
14000	219.96	218.76	215.24	213.85	213.29	213.07
15000	235.67	234.39	230.62	229.13	228.53	228.29
16000	251.38	250.01	245.99	244.40	243.76	243.51
17000	267.09	265.64	261.37	259.68	259.00	258.73
18000	282.81	281.26	276.74	274.95	274.33	273.95
19000	298.52	296.89	292.11	290.23	289.47	289.17
20000	314.23	312.52	307.49	305.50	304.71	304.38
21000	329.94	328.14	322.86	320.78	319.94	319.60
22000	345.65	343.77	338.24	336.05	335.18	334.82
23000	361.36	359.39	353.61	351.33	350.41	350.04
24000	377.07	375.02	368.99	366.60	365.65	365.26
25000	392.79	390.64	384.36	381.88	380.88	380.48
30000	471.34	468.77	461.23	458.25	457.06	456.58
35000	549.90	546.90	538.10	534.63	533.23	532.67
40000	628.46	625.03	614.98	611.00	609.41	608.77
45000	707.01	703.16	691.85	687.38	685.59	684.86
50000	785.57	781.29	768.72	763.75	761.76	760.96
55000	864.13	859.42	845.59	840.13	837.94	837.06
60000	942.69	937.55	922.46	916.50	914.11	913.15
65000	1021.24	1015.68	999.34	992.88	990.29	989.25
70000	1099.80	1093.80	1076.21	1069.25	1066.47	1065.34
75000	1178.36	1171.93	1153.08	1145.63	1142.64	1141.44
80000	1256.91	1250.06	1229.95	1222.00	1218.82	1217.54
85000	1335.47	1328.19	1306.82	1298.38	1294.99	1293.63
90000	1414.03	1406.32	1383.69	1374.75	1371.17	1369.73
95000	1492.58	1484.45	1460.57	1451.13	1447.35	1445.82
100000	1571.14	1562.58	1537.44	1527.50	1523.52	1521.92
200000	3142.28	3125.16	3074.88	3055.01	3047.05	3043.84
300000	4713.42	4687.73	4612.32	4582.51	4570.57	4565.76
400000	6284.56	6250.31	6149.75	6110.01	6094.09	6087.68
500000	7855.71	7812.89	7687.19	7637.52	7617.61	7609.60

18 1/2%

MONTHLY PAYMENT

Necessary to amortize a loan

TERM / AMOUNT	1 YEAR	2 YEARS	3 YEARS	4 YEARS	5 YEARS	6 YEARS
500	45.96	25.08	18.20	14.82	12.83	11.55
600	55.15	30.10	21.84	17.78	15.40	13.85
700	64.34	35.12	25.48	20.75	17.97	16.16
800	73.53	40.13	29.12	23.71	20.53	18.47
900	82.73	45.15	32.76	26.67	23.10	20.78
1000	91.92	50.17	36.40	29.64	25.67	23.09
2000	183.84	100.33	72.81	59.27	51.33	46.18
3000	275.76	150.50	109.21	88.91	77.00	69.27
4000	367.67	200.66	145.62	118.55	102.67	92.37
5000	459.59	250.83	182.02	148.10	128.33	115.46
6000	551.51	301.00	218.42	177.82	154.00	138.55
7000	643.43	351.16	254.83	207.46	179.66	161.64
8000	735.35	401.33	291.23	237.10	205.33	184.73
9000	827.27	451.50	327.63	266.73	231.00	207.82
10000	919.18	501.66	364.04	296.37	256.66	230.91
11000	1011.10	551.83	400.44	326.01	282.33	254.01
12000	1103.02	601.99	436.85	355.64	308.00	277.10
13000	1194.94	652.16	473.25	385.28	333.66	300.19
14000	1286.86	702.33	509.65	414.92	359.33	323.28
15000	1378.78	752.49	546.06	444.55	384.99	346.37
16000	1470.69	802.66	582.46	474.19	410.66	369.46
17000	1562.61	852.82	618.86	503.83	436.33	392.55
18000	1654.53	902.99	655.27	533.47	461.99	415.65
19000	1746.45	953.16	691.67	563.10	487.66	438.74
20000	1838.37	1003.32	728.08	592.74	513.33	461.83
21000	1930.29	1053.49	764.48	622.38	538.99	484.92
22000	2022.20	1103.65	800.88	652.01	564.66	508.01
23000	2114.12	1153.82	837.29	681.65	590.32	531.10
24000	2206.04	1203.99	873.69	711.29	615.99	554.19
25000	2297.96	1254.15	910.09	740.92	641.66	577.29
30000	2757.55	1504.98	1092.11	889.11	769.99	692.74
35000	3217.14	1755.81	1274.13	1037.29	898.32	808.20
40000	3676.73	2006.64	1456.15	1185.48	1026.65	923.66
45000	4136.33	2257.48	1638.17	1333.66	1154.98	1039.11
50000	4595.92	2508.31	1820.19	1481.85	1283.31	1154.57
55000	5055.51	2759.14	2002.21	1630.03	1411.64	1270.03
60000	5515.10	3009.97	2184.23	1778.22	1539.97	1385.48
65000	5974.69	3260.80	2366.25	1926.40	1668.31	1500.94
70000	6434.28	3511.63	2548.26	2074.59	1796.64	1616.40
75000	6893.88	3762.46	2730.28	2222.77	1924.97	1731.85
80000	7353.47	4013.29	2912.30	2370.96	2053.30	1847.31
85000	7813.06	4264.12	3094.32	2519.14	2181.63	1962.77
90000	8272.65	4514.95	3276.34	2667.33	2309.96	2078.22
95000	8732.24	4765.78	3458.36	2815.51	2438.29	2193.68
100000	9191.83	5016.61	3640.38	2963.70	2566.62	2309.14
200000	18383.70	10033.20	7280.75	5927.39	5133.25	4618.28
300000	27575.50	15049.80	10921.10	8891.09	7699.87	6927.42
400000	36767.30	20066.40	14561.50	11854.80	10266.50	9236.55
500000	45959.20	25083.10	18201.90	14818.50	12833.10	11545.70

MONTHLY PAYMENT

Necessary to amortize a loan

18 1/2%

TERM / AMOUNT	7 YEARS	8 YEARS	9 YEARS	10 YEARS	11 YEARS	12 YEARS
500	10.66	10.01	9.54	9.17	8.89	8.67
600	12.79	12.02	11.44	11.01	10.67	10.40
700	14.92	14.02	13.35	12.84	12.44	12.13
800	17.05	16.02	15.26	14.67	14.22	13.86
900	19.18	18.02	17.16	16.51	16.00	15.60
1000	21.31	20.03	19.07	18.34	17.78	17.33
2000	42.62	40.05	38.14	36.68	35.55	34.66
3000	63.94	60.08	57.21	55.03	53.33	51.99
4000	85.25	80.11	76.28	73.37	71.10	69.32
5000	106.56	100.14	95.35	91.71	88.88	86.66
6000	127.87	120.17	114.43	110.05	106.66	103.99
7000	149.18	140.19	133.50	128.39	124.43	121.32
8000	170.50	160.22	152.57	146.73	142.21	138.65
9000	191.81	180.25	171.64	165.08	159.98	155.98
10000	213.12	200.28	190.71	183.42	177.76	173.31
11000	234.43	220.30	209.78	201.76	195.54	190.64
12000	255.74	240.33	228.85	220.10	213.31	207.97
13000	277.06	260.36	247.92	238.44	231.09	225.31
14000	298.37	280.38	266.99	256.78	248.86	242.64
15000	319.68	300.41	286.06	275.13	266.64	259.97
16000	340.99	320.44	305.13	293.47	284.42	277.30
17000	362.30	340.47	324.20	311.81	302.19	294.63
18000	383.62	360.49	343.28	330.15	319.97	311.96
19000	404.93	380.52	362.35	348.49	337.74	329.29
20000	426.24	400.55	381.42	366.83	355.52	346.62
21000	447.55	420.58	400.49	385.18	373.30	363.95
22000	468.86	440.60	419.56	403.52	391.07	381.29
23000	490.18	460.63	438.63	421.86	408.85	398.62
24000	511.49	480.66	457.70	440.20	426.62	415.95
25000	532.80	500.69	476.77	458.54	444.40	433.28
30000	639.36	600.82	572.13	550.25	533.28	519.94
35000	745.92	700.96	667.48	641.96	622.16	606.59
40000	852.48	801.10	762.83	733.67	711.04	693.25
45000	959.04	901.24	858.19	825.38	799.92	779.90
50000	1065.60	1001.37	953.54	917.08	888.80	866.56
55000	1172.16	1101.51	1048.90	1008.79	977.68	953.21
60000	1278.72	1201.65	1144.25	1100.50	1066.56	1039.87
65000	1385.28	1301.78	1239.60	1192.21	1155.44	1126.52
70000	1491.84	1401.92	1334.96	1283.92	1244.32	1213.18
75000	1598.40	1502.06	1430.31	1375.63	1333.20	1299.84
80000	1704.96	1602.20	1525.67	1467.33	1422.08	1386.49
85000	1811.52	1702.33	1621.02	1559.04	1510.96	1473.15
90000	1918.08	1802.47	1716.37	1650.75	1599.84	1559.80
95000	2024.63	1902.61	1811.73	1742.46	1688.72	1646.46
100000	2131.19	2002.75	1907.08	1834.17	1777.60	1733.12
200000	4262.39	4005.49	3814.17	3668.33	3555.20	3466.23
300000	6393.58	6008.24	5721.25	5502.50	5332.80	5199.35
400000	8524.78	8010.98	7628.33	7336.67	7110.40	6932.46
500000	10656.00	10013.70	9535.42	9170.83	8888.00	8665.58

18 1/2% MONTHLY PAYMENT

Necessary to amortize a loan

TERM / AMOUNT	13 YEARS	14 YEARS	15 YEARS	16 YEARS	17 YEARS	18 YEARS
500	8.49	8.35	8.23	8.14	8.06	8.00
600	10.19	10.02	9.88	9.77	9.68	9.60
700	11.88	11.69	11.53	11.40	11.29	11.20
800	13.58	13.36	13.17	13.02	12.90	12.80
900	15.28	15.02	14.82	14.65	14.52	14.40
1000	16.98	16.69	16.47	16.28	16.13	16.00
2000	33.96	33.39	32.93	32.56	32.26	32.01
3000	50.93	50.08	49.40	48.84	48.38	48.01
4000	67.91	66.78	65.86	65.12	64.51	64.02
5000	84.89	83.47	82.33	81.40	80.64	80.02
6000	101.87	100.16	98.79	97.68	96.77	96.03
7000	118.84	116.86	115.26	113.96	112.90	112.03
8000	135.82	133.55	131.72	130.24	129.03	128.03
9000	152.80	150.25	148.19	146.52	145.15	144.04
10000	169.78	166.94	164.65	162.80	161.28	160.04
11000	186.75	183.64	181.12	179.08	177.41	176.05
12000	203.73	200.33	197.58	195.35	193.54	192.05
13000	220.71	217.02	214.05	211.63	209.67	208.06
14000	237.69	233.72	230.51	227.91	225.79	224.06
15000	254.66	250.41	246.98	244.19	241.92	240.06
16000	271.64	267.11	263.44	260.47	258.05	256.07
17000	288.62	283.80	279.91	276.75	274.18	272.07
18000	305.60	300.49	296.37	293.03	290.31	288.08
19000	322.57	317.19	312.84	309.31	306.43	304.08
20000	339.55	333.88	329.31	325.59	322.56	320.09
21000	356.53	350.58	345.77	341.87	338.69	336.09
22000	373.51	367.27	362.24	358.15	354.82	352.09
23000	390.48	383.96	378.70	374.43	370.95	368.10
24000	407.46	400.66	395.17	390.71	387.08	384.10
25000	424.44	417.35	411.63	406.99	403.20	400.11
30000	509.33	500.82	493.96	488.39	483.84	480.13
35000	594.21	584.29	576.28	569.78	564.49	560.15
40000	679.10	667.76	658.61	651.18	645.13	640.17
45000	763.99	751.23	740.94	732.58	725.77	720.19
50000	848.88	834.70	823.26	813.98	806.41	800.21
55000	933.77	918.17	905.59	895.37	887.05	880.23
60000	1018.65	1001.64	987.91	976.77	967.69	960.26
65000	1103.54	1085.11	1070.24	1058.17	1048.33	1040.28
70000	1188.43	1168.58	1152.57	1139.57	1128.97	1120.30
75000	1273.32	1252.05	1234.89	1220.96	1209.61	1200.32
80000	1358.20	1335.52	1317.22	1302.36	1290.25	1280.34
85000	1443.09	1419.00	1399.55	1383.76	1370.89	1360.36
90000	1527.98	1502.47	1481.87	1465.16	1451.53	1440.38
95000	1612.87	1585.94	1564.20	1546.56	1532.17	1520.40
100000	1697.75	1669.41	1646.52	1627.95	1612.81	1600.43
200000	3395.51	3338.81	3293.05	3255.91	3225.63	3200.85
300000	5093.26	5008.22	4939.57	4883.86	4838.44	4801.28
400000	6791.02	6677.62	6586.10	6511.81	6451.25	6401.70
500000	8488.77	8347.03	8232.62	8139.76	8064.06	8002.13

MONTHLY PAYMENT

Necessary to amortize a loan

18 1/2%

TERM / AMOUNT	19 YEARS	20 YEARS	25 YEARS	30 YEARS	35 YEARS	40 YEARS
500	7.95	7.91	7.79	7.74	7.72	7.71
600	9.54	9.49	9.34	9.29	9.27	9.26
700	11.13	11.07	10.90	10.84	10.81	10.80
800	12.72	12.66	12.46	12.38	12.35	12.34
900	14.31	14.24	14.02	13.93	13.90	13.88
1000	15.90	15.82	15.57	15.48	15.44	15.43
2000	31.81	31.64	31.15	30.96	30.88	30.85
3000	47.71	47.46	46.72	46.44	46.33	46.28
4000	63.61	63.28	62.30	61.92	61.77	61.71
5000	79.51	79.09	77.87	77.40	77.21	77.13
6000	95.42	94.91	93.45	92.88	92.65	92.56
7000	111.32	110.73	109.02	108.36	108.09	107.99
8000	127.22	126.55	124.60	123.84	123.53	123.41
9000	143.12	142.37	140.17	139.32	138.98	138.84
10000	159.03	158.19	155.75	154.79	154.42	154.27
11000	174.93	174.01	171.32	170.27	169.86	169.69
12000	190.83	189.83	186.90	185.75	185.30	185.12
13000	206.73	205.65	202.47	201.23	200.74	200.55
14000	222.64	221.47	218.05	216.71	216.18	215.97
15000	238.54	237.29	233.62	232.19	231.63	231.40
16000	254.44	253.10	249.20	247.67	247.07	246.83
17000	270.34	268.92	264.77	263.15	262.51	262.25
18000	286.25	284.74	280.35	278.63	277.95	277.68
19000	302.15	300.56	295.92	294.11	293.39	293.11
20000	318.05	316.38	311.50	309.59	308.83	308.53
21000	333.96	332.20	327.07	325.07	324.28	323.96
22000	349.86	348.02	342.65	340.55	339.72	339.39
23000	365.76	363.84	358.22	356.03	355.16	354.81
24000	381.66	379.66	373.80	371.51	370.60	370.24
25000	397.57	395.47	389.37	386.99	386.04	385.67
30000	477.08	474.57	467.25	464.38	463.25	462.80
35000	556.59	553.66	545.12	541.78	540.46	539.93
40000	636.10	632.76	622.99	619.18	617.67	617.07
45000	715.62	711.85	700.87	696.58	694.88	694.20
50000	795.13	790.95	778.74	773.97	772.08	771.33
55000	874.64	870.04	856.62	851.37	849.29	848.47
60000	954.16	949.14	934.49	928.77	926.50	925.60
65000	1033.67	1028.23	1012.36	1006.16	1003.71	1002.73
70000	1113.18	1107.33	1090.24	1083.56	1080.92	1079.87
75000	1192.69	1186.42	1168.11	1160.96	1158.13	1157.00
80000	1272.21	1265.52	1245.99	1238.36	1235.33	1234.13
85000	1351.72	1344.61	1323.86	1315.75	1312.54	1311.26
90000	1431.23	1423.71	1401.74	1393.15	1389.75	1388.40
95000	1510.75	1502.80	1479.61	1470.55	1466.96	1465.53
100000	1590.26	1581.90	1557.48	1547.94	1544.17	1542.66
200000	3180.52	3163.79	3114.97	3095.89	3088.34	3085.33
300000	4770.78	4745.69	4672.45	4643.83	4632.50	4627.99
400000	6361.04	6327.59	6229.94	6191.78	6176.67	6170.66
500000	7951.30	7909.48	7787.42	7739.72	7720.84	7713.32

18 3/4%

MONTHLY PAYMENT

Necessary to amortize a loan

TERM / AMOUNT	1 YEAR	2 YEARS	3 YEARS	4 YEARS	5 YEARS	6 YEARS
500	46.02	25.14	18.26	14.88	12.90	11.62
600	55.22	30.17	21.92	17.86	15.48	13.94
700	64.43	35.20	25.57	20.84	18.06	16.26
800	73.63	40.23	29.22	23.81	20.64	18.59
900	82.83	45.26	32.88	26.79	23.22	20.91
1000	92.04	50.29	36.53	29.77	25.80	23.23
2000	184.07	100.57	73.06	59.54	51.61	46.47
3000	276.11	150.86	109.59	89.31	77.41	69.70
4000	368.15	201.15	146.12	119.07	103.21	92.94
5000	460.19	251.44	182.65	148.84	129.02	116.17
6000	552.22	301.72	219.18	178.61	154.82	139.40
7000	644.26	352.01	255.71	208.38	180.62	162.64
8000	736.30	402.30	292.24	238.15	206.43	185.87
9000	828.34	452.59	328.77	267.92	232.23	209.10
10000	920.37	502.87	365.30	297.68	258.03	232.34
11000	1012.41	553.16	401.83	327.45	283.84	255.57
12000	1104.45	603.45	438.36	357.22	309.64	278.81
13000	1196.48	653.73	474.89	386.99	335.44	302.04
14000	1288.52	704.02	511.42	416.76	361.24	325.27
15000	1380.56	754.31	547.95	446.53	387.05	348.51
16000	1472.60	804.60	584.48	476.29	412.85	371.74
17000	1564.63	854.88	621.01	506.06	438.65	394.98
18000	1656.67	905.17	657.54	535.83	464.46	418.21
19000	1748.71	955.46	694.06	565.60	490.26	441.44
20000	1840.74	1005.74	730.59	595.37	516.06	464.68
21000	1932.78	1056.03	767.12	625.14	541.87	487.91
22000	2024.82	1106.32	803.65	654.90	567.67	511.14
23000	2116.86	1156.61	840.18	684.67	593.47	534.38
24000	2208.89	1206.89	876.71	714.44	619.28	557.61
25000	2300.93	1257.18	913.24	744.21	645.08	580.85
30000	2761.12	1508.62	1095.89	893.05	774.10	697.01
35000	3221.30	1760.05	1278.54	1041.89	903.11	813.18
40000	3681.49	2011.49	1461.19	1190.73	1032.13	929.35
45000	4141.67	2262.92	1643.84	1339.57	1161.14	1045.52
50000	4601.86	2514.36	1826.49	1488.42	1290.16	1161.69
55000	5062.05	2765.79	2009.13	1637.26	1419.17	1277.86
60000	5522.23	3017.23	2191.78	1786.10	1548.19	1394.03
65000	5982.42	3268.67	2374.43	1934.94	1677.21	1510.20
70000	6442.61	3520.10	2557.08	2083.78	1806.22	1626.37
75000	6902.79	3771.54	2739.73	2232.62	1935.24	1742.53
80000	7362.98	4022.97	2922.38	2381.47	2064.25	1858.70
85000	7823.16	4274.41	3105.02	2530.31	2193.27	1974.87
90000	8283.35	4525.85	3287.67	2679.15	2322.28	2091.04
95000	8743.54	4777.28	3470.32	2827.99	2451.30	2207.21
100000	9203.72	5028.72	3652.97	2976.83	2580.32	2323.38
200000	18407.40	10057.40	7305.94	5953.67	5160.63	4646.76
300000	27611.20	15086.20	10958.90	8930.50	7740.95	6970.14
400000	36814.90	20114.90	14611.90	11907.30	10321.30	9293.52
500000	46018.60	25143.60	18264.90	14884.20	12901.60	11616.90

MONTHLY PAYMENT
Necessary to amortize a loan

18 3/4%

TERM / AMOUNT	7 YEARS	8 YEARS	9 YEARS	10 YEARS	11 YEARS	12 YEARS
500	10.73	10.09	9.61	9.25	8.97	8.75
600	12.88	12.11	11.54	11.10	10.77	10.50
700	15.02	14.13	13.46	12.95	12.56	12.25
800	17.17	16.14	15.38	14.80	14.35	14.00
900	19.31	18.16	17.31	16.65	16.15	15.75
1000	21.46	20.18	19.23	18.50	17.94	17.50
2000	42.92	40.36	38.46	37.01	35.89	35.00
3000	64.38	60.54	57.69	55.51	53.83	52.51
4000	85.84	80.72	76.91	74.02	71.77	70.01
5000	107.30	100.90	96.14	92.52	89.71	87.51
6000	128.76	121.08	115.37	111.03	107.66	105.01
7000	150.22	141.26	134.60	129.53	125.60	122.52
8000	171.68	161.44	153.83	148.03	143.54	140.02
9000	193.14	181.62	173.06	166.54	161.49	157.52
10000	214.60	201.80	192.29	185.04	179.43	175.02
11000	236.06	221.98	211.52	203.55	197.37	192.52
12000	257.52	242.16	230.74	222.05	215.31	210.03
13000	278.98	262.35	249.97	240.55	233.26	227.53
14000	300.44	282.53	269.20	259.06	251.20	245.03
15000	321.90	302.71	288.43	277.56	269.14	262.53
16000	343.36	322.89	307.66	296.07	287.09	280.03
17000	364.82	343.07	326.89	314.57	305.03	297.54
18000	386.28	363.25	346.12	333.07	322.97	315.04
19000	407.73	383.43	365.34	351.58	340.91	332.54
20000	429.19	403.61	384.57	370.08	358.86	350.04
21000	450.65	423.79	403.80	388.59	376.80	367.54
22000	472.11	443.97	423.03	407.09	394.74	385.05
23000	493.57	464.15	442.26	425.60	412.69	402.55
24000	515.03	484.33	461.49	444.10	430.63	420.05
25000	536.49	504.51	480.72	462.60	448.57	437.55
30000	643.79	605.41	576.86	555.12	538.29	525.06
35000	751.09	706.31	673.00	647.65	628.00	612.57
40000	858.39	807.22	769.15	740.17	717.71	700.08
45000	965.69	908.12	865.29	832.69	807.43	787.59
50000	1072.99	1009.02	961.43	925.21	897.14	875.10
55000	1180.28	1109.92	1057.58	1017.73	986.86	962.61
60000	1287.58	1210.82	1153.72	1110.25	1076.57	1050.12
65000	1394.88	1311.72	1249.86	1202.77	1166.28	1137.63
70000	1502.18	1412.63	1346.01	1295.29	1256.00	1225.15
75000	1609.48	1513.53	1442.15	1387.81	1345.71	1312.66
80000	1716.78	1614.43	1538.29	1480.33	1435.43	1400.17
85000	1824.07	1715.33	1634.44	1572.85	1525.14	1487.68
90000	1931.37	1816.23	1730.58	1665.37	1614.86	1575.19
95000	2038.67	1917.13	1826.72	1757.89	1704.57	1662.70
100000	2145.97	2018.04	1922.86	1850.41	1794.28	1750.21
200000	4291.94	4036.07	3845.73	3700.83	3588.57	3500.41
300000	6437.91	6054.11	5768.59	5551.24	5382.85	5250.62
400000	8583.88	8072.15	7691.46	7401.65	7177.14	7000.83
500000	10729.90	10090.20	9614.32	9252.07	8971.42	8751.04

18 3/4%

MONTHLY PAYMENT
Necessary to amortize a loan

TERM / AMOUNT	13 YEARS	14 YEARS	15 YEARS	16 YEARS	17 YEARS	18 YEARS
500	8.58	8.44	8.32	8.23	8.16	8.10
600	10.29	10.12	9.99	9.88	9.79	9.72
700	12.01	11.81	11.65	11.52	11.42	11.34
800	13.72	13.50	13.32	13.17	13.05	12.96
900	15.44	15.19	14.98	14.82	14.68	14.57
1000	17.15	16.87	16.65	16.46	16.32	16.19
2000	34.30	33.74	33.29	32.93	32.63	32.39
3000	51.46	50.62	49.94	49.39	48.95	48.58
4000	68.61	67.49	66.59	65.86	65.26	64.78
5000	05.70	04.30	03.20	02.02	01.50	00.97
6000	102.91	101.23	99.88	98.78	97.89	97.16
7000	120.07	118.11	116.53	115.25	114.21	113.36
8000	137.22	134.98	133.17	131.71	130.52	129.55
9000	154.37	151.85	149.82	148.18	146.84	145.74
10000	171.52	168.72	166.47	164.64	163.15	161.94
11000	188.68	185.60	183.11	181.10	179.47	178.13
12000	205.83	202.47	199.76	197.57	195.78	194.33
13000	222.98	219.34	216.41	214.03	212.10	210.52
14000	240.13	236.21	233.05	230.50	228.41	226.71
15000	257.28	253.08	249.70	246.96	244.73	242.91
16000	274.44	269.96	266.35	263.42	261.04	259.10
17000	291.59	286.83	282.99	279.89	277.36	275.29
18000	308.74	303.70	299.64	296.35	293.67	291.49
19000	325.89	320.57	316.29	312.82	309.99	307.68
20000	343.05	337.45	332.93	329.28	326.30	323.88
21000	360.20	354.32	349.58	345.74	342.62	340.07
22000	377.35	371.19	366.23	362.21	358.94	356.26
23000	394.50	388.06	382.87	378.67	375.25	372.46
24000	411.65	404.94	399.52	395.13	391.57	388.65
25000	428.81	421.81	416.17	411.60	407.88	404.84
30000	514.57	506.17	499.40	493.92	489.46	485.81
35000	600.33	590.53	582.63	576.24	571.03	566.78
40000	686.09	674.89	665.87	658.56	652.61	647.75
45000	771.85	759.25	749.10	740.88	734.18	728.72
50000	857.61	843.61	832.33	823.20	815.76	809.69
55000	943.37	927.98	915.57	905.52	897.34	890.66
60000	1029.14	1012.34	998.80	987.84	978.91	971.63
65000	1114.90	1096.70	1082.03	1070.15	1060.49	1052.59
70000	1200.66	1181.06	1165.27	1152.47	1142.06	1133.56
75000	1286.42	1265.42	1248.50	1234.79	1223.64	1214.53
80000	1372.18	1349.78	1331.73	1317.11	1305.22	1295.50
85000	1457.94	1434.14	1414.97	1399.43	1386.79	1376.47
90000	1543.70	1518.51	1498.20	1481.75	1468.37	1457.44
95000	1629.46	1602.87	1581.44	1564.07	1549.94	1538.41
100000	1715.23	1687.23	1664.67	1646.39	1631.52	1619.38
200000	3430.45	3374.46	3329.34	3292.78	3263.04	3238.75
300000	5145.68	5061.68	4994.01	4939.18	4894.56	4858.13
400000	6860.90	6748.91	6658.67	6585.57	6526.08	6477.51
500000	8576.13	8436.14	8323.34	8231.96	8157.60	8096.88

MONTHLY PAYMENT

Necessary to amortize a loan

18 3/4%

TERM / AMOUNT	19 YEARS	20 YEARS	25 YEARS	30 YEARS	35 YEARS	40 YEARS
500	8.05	8.01	7.89	7.84	7.82	7.82
600	9.66	9.61	9.47	9.41	9.39	9.38
700	11.27	11.21	11.04	10.98	10.95	10.94
800	12.88	12.81	12.62	12.55	12.52	12.51
900	14.48	14.41	14.20	14.12	14.08	13.07
1000	16.09	16.01	15.78	15.68	15.65	15.63
2000	32.19	32.03	31.55	31.37	31.30	31.27
3000	48.28	48.04	47.33	47.05	46.94	46.90
4000	64.38	64.05	63.10	62.74	62.59	62.54
5000	80.47	80.06	78.88	78.42	78.24	78.17
6000	96.57	96.08	94.65	94.10	93.89	93.81
7000	112.66	112.09	110.43	109.79	109.54	109.44
8000	128.75	128.10	126.21	125.47	125.19	125.07
9000	144.85	144.11	141.98	141.16	140.83	140.71
10000	160.94	160.13	157.76	156.84	156.48	156.34
11000	177.04	176.14	173.53	172.53	172.13	171.98
12000	193.13	192.15	189.31	188.21	187.78	187.61
13000	209.23	208.17	205.08	203.89	203.43	203.24
14000	225.32	224.18	220.86	219.58	219.08	218.88
15000	241.42	240.19	236.64	235.26	234.72	234.51
16000	257.51	256.20	252.41	250.95	250.37	250.15
17000	273.60	272.22	268.19	266.63	266.02	265.78
18000	289.70	288.23	283.96	282.31	281.67	281.42
19000	305.79	304.24	299.74	298.00	297.32	297.05
20000	321.89	320.25	315.51	313.68	312.97	312.68
21000	337.98	336.27	331.29	329.37	328.61	328.32
22000	354.08	352.28	347.06	345.05	344.26	343.95
23000	370.17	368.29	362.84	360.73	359.91	359.59
24000	386.26	384.30	378.62	376.42	375.56	375.22
25000	402.36	400.32	394.39	392.10	391.21	390.85
30000	482.83	480.38	473.27	470.52	469.45	469.03
35000	563.30	560.44	552.15	548.94	547.69	547.20
40000	643.77	640.51	631.03	627.36	625.93	625.37
45000	724.24	720.57	709.90	705.78	704.17	703.54
50000	804.72	800.63	788.78	784.20	782.41	781.71
55000	885.19	880.70	867.66	862.62	860.65	859.88
60000	965.66	960.76	946.54	941.05	938.90	938.05
65000	1046.13	1040.82	1025.42	1019.47	1017.14	1016.22
70000	1126.60	1120.89	1104.30	1097.89	1095.38	1094.39
75000	1207.07	1200.95	1183.17	1176.31	1173.62	1172.56
80000	1287.54	1281.01	1262.05	1254.73	1251.86	1250.73
85000	1368.02	1361.08	1340.93	1333.15	1330.10	1328.90
90000	1448.49	1441.14	1419.81	1411.57	1408.34	1407.07
95000	1528.96	1521.20	1498.69	1489.99	1486.58	1485.25
100000	1609.43	1601.27	1577.56	1568.41	1564.83	1563.42
200000	3218.86	3202.53	3155.13	3136.82	3129.65	3126.83
300000	4828.29	4803.80	4732.69	4705.22	4694.48	4690.25
400000	6437.72	6405.06	6310.26	6273.63	6259.30	6253.67
500000	8047.15	8006.33	7887.82	7842.04	7824.13	7817.08

19%

MONTHLY PAYMENT

Necessary to amortize a loan

TERM / AMOUNT	1 YEAR	2 YEARS	3 YEARS	4 YEARS	5 YEARS	6 YEARS
500	46.08	25.20	18.33	14.95	12.97	11.69
600	55.29	30.25	21.99	17.94	15.56	14.03
700	64.51	35.29	25.66	20.93	18.16	16.36
800	73.73	40.33	29.32	23.92	20.75	18.70
900	82.94	45.37	32.99	26.91	23.35	21.04
1000	92.16	50.41	36.66	29.90	25.94	23.38
2000	184.31	100.82	73.31	59.80	51.88	46.75
3000	276.47	151.23	109.97	89.70	77.82	70.13
4000	368.63	201.63	146.62	119.60	103.76	93.51
5000	460.78	252.04	183.28	149.50	129.70	116.88
6000	552.94	302.45	219.94	179.40	155.64	140.26
7000	645.09	352.86	256.59	209.30	181.58	163.64
8000	737.25	403.27	293.25	239.20	207.52	187.01
9000	829.41	453.68	329.90	269.10	233.47	210.39
10000	921.56	504.09	366.56	299.00	259.41	233.77
11000	1013.72	554.49	403.22	328.90	285.35	257.14
12000	1105.88	604.90	439.87	358.80	311.29	280.52
13000	1198.03	655.31	476.53	388.70	337.23	303.90
14000	1290.19	705.72	513.18	418.60	363.17	327.27
15000	1382.35	756.13	549.84	448.50	389.11	350.65
16000	1474.50	806.54	586.50	478.40	415.05	374.03
17000	1566.66	856.94	623.15	508.30	440.99	397.40
18000	1658.81	907.35	659.81	538.20	466.93	420.78
19000	1750.97	957.76	696.46	568.10	492.87	444.16
20000	1843.13	1008.17	733.12	598.00	518.81	467.53
21000	1935.28	1058.58	769.78	627.90	544.75	490.91
22000	2027.44	1108.99	806.43	657.80	570.69	514.29
23000	2119.60	1159.40	843.09	687.70	596.63	537.66
24000	2211.75	1209.80	879.74	717.60	622.57	561.04
25000	2303.91	1260.21	916.40	747.50	648.51	584.42
30000	2764.69	1512.25	1099.68	897.00	778.22	701.30
35000	3225.47	1764.30	1282.96	1046.50	907.92	818.18
40000	3686.25	2016.34	1466.24	1196.00	1037.62	935.07
45000	4147.04	2268.38	1649.52	1345.50	1167.32	1051.95
50000	4607.82	2520.42	1832.80	1495.00	1297.03	1168.83
55000	5068.60	2772.47	2016.08	1644.50	1426.73	1285.72
60000	5529.38	3024.51	2199.36	1794.00	1556.43	1402.60
65000	5990.16	3276.55	2382.64	1943.50	1686.13	1519.48
70000	6450.94	3528.59	2565.92	2093.00	1815.84	1636.37
75000	6911.73	3780.64	2749.20	2242.50	1945.54	1753.25
80000	7372.51	4032.68	2932.48	2392.00	2075.24	1870.13
85000	7833.29	4284.72	3115.75	2541.50	2204.94	1987.02
90000	8294.07	4536.76	3299.03	2691.01	2334.65	2103.90
95000	8754.85	4788.81	3482.31	2840.51	2464.35	2220.79
100000	9215.63	5040.85	3665.59	2990.01	2594.05	2337.67
200000	18431.30	10081.70	7331.19	5980.01	5188.10	4675.34
300000	27646.90	15122.50	10996.80	8970.02	7782.15	7013.01
400000	36862.50	20163.40	14662.40	11960.00	10376.20	9350.67
500000	46078.20	25204.20	18328.00	14950.00	12970.30	11688.30

MONTHLY PAYMENT

Necessary to amortize a loan

19%

TERM / AMOUNT	7 YEARS	8 YEARS	9 YEARS	10 YEARS	11 YEARS	12 YEARS
500	10.80	10.17	9.69	9.33	9.06	8.84
600	12.96	12.20	11.63	11.20	10.87	10.60
700	15.13	14.23	13.57	13.07	12.68	12.37
800	17.29	16.27	15.51	14.93	14.49	14.14
900	19.45	18.30	17.45	16.80	16.30	15.91
1000	21.61	20.33	19.39	18.67	18.11	17.67
2000	43.22	40.67	38.77	37.33	36.22	35.35
3000	64.82	61.00	58.16	56.00	54.33	53.02
4000	86.43	81.34	77.55	74.67	72.44	70.69
5000	108.04	101.67	96.94	93.34	90.55	88.37
6000	129.65	122.00	116.32	112.00	108.66	106.04
7000	151.26	142.34	135.71	130.67	126.77	123.72
8000	172.86	162.67	155.10	149.34	144.88	141.39
9000	194.47	183.01	174.48	168.01	162.99	159.06
10000	216.08	203.34	193.87	186.67	181.10	176.74
11000	237.69	223.67	213.26	205.34	199.21	194.41
12000	259.30	244.01	232.65	224.01	217.32	212.08
13000	280.90	264.34	252.03	242.67	235.43	229.76
14000	302.51	284.67	271.42	261.34	253.54	247.43
15000	324.12	305.01	290.81	180.01	271.66	265.10
16000	345.73	325.34	310.19	298.68	289.77	282.78
17000	367.34	345.68	329.58	317.34	307.88	300.45
18000	388.94	366.01	348.97	336.01	325.99	318.13
19000	410.55	386.34	368.35	354.68	344.10	335.80
20000	432.16	406.68	387.74	373.34	362.21	353.47
21000	453.77	427.01	407.13	392.01	380.32	371.15
22000	475.38	447.34	426.52	410.68	398.43	388.82
23000	496.98	467.68	445.90	429.35	416.54	406.49
24000	518.59	488.01	465.29	448.01	434.65	424.17
25000	540.20	508.35	484.68	466.68	452.76	441.84
30000	648.24	610.02	581.61	560.02	543.31	530.21
35000	756.28	711.68	678.55	653.35	633.86	618.58
40000	864.32	813.35	775.48	746.69	724.41	706.95
45000	972.36	915.02	872.42	840.03	814.96	795.31
50000	1080.40	1016.69	969.35	933.36	905.52	883.68
55000	1188.44	1118.36	1066.29	1026.70	996.07	972.05
60000	1296.48	1220.03	1163.22	1120.03	1086.62	1060.42
65000	1404.52	1321.70	1260.16	1213.37	1177.17	1148.79
70000	1512.56	1423.37	1357.09	1306.71	1267.72	1237.15
75000	1620.60	1525.04	1454.03	1400.04	1358.27	1325.52
80000	1728.64	1626.71	1550.96	1493.38	1448.82	1413.89
85000	1836.68	1728.38	1647.90	1586.71	1539.38	1502.26
90000	1944.72	1830.05	1744.84	1680.05	1629.93	1590.63
95000	2052.76	1931.71	1841.77	1773.39	1720.48	1679.00
100000	2160.80	2033.38	1938.71	1866.72	1811.03	1767.36
200000	4321.60	4066.77	3877.41	3733.44	3622.06	3534.73
300000	6482.40	6100.15	5816.12	5600.17	5433.09	5302.09
400000	8643.19	8133.54	7754.82	7466.89	7244.12	7069.45
500000	10804.00	10166.90	9693.53	9333.61	9055.15	8836.82

19%

MONTHLY PAYMENT
Necessary to amortize a loan

TERM / AMOUNT	13 YEARS	14 YEARS	15 YEARS	16 YEARS	17 YEARS	18 YEARS
500	8.66	8.53	8.41	8.32	8.25	8.19
600	10.40	10.23	10.10	9.99	9.90	9.83
700	12.13	11.94	11.78	11.65	11.55	11.47
800	13.86	13.64	13.46	13.32	13.20	13.11
900	15.59	15.35	15.15	14.98	14.85	14.75
1000	17.33	17.05	16.83	16.65	16.50	16.38
2000	34.66	34.10	33.66	33.30	33.01	32.77
3000	51.98	51.15	50.49	49.95	49.51	59.15
4000	69.31	68.20	67.32	66.60	66.01	65.54
5000	86.64	85.26	84.14	83.24	82.51	81.92
6000	103.97	102.31	100.97	99.89	99.02	98.30
7000	121.29	119.36	117.80	116.54	115.52	114.69
8000	138.62	136.41	134.63	133.19	132.02	131.07
9000	155.95	153.46	151.46	149.84	148.53	147.46
10000	173.28	170.51	168.29	166.49	165.03	163.84
11000	190.60	187.56	185.12	183.14	181.53	180.22
12000	207.93	204.61	201.95	199.79	198.03	196.61
13000	225.26	221.67	218.77	216.44	214.54	212.99
14000	242.59	238.72	235.60	233.09	231.04	229.37
15000	259.91	255.77	252.43	249.73	247.54	245.76
16000	277.24	272.82	269.26	266.38	264.05	262.14
17000	294.57	289.87	286.09	283.03	280.55	278.53
18000	311.90	306.92	302.92	299.68	297.05	294.91
19000	329.23	323.97	319.75	316.33	313.55	311.29
20000	346.55	341.02	336.58	332.98	330.06	327.68
21000	363.88	358.07	353.40	349.63	346.56	344.06
22000	381.21	375.13	370.23	366.28	363.06	360.44
23000	398.54	392.18	387.06	382.93	379.57	376.83
24000	415.86	409.23	403.89	399.57	396.07	393.21
25000	433.19	426.28	420.72	416.22	412.57	409.60
30000	519.83	511.53	504.86	499.47	495.09	491.52
35000	606.47	596.79	589.01	582.71	577.60	573.43
40000	693.11	682.05	673.15	665.96	660.12	655.35
45000	779.74	767.30	757.29	749.20	742.63	737.27
50000	866.38	852.56	841.44	832.45	825.14	819.19
55000	953.02	937.81	925.58	915.69	907.66	901.11
60000	1039.66	1023.07	1009.73	998.94	990.17	983.03
65000	1126.29	1108.32	1093.87	1082.18	1072.69	1064.95
70000	1212.93	1193.58	1178.01	1165.42	1155.20	1146.87
75000	1299.57	1278.84	1262.16	1248.67	1237.72	1228.79
80000	1386.21	1364.09	1346.30	1331.91	1320.23	1310.71
85000	1472.85	1449.35	1430.44	1415.16	1402.74	1392.63
90000	1559.49	1534.60	1514.59	1498.40	1485.26	1474.55
95000	1646.12	1619.86	1598.73	1581.65	1567.77	1556.46
100000	1732.76	1705.11	1682.88	1664.89	1650.29	1638.38
200000	3465.52	3410.23	3365.75	3329.78	3300.57	3276.77
300000	5198.28	5115.34	5048.63	4994.68	4950.86	4915.15
400000	6931.05	6820.45	6731.50	6659.57	6601.15	6553.53
500000	8663.81	8525.57	8414.38	8324.46	8251.43	8191.92

MONTHLY PAYMENT

Necessary to amortize a loan

19%

TERM / AMOUNT	19 YEARS	20 YEARS	25 YEARS	30 YEARS	35 YEARS	40 YEARS
500	8.14	8.10	7.99	7.94	7.93	7.92
600	9.77	9.72	9.59	9.53	9.51	9.51
700	11.40	11.34	11.18	11.12	11.10	11.09
800	13.03	12.97	12.78	12.71	12.68	12.67
900	14.66	14.59	14.38	14.30	14.27	14.26
1000	16.29	16.21	15.98	15.89	15.85	15.84
2000	32.57	32.41	31.95	31.78	31.71	31.68
3000	48.86	48.62	47.93	47.67	47.56	47.53
4000	65.15	64.83	63.91	63.56	63.42	63.37
5000	81.43	81.03	79.88	79.44	79.27	79.21
6000	97.72	97.24	95.86	95.33	95.13	95.05
7000	114.01	113.45	111.84	111.22	110.99	110.89
8000	130.29	129.66	127.81	127.11	126.84	126.73
9000	146.58	145.86	143.79	143.00	142.70	142.58
10000	162.87	162.07	159.77	158.89	158.55	158.42
11000	179.15	178.28	175.75	174.78	174.40	174.26
12000	195.44	194.48	191.72	190.67	190.26	190.10
13000	211.73	210.69	207.70	206.56	206.11	205.94
14000	228.01	226.90	223.68	222.45	221.97	221.78
15000	244.30	243.10	239.65	238.33	237.82	237.63
16000	260.59	259.31	255.63	254.22	253.68	253.47
17000	276.87	275.52	271.61	270.11	269.53	269.31
18000	293.16	291.72	287.58	286.00	285.39	285.15
19000	309.44	307.93	303.56	301.89	301.24	300.99
20000	325.73	324.14	319.54	317.78	317.10	316.84
21000	342.02	340.34	335.51	333.67	332.95	332.68
22000	358.30	356.55	351.49	349.56	348.81	348.52
23000	374.59	372.76	367.47	365.45	364.66	364.36
24000	390.88	388.96	383.44	381.33	380.52	380.20
25000	407.16	405.17	399.42	397.22	396.37	396.04
30000	488.60	486.21	479.30	476.67	475.65	475.25
35000	570.03	567.24	559.19	556.11	554.92	554.46
40000	651.46	648.27	639.07	635.56	634.20	633.67
45000	732.90	729.31	718.96	715.00	713.47	712.88
50000	814.33	810.34	798.84	794.45	792.75	792.09
55000	895.76	891.38	878.72	873.89	872.02	871.30
60000	977.19	972.41	958.61	953.34	951.30	950.51
65000	1058.63	1053.44	1038.49	1032.78	1030.57	1029.71
70000	1140.06	1134.48	1118.38	1112.22	1109.85	1108.92
75000	1221.49	1215.51	1198.26	1191.67	1189.12	1188.13
80000	1302.92	1296.55	1278.14	1271.11	1268.40	1267.34
85000	1384.36	1377.58	1358.03	1350.56	1347.67	1346.55
90000	1465.79	1458.62	1437.91	1430.00	1426.95	1425.76
95000	1547.22	1539.65	1517.80	1509.45	1506.22	1504.97
100000	1628.65	1620.68	1597.68	1588.89	1585.49	1584.17
200000	3257.31	3241.37	3195.36	3177.78	3170.99	3168.35
300000	4885.96	4862.05	4793.04	4766.68	4756.48	4752.52
400000	6514.62	6482.74	6390.72	6355.57	6341.98	6336.70
500000	8143.27	8103.42	7988.40	7944.46	7927.47	7920.87

19 1/4%

MONTHLY PAYMENT
Necessary to amortize a loan

TERM / AMOUNT	1 YEAR	2 YEARS	3 YEARS	4 YEARS	5 YEARS	6 YEARS
500	46.14	25.27	18.39	15.02	13.04	11.76
600	55.37	30.32	22.07	18.02	15.65	14.11
700	64.59	35.37	25.75	21.02	18.25	16.46
800	73.82	40.42	29.43	24.03	20.86	18.82
900	83.05	45.48	33.10	27.03	23.47	21.17
1000	92.28	50.53	36.78	30.03	26.08	23.52
2000	184.55	101.06	73.57	60.06	52.16	47.04
3000	276.83	151.59	110.35	90.10	78.23	70.56
4000	369.10	202.12	147.13	120.13	104.13	94.08
5000	461.38	252.65	183.91	150.16	130.39	117.60
6000	553.66	303.18	220.70	180.19	156.47	141.12
7000	645.93	353.71	257.48	210.23	182.55	164.64
8000	738.21	404.24	294.26	240.26	208.63	188.16
9000	830.48	454.77	331.04	270.29	234.71	211.68
10000	922.76	505.30	367.83	300.32	260.78	235.20
11000	1015.04	555.83	404.61	330.35	286.86	258.72
12000	1107.31	606.36	441.39	360.39	312.94	282.24
13000	1199.59	656.89	478.17	390.42	339.02	305.76
14000	1291.86	707.42	514.96	420.45	365.10	329.28
15000	1384.14	757.95	551.74	450.48	391.18	352.80
16000	1476.42	808.48	588.52	480.52	417.25	376.32
17000	1568.69	859.01	625.30	510.55	443.33	399.84
18000	1660.97	909.54	662.09	540.58	469.41	423.36
19000	1753.24	960.07	698.87	570.61	495.49	446.88
20000	1845.52	1010.60	735.65	600.64	521.57	470.40
21000	1937.80	1061.13	772.43	630.68	547.65	493.92
22000	2030.07	1111.66	809.22	660.71	573.72	517.44
23000	2122.35	1162.19	846.00	690.74	599.80	540.96
24000	2214.62	1212.72	882.78	720.77	625.88	564.48
25000	2306.90	1263.25	919.56	750.81	651.96	588.00
30000	2768.28	1515.91	1103.48	900.97	782.35	705.60
35000	3229.66	1768.56	1287.39	1051.13	912.74	823.20
40000	3691.04	2021.21	1471.30	1201.29	1043.13	940.80
45000	4152.42	2273.86	1655.22	1351.45	1173.52	1058.40
50000	4613.80	2526.51	1839.13	1501.61	1303.92	1176.00
55000	5075.18	2779.16	2023.04	1651.77	1434.31	1293.60
60000	5536.56	3031.81	2206.95	1801.93	1564.70	1411.21
65000	5997.94	3284.46	2390.87	1952.09	1695.09	1528.81
70000	6459.32	3537.11	2574.78	2102.25	1825.48	1646.41
75000	6920.70	3789.76	2758.69	2252.42	1955.87	1764.01
80000	7382.08	4042.41	2942.60	2402.58	2086.26	1881.61
85000	7843.46	4295.07	3126.52	2552.74	2216.66	1999.21
90000	8304.84	4547.72	3310.43	2702.90	2347.05	2116.81
95000	8766.22	4800.37	3494.34	2853.06	2477.44	2234.41
100000	9227.60	5053.02	3678.26	3003.22	2607.83	2352.01
200000	18455.20	10106.00	7356.51	6006.44	5215.66	4704.02
300000	27682.80	15159.10	11034.80	9009.66	7823.49	7056.03
400000	36910.40	20212.10	14713.00	12012.90	10431.30	9408.03
500000	46138.00	25265.10	18391.30	15016.10	13039.20	11760.00

MONTHLY PAYMENT

Necessary to amortize a loan

19 1/4%

TERM / AMOUNT	7 YEARS	8 YEARS	9 YEARS	10 YEARS	11 YEARS	12 YEARS
500	10.88	10.24	9.77	9.42	9.14	8.92
600	13.05	12.29	11.73	11.30	10.97	10.71
700	15.23	14.34	13.68	13.18	12.79	12.49
800	17.41	16.39	15.64	15.06	14.62	14.28
900	19.58	18.44	17.59	16.95	16.45	16.06
1000	21.76	20.49	19.55	18.83	18.28	17.85
2000	43.51	40.98	39.09	37.66	36.56	35.69
3000	65.27	61.46	58.64	56.49	54.84	53.54
4000	87.03	81.95	78.18	75.32	73.11	71.38
5000	108.78	102.44	97.73	94.15	91.39	89.23
6000	130.54	122.93	117.28	112.99	109.67	107.08
7000	152.30	143.42	136.82	131.82	127.95	124.92
8000	174.06	163.90	156.37	150.65	146.23	142.77
9000	195.81	184.39	175.92	169.48	164.51	160.61
10000	217.57	204.88	195.46	188.31	182.78	178.46
11000	239.33	225.37	215.01	207.14	201.06	196.30
12000	261.08	245.86	234.55	225.97	219.34	214.15
13000	282.84	266.34	254.18	244.80	237.62	232.00
14000	304.60	286.83	273.65	255.90	255.90	249.84
15000	326.35	307.32	293.19	282.46	274.18	267.69
16000	348.11	327.81	312.74	301.30	292.46	285.53
17000	369.87	348.29	332.28	320.13	310.73	303.38
18000	391.62	368.78	351.83	338.96	329.01	321.23
19000	413.38	389.27	371.38	357.79	347.29	339.07
20000	435.14	409.76	390.92	376.62	365.57	356.92
21000	456.89	430.25	410.47	395.45	383.85	374.76
22000	478.65	450.73	430.01	414.28	402.13	392.61
23000	500.41	471.22	449.56	433.11	420.40	410.45
24000	522.16	491.71	469.11	451.94	438.68	428.30
25000	543.92	512.20	488.65	470.77	456.96	446.15
30000	652.71	614.64	586.38	564.93	548.35	535.38
35000	761.49	717.08	684.11	659.08	639.75	624.60
40000	870.27	819.52	781.84	753.24	731.14	713.83
45000	979.06	921.96	879.57	847.39	822.53	803.06
50000	1087.84	1024.39	977.30	941.55	913.92	892.29
55000	1196.63	1126.83	1075.03	1035.70	1005.31	981.52
60000	1305.41	1229.27	1172.77	1129.86	1096.71	1070.75
65000	1414.19	1331.71	1270.50	1224.01	1188.10	1159.98
70000	1522.98	1434.15	1368.23	1318.17	1279.49	1249.21
75000	1631.76	1536.59	1465.96	1412.32	1370.88	1338.44
80000	1740.55	1639.03	1563.69	1506.47	1461.27	1427.67
85000	1849.33	1741.47	1661.42	1600.63	1553.67	1516.90
90000	1958.11	1843.91	1759.15	1694.78	1645.06	1606.13
95000	2066.90	1946.35	1856.88	1788.94	1736.45	1695.36
100000	2175.68	2048.79	1954.61	1883.09	1827.84	1784.58
200000	4351.36	4097.58	3909.22	3766.19	3655.68	3569.17
300000	6527.05	6146.37	5863.83	5649.28	5483.53	5353.75
400000	8702.73	8195.16	7818.43	7532.37	7311.37	7138.34
500000	10878.40	10243.90	9773.04	9415.47	9139.21	8922.92

19 1/4%

MONTHLY PAYMENT

Necessary to amortize a loan

TERM AMOUNT	13 YEARS	14 YEARS	15 YEARS	16 YEARS	17 YEARS	18 YEARS
500	8.75	8.62	8.51	8.42	8.35	8.29
600	10.50	10.34	10.21	10.10	10.01	9.94
700	12.25	12.06	11.91	11.78	11.68	11.60
800	14.00	13.78	13.61	13.47	13.35	13.26
900	15.75	15.51	15.31	15.15	15.02	14.92
1000	17.50	17.23	17.01	16.83	16.69	16.57
2000	35.01	34.46	34.02	33.67	33.38	33.15
3000	52.51	51.69	51.03	50.50	50.07	49.72
4000	70.01	68.92	68.05	67.34	66.76	66.30
5000	87.52	86.15	85.06	84.17	83.40	02.07
6000	105.02	103.38	102.07	101.01	100.15	99.45
7000	122.53	120.61	119.08	117.84	116.84	116.02
8000	140.03	137.85	136.09	134.68	133.53	132.60
9000	157.53	155.08	153.10	151.51	150.22	149.17
10000	175.04	172.31	170.11	168.35	166.91	165.75
11000	192.54	189.54	187.13	185.18	183.60	182.32
12000	210.04	206.77	204.14	202.01	200.29	198.89
13000	227.55	224.00	221.15	218.85	216.98	215.47
14000	245.05	241.23	238.16	235.68	233.68	232.04
15000	262.55	258.46	255.17	252.52	250.37	248.62
16000	280.06	275.69	272.18	269.35	267.06	265.19
17000	297.56	292.92	289.19	286.19	283.75	281.77
18000	315.07	310.15	306.21	303.02	300.44	298.34
19000	332.57	327.38	323.22	319.86	317.13	314.92
20000	350.07	344.61	340.23	336.69	333.82	331.49
21000	367.58	361.84	357.24	353.53	350.51	348.06
22000	385.08	379.07	374.25	370.36	367.20	364.64
23000	402.58	396.30	391.26	387.19	383.90	381.21
24000	420.09	413.54	408.27	404.03	400.59	397.79
25000	437.59	430.77	425.29	420.86	417.28	414.36
30000	525.11	516.92	510.34	505.04	500.73	497.23
35000	612.63	603.07	595.40	589.21	584.19	580.11
40000	700.14	689.23	680.46	673.38	667.64	662.98
45000	787.66	775.38	765.52	757.55	751.10	745.85
50000	875.18	861.53	850.57	841.73	834.56	828.72
55000	962.70	947.68	935.63	925.90	918.01	911.60
60000	1050.22	1033.84	1020.69	1010.07	1001.47	994.47
65000	1137.73	1119.99	1105.74	1094.24	1084.92	1077.34
70000	1225.25	1206.14	1190.80	1178.42	1168.38	1160.21
75000	1312.77	1292.30	1275.86	1262.59	1251.83	1243.08
80000	1400.29	1378.45	1360.91	1346.76	1335.29	1325.96
85000	1487.81	1464.60	1445.97	1430.93	1418.74	1408.83
90000	1575.33	1550.76	1531.03	1515.11	1502.20	1491.70
95000	1662.84	1636.91	1616.09	1599.28	1585.65	1574.57
100000	1750.36	1723.06	1701.14	1683.45	1669.11	1657.45
200000	3500.72	3446.12	3402.29	3366.90	3338.22	3314.89
300000	5251.08	5169.19	5103.43	5050.35	5007.33	4972.34
400000	7001.44	6892.25	6804.57	6733.81	6676.44	6629.78
500000	8751.81	8615.31	8505.72	8417.26	8345.55	8287.23

MONTHLY PAYMENT

Necessary to amortize a loan

19 1/4%

TERM AMOUNT	19 YEARS	20 YEARS	25 YEARS	30 YEARS	35 YEARS	40 YEARS
500	8.24	8.20	8.09	8.05	8.03	8.02
600	9.89	9.84	9.71	9.66	9.64	9.63
700	11.54	11.48	11.32	11.27	11.24	11.23
800	13.18	13.12	12.94	12.88	12.85	12.84
900	14.83	14.76	14.56	14.48	14.46	14.44
1000	16.48	16.40	16.18	16.09	16.06	16.05
2000	32.96	32.80	32.36	32.19	32.12	32.10
3000	49.44	49.20	48.53	48.28	48.19	48.15
4000	65.92	65.61	64.71	64.38	64.25	64.20
5000	82.40	82.01	80.89	80.47	80.31	80.25
6000	98.88	98.41	97.07	96.56	96.37	96.30
7000	115.36	114.81	113.25	112.66	112.43	112.35
8000	131.83	131.21	129.43	128.75	128.49	128.40
9000	148.31	147.61	145.60	144.85	144.56	144.45
10000	164.79	164.02	161.78	160.94	160.62	160.49
11000	181.27	180.42	177.96	177.03	176.68	176.54
12000	197.75	196.82	194.14	193.13	192.74	192.59
13000	214.23	213.22	210.32	209.22	208.80	208.64
14000	230.71	229.62	226.50	225.32	224.87	224.69
15000	247.19	246.02	242.67	241.41	240.93	240.74
16000	263.67	262.42	258.85	257.50	256.99	256.79
17000	280.15	278.83	275.03	273.60	273.05	272.84
18000	296.63	295.23	291.21	289.69	289.11	288.89
19000	313.11	311.63	307.39	305.79	305.17	304.94
20000	329.59	328.03	323.57	321.88	321.24	320.99
21000	346.07	344.43	339.74	337.97	337.30	337.04
22000	362.55	360.83	355.92	354.07	353.36	353.09
23000	379.02	377.24	372.10	370.16	369.42	369.14
24000	395.50	393.64	388.28	386.26	385.48	385.19
25000	411.98	410.04	404.46	402.35	401.54	401.24
30000	494.38	492.05	485.35	482.82	481.85	481.48
35000	576.78	574.05	566.24	563.29	562.16	561.73
40000	659.17	656.06	647.13	643.76	642.47	641.98
45000	741.57	738.07	728.02	724.23	722.78	722.22
50000	823.97	820.08	808.91	804.70	803.09	802.47
55000	906.36	902.08	889.81	885.17	883.40	882.72
60000	988.76	984.09	970.70	965.64	963.71	962.96
65000	1071.15	1066.10	1051.59	1046.11	1044.01	1043.21
70000	1153.55	1148.11	1132.48	1126.58	1124.32	1123.46
75000	1235.95	1230.11	1213.37	1207.05	1204.63	1203.70
80000	1318.34	1312.12	1294.26	1287.52	1284.94	1283.95
85000	1400.74	1394.13	1375.15	1367.99	1365.25	1364.20
90000	1483.14	1476.14	1456.04	1448.46	1445.56	1444.45
95000	1565.53	1558.14	1536.94	1528.93	1525.87	1524.69
100000	1647.93	1640.15	1617.83	1609.40	1606.18	1604.94
200000	3295.86	3280.30	3235.66	3218.79	3212.35	3209.88
300000	4943.79	4920.45	4853.48	4828.19	4818.53	4814.82
400000	6591.72	6560.61	6471.31	6437.59	6424.70	6419.76
500000	8239.65	8200.76	8089.14	8046.98	8030.88	8024.70

19 1/2%

MONTHLY PAYMENT

Necessary to amortize a loan

TERM / AMOUNT	1 YEAR	2 YEARS	3 YEARS	4 YEARS	5 YEARS	6 YEARS
500	46.20	25.33	18.45	15.08	13.11	11.83
600	55.44	30.39	22.15	18.10	15.73	14.20
700	64.68	35.46	25.84	21.12	18.35	16.56
800	73.92	40.52	29.53	24.13	20.97	18.93
900	83.16	45.59	33.22	27.15	23.59	21.30
1000	92.40	50.65	36.91	30.16	26.22	23.66
2000	184.79	101.30	73.82	60.33	52.43	47.33
3000	277.19	151.96	110.73	90.49	78.65	70.99
4000	369.58	202.61	147.64	120.66	104.87	94.66
5000	461.98	253.26	184.55	150.82	131.08	118.32
6000	554.37	303.91	221.46	180.99	157.30	141.98
7000	646.77	354.56	258.37	211.15	183.52	165.65
8000	739.16	405.22	295.27	241.32	209.73	189.31
9000	831.56	455.87	332.18	271.48	235.95	212.98
10000	923.95	506.52	369.09	301.65	262.16	236.64
11000	1016.35	557.17	406.00	331.81	288.38	260.30
12000	1108.74	607.82	442.91	361.98	314.60	283.97
13000	1201.14	658.47	479.82	392.14	340.81	307.63
14000	1293.53	709.13	516.73	422.30	367.03	331.29
15000	1385.93	759.78	553.64	452.47	393.25	354.96
16000	1478.33	810.43	590.55	482.63	419.46	378.62
17000	1570.72	861.08	627.46	512.80	445.68	402.29
18000	1663.12	911.73	664.37	542.96	471.90	425.95
19000	1755.51	962.39	701.28	573.13	498.11	449.61
20000	1847.91	1013.04	738.19	603.29	524.33	473.28
21000	1940.30	1063.69	775.10	633.46	550.55	496.94
22000	2032.70	1114.34	812.01	663.62	576.76	520.61
23000	2125.09	1164.99	848.91	693.79	602.98	544.27
24000	2217.49	1215.64	885.82	723.95	629.20	567.93
25000	2309.88	1266.30	922.73	754.12	655.41	591.60
30000	2771.86	1519.56	1107.28	904.94	786.49	709.92
35000	3233.84	1772.82	1291.83	1055.76	917.58	828.24
40000	3695.81	2026.07	1476.37	1206.58	1048.66	946.56
45000	4157.79	2279.33	1660.92	1357.41	1179.74	1064.87
50000	4619.77	2532.59	1845.46	1508.23	1310.82	1183.19
55000	5081.74	2785.85	2030.01	1659.05	1441.90	1301.51
60000	5543.72	3039.11	2213.56	1809.88	1572.99	1419.83
65000	6005.70	3292.37	2399.10	1960.70	1704.07	1538.15
70000	6467.67	3545.63	2583.65	2111.52	1835.15	1656.47
75000	6929.65	3798.89	2768.20	2262.34	1966.23	1774.79
80000	7391.63	4052.15	2952.74	2413.17	2097.31	1893.11
85000	7853.60	4305.41	3137.29	2563.99	2228.40	2011.43
90000	8315.58	4558.67	3321.84	2714.81	2359.48	2129.75
95000	8777.56	4811.93	3506.38	2865.64	2490.56	2248.07
100000	9239.53	5065.19	3690.93	3016.46	2621.64	2366.39
200000	18479.10	10130.40	7381.86	6032.92	5243.29	4732.78
300000	27718.60	15195.60	11072.80	9049.38	7864.93	7099.16
400000	36958.10	20260.70	14763.70	12065.80	10486.60	9465.55
500000	46197.70	25325.90	18454.60	15082.30	13108.20	11831.90

MONTHLY PAYMENT

Necessary to amortize a loan

19 1/2%

TERM / AMOUNT	7 YEARS	8 YEARS	9 YEARS	10 YEARS	11 YEARS	12 YEARS
500	10.95	10.32	9.85	9.50	9.22	9.01
600	13.14	12.39	11.82	11.40	11.07	10.81
700	15.33	14.45	13.79	13.30	12.91	12.61
800	17.52	16.51	15.76	15.20	14.76	14.41
900	19.72	18.58	17.74	17.10	16.60	16.22
1000	21.91	20.64	19.71	19.00	18.45	18.02
2000	43.81	41.28	39.41	37.99	36.89	36.04
3000	65.72	61.93	59.12	56.99	55.34	54.06
4000	87.62	82.57	78.82	75.98	73.79	72.07
5000	109.53	103.21	98.53	94.98	92.24	90.09
6000	131.44	123.86	118.23	113.97	110.68	108.11
7000	153.34	144.50	137.94	132.97	129.13	126.13
8000	175.25	165.14	157.65	151.96	147.58	144.15
9000	197.16	185.78	177.35	170.96	166.02	162.17
10000	219.06	206.43	197.06	189.95	184.47	180.19
11000	240.97	227.07	216.76	208.95	202.92	198.21
12000	262.87	247.71	236.47	227.94	221.37	216.22
13000	284.78	268.35	256.17	246.94	239.81	234.24
14000	306.69	288.99	275.88	265.93	258.26	252.26
15000	328.59	309.64	295.59	284.93	276.71	270.28
16000	350.50	330.28	315.29	303.92	295.15	288.30
17000	372.40	350.92	335.00	322.92	313.60	306.32
18000	394.31	371.56	354.70	341.91	332.05	324.34
19000	416.22	392.21	374.41	360.91	350.50	342.35
20000	438.12	412.85	394.11	379.90	368.94	360.37
21000	460.03	433.49	413.82	398.90	387.39	378.39
22000	481.94	454.13	433.52	417.90	405.84	396.41
23000	503.84	474.78	453.23	436.89	424.28	414.43
24000	525.75	495.42	472.94	455.89	442.73	432.45
25000	547.65	516.06	492.64	474.88	461.18	450.47
30000	657.18	619.27	591.17	569.86	553.41	540.56
35000	766.71	722.49	689.70	664.83	645.65	630.65
40000	876.25	825.70	788.23	759.81	737.89	720.75
45000	985.78	928.91	886.75	854.79	830.12	810.84
50000	1095.31	1032.12	985.28	949.76	922.36	900.93
55000	1204.84	1135.34	1083.81	1044.74	1014.59	991.03
60000	1314.37	1238.55	1182.34	1139.71	1106.83	1081.12
65000	1423.90	1341.76	1280.87	1234.69	1199.06	1171.21
70000	1533.43	1444.97	1379.40	1329.67	1291.30	1261.31
75000	1642.96	1548.18	1477.92	1424.64	1383.53	1351.40
80000	1752.49	1651.40	1576.45	1519.62	1475.77	1441.49
85000	1862.02	1754.61	1674.98	1614.59	1568.01	1531.59
90000	1971.55	1857.82	1773.51	1709.57	1660.24	1621.68
95000	2081.08	1961.03	1872.04	1804.55	1752.48	1711.77
100000	2190.61	2064.25	1970.57	1899.52	1844.71	1801.86
200000	4381.22	4128.49	3941.13	3799.04	3689.42	3603.73
300000	6571.83	6192.74	5911.70	5698.57	5534.14	5405.59
400000	8762.45	8256.98	7882.26	7598.09	7378.85	7207.46
500000	10953.10	10321.20	9852.83	9497.61	9223.56	9009.32

19 1/2%

MONTHLY PAYMENT

Necessary to amortize a loan

TERM / AMOUNT	13 YEARS	14 YEARS	15 YEARS	16 YEARS	17 YEARS	18 YEARS
500	8.84	8.71	8.60	8.51	8.44	8.38
600	10.61	10.45	10.32	10.21	10.13	10.06
700	12.38	12.19	12.04	11.91	11.82	11.74
800	14.14	13.93	13.76	13.62	13.50	13.41
900	15.91	15.67	15.48	15.32	15.19	15.09
1000	17.68	17.41	17.19	17.02	16.88	16.77
2000	35.36	34.82	34.39	34.04	33.76	33.53
3000	53.04	52.23	51.58	51.06	50.64	50.30
4000	70.72	69.64	68.78	68.08	67.52	67.06
5000	88.40	87.05	85.97	85.10	84.40	83.83
6000	106.08	104.46	103.17	102.12	101.28	100.59
7000	123.76	121.88	120.36	119.15	118.16	117.36
8000	141.44	139.29	137.56	136.17	135.04	134.13
9000	159.12	156.70	154.75	153.19	151.92	150.89
10000	176.80	174.11	171.95	170.21	168.80	167.66
11000	194.48	191.52	189.14	187.23	185.68	184.42
12000	212.16	200.93	206.34	204.25	202.56	201.19
13000	229.84	226.34	223.53	221.27	219.44	217.95
14000	247.52	243.75	240.73	238.29	236.32	234.72
15000	265.20	261.16	257.92	255.31	253.20	251.48
16000	282.88	278.57	275.12	272.33	270.08	268.25
17000	300.56	295.98	292.31	289.35	286.96	285.02
18000	318.24	313.39	309.51	306.37	303.84	301.78
19000	335.92	330.80	326.70	323.39	320.72	318.55
20000	353.60	348.21	343.89	340.41	337.60	335.31
21000	371.28	365.63	361.09	357.43	354.48	352.08
22000	388.97	383.04	378.28	374.46	371.36	368.84
23000	406.65	400.45	395.48	391.48	388.24	385.61
24000	424.33	417.86	412.67	408.50	405.12	402.37
25000	442.01	435.27	429.87	425.52	422.00	419.14
30000	530.41	522.32	515.84	510.62	506.40	502.97
35000	618.81	609.38	601.81	595.72	590.80	586.80
40000	707.21	696.43	687.79	680.83	675.20	670.62
45000	795.61	783.48	773.76	765.93	759.59	754.45
50000	884.01	870.54	859.74	851.03	843.99	838.28
55000	972.41	957.59	945.71	936.14	928.39	922.11
60000	1060.81	1044.64	1031.68	1021.24	1012.79	1005.93
65000	1149.21	1131.70	1117.66	1106.34	1097.19	1089.76
70000	1237.61	1218.75	1203.63	1191.45	1181.59	1173.59
75000	1326.02	1305.80	1289.60	1276.55	1265.99	1257.42
80000	1414.42	1392.86	1375.58	1361.65	1350.39	1341.25
85000	1502.82	1479.91	1461.55	1446.76	1434.79	1425.07
90000	1591.22	1566.96	1547.52	1531.86	1519.19	1508.90
95000	1679.62	1654.02	1633.50	1616.96	1603.59	1592.73
100000	1768.02	1741.07	1719.47	1702.07	1687.99	1676.56
200000	3536.04	3482.14	3438.94	3404.13	3375.97	3353.12
300000	5304.06	5223.21	5158.41	5106.20	5063.96	5029.67
400000	7072.08	6964.28	6877.88	6808.27	6751.95	6706.23
500000	8840.10	8705.35	8597.35	8510.33	8439.94	8382.79

MONTHLY PAYMENT

Necessary to amortize a loan

19 1/2%

TERM / AMOUNT	19 YEARS	20 YEARS	25 YEARS	30 YEARS	35 YEARS	40 YEARS
500	8.34	8.30	8.19	8.15	8.13	8.13
600	10.00	9.96	9.83	9.78	9.76	9.75
700	11.67	11.62	11.47	11.41	11.39	11.38
800	13.34	13.28	13.10	13.04	13.01	13.01
900	15.01	14.94	14.74	14.67	14.64	14.63
1000	16.67	16.60	16.38	16.30	16.27	16.26
2000	33.35	33.19	32.76	32.60	32.54	32.51
3000	50.02	49.79	49.14	48.90	48.81	48.77
4000	66.69	66.39	65.52	65.20	65.07	65.03
5000	83.36	82.98	81.90	81.50	81.34	81.29
6000	100.04	99.58	98.28	97.80	97.61	97.54
7000	116.71	116.18	114.66	114.09	113.88	113.80
8000	133.38	132.77	131.04	130.39	130.15	130.06
9000	150.05	149.37	147.42	146.69	146.42	146.31
10000	166.73	165.97	163.80	162.99	162.69	162.57
11000	183.40	182.56	180.18	179.29	178.96	178.83
12000	200.07	199.16	196.56	195.59	195.22	195.09
13000	216.74	215.76	212.94	211.89	211.49	211.34
14000	233.42	232.35	229.32	228.19	227.76	227.60
15000	250.09	248.95	245.70	244.49	244.03	243.86
16000	266.76	265.55	262.08	260.79	260.30	260.11
17000	283.43	282.14	278.46	277.09	276.57	276.37
18000	300.11	298.74	294.84	293.39	292.84	292.63
19000	316.78	315.34	311.22	309.69	309.11	308.89
20000	333.45	331.93	327.60	325.98	325.37	325.14
21000	350.12	348.53	343.98	342.28	341.64	341.40
22000	366.80	365.13	360.36	358.58	357.91	357.66
23000	383.47	381.72	376.74	374.88	374.18	373.91
24000	400.14	398.32	393.12	391.18	390.45	390.17
25000	416.81	414.92	409.50	407.48	406.72	406.43
30000	500.18	497.90	491.40	488.98	488.06	487.71
35000	583.54	580.88	573.30	570.47	569.40	569.00
40000	666.90	663.87	655.20	651.97	650.75	650.28
45000	750.27	746.85	737.10	733.46	732.09	731.57
50000	833.63	829.83	819.00	814.96	813.43	812.85
55000	916.99	912.82	900.90	896.46	894.78	894.14
60000	1000.35	995.80	982.80	977.95	976.12	975.32
65000	1083.72	1078.78	1064.70	1059.45	1057.46	1056.71
70000	1167.08	1161.77	1146.60	1140.94	1138.81	1138.00
75000	1250.44	1244.75	1228.50	1222.44	1220.15	1219.28
80000	1333.80	1327.73	1310.40	1303.94	1301.49	1300.57
85000	1417.17	1410.71	1392.30	1385.43	1382.84	1381.85
90000	1500.53	1493.70	1474.21	1466.93	1464.18	1463.14
95000	1583.89	1576.68	1556.11	1548.42	1545.52	1544.42
100000	1667.25	1659.66	1638.01	1629.92	1626.87	1625.71
200000	3334.51	3319.33	3276.01	3259.84	3253.73	3251.42
300000	5001.76	4978.99	4914.02	4889.76	4880.60	4877.13
400000	6669.02	6638.66	6552.02	6519.68	6507.47	6502.84
500000	8336.27	8298.32	8190.03	8149.60	8134.33	8128.54

19 3/4%

MONTHLY PAYMENT

Necessary to amortize a loan

TERM / AMOUNT	1 YEAR	2 YEARS	3 YEARS	4 YEARS	5 YEARS	6 YEARS
500	46.26	25.39	18.52	15.15	13.18	11.90
600	55.51	30.46	22.22	18.18	15.81	14.28
700	64.76	35.54	25.93	21.21	18.45	16.67
800	74.01	40.62	29.63	24.24	21.08	19.05
900	83.26	45.70	33.33	27.27	23.72	21.43
1000	92.51	50.77	37.04	30.30	26.35	23.81
2000	185.03	101.55	74.07	60.59	52.71	47.62
3000	277.54	152.32	111.11	90.89	79.06	71.42
4000	370.06	203.10	148.15	121.19	105.42	95.23
5000	462.57	253.87	185.18	151.49	131.78	119.04
6000	555.09	304.64	222.22	181.78	158.13	142.85
7000	647.60	355.42	259.25	212.08	184.49	166.66
8000	740.12	406.19	296.29	242.38	210.84	190.47
9000	832.63	456.96	333.33	272.68	237.20	214.27
10000	925.15	507.74	370.36	302.97	263.55	238.08
11000	1017.66	558.51	407.40	333.27	289.90	201.09
12000	1110.18	609.28	444.44	363.57	316.26	285.70
13000	1202.69	660.06	481.47	393.87	342.61	309.51
14000	1295.21	710.83	518.51	424.16	368.97	333.31
15000	1387.72	761.61	555.54	454.46	395.32	357.12
16000	1480.24	812.38	592.58	484.76	421.68	380.93
17000	1572.75	863.15	629.62	515.05	448.03	404.74
18000	1665.27	913.93	666.65	545.35	474.39	428.55
19000	1757.78	864.70	703.69	575.65	500.74	452.35
20000	1850.30	1015.47	740.73	605.95	527.10	476.16
21000	1942.81	1066.25	777.76	636.24	553.45	499.97
22000	2035.32	1117.02	814.80	666.54	579.81	523.78
23000	2127.84	1167.79	851.83	696.84	606.16	547.59
24000	2220.35	1218.57	888.87	727.14	632.52	571.40
25000	2312.87	1269.34	925.91	757.43	658.87	595.20
30000	2775.44	1523.21	1111.09	908.92	790.65	714.24
35000	3238.02	1777.08	1296.27	1060.41	922.42	833.28
40000	3700.59	2030.95	1481.45	1211.89	1054.20	952.33
45000	992.52	935.89	893.96	862.20	837.74	818.64
50000	1102.79	1039.88	993.29	958.01	930.82	909.60
55000	1213.07	1143.87	1092.62	1053.81	1023.90	1000.56
60000	1323.35	1247.85	1191.95	1149.61	1116.99	1091.52
65000	6013.46	3300.29	2407.36	1969.32	1713.07	1547.53
70000	6476.03	3554.16	2592.54	2120.81	1844.85	1666.57
75000	6938.61	3808.03	2777.72	2272.30	1976.62	1785.61
80000	7401.18	4061.90	2962.90	2423.78	2108.40	1904.65
85000	7863.76	4315.76	3148.08	2575.27	2240.17	2023.69
90000	8326.33	4569.63	3333.27	2726.76	2371.95	2142.73
95000	8788.90	4823.50	3518.45	2878.24	2503.72	2261.77
100000	9251.48	5077.37	3703.63	3029.73	2635.49	2380.81
200000	18503.00	10154.70	7407.26	6059.46	5270.99	4761.62
300000	27754.40	15232.10	11110.90	9089.19	7906.48	7142.43
400000	37005.90	20309.50	14814.50	12118.90	10542.00	9523.25
500000	46257.40	25386.80	18518.10	15148.60	13177.50	11904.10

MONTHLY PAYMENT

Necessary to amortize a loan

19 3/4%

TERM / AMOUNT	7 YEARS	8 YEARS	9 YEARS	10 YEARS	11 YEARS	12 YEARS
500	11.03	10.40	9.93	9.58	9.31	9.10
600	13.23	12.48	11.92	11.50	11.17	10.92
700	15.44	14.56	13.91	13.41	13.03	12.73
800	17.64	16.64	15.89	15.33	14.89	14.55
900	19.85	18.72	17.88	17.24	16.75	16.37
1000	22.06	20.80	19.87	19.16	18.62	18.19
2000	44.11	41.60	39.73	38.32	37.23	36.38
3000	66.17	62.39	59.60	57.48	55.85	54.58
4000	88.22	83.19	79.46	76.64	74.47	72.77
5000	110.29	103.99	99.33	95.80	93.08	90.96
6000	132.34	123.79	119.20	114.96	111.70	109.15
7000	154.39	145.58	139.06	134.12	130.32	127.34
8000	176.45	166.38	158.93	153.28	148.93	145.54
9000	198.50	187.18	178.79	172.44	167.55	163.73
10000	220.56	207.98	198.66	191.60	186.16	181.92
11000	242.62	228.77	218.52	210.76	204.78	200.11
12000	264.67	249.57	238.39	229.92	223.40	218.31
13000	286.73	270.37	258.26	249.08	242.01	236.50
14000	308.78	291.17	278.12	268.24	260.63	254.69
15000	330.84	311.96	297.99	287.40	279.25	272.88
16000	352.89	332.76	317.85	306.56	297.86	291.07
17000	374.95	353.56	337.72	325.72	316.48	309.27
18000	397.01	374.36	357.58	344.88	335.10	327.46
19000	419.06	395.15	377.45	364.04	353.71	345.65
20000	441.12	415.95	397.32	383.20	372.33	363.84
21000	463.17	436.75	417.18	402.36	390.95	382.03
22000	485.23	457.55	437.05	421.52	409.56	400.23
23000	507.29	478.34	456.91	440.68	428.18	418.42
24000	529.34	499.14	476.78	459.84	446.79	436.61
25000	551.40	519.94	496.65	479.00	465.41	454.80
30000	661.68	623.93	595.97	574.80	558.49	545.76
35000	771.96	727.91	695.30	670.60	651.58	636.72
40000	882.24	831.90	794.63	766.40	744.66	727.68
45000	4163.16	2284.82	1666.63	1363.38	1185.97	1071.37
50000	4625.74	2538.68	1851.81	1514.86	1317.75	1190.41
55000	5088.31	2792.55	2037.00	1666.35	1449.52	1309.45
60000	5550.89	3046.42	2222.18	1817.84	1581.30	1428.49
65000	1433.63	1351.84	1291.28	1245.41	1210.07	1182.48
70000	1543.91	1455.83	1390.61	1341.21	1303.15	1273.44
75000	1654.19	1559.82	1489.93	1437.01	1396.23	1364.40
80000	1764.47	1663.80	1589.26	1532.81	1489.31	1455.36
85000	1874.75	1767.79	1688.59	1628.61	1582.40	1546.33
90000	1985.03	1871.78	1787.92	1724.41	1675.48	1637.29
95000	2095.31	1975.77	1887.25	1820.21	1768.56	1728.25
100000	2205.59	2079.75	1986.58	1916.01	1861.64	1819.21
200000	4411.18	4159.51	3973.16	3832.02	3723.29	3638.41
300000	6616.77	6239.26	5959.74	5748.03	5584.93	5457.62
400000	8822.36	8319.02	7946.31	7664.04	7446.57	7276.82
500000	11027.90	10398.80	9932.89	9580.05	9308.21	9096.03

19 3/4%

MONTHLY PAYMENT

Necessary to amortize a loan

TERM / AMOUNT	13 YEARS	14 YEARS	15 YEARS	16 YEARS	17 YEARS	18 YEARS
500	8.93	8.80	8.69	8.60	8.53	8.48
600	10.71	10.55	10.43	10.32	10.24	10.17
700	12.50	12.31	12.17	12.05	11.95	11.87
800	14.29	14.07	13.90	13.77	13.66	13.57
900	16.07	15.83	15.64	15.49	15.36	15.26
1000	17.86	17.59	17.38	17.21	17.07	16.96
2000	35.71	35.18	34.76	34.41	34.14	33.91
3000	53.57	52.77	52.14	51.62	51.21	50.87
4000	71.43	70.37	69.51	68.83	68.28	67.83
5000	89.29	87.96	86.89	86.04	85.35	84.79
6000	107.14	105.55	104.27	103.24	102.42	101.74
7000	125.00	123.14	121.65	120.45	119.48	118.70
8000	142.86	140.73	139.03	137.66	136.55	135.66
9000	160.72	158.32	156.41	154.87	153.62	152.62
10000	178.57	175.91	173.79	172.07	170.69	169.57
11000	196.43	193.51	191.16	189.28	187.76	186.53
12000	214.29	211.10	208.54	206.49	204.83	203.49
13000	232.15	228.69	225.92	223.70	221.90	220.44
14000	250.00	246.28	243.30	240.90	238.97	237.40
15000	267.86	263.87	260.68	258.11	256.04	254.36
16000	285.72	281.46	278.06	275.32	273.11	271.32
17000	303.58	299.05	295.44	292.53	290.18	288.27
18000	321.43	316.65	312.81	309.73	307.25	305.23
19000	339.29	334.24	330.19	326.94	324.32	322.19
20000	357.15	351.83	347.57	344.15	341.38	339.14
21000	375.01	369.42	364.95	361.36	358.45	356.10
22000	392.86	387.01	382.33	378.56	375.52	373.06
23000	410.72	404.60	399.71	395.77	392.59	390.02
24000	428.58	422.19	417.09	412.98	409.66	406.97
25000	446.44	439.79	434.46	430.19	426.73	423.93
30000	535.72	527.74	521.36	516.22	512.08	508.72
35000	625.01	615.70	608.25	602.26	597.42	593.50
40000	714.30	703.66	695.14	688.30	682.77	678.29
45000	803.58	791.61	782.03	774.33	768.11	763.08
50000	892.87	879.57	868.93	860.37	853.46	847.86
55000	982.16	967.53	955.82	946.41	938.81	932.65
60000	1071.44	1055.48	1042.71	1032.44	1024.15	1017.43
65000	1160.73	1143.44	1129.61	1118.48	1109.50	1102.22
70000	1250.02	1231.40	1216.50	1204.52	1194.84	1187.01
75000	1339.31	1319.35	1303.39	1290.55	1280.19	1271.79
80000	1428.59	1407.31	1390.28	1376.59	1365.53	1356.58
85000	1517.88	1495.27	1477.18	1462.63	1450.88	1441.36
90000	1607.17	1583.22	1564.07	1548.66	1536.23	1526.15
95000	1696.45	1671.18	1650.96	1634.70	1621.57	1610.94
100000	1785.74	1759.14	1737.85	1720.74	1706.92	1695.72
200000	3571.48	3518.28	3475.71	3441.48	3413.84	3391.44
300000	5357.22	5277.41	5213.56	5162.22	5120.76	5087.17
400000	7142.97	7036.55	6951.42	6882.96	6827.67	6782.89
500000	8928.71	8795.69	8689.27	8603.69	8534.59	8478.61

MONTHLY PAYMENT

Necessary to amortize a loan

19 3/4%

TERM / AMOUNT	19 YEARS	20 YEARS	25 YEARS	30 YEARS	35 YEARS	40 YEARS
500	8.43	8.40	8.29	8.25	8.24	8.23
600	10.12	10.08	9.95	9.90	9.89	9.88
700	11.81	11.75	11.61	11.55	11.53	11.53
800	13.49	13.43	13.27	13.20	13.18	13.17
900	15.18	15.11	14.92	14.85	14.83	14.82
1000	16.87	16.79	16.58	16.50	16.48	16.46
2000	33.73	33.58	33.16	33.01	32.95	32.93
3000	50.60	50.38	49.75	49.51	49.43	49.39
4000	67.47	67.17	66.33	66.02	65.90	65.86
5000	84.33	83.96	82.91	82.52	82.38	82.32
6000	101.20	100.75	99.49	99.03	98.85	98.79
7000	118.06	117.55	116.08	115.53	115.33	115.25
8000	134.93	134.34	132.66	132.04	131.81	131.72
9000	151.80	151.13	149.24	148.54	148.28	148.18
10000	168.66	167.92	165.82	165.05	164.76	164.65
11000	185.53	184.71	182.40	181.55	181.23	181.11
12000	202.40	201.51	198.99	198.06	197.71	197.58
13000	219.26	218.30	215.57	214.56	214.18	214.04
14000	236.13	235.09	232.15	231.07	230.66	230.51
15000	252.99	251.88	248.73	247.57	247.14	246.97
16000	269.86	268.68	265.31	264.07	263.61	263.44
17000	286.73	285.47	281.90	280.58	280.09	279.90
18000	303.59	302.59	298.48	297.08	296.56	296.37
19000	320.46	319.05	315.06	313.59	313.04	312.83
20000	337.33	335.85	331.64	330.09	329.51	329.30
21000	354.19	352.64	348.23	346.60	345.99	345.76
22000	371.06	369.43	364.81	363.10	362.47	362.23
23000	387.92	386.22	381.39	379.61	378.94	378.69
24000	404.79	403.01	397.97	396.11	395.42	395.16
25000	421.66	419.81	414.55	412.62	411.89	411.62
30000	505.99	503.77	497.46	495.14	494.27	493.95
35000	590.32	587.73	580.38	577.66	576.65	576.27
40000	674.65	671.69	663.29	660.18	659.03	658.59
45000	758.98	755.65	746.20	742.71	741.41	740.92
50000	843.31	839.61	829.11	825.23	823.78	823.24
55000	927.65	923.57	912.02	907.75	906.16	905.57
60000	1011.98	1007.53	994.93	990.28	988.54	987.89
65000	1096.31	1091.49	1077.84	1072.80	1070.92	1070.21
70000	1180.64	1175.46	1160.75	1155.32	1153.30	1152.54
75000	1264.97	1259.42	1243.66	1237.85	1235.68	1234.86
80000	1349.30	1343.38	1326.57	1320.37	1318.05	1317.19
85000	1433.63	1427.34	1409.48	1402.89	1400.43	1399.51
90000	1517.96	1511.30	1492.39	1485.41	1482.81	1481.84
95000	1602.30	1595.26	1575.30	1567.94	1565.19	1564.16
100000	1686.63	1679.22	1658.21	1650.46	1647.57	1646.48
200000	3373.25	3358.45	3316.43	3300.92	3295.14	3292.97
300000	5059.88	5037.67	4974.64	4951.38	4942.70	4939.45
400000	6746.51	6716.89	6632.86	6601.84	6590.27	6585.94
500000	8433.13	8396.11	8291.07	8252.30	8237.84	8232.42

20%

MONTHLY PAYMENT

Necessary to amortize a loan

TERM AMOUNT	1 YEAR	2 YEARS	3 YEARS	4 YEARS	5 YEARS	6 YEARS
500	46.32	25.45	18.58	15.22	13.25	11.98
600	55.58	30.54	22.30	18.26	15.90	14.37
700	64.84	35.63	26.01	21.30	18.55	16.77
800	74.11	40.72	29.73	24.34	21.20	19.16
900	83.37	45.81	33.45	27.39	23.84	21.56
1000	92.63	50.90	37.16	30.43	26.49	23.95
2000	185.27	101.79	74.33	60.86	52.99	47.91
3000	277.90	152.69	111.49	91.29	79.48	71.86
4000	370.54	203.58	148.65	121.72	105.98	95.81
5000	463.17	254.48	185.82	152.15	132.47	119.76
6000	555.81	305.38	222.98	182.58	158.96	143.72
7000	648.44	356.27	260.15	213.01	185.46	167.67
8000	741.08	407.17	297.31	243.44	211.95	191.62
9000	833.71	458.06	334.47	273.87	238.45	215.58
10000	926.35	508.96	371.64	304.30	264.94	239.53
11000	1018.98	559.85	408.80	334.73	291.43	263.48
12000	1111.62	610.75	445.96	365.17	317.93	287.43
13000	1204.25	661.65	483.13	395.60	344.42	311.39
14000	1296.88	712.54	520.29	426.03	370.92	335.34
15000	1389.52	763.44	557.45	456.46	397.41	359.29
16000	1482.15	814.33	594.62	486.89	423.90	383.25
17000	1574.79	865.23	631.78	517.32	450.40	407.20
18000	1667.42	916.13	668.95	547.75	476.89	431.15
19000	1760.06	967.02	706.11	578.18	503.38	455.10
20000	1852.69	1017.92	743.27	608.61	529.88	479.06
21000	1945.33	1068.81	780.44	639.04	556.37	503.01
22000	2037.96	1119.71	817.60	669.47	582.87	526.96
23000	2130.60	1170.60	854.76	699.90	609.36	550.92
24000	2223.23	1221.50	891.93	730.33	635.85	574.87
25000	2315.86	1272.40	929.09	760.76	662.35	598.82
30000	2779.04	1526.88	1114.91	912.91	794.82	718.59
35000	3242.21	1781.35	1300.73	1065.06	927.29	838.35
40000	3705.38	2035.83	1486.54	1217.22	1059.76	958.11
45000	4168.56	2290.31	1672.36	1369.37	1192.23	1077.88
50000	4631.73	2544.79	1858.18	1521.52	1324.69	1197.64
55000	5094.90	2799.27	2044.00	1673.67	1457.16	1317.41
60000	5558.08	3053.75	2229.82	1825.82	1589.63	1437.17
65000	6021.25	3308.23	2415.63	1977.98	1722.10	1556.93
70000	6484.42	3562.71	2601.45	2130.13	1854.57	1676.70
75000	6947.59	3817.19	2787.27	2282.28	1987.04	1796.46
80000	7410.77	4071.67	2973.09	2434.43	2119.51	1916.23
85000	7873.94	4326.15	3158.91	2586.58	2251.98	2035.99
90000	8337.11	4580.63	3344.73	2738.73	2384.45	2155.76
95000	8800.29	4835.11	3530.54	2890.89	2516.92	2275.52
100000	9263.46	5089.59	3716.36	3043.04	2649.39	2395.28
200000	18526.90	10179.20	7432.72	6086.08	5298.78	4790.57
300000	27790.40	15268.80	11149.10	9129.12	7948.17	7185.85
400000	37053.80	20358.30	14865.40	12172.20	10597.60	9581.14
500000	46317.30	25447.90	18581.80	15215.20	13247.00	11976.40

MONTHLY PAYMENT

Necessary to amortize a loan

20%

TERM / AMOUNT	7 YEARS	8 YEARS	9 YEARS	10 YEARS	11 YEARS	12 YEARS
500	11.10	10.48	10.01	9.66	9.39	9.18
600	13.32	12.57	12.02	11.60	11.27	11.02
700	15.54	14.67	14.02	13.53	13.15	12.86
800	17.77	16.76	16.02	15.46	15.03	14.69
900	19.99	18.86	18.02	17.39	16.91	16.53
1000	22.21	20.95	20.03	19.33	18.79	18.37
2000	44.41	41.91	40.05	38.65	37.57	36.73
3000	66.62	62.86	60.08	57.98	56.36	55.10
4000	88.82	83.81	80.11	77.30	75.15	73.46
5000	111.03	104.77	100.13	96.63	93.93	91.83
6000	133.24	125.72	120.16	115.95	112.72	110.20
7000	155.44	146.67	140.19	135.28	131.50	128.56
8000	177.65	167.63	160.21	154.61	150.29	146.93
9000	199.86	188.58	180.24	173.93	169.08	165.30
10000	222.06	209.53	200.27	193.26	187.86	183.66
11000	244.27	230.49	220.29	212.58	206.65	202.03
12000	266.48	251.44	240.32	231.91	225.44	220.39
13000	288.68	272.39	260.35	251.23	244.22	238.76
14000	310.89	293.35	280.37	270.56	263.01	257.13
15000	333.09	314.30	300.40	289.88	281.80	275.49
16000	355.30	335.25	320.42	309.21	300.58	293.86
17000	377.51	356.21	340.45	328.54	319.37	312.22
18000	399.71	377.16	360.48	347.86	338.15	330.59
19000	421.92	398.11	380.50	367.19	356.94	348.96
20000	444.12	419.06	400.53	386.51	375.73	367.32
21000	466.33	440.02	420.56	405.84	394.51	385.69
22000	488.54	460.97	440.58	425.16	413.30	404.05
23000	510.74	481.92	460.61	444.49	432.09	422.42
24000	532.95	502.88	480.64	463.81	450.87	440.79
25000	555.16	523.83	500.66	483.14	469.66	459.15
30000	666.19	628.60	600.80	579.77	563.59	550.98
35000	777.22	733.36	700.93	676.40	657.52	642.81
40000	888.25	838.13	801.06	773.02	751.45	734.64
45000	999.28	942.89	901.19	869.65	845.39	826.47
50000	1110.31	1047.66	1001.33	966.28	939.62	918.31
55000	1221.34	1152.43	1101.46	1062.91	1033.25	1010.14
60000	1332.37	1257.19	1201.59	1159.53	1127.18	1101.97
65000	1443.40	1361.96	1301.72	1256.16	1221.11	1193.80
70000	1554.43	1466.72	1401.86	1352.79	1315.04	1285.63
75000	1665.47	1571.49	1501.99	1449.42	1408.98	1377.46
80000	1776.50	1676.26	1602.12	1546.05	1502.91	1469.29
85000	1887.53	1781.02	1702.25	1642.67	1596.84	1561.12
90000	1998.56	1885.79	1802.39	1739.30	1690.77	1652.95
95000	2109.59	1990.55	1902.52	1835.93	1784.70	1744.78
100000	2220.62	2095.32	2002.65	1932.56	1878.63	1836.61
200000	4441.24	4190.64	4005.30	3865.12	3757.27	3673.22
300000	6661.86	6285.96	6007.95	5797.67	5635.90	5509.83
400000	8882.48	8381.28	8010.60	7730.23	7514.54	7346.44
500000	11103.10	10476.60	10013.30	9662.79	9393.17	9183.04

20%

MONTHLY PAYMENT

Necessary to amortize a loan

TERM / AMOUNT	13 YEARS	14 YEARS	15 YEARS	16 YEARS	17 YEARS	18 YEARS
500	9.02	8.89	8.78	8.70	8.63	8.57
600	10.82	10.66	10.54	10.44	10.36	10.29
700	12.62	12.44	12.29	12.18	12.08	12.00
800	14.43	14.22	14.05	13.92	13.81	13.72
900	16.23	16.00	15.81	15.66	15.53	15.43
1000	18.04	17.77	17.56	17.39	17.26	17.15
2000	36.07	35.55	35.13	34.79	34.52	34.30
3000	54.11	53.32	52.69	52.18	51.78	51.45
4000	72.14	71.09	70.25	69.58	69.04	68.60
5000	90.18	88.86	87.81	86.97	86.30	85.75
6000	108.21	106.64	105.38	104.37	103.55	102.90
7000	126.25	124.41	122.94	121.76	120.81	120.05
8000	144.28	142.18	140.50	139.16	138.07	137.20
9000	162.32	159.95	158.07	156.55	155.33	154.34
10000	180.35	177.73	175.63	173.95	172.59	171.49
11000	198.39	195.50	193.19	191.34	189.85	188.64
12000	216.42	213.27	210.76	208.74	207.11	205.79
13000	234.46	231.05	228.32	226.13	224.37	222.94
14000	252.49	248.82	245.88	243.53	241.63	240.09
15000	270.53	266.59	263.45	260.92	258.89	257.24
16000	288.56	284.36	281.01	278.32	276.14	274.39
17000	306.60	302.14	298.57	295.71	293.40	291.54
18000	324.63	319.91	316.13	313.10	310.66	308.69
19000	342.67	337.68	333.70	330.50	327.92	325.84
20000	360.71	355.45	351.26	347.89	345.18	342.99
21000	378.74	373.23	368.82	365.29	362.44	360.14
22000	396.78	391.00	386.39	382.68	379.70	377.29
23000	414.81	408.77	403.95	400.08	396.96	394.44
24000	432.85	426.54	421.51	417.47	414.22	411.59
25000	450.88	444.32	439.07	434.87	431.48	428.73
30000	541.06	533.18	526.89	521.84	517.77	514.48
35000	631.23	622.04	614.70	608.81	604.07	600.23
40000	721.41	710.91	702.52	695.79	690.36	685.98
45000	811.59	799.77	790.33	782.76	776.66	771.72
50000	901.76	888.63	878.15	869.73	862.95	857.47
55000	991.94	977.50	965.96	956.71	949.25	943.22
60000	1082.11	1066.36	1053.78	1043.68	1035.54	1028.96
65000	1172.29	1155.22	1141.59	1130.65	1121.84	1114.71
70000	1262.47	1244.09	1229.41	1217.63	1208.13	1200.46
75000	1352.64	1332.95	1317.22	1304.60	1294.43	1286.20
80000	1442.82	1421.81	1405.04	1391.57	1380.72	1371.95
85000	1532.99	1510.68	1492.85	1478.55	1467.02	1457.70
90000	1623.17	1599.54	1580.67	1565.52	1553.31	1543.44
95000	1713.35	1688.40	1668.48	1652.49	1639.61	1629.19
100000	1803.52	1777.27	1756.30	1739.47	1725.90	1714.94
200000	3607.05	3554.53	3512.59	3478.93	3451.81	3429.87
300000	5410.57	5331.80	5268.89	5218.40	5177.71	5144.81
400000	7214.09	7109.06	7025.19	6957.87	6903.61	6859.75
500000	9017.61	8886.33	8781.48	8697.33	8629.51	8574.68

MONTHLY PAYMENT

Necessary to amortize a loan

20 %

TERM / AMOUNT	19 YEARS	20 YEARS	25 YEARS	30 YEARS	35 YEARS	40 YEARS
500	8.53	8.49	8.39	8.36	8.34	8.34
600	10.24	10.19	10.07	10.03	10.01	10.00
700	11.94	11.89	11.75	11.70	11.68	11.67
800	13.65	13.59	13.43	13.37	13.35	13.34
900	15.35	15.29	15.11	15.04	15.01	15.01
1000	17.06	16.99	16.78	16.71	16.68	16.67
2000	34.12	33.98	33.57	33.42	33.37	33.35
3000	51.18	50.96	50.35	50.13	50.05	50.02
4000	68.24	67.95	67.14	66.84	66.73	66.69
5000	85.30	84.94	83.92	83.55	83.41	83.36
6000	102.36	101.93	100.71	100.26	100.10	100.04
7000	119.42	118.92	117.49	116.97	116.78	116.71
8000	136.48	135.91	134.28	133.68	133.46	133.38
9000	153.54	152.89	151.06	150.39	150.15	150.05
10000	170.61	169.88	167.85	167.10	166.83	166.73
11000	187.67	186.87	184.63	183.81	183.51	183.40
12000	204.73	203.86	201.41	200.52	200.19	200.07
13000	221.79	220.85	218.20	217.23	216.88	216.74
14000	238.85	237.84	234.98	233.94	233.56	233.42
15000	255.91	254.82	251.77	250.65	250.24	250.09
16000	272.97	271.81	268.55	267.36	266.93	266.76
17000	290.03	288.80	285.34	284.07	283.61	283.44
18000	307.09	305.79	302.12	300.78	300.29	300.11
19000	324.15	322.78	318.91	317.49	316.97	316.78
20000	341.21	339.77	335.69	334.20	333.66	333.45
21000	358.27	356.75	352.48	350.91	350.34	350.13
22000	375.33	373.74	369.26	367.62	367.02	366.80
23000	392.39	390.73	386.04	384.33	383.70	383.47
24000	409.45	407.72	402.83	401.04	400.39	400.14
25000	426.51	424.71	419.61	417.76	417.07	416.82
30000	511.81	509.65	503.54	501.31	500.48	500.18
35000	597.12	594.59	587.46	584.86	583.90	583.54
40000	682.42	679.53	671.38	668.41	667.31	666.91
45000	767.72	764.47	755.30	751.96	750.73	750.27
50000	853.02	849.41	839.23	835.51	834.14	833.63
55000	938.33	934.35	923.15	919.06	917.55	917.00
60000	1023.63	1019.29	1007.07	1002.61	1000.97	1000.36
65000	1108.93	1104.24	1090.99	1086.16	1084.38	1083.72
70000	1194.23	1189.18	1174.92	1169.71	1167.79	1167.08
75000	1279.54	1274.12	1258.84	1253.26	1251.21	1250.45
80000	1364.84	1359.06	1342.76	1336.81	1334.62	1333.81
85000	1450.14	1444.00	1426.68	1420.37	1418.04	1417.17
90000	1535.44	1528.94	1510.61	1503.92	1501.45	1500.54
95000	1620.74	1613.88	1594.53	1587.47	1584.86	1583.90
100000	1706.05	1698.82	1678.45	1671.02	1668.28	1667.26
200000	3412.09	3397.65	3356.90	3342.04	3336.56	3334.53
300000	5118.14	5096.47	5035.36	5013.06	5004.83	5001.79
400000	6824.19	6795.30	6713.81	6684.07	6673.11	6669.06
500000	8530.23	8494.12	8392.26	8355.09	8341.39	8336.32

20 1/2% MONTHLY PAYMENT

Necessary to amortize a loan

TERM / AMOUNT	1 YEAR	2 YEARS	3 YEARS	4 YEARS	5 YEARS	6 YEARS
500	46.44	25.57	18.71	15.35	13.39	12.12
600	55.72	30.68	22.45	18.42	16.06	14.55
700	65.01	35.80	26.19	21.49	18.74	16.97
800	74.30	40.91	29.94	24.56	21.42	19.39
900	83.59	46.03	33.68	27.63	24.10	21.82
1000	92.87	51.14	37.42	30.70	26.77	24.24
2000	185.75	102.28	74.84	61.39	53.55	48.49
3000	278.62	153.42	112.26	92.09	80.32	72.73
4000	371.50	204.56	149.68	122.79	107.09	96.97
5000	464.37	255.70	187.10	153.49	133.87	121.22
6000	557.25	306.84	224.51	184.19	160.64	145.46
7000	650.12	357.98	261.93	214.88	187.41	169.71
8000	742.99	409.12	299.35	245.58	214.18	193.95
9000	835.87	460.27	336.77	276.28	240.96	218.19
10000	928.74	511.41	374.19	306.98	267.73	242.44
11000	1021.62	562.55	411.61	337.67	294.50	266.68
12000	1114.49	613.69	449.03	368.37	321.28	290.92
13000	1207.37	664.83	486.45	399.07	348.05	315.17
14000	1300.24	715.97	523.87	429.77	374.82	339.41
15000	1393.11	767.11	561.28	460.46	401.59	363.65
16000	1485.99	818.25	598.70	491.16	428.37	387.90
17000	1578.86	869.39	636.12	521.86	455.14	412.14
18000	1671.74	920.53	673.54	552.55	481.91	436.38
19000	1764.61	971.67	710.96	583.25	508.69	460.63
20000	1857.49	1022.81	748.38	613.95	535.46	484.87
21000	1950.36	1073.95	785.80	644.65	562.23	509.12
22000	2043.23	1125.09	823.22	675.34	589.00	533.36
23000	2136.11	1176.23	860.64	706.04	615.78	557.60
24000	2228.98	1227.37	898.05	736.74	642.55	581.85
25000	2321.86	1278.51	935.47	767.44	669.32	606.09
30000	2786.23	1534.22	1122.57	920.92	803.19	727.31
35000	3250.60	1789.92	1309.66	1074.41	937.05	848.53
40000	3714.97	2045.62	1496.76	1227.90	1070.92	969.74
45000	4179.34	2301.32	1683.85	1381.39	1204.78	1090.96
50000	4643.71	2557.03	1870.95	1534.87	1338.65	1212.18
55000	5108.09	2812.73	2058.04	1688.36	1472.51	1333.40
60000	5572.46	3068.43	2245.14	1841.85	1606.37	1454.61
65000	6036.83	3324.13	2432.23	1995.34	1740.24	1575.83
70000	6501.20	3579.84	2619.33	2148.82	1874.10	1697.05
75000	6965.57	3835.54	2806.42	2302.31	2007.97	1818.27
80000	7429.94	4091.24	2993.51	2455.80	2141.83	1939.49
85000	7894.31	4346.95	3180.61	2609.28	2275.70	2060.70
90000	8358.69	4602.65	3367.70	2762.77	2409.56	2181.92
95000	8823.06	4858.35	3554.80	2916.26	2543.43	2303.14
100000	9287.43	5114.05	3741.89	3069.75	2677.29	2424.36
200000	18574.90	10228.10	7483.79	6139.49	5354.58	4848.72
300000	27862.30	15342.20	11225.70	9209.24	8031.87	7273.07
400000	37149.70	20456.20	14967.60	12279.00	10709.20	9697.43
500000	46437.10	25570.30	18709.50	15348.70	13386.50	12121.80

MONTHLY PAYMENT

Necessary to amortize a loan

20 1/2%

TERM / AMOUNT	7 YEARS	8 YEARS	9 YEARS	10 YEARS	11 YEARS	12 YEARS
500	11.25	10.63	10.17	9.83	9.56	9.36
600	13.51	12.76	12.21	11.80	11.48	11.23
700	15.76	14.89	14.24	13.76	13.39	13.10
800	18.01	17.01	16.28	15.73	15.30	14.97
900	20.26	19.14	18.31	17.69	17.22	16.84
1000	22.51	21.27	20.35	19.66	19.13	18.72
2000	45.02	42.53	40.70	39.32	38.26	37.43
3000	67.52	63.80	61.05	58.97	57.38	56.15
4000	90.03	85.06	81.40	78.63	76.51	74.86
5000	112.54	106.33	101.75	98.29	95.64	93.58
6000	135.05	127.60	122.10	117.95	114.77	112.30
7000	157.56	148.86	142.45	137.61	133.90	131.01
8000	180.07	170.13	162.80	157.27	153.02	149.73
9000	202.57	191.40	183.15	176.92	172.15	168.44
10000	225.08	212.66	203.50	196.58	191.28	187.16
11000	247.59	233.93	223.85	216.24	210.41	205.88
12000	270.10	255.19	244.20	235.90	229.54	224.59
13000	292.61	276.46	264.55	255.56	248.66	243.31
14000	315.12	297.73	284.90	275.22	267.79	262.02
15000	337.62	318.99	305.24	294.87	286.92	280.74
16000	360.13	340.26	325.59	314.53	306.05	299.46
17000	382.64	361.52	345.94	334.19	325.18	318.17
18000	405.15	382.79	366.29	353.85	344.30	336.89
19000	427.66	404.06	386.64	373.51	363.43	355.60
20000	450.17	425.32	406.99	393.17	382.56	374.32
21000	472.67	446.59	427.34	412.82	401.69	393.03
22000	495.18	467.85	447.69	432.48	420.82	411.75
23000	517.69	489.12	468.04	452.14	439.94	430.47
24000	540.20	510.39	488.39	471.80	459.07	449.18
25000	562.71	531.65	508.74	491.46	478.20	467.90
30000	675.25	637.98	610.49	589.75	573.84	561.48
35000	787.79	744.31	712.24	688.04	669.48	655.06
40000	900.33	850.64	813.98	786.33	765.12	748.64
45000	1012.87	956.97	915.73	884.62	860.76	842.22
50000	1125.41	1063.30	1017.48	982.91	956.40	935.80
55000	1237.96	1169.63	1119.23	1081.20	1052.04	1029.38
60000	1350.50	1275.97	1220.98	1179.50	1147.68	1122.95
65000	1463.04	1382.30	1322.72	1277.79	1243.32	1216.53
70000	1575.58	1488.63	1424.47	1376.08	1338.96	1310.11
75000	1688.12	1594.96	1526.22	1474.37	1434.60	1403.69
80000	1800.66	1701.29	1627.97	1572.66	1530.23	1497.27
85000	1913.20	1807.62	1729.72	1670.95	1625.87	1590.85
90000	2025.75	1913.95	1831.46	1769.24	1721.51	1684.43
95000	2138.29	2020.28	1933.21	1867.53	1817.15	1778.01
100000	2250.83	2126.61	2034.96	1965.83	1912.79	1871.59
200000	4501.66	4253.22	4069.92	3931.65	3825.59	3743.18
300000	6752.48	6379.83	6104.88	5897.48	5738.38	5614.77
400000	9003.31	8506.44	8139 84	7863.30	7651.17	7486.36
500000	11254.10	10633.00	10174.80	9829 13	9563.97	9357.95

20 1/2% MONTHLY PAYMENT

Necessary to amortize a loan

TERM / AMOUNT	13 YEARS	14 YEARS	15 YEARS	16 YEARS	17 YEARS	18 YEARS
500	9.20	9.07	8.97	8.89	8.82	8.77
600	11.04	10.88	10.76	10.66	10.58	10.52
700	12.87	12.70	12.55	12.44	12.35	12.27
800	14.71	14.51	14.35	14.22	14.11	14.03
900	16.55	16.32	16.14	15.99	15.88	15.78
1000	18.39	18.14	17.93	17.77	17.64	17.54
2000	36.79	36.27	35.87	35.54	35.28	35.07
3000	55.18	54.41	53.80	53.31	52.92	52.61
4000	73.57	72.55	71.73	71.08	70.56	70.14
5000	91.96	90.68	89.67	88.85	88.20	87.68
6000	110.36	108.82	107.60	106.63	105.84	105.21
7000	128.75	126.96	125.53	124.40	123.48	122.75
8000	147.14	145.10	143.47	142.17	141.12	140.28
9000	165.53	163.23	161.40	159.94	158.76	157.82
10000	183.93	181.37	179.34	177.71	176.40	175.35
11000	202.32	199.51	197.27	195.48	194.04	192.89
12000	220.71	217.64	215.20	213.25	211.68	210.42
13000	239.10	235.78	233.14	231.02	229.32	227.96
14000	257.50	253.92	251.07	248.79	246.96	245.49
15000	275.89	272.05	269.00	266.56	264.60	263.03
16000	294.28	290.19	286.94	284.33	282.24	280.56
17000	312.67	308.33	304.87	302.10	299.88	298.10
18000	331.07	326.47	322.80	319.88	317.51	315.63
19000	349.46	344.60	340.74	337.65	335.16	333.17
20000	367.85	362.74	358.67	355.42	352.81	350.70
21000	386.25	380.88	376.60	373.19	370.45	368.24
22000	404.64	399.01	394.54	390.96	388.09	385.77
23000	423.03	417.15	412.47	408.73	405.73	403.31
24000	441.42	435.29	430.40	426.50	423.37	420.84
25000	459.82	453.42	448.34	444.27	441.01	438.38
30000	551.78	544.11	538.00	533.12	529.21	526.05
35000	643.74	634.79	627.67	621.98	617.41	613.73
40000	735.70	725.48	717.34	710.83	705.61	701.40
45000	827.67	816.16	807.01	799.69	793.81	789.08
50000	919.63	906.85	896.67	888.54	882.01	876.75
55000	1011.59	997.53	986.34	977.39	970.21	964.43
60000	1103.56	1088.22	1076.01	1066.25	1058.41	1052.11
65000	1195.52	1178.90	1165.68	1155.10	1146.62	1139.78
70000	1287.48	1269.58	1255.34	1243.96	1234.82	1227.46
75000	1379.44	1360.27	1345.01	1332.81	1323.02	1315.13
80000	1471.41	1450.95	1434.68	1421.66	1411.22	1402.81
85000	1563.37	1541.64	1524.35	1510.52	1499.42	1490.48
90000	1655.33	1632.32	1614.01	1599.37	1587.62	1578.16
95000	1747.30	1723.01	1703.68	1688.23	1675.82	1665.83
100000	1839.26	1813.69	1793.35	1777.08	1764.02	1753.51
200000	3678.52	3627.38	3586.70	3554.16	3528.05	3507.02
300000	5517.78	5441.08	5380.04	5331.24	5292.07	5260.53
400000	7357.04	7254.77	7173.39	7108.32	7056.09	7014.03
500000	9196.30	9068.46	8966.74	8885.40	8820.12	8767.54

MONTHLY PAYMENT

Necessary to amortize a loan

20 1/2%

TERM / AMOUNT	19 YEARS	20 YEARS	25 YEARS	30 YEARS	35 YEARS	40 YEARS
500	8.73	8.69	8.60	8.56	8.55	8.54
600	10.47	10.43	10.31	10.27	10.26	10.25
700	12.22	12.17	12.03	11.99	11.97	11.96
800	13.96	13.91	13.75	13.70	13.68	13.67
900	15.71	15.64	15.47	15.41	15.39	15.38
1000	17.45	17.38	17.19	17.12	17.10	17.09
2000	34.90	34.76	34.38	34.24	34.19	34.18
3000	52.35	52.14	51.57	51.37	51.29	51.27
4000	69.80	69.53	68.76	68.49	68.39	68.35
5000	87.25	86.91	85.95	85.61	85.49	85.44
6000	104.70	104.29	103.14	102.73	102.58	102.53
7000	122.15	121.67	120.33	119.85	119.68	119.62
8000	139.60	139.05	137.52	136.97	136.78	136.71
9000	157.05	156.43	154.71	154.10	153.88	153.80
10000	174.50	173.82	171.90	171.22	170.97	170.88
11000	191.95	191.20	189.09	188.34	188.07	187.97
12000	209.40	208.58	206.28	205.46	205.17	205.06
13000	226.85	225.96	223.47	222.58	222.26	222.15
14000	244.30	243.34	240.66	239.71	239.36	239.24
15000	261.75	260.72	257.85	256.83	256.46	256.33
16000	279.20	278.11	275.04	273.95	273.56	273.41
17000	296.65	295.49	292.23	291.07	290.65	290.50
18000	314.10	312.87	309.42	308.19	307.75	307.59
19000	331.55	330.25	326.61	325.31	324.85	324.68
20000	349.00	347.63	343.80	342.44	341.95	341.77
21000	366.45	365.01	360.99	359.56	359.04	358.86
22000	383.91	382.39	378.18	376.68	376.14	375.94
23000	401.36	399.78	395.37	393.80	393.24	393.03
24000	418.81	417.16	412.56	410.92	410.33	410.12
25000	436.26	434.54	429.75	428.05	427.43	427.21
30000	523.51	521.45	515.70	513.65	512.92	512.65
35000	610.76	608.35	601.65	599.26	598.40	598.09
40000	698.01	695.26	687.60	684.87	683.89	683.54
45000	785.26	782.17	773.55	770.48	769.38	768.98
50000	872.51	869.08	859.50	856.09	854.86	854.42
55000	959.76	955.99	945.45	941.70	940.35	939.86
60000	1047.01	1042.89	1031.40	1027.31	1025.83	1025.30
65000	1134.26	1129.80	1117.35	1112.92	1111.32	1110.74
70000	1221.51	1216.71	1203.31	1198.53	1196.81	1196.19
75000	1308.77	1303.62	1289.26	1284.14	1282.29	1281.63
80000	1396.02	1390.52	1375.21	1369.74	1367.78	1367.07
85000	1483.27	1477.43	1461.16	1455.35	1453.27	1452.51
90000	1570.52	1564.34	1547.11	1540.96	1538.75	1537.95
95000	1657.77	1651.25	1633.06	1626.57	1624.24	1623.39
100000	1745.02	1738.15	1719.01	1712.18	1709.72	1708.84
200000	3490.04	3476.31	3438.01	3424.36	3419.45	3417.67
300000	5235.06	5214.46	5157.02	5136.54	5129.17	5126.51
400000	6980.08	6952.62	6876.03	6848.72	6838.90	6835.35
500000	8725.10	8690.77	8595.04	8560.91	8548.62	8544.18

21%

MONTHLY PAYMENT

Necessary to amortize a loan

TERM / AMOUNT	1 YEAR	2 YEARS	3 YEARS	4 YEARS	5 YEARS	6 YEARS
500	46.56	25.69	18.84	15.48	13.53	12.27
600	55.87	30.83	22.61	18.58	16.23	14.72
700	65.18	35.97	26.37	21.68	18.94	17.18
800	74.49	41.11	30.14	24.77	21.64	19.63
900	83.80	46.25	33.91	27.87	24.35	22.08
1000	93.11	51.39	37.68	30.97	27.05	24.54
2000	186.23	102.77	75.35	61.93	54.11	49.07
3000	279.34	154.16	113.03	92.90	81.16	73.61
4000	372.45	205.54	150.70	123.86	108.21	98.14
5000	465.57	256.93	188.38	154.83	135.27	122.68
6000	558.68	308.31	226.05	185.79	162.32	147.22
7000	651.80	359.70	263.73	216.76	180.37	171.75
8000	744.91	411.08	301.40	247.73	216.43	196.29
9000	838.02	462.47	339.08	278.69	243.48	220.82
10000	931.14	513.86	376.75	309.66	270.53	245.36
11000	1024.25	565.24	414.43	340.62	297.59	269.90
12000	1117.36	616.63	452.10	371.59	324.64	294.43
13000	1210.48	668.01	489.78	402.55	351.69	318.97
14000	1303.59	719.40	527.45	433.52	378.75	343.50
15000	1396.70	770.78	565.13	464.49	405.80	368.04
16000	1489.82	822.17	602.80	495.45	432.85	392.58
17000	1582.93	873.55	640.48	526.42	459.91	417.11
18000	1676.04	924.94	678.15	557.38	486.96	441.65
19000	1769.16	976.33	715.83	588.35	514.01	466.18
20000	1862.27	1027.71	753.50	619.31	541.07	490.72
21000	1955.38	1079.10	791.18	650.28	568.12	515.26
22000	2048.50	1130.48	828.85	681.24	595.17	539.79
23000	2141.61	1181.87	866.53	712.21	622.23	564.33
24000	2234.72	1233.25	904.20	743.18	649.28	588.86
25000	2327.84	1284.64	941.88	774.14	676.33	613.40
30000	2793.41	1541.57	1130.25	928.97	811.60	736.08
35000	3258.97	1798.49	1318.62	1083.80	946.87	858.76
40000	3724.54	2055.42	1507.00	1238.63	1082.13	981.44
45000	4190.11	2312.35	1695.37	1393.45	1217.40	1104.12
50000	4655.68	2569.28	1883.75	1548.28	1352.67	1226.80
55000	5121.24	2826.20	2072.12	1703.11	1487.93	1349.48
60000	5586.81	3083.13	2260.50	1857.94	1623.20	1472.16
65000	6052.38	3340.06	2448.87	2012.77	1758.47	1594.84
70000	6517.95	3596.99	2637.25	2167.59	1893.73	1717.52
75000	6983.51	3853.91	2825.62	2322.42	2029.00	1840.20
80000	7449.08	4110.84	3014.00	2477.25	2164.26	1962.88
85000	7914.65	4367.77	3202.37	2632.08	2299.53	2085.56
90000	8380.22	4624.70	3390.75	2786.91	2434.80	2208.24
95000	8845.79	4881.63	3579.12	2941.74	2570.06	2330.92
100000	9311.35	5138.55	3767.50	3096.56	2705.33	2453.60
200000	18622.70	10277.10	7535.00	6193.13	5410.66	4907.19
300000	27934.10	15415.70	11302.50	9289.69	8115.99	7360.79
400000	37245.40	20554.20	15070.00	12386.30	10821.30	9814.38
500000	46556.80	25692.80	18837.50	15482.80	13526.70	12268.00

MONTHLY PAYMENT

Necessary to amortize a loan

21%

TERM / AMOUNT	7 YEARS	8 YEARS	9 YEARS	10 YEARS	11 YEARS	12 YEARS
500	11.41	10.79	10.34	10.00	9.74	9.53
600	13.69	12.95	12.40	12.00	11.68	11.44
700	15.97	15.11	14.47	14.00	13.63	13.35
800	18.25	17.26	16.54	15.99	15.58	15.25
900	20.53	19.42	18.61	17.99	17.52	17.16
1000	22.81	21.58	20.67	19.99	19.47	19.07
2000	45.62	43.16	41.35	39.99	38.94	38.14
3000	68.44	64.74	62.02	59.98	58.42	57.20
4000	91.25	86.32	82.70	79.97	77.89	76.27
5000	114.06	107.91	103.37	99.97	97.36	95.34
6000	136.87	129.49	124.05	119.96	116.83	114.41
7000	159.69	151.07	144.72	139.95	136.30	133.48
8000	182.50	172.65	165.40	159.95	155.77	152.54
9000	205.31	194.23	186.07	179.94	175.25	171.61
10000	228.12	215.81	206.75	199.93	194.72	190.68
11000	250.93	237.39	227.42	219.93	214.19	209.75
12000	273.75	258.97	248.10	239.92	233.66	228.82
13000	296.56	280.55	268.77	259.91	253.13	247.88
14000	319.37	302.13	289.45	279.90	272.61	266.95
15000	342.18	323.72	310.12	299.90	292.08	286.02
16000	365.00	345.30	330.80	319.89	311.55	305.09
17000	387.81	366.88	351.47	339.88	331.02	324.16
18000	410.62	388.46	372.15	359.88	350.49	343.22
19000	433.43	410.04	392.82	379.87	369.96	362.29
20000	456.24	431.62	413.50	399.86	389.44	381.36
21000	479.06	453.20	434.17	419.86	408.91	400.43
22000	501.87	474.78	454.85	439.85	428.38	419.50
23000	524.68	496.36	475.52	459.84	447.85	438.56
24000	547.49	517.94	496.20	479.84	467.32	457.63
25000	570.31	539.53	516.87	499.83	486.80	476.70
30000	684.37	647.43	620.25	599.79	584.15	572.04
35000	798.43	755.33	723.62	699.76	681.51	667.38
40000	912.49	863.24	826.99	799.73	778.87	762.72
45000	1026.55	971.14	930.37	899.69	876.23	858.06
50000	1140.61	1079.05	1033.74	999.66	973.59	953.40
55000	1254.67	1186.95	1137.12	1099.62	1070.95	1048.74
60000	1368.73	1294.86	1240.49	1199.59	1168.31	1144.08
65000	1482.79	1402.76	1343.87	1299.55	1265.67	1239.42
70000	1596.85	1510.67	1447.24	1399.52	1363.02	1334.76
75000	1710.91	1618.57	1550.61	1499.49	1460.38	1430.10
80000	1824.98	1726.48	1653.99	1599.45	1557.74	1525.44
85000	1939.04	1834.38	1757.36	1699.42	1655.10	1620.78
90000	2053.10	1942.29	1860.74	1799.38	1752.46	1716.12
95000	2167.16	2050.19	1964.11	1899.35	1849.82	1811.46
100000	2881.22	2158.10	2067.48	1999.31	1947.18	1906.80
200000	4562.44	4316.20	4134.97	3998.63	3894.36	3813.60
300000	6843.66	6474.30	6202.45	5997.94	5841.54	5720.40
400000	9124.88	8632.39	8269.94	7997.26	7788.71	7627.20
500000	11406.10	10790.50	10337.40	9996.58	9735.89	9534.00

21%

MONTHLY PAYMENT

Necessary to amortize a loan

TERM / AMOUNT	13 YEARS	14 YEARS	15 YEARS	16 YEARS	17 YEARS	18 YEARS
500	9.38	9.25	9.15	9.07	9.01	8.96
600	11.25	11.10	10.98	10.89	10.81	10.75
700	13.13	12.95	12.81	12.70	12.62	12.55
800	15.00	14.80	14.64	14.52	14.42	14.34
900	16.88	16.65	16.48	16.33	16.22	16.13
1000	18.75	18.50	18.31	18.15	18.02	17.92
2000	37.50	37.01	36.61	36.30	36.05	35.85
3000	56.26	55.51	54.92	54.45	54.07	53.77
4000	75.01	74.01	73.22	72.60	72.09	71.69
5000	93.76	92.52	91.53	90.75	90.12	89.61
6000	112.51	111.02	109.84	108.89	108.14	107.54
7000	131.27	129.52	128.14	127.04	126.16	125.46
8000	150.02	148.03	146.45	145.19	144.19	143.38
9000	168.77	166.53	164.76	163.34	162.21	161.30
10000	187.52	185.03	183.06	181.49	180.23	179.23
11000	206.27	203.54	201.37	199.64	198.26	197.15
12000	225.03	222.04	219.67	217.79	216.28	215.07
13000	243.78	240.54	237.98	235.94	234.30	232.99
14000	262.53	259.05	256.29	254.09	252.33	250.92
15000	281.28	277.55	274.59	272.24	270.35	268.84
16000	300.04	296.05	292.90	290.38	288.37	286.76
17000	318.79	314.56	311.20	308.53	306.40	304.69
18000	337.54	333.06	329.51	326.68	324.42	322.61
19000	356.29	351.56	347.82	344.83	342.44	340.53
20000	375.04	370.07	366.12	362.98	360.47	358.45
21000	393.80	388.57	384.43	381.13	378.49	376.38
22000	412.55	407.07	402.74	399.28	396.51	394.30
23000	431.30	425.58	421.04	417.43	414.54	412.22
24000	450.05	444.08	439.35	435.58	432.56	430.14
25000	468.81	462.58	457.65	453.73	450.58	448.07
30000	562.57	555.10	549.18	544.47	540.70	537.68
35000	656.33	647.62	640.71	635.22	630.82	627.29
40000	750.09	740.14	732.25	725.96	720.94	716.91
45000	843.85	832.65	823.78	816.71	811.05	806.52
50000	937.61	925.17	915.31	907.45	901.17	896.13
55000	1031.37	1017.69	1006.84	998.20	991.29	985.75
60000	1125.13	1110.20	1098.37	1088.94	1081.40	1075.36
65000	1218.89	1202.72	1189.90	1179.68	1171.52	1164.97
70000	1312.66	1295.24	1281.43	1270.43	1261.64	1254.58
75000	1406.42	1387.75	1372.96	1361.17	1351.75	1344.20
80000	1500.18	1480.27	1464.49	1451.92	1441.87	1433.81
85000	1593.94	1572.79	1556.02	1542.66	1531.99	1523.42
90000	1687.70	1665.30	1647.55	1633.41	1622.10	1613.04
95000	1781.46	1757.82	1739.08	1724.15	1712.22	1702.65
100000	1875.22	1850.34	1830.61	1814.90	1802.34	1792.26
200000	3750.44	3700.68	3661.22	3629.80	3604.67	3584.53
300000	5625.67	5551.01	5491.83	5444.70	5407.01	5376.79
400000	7500.89	7401.35	7322.45	7259.60	7209.35	7169.05
500000	9376.11	9251.69	9153.06	9074.50	9011.69	8961.32

MONTHLY PAYMENT

Necessary to amortize a loan

21%

TERM / AMOUNT	19 YEARS	20 YEARS	25 YEARS	30 YEARS	35 YEARS	40 YEARS
500	8.92	8.89	8.80	8.77	8.76	8.75
600	10.71	10.67	10.56	10.52	10.51	10.50
700	12.49	12.44	12.32	12.27	12.26	12.25
800	14.27	14.22	14.08	14.03	14.01	14.00
900	16.06	16.00	15.84	15.78	15.76	15.75
1000	17.84	17.78	17.60	17.53	17.51	17.50
2000	35.68	35.55	35.19	35.07	35.02	35.01
3000	53.53	53.33	52.79	52.60	52.54	52.51
4000	71.37	71.11	70.39	70.14	70.05	70.02
5000	89.21	88.88	87.98	87.67	87.56	87.52
6000	107.05	106.66	105.58	105.20	105.07	105.03
7000	124.89	124.44	123.18	122.74	122.58	122.53
8000	142.73	142.21	140.77	140.27	140.10	140.03
9000	160.58	159.99	158.37	157.81	157.61	157.54
10000	178.42	177.76	175.97	175.34	175.12	175.04
11000	196.26	195.54	193.56	192.87	192.63	192.55
12000	214.10	213.32	211.16	210.41	210.14	210.05
13000	231.94	231.09	228.76	227.94	227.66	227.56
14000	249.78	248.87	246.35	245.48	245.17	245.06
15000	267.63	266.65	263.95	263.01	262.68	262.56
16000	285.47	284.42	281.55	280.54	280.19	280.07
17000	303.31	302.20	299.14	298.08	297.70	297.57
18000	321.15	319.98	316.74	315.61	315.22	315.08
19000	338.99	337.75	334.34	333.15	332.73	332.58
20000	356.83	355.53	351.93	350.68	350.24	350.09
21000	374.68	373.31	369.53	368.21	367.75	367.59
22000	392.52	391.08	387.13	385.75	385.26	385.09
23000	410.36	408.86	404.72	403.28	402.78	402.60
24000	428.20	426.63	422.32	420.82	420.29	420.10
25000	446.04	444.41	439.92	438.35	437.80	437.61
30000	535.25	533.29	527.90	526.02	525.36	525.13
35000	624.46	622.18	615.88	613.69	612.92	612.65
40000	713.67	711.06	703.87	701.36	700.48	700.17
45000	802.87	799.94	791.85	789.03	788.04	787.69
50000	892.08	888.82	879.83	876.70	875.60	875.21
55000	981.29	977.70	967.81	964.37	963.16	962.73
60000	1070.50	1066.59	1055.80	1052.04	1050.72	1050.25
65000	1159.71	1155.47	1143.78	1139.71	1138.28	1137.78
70000	1248.92	1244.35	1231.76	1227.38	1225.84	1225.30
75000	1338.12	1333.23	1319.75	1315.05	1313.40	1312.82
80000	1427.33	1422.11	1407.73	1402.72	1400.96	1400.34
85000	1516.54	1511.00	1495.71	1490.39	1488.52	1487.86
90000	1605.75	1599.88	1583.70	1578.06	1576.08	1575.38
95000	1694.96	1688.76	1671.68	1665.73	1663.64	1662.90
100000	1784.17	1777.64	1759.66	1753.40	1751.20	1750.42
200000	3568.33	3555.29	3519.32	3506.80	3502.40	3500.85
300000	5352.50	5332.93	5278.99	5260.20	5253.60	5251.27
400000	7136.66	7110.57	7038.65	7013.60	7004.80	7001.69
500000	8920.83	8888.21	8798.31	8767.00	8756.00	8752.12

21 1/2%

MONTHLY PAYMENT
Necessary to amortize a loan

TERM / AMOUNT	1 YEAR	2 YEARS	3 YEARS	4 YEARS	5 YEARS	6 YEARS
500	46.68	25.82	18.97	15.62	13.67	12.42
600	56.01	30.98	22.76	18.74	16.40	14.90
700	65.35	36.14	26.55	21.86	19.13	17.38
800	74.68	41.31	30.35	24.99	21.87	19.86
900	84.02	46.47	34.14	28.11	24.60	22.35
1000	93.35	51.63	37.93	31.24	27.34	24.83
2000	186.71	103.26	75.86	62.47	54.67	49.66
3000	280.06	154.90	113.80	93.71	82.01	74.49
4000	373.42	206.53	151.73	124.94	109.34	99.32
5000	466.77	258.16	189.66	156.18	136.68	124.15
6000	560.12	309.79	227.59	187.41	164.01	148.98
7000	653.48	361.42	265.53	218.65	191.35	173.81
8000	746.83	413.05	303.46	249.88	218.68	198.64
9000	840.19	464.68	341.39	281.12	246.02	223.47
10000	933.54	516.32	379.32	312.35	273.35	248.30
11000	1026.89	567.95	417.26	343.59	300.69	273.13
12000	1120.25	619.58	455.19	374.82	328.02	297.96
13000	1213.60	671.21	493.12	406.06	355.36	322.79
14000	1306.95	722.84	531.05	437.29	382.70	347.62
15000	1400.31	774.47	568.98	468.53	410.03	372.45
16000	1493.66	826.11	606.92	499.76	437.37	397.28
17000	1587.02	877.74	644.85	531.00	464.70	422.11
18000	1680.37	929.37	682.78	562.23	492.04	446.94
19000	1773.72	981.00	720.71	593.47	519.37	471.77
20000	1867.08	1032.63	758.65	624.71	546.71	496.60
21000	1960.43	1084.26	796.58	655.94	574.04	521.43
22000	2053.78	1135.89	834.51	687.18	601.38	546.26
23000	2147.14	1187.53	872.44	718.41	628.71	571.09
24000	2240.49	1239.16	910.37	749.65	656.05	595.93
25000	2333.85	1290.79	948.31	780.88	683.38	620.76
30000	2800.62	1548.95	1137.97	937.06	820.06	744.91
35000	3267.38	1807.10	1327.63	1093.23	956.74	869.06
40000	3734.15	2065.26	1517.29	1249.41	1093.41	993.21
45000	4200.92	2323.42	1706.95	1405.59	1230.09	1117.36
50000	4667.69	2581.58	1896.61	1561.76	1366.77	1241.51
55000	5134.46	2839.73	2086.27	1717.94	1503.45	1365.66
60000	5601.23	3097.89	2275.94	1874.11	1640.12	1489.81
65000	6068.00	3356.05	2465.60	2030.29	1776.80	1613.96
70000	6534.77	3614.21	2655.26	2186.47	1913.48	1738.11
75000	7001.54	3872.37	2844.92	2342.64	2050.15	1862.26
80000	7468.31	4130.52	3034.58	2498.82	2186.83	1986.42
85000	7935.08	4388.68	3224.24	2655.00	2323.51	2110.57
90000	8401.84	4646.84	3413.90	2811.17	2460.18	2234.72
95000	8868.61	4905.00	3603.56	2967.35	2596.86	2358.87
100000	9335.38	5163.15	3793.23	3123.52	2733.54	2483.02
200000	18670.80	10326.30	7586.45	6247.05	5467.07	4966.04
300000	28006.20	15489.50	11379.70	9370.57	8200.61	7449.06
400000	37341.50	20652.60	15172.90	12494.10	10934.10	9932.08
500000	46676.90	25815.80	18966.10	15617.60	13667.70	12415.10

MONTHLY PAYMENT

Necessary to amortize a loan

21 1/2%

TERM / AMOUNT	7 YEARS	8 YEARS	9 YEARS	10 YEARS	11 YEARS	12 YEARS
500	11.56	10.95	10.50	10.17	9.91	9.71
600	13.87	13.14	12.60	12.20	11.89	11.65
700	16.18	15.33	14.70	14.23	13.87	13.60
800	18.49	17.52	16.80	16.26	15.85	15.54
900	20.81	19.71	18.90	18.30	17.84	17.48
1000	23.12	21.90	21.00	20.33	19.82	19.42
2000	46.24	43.80	42.00	40.66	39.64	38.84
3000	69.35	65.69	63.01	60.99	59.45	58.27
4000	92.47	87.59	84.01	81.32	79.27	77.69
5000	115.59	109.49	105.01	101.65	99.09	97.11
6000	138.71	131.39	126.01	121.98	118.91	116.53
7000	161.83	153.29	147.02	142.31	138.73	135.96
8000	184.95	175.18	168.02	162.64	158.54	155.38
9000	208.06	197.08	189.02	182.97	178.36	174.80
10000	231.18	218.98	210.02	203.30	198.18	194.22
11000	254.30	240.88	231.03	223.63	218.00	213.65
12000	277.42	262.78	252.03	243.96	237.82	233.07
13000	300.54	284.67	273.03	264.29	257.63	252.49
14000	323.65	306.57	294.03	284.63	277.45	271.91
15000	346.77	328.47	315.04	304.96	297.27	291.34
16000	369.89	350.37	336.04	325.29	317.09	310.76
17000	393.01	372.27	357.04	345.62	336.91	330.18
18000	416.13	394.16	378.04	365.95	356.72	349.60
19000	439.24	416.06	399.04	386.28	376.54	369.03
20000	462.36	437.96	420.05	406.61	396.36	388.45
21000	485.48	459.86	441.05	426.94	416.18	407.87
22000	508.60	481.76	462.05	447.27	436.00	427.29
23000	531.72	503.65	483.05	467.60	455.81	446.72
24000	554.84	525.55	504.06	487.93	475.63	466.14
25000	577.95	547.45	525.06	508.26	495.45	485.56
30000	693.54	656.94	630.07	609.91	594.54	582.67
35000	809.13	766.43	735.08	711.56	693.63	679.78
40000	924.73	875.92	840.09	813.21	792.72	776.90
45000	1040.32	985.41	945.10	914.87	891.81	874.01
50000	1155.91	1094.90	1050.12	1016.52	990.90	971.12
55000	1271.50	1204.39	1155.13	1118.17	1089.99	1068.23
60000	1387.09	1313.88	1260.14	1219.82	1189.08	1165.34
65000	1502.68	1423.37	1365.15	1321.47	1288.17	1262.45
70000	1618.27	1532.86	1470.16	1423.12	1387.26	1359.57
75000	1733.86	1642.35	1575.17	1524.77	1486.35	1456.68
80000	1849.45	1751.84	1680.18	1626.43	1585.43	1553.79
85000	1965.04	1861.33	1785.20	1728.08	1684.52	1650.90
90000	2080.63	1970.82	1890.21	1829.73	1783.61	1748.01
95000	2196.22	2080.31	1995.22	1931.38	1882.70	1845.13
100000	2311.81	2189.80	2100.23	2033.03	1981.79	1942.24
200000	4623.63	4379.60	4200.46	4066.07	3963.59	3884.47
300000	6935.44	6569.41	6300.69	6099.10	5945.38	5826.71
400000	9247.25	8759.21	8400.92	8132.13	7927.17	7768.95
500000	11559.10	10949.00	10501.20	10165.20	9908.97	9711.19

21 1/2%

MONTHLY PAYMENT
Necessary to amortize a loan

TERM / AMOUNT	13 YEARS	14 YEARS	15 YEARS	16 YEARS	17 YEARS	18 YEARS
500	9.56	9.44	9.34	9.26	9.20	9.16
600	11.47	11.32	11.21	11.12	11.05	10.99
700	13.38	13.21	13.08	12.97	12.89	12.82
800	15.29	15.10	14.94	14.82	14.73	14.65
900	17.20	16.98	16.81	16.68	16.57	16.48
1000	19.11	18.87	18.68	18.53	18.41	18.31
2000	38.23	37.74	37.36	37.06	36.82	36.62
3000	57.34	56.62	56.04	55.59	55.23	54.94
4000	76.46	75.49	74.72	74.12	73.63	73.25
5000	95.57	94.36	93.40	92.65	92.04	91.56
6000	114.69	113.23	112.09	111.18	110.45	109.87
7000	133.80	132.10	130.77	129.70	128.86	128.18
8000	152.91	150.98	149.45	148.23	147.27	146.50
9000	172.03	169.85	168.13	166.76	165.68	164.81
10000	191.14	188.72	186.81	185.29	184.08	183.12
11000	210.26	207.59	205.49	203.82	202.49	201.43
12000	229.37	226.46	224.17	222.35	220.90	219.74
13000	248.48	245.34	242.85	240.88	239.31	238.06
14000	267.60	264.21	261.53	259.41	257.72	256.37
15000	286.71	283.08	280.21	277.94	276.13	274.68
16000	305.83	301.95	298.89	296.47	294.53	292.99
17000	324.94	320.82	317.57	315.00	312.94	311.30
18000	344.05	339.70	336.26	333.53	331.35	329.62
19000	363.17	358.57	354.94	352.05	349.76	347.93
20000	382.28	377.44	373.62	370.58	368.17	366.24
21000	401.40	396.31	392.30	389.11	386.58	384.55
22000	420.51	415.18	410.98	407.64	404.99	402.86
23000	439.62	434.06	429.66	426.17	423.39	421.18
24000	458.74	452.93	448.34	444.70	441.80	439.49
25000	477.85	471.80	467.02	463.23	460.21	457.80
30000	573.42	566.16	560.43	555.88	552.25	549.36
35000	668.99	660.52	653.83	648.52	644.29	640.92
40000	764.56	754.88	747.23	741.17	736.34	732.48
45000	860.13	849.24	840.64	833.81	828.38	824.04
50000	955.70	943.60	934.04	926.46	920.42	915.60
55000	1051.27	1037.96	1027.45	1019.10	1012.46	1007.16
60000	1146.85	1132.32	1120.85	1111.75	1104.50	1098.72
65000	1242.42	1226.68	1214.25	1204.40	1196.55	1190.28
70000	1337.99	1321.04	1307.66	1297.04	1288.59	1281.84
75000	1433.56	1415.40	1401.06	1389.69	1380.63	1373.40
80000	1529.13	1509.76	1494.47	1482.33	1472.67	1464.95
85000	1624.70	1604.12	1587.87	1574.98	1564.71	1556.51
90000	1720.27	1698.48	1681.28	1667.63	1656.76	1648.07
95000	1815.84	1792.84	1774.68	1760.27	1748.80	1739.63
100000	1911.41	1887.20	1868.08	1852.92	1840.84	1831.19
200000	3822.82	3774.40	3736.17	3705.83	3681.68	3662.39
300000	5734.23	5661.60	5604.25	5558.75	5522.52	5493.58
400000	7645.63	7548.81	7472.34	7411.67	7363.36	7324.77
500000	9557.04	9436.01	9340.42	9264.58	9204.19	9155.97

MONTHLY PAYMENT

Necessary to amortize a loan

21 1/2%

TERM / AMOUNT	19 YEARS	20 YEARS	25 YEARS	30 YEARS	35 YEARS	40 YEARS
500	9.12	9.09	9.00	8.97	8.96	8.96
600	10.94	10.90	10.80	10.77	10.76	10.75
700	12.76	12.72	12.60	12.56	12.55	12.54
800	14.59	14.54	14.40	14.36	14.34	14.34
900	16.41	16.36	16.20	16.15	16.13	16.13
1000	18.23	18.17	18.00	17.95	17.93	17.92
2000	36.47	36.35	36.01	35.89	35.85	35.84
3000	54.70	54.52	54.01	53.84	53.78	53.76
4000	72.94	72.69	72.02	71.79	71.71	71.68
5000	91.17	90.86	90.02	89.73	89.64	89.60
6000	109.41	109.04	108.03	107.68	107.56	107.52
7000	127.64	127.21	126.03	125.63	125.49	125.44
8000	145.88	145.38	144.03	143.57	143.42	143.36
9000	164.11	163.56	162.04	161.52	161.34	161.28
10000	182.35	181.73	180.04	179.47	179.27	179.20
11000	200.58	199.90	198.05	197.41	197.20	197.12
12000	218.82	218.07	216.05	215.36	215.12	215.04
13000	237.05	236.25	234.05	233.31	233.05	232.96
14000	255.29	254.42	252.06	251.25	250.98	250.88
15000	273.52	272.59	270.06	269.20	268.91	268.80
16000	291.76	290.77	288.07	287.15	286.83	286.72
17000	309.99	308.94	306.07	305.09	304.76	304.64
18000	328.23	327.11	324.07	323.04	322.69	322.56
19000	346.46	345.28	342.08	340.99	340.61	340.48
20000	364.70	363.46	360.08	358.93	358.54	358.41
21000	382.93	381.63	378.09	376.88	376.47	376.33
22000	401.16	399.80	396.09	394.83	394.39	394.25
23000	419.40	417.98	414.09	412.77	412.32	412.17
24000	437.63	436.15	432.10	430.72	430.25	430.09
25000	455.87	454.32	450.10	448.67	448.18	448.01
30000	547.04	545.18	540.12	538.40	537.81	537.61
35000	638.22	636.05	630.14	628.13	627.45	627.21
40000	729.39	726.91	720.16	717.87	717.08	716.81
45000	820.56	817.78	810.19	807.60	806.72	806.41
50000	911.74	908.64	900.21	897.34	896.35	896.01
55000	1012.91	999.51	990.23	987.07	985.99	985.61
60000	1094.08	1090.37	1080.25	1076.80	1075.62	1075.21
65000	1185.26	1181.23	1170.27	1166.54	1165.26	1164.81
70000	1276.43	1272.10	1260.29	1256.27	1254.89	1254.42
75000	1367.60	1362.96	1350.31	1346.00	1344.53	1344.02
80000	1458.78	1453.82	1440.33	1435.74	1434.16	1433.62
85000	1549.95	1544.69	1530.35	1525.47	1523.80	1523.22
90000	1641.13	1635.55	1620.37	1615.20	1613.43	1612.82
95000	1732.30	1726.42	1710.39	1704.94	1703.07	1702.42
100000	1823.47	1817.28	1800.41	1794.67	1792.70	1792.02
200000	3646.95	3634.56	3600.82	3589.34	3585.40	3584.05
300000	5470.42	5451.84	5401.23	5384.01	5378.10	5376.07
400000	7293.89	7269.12	7201.64	7178.68	7170.80	7168.09
500000	9117.36	9086.41	9002.05	8973.35	8963.50	8960.11

22%

MONTHLY PAYMENT

Necessary to amortize a loan

TERM / AMOUNT	1 YEAR	2 YEARS	3 YEARS	4 YEARS	5 YEARS	6 YEARS
500	46.80	25.94	19.10	15.75	13.81	12.56
600	56.16	31.13	22.91	18.90	16.57	15.08
700	65.52	36.31	26.73	22.05	19.33	17.59
800	74.88	41.50	30.55	25.20	22.10	20.10
900	84.24	46.69	34.37	28.36	24.86	22.61
1000	93.59	51.88	38.19	31.51	27.62	25.13
2000	187.19	103.76	76.38	63.01	55.24	50.25
3000	280.78	155.64	114.57	94.52	82.86	75.38
4000	374.38	207.51	152.76	126.03	110.48	100.51
5000	467.97	259.39	190.95	157.53	138.10	125.63
6000	561.57	311.27	229.14	189.04	165.71	150.76
7000	655.16	363.15	267.33	220.54	193.33	175.88
8000	748.76	415.03	305.52	252.05	220.95	201.01
9000	842.35	466.90	343.72	283.56	248.57	226.14
10000	935.95	518.78	381.91	315.06	276.19	251.26
11000	1029.54	570.66	420.10	346.57	303.81	276.39
12000	1123.13	622.54	458.29	378.07	331.43	301.51
13000	1216.73	674.42	496.48	409.58	359.05	326.64
14000	1310.32	726.30	534.67	441.09	386.67	351.77
15000	1403.92	778.17	572.86	472.59	414.28	376.89
16000	1497.51	830.05	611.05	504.10	441.90	402.02
17000	1591.11	881.93	649.24	535.60	469.52	427.15
18000	1684.70	933.81	687.43	567.11	497.14	452.27
19000	1778.30	985.69	725.62	598.62	524.76	477.40
20000	1871.89	1037.57	763.81	630.12	552.38	502.52
21000	1965.49	1089.44	802.00	661.63	580.00	527.65
22000	2059.08	1141.32	840.19	693.14	607.62	552.78
23000	2152.68	1193.20	878.38	724.64	635.24	577.90
24000	2246.27	1245.08	916.57	756.15	662.86	603.03
25000	2339.86	1296.96	954.76	787.65	690.47	628.15
30000	2807.84	1556.35	1145.72	945.18	828.57	753.79
35000	3275.81	1815.74	1336.67	1102.71	966.66	879.42
40000	3743.78	2075.13	1527.62	1260.25	1104.76	1005.05
45000	4211.76	2334.52	1718.57	1417.78	1242.85	1130.68
50000	4679.73	2593.91	1909.53	1575.31	1380.95	1256.31
55000	5147.70	2853.30	2100.48	1732.84	1519.04	1381.94
60000	5615.67	3112.70	2291.43	1890.37	1657.14	1507.57
65000	6083.65	3372.09	2482.38	2047.90	1795.23	1633.20
70000	6551.62	3631.48	2673.34	2205.43	1933.33	1758.83
75000	7019.59	3890.87	2864.29	2362.96	2071.42	1884.46
80000	7487.57	4150.26	3055.24	2520.49	2209.52	2010.09
85000	7955.54	4409.65	3246.19	2678.02	2347.61	2135.72
90000	8423.51	4669.04	3437.15	2835.55	2485.71	2261.35
95000	8891.48	4928.43	3628.10	2993.08	2623.80	2386.98
100000	9359.46	5187.83	3819.05	3150.61	2761.89	2512.62
200000	18718.90	10375.70	7638.10	6301.23	5523.79	5025.23
300000	28078.40	15563.50	11457.20	9451.84	8285.68	7537.85
400000	37437.80	20751.30	15276.20	12602.50	11047.60	10050.50
500000	46797.30	25939.10	19095.30	15753.10	13809.50	12563.10

MONTHLY PAYMENT

Necessary to amortize a loan

22%

TERM / AMOUNT	7 YEARS	8 YEARS	9 YEARS	10 YEARS	11 YEARS	12 YEARS
500	11.71	11.11	10.67	10.33	10.08	9.89
600	14.06	13.33	12.80	12.40	12.10	11.87
700	16.40	15.55	14.93	14.47	14.12	13.85
800	18.74	17.77	17.07	16.54	16.13	15.82
900	21.08	20.00	19.20	18.60	18.15	17.80
1000	23.43	22.22	21.33	20.67	20.17	19.78
2000	46.85	44.43	42.66	41.34	40.33	39.56
3000	70.28	66.65	64.00	62.01	60.50	59.34
4000	93.70	88.87	85.33	82.68	80.67	79.12
5000	117.13	111.09	106.66	103.35	100.83	98.89
6000	140.56	133.30	127.99	124.02	121.00	118.67
7000	163.98	155.52	149.32	144.69	141.16	138.45
8000	187.41	177.74	170.66	165.36	161.33	158.23
9000	210.83	199.95	191.99	186.03	181.50	178.01
10000	234.26	222.17	213.32	206.70	201.66	197.79
11000	257.69	244.39	234.65	227.37	221.83	217.57
12000	281.11	266.61	255.98	248.04	242.00	237.35
13000	304.54	288.82	277.32	268.71	262.16	257.13
14000	327.96	311.04	298.65	289.38	282.33	276.91
15000	351.39	333.26	319.98	310.05	302.49	296.68
16000	374.82	355.47	341.31	330.72	322.66	316.46
17000	398.24	377.69	362.64	351.39	342.83	336.24
18000	421.67	399.91	383.97	372.06	362.99	356.02
19000	445.09	422.13	405.31	392.72	383.16	375.80
20000	468.52	444.34	426.64	413.39	403.33	395.58
21000	491.95	466.56	447.97	434.06	423.49	415.36
22000	515.37	488.78	469.30	454.73	443.66	435.14
23000	538.80	510.99	490.63	475.40	463.83	454.92
24000	562.22	533.21	511.97	496.07	483.99	474.70
25000	585.65	555.43	533.30	516.74	504.16	494.47
30000	702.78	666.51	639.96	620.09	604.99	593.37
35000	819.91	777.60	746.62	723.44	705.82	692.26
40000	937.04	888.68	853.28	826.79	806.65	791.16
45000	1054.17	999.77	959.94	930.14	907.48	890.05
50000	1171.30	1110.85	1066.60	1033.49	1008.31	988.95
55000	1288.43	1221.94	1173.26	1136.83	1109.15	1087.84
60000	1405.56	1333.03	1279.92	1240.18	1209.98	1186.74
65000	1522.69	1444.11	1386.57	1343.53	1310.81	1285.63
70000	1639.82	1555.20	1493.23	1446.88	1411.64	1384.53
75000	1756.95	1666.28	1599.89	1550.23	1512.47	1483.42
80000	1874.08	1777.37	1706.55	1653.58	1613.30	1582.32
85000	1991.21	1888.45	1813.21	1756.92	1714.14	1681.21
90000	2108.34	1999.54	1919.87	1860.27	1814.97	1780.11
95000	2225.47	2110.62	2026.53	1963.62	1915.80	1879.00
100000	2342.60	2221.71	2133.19	2066.97	2016.63	1977.89
200000	4685.19	4443.42	4266.38	4133.94	4033.26	3955.79
300000	7027.79	6665.13	6399.58	6200.91	6049.89	5933.68
400000	9370.39	8886.84	8532.77	8267.88	8066.52	7911.58
500000	11713.00	11108.50	10666.00	10334.90	10083.10	9889.47

22%

MONTHLY PAYMENT

Necessary to amortize a loan

TERM / AMOUNT	13 YEARS	14 YEARS	15 YEARS	16 YEARS	17 YEARS	18 YEARS
500	9.74	9.62	9.53	9.46	9.40	9.35
600	11.69	11.55	11.43	11.35	11.28	11.22
700	13.63	13.47	13.34	13.24	13.16	13.09
800	15.58	15.39	15.25	15.13	15.04	14.96
900	17.53	17.32	17.15	17.02	16.92	16.83
1000	19.48	19.24	19.06	18.91	18.80	18.70
2000	38.96	38.49	38.12	37.82	37.59	37.41
3000	58.43	57.73	57.17	56.73	56.39	56.11
4000	77.91	76.97	76.23	75.64	75.18	74.81
5000	97.39	96.21	95.29	94.56	93.98	93.51
6000	116.87	115.46	114.35	113.47	112.77	112.22
7000	136.35	134.70	133.40	132.38	131.57	130.92
8000	155.83	153.94	152.46	151.29	150.36	149.62
9000	175.30	173.19	171.52	170.20	169.16	168.33
10000	194.78	192.43	190.58	189.11	187.95	187.03
11000	214.28	211.67	209.63	208.02	206.75	205.73
12000	233.74	230.91	228.69	226.94	225.54	224.44
13000	253.22	250.16	247.75	245.85	244.34	243.14
14000	272.69	269.40	266.81	264.76	263.13	261.84
15000	292.17	288.64	285.86	283.67	281.93	280.54
16000	311.65	307.88	304.92	302.58	300.72	299.25
17000	331.13	327.13	323.98	321.49	319.52	317.95
18000	350.61	346.37	343.04	340.40	338.31	336.65
19000	370.08	365.61	362.09	359.31	357.11	355.36
20000	389.56	384.86	381.15	378.23	375.90	374.06
21000	409.04	404.10	400.21	397.14	394.70	392.76
22000	428.52	423.34	419.27	416.05	413.49	411.46
23000	448.00	442.58	438.32	434.96	432.29	430.17
24000	467.47	461.83	457.38	453.87	451.08	448.87
25000	486.95	481.07	476.44	472.78	469.88	467.57
30000	584.34	577.28	571.73	567.34	563.86	561.09
35000	681.73	673.50	667.02	661.89	657.83	654.60
40000	779.12	769.71	762.30	756.45	751.81	748.12
45000	876.51	865.92	857.59	851.01	845.78	841.63
50000	973.91	962.14	952.88	945.56	939.76	935.14
55000	1071.30	1058.35	1048.17	1040.12	1033.73	1028.66
60000	1168.69	1154.56	1143.45	1134.67	1127.71	1122.17
65000	1266.08	1250.78	1238.74	1229.23	1221.69	1215.69
70000	1363.47	1346.99	1334.03	1323.79	1315.66	1309.20
75000	1460.86	1443.21	1429.32	1418.34	1409.64	1402.72
80000	1558.25	1539.42	1524.61	1512.90	1503.61	1496.23
85000	1655.64	1635.63	1619.89	1607.45	1597.59	1589.75
90000	1753.03	1731.85	1715.18	1702.01	1691.57	1683.26
95000	1850.42	1828.06	1810.47	1796.57	1785.54	1776.77
100000	1947.81	1924.27	1905.76	1891.12	1879.52	1870.29
200000	3895.62	3848.55	3811.51	3782.25	3759.04	3740.58
300000	5843.43	5772.82	5717.27	5673.37	5638.55	5610.87
400000	7791.24	7697.09	7623.03	7564.49	7518.07	7481.16
500000	9739.05	9621.37	9528.78	9455.61	9397.59	9351.44

MONTHLY PAYMENT

Necessary to amortize a loan

22%

TERM AMOUNT	19 YEARS	20 YEARS	25 YEARS	30 YEARS	35 YEARS	40 YEARS
500	9.31	9.29	9.21	9.18	9.17	9.17
600	11.18	11.14	11.05	11.02	11.01	11.00
700	13.04	13.00	12.89	12.85	12.84	12.84
800	14.90	14.86	14.73	14.69	14.67	14.67
900	16.77	16.71	16.57	16.52	16.51	16.50
1000	18.63	18.57	18.41	18.36	18.34	18.34
2000	37.26	37.14	36.82	36.72	36.68	36.67
3000	55.89	55.71	55.24	55.08	55.03	55.01
4000	74.52	74.28	73.65	73.44	73.37	73.35
5000	93.15	92.85	92.06	91.80	91.71	91.68
6000	111.78	111.42	110.48	110.16	110.05	110.02
7000	130.41	129.99	128.89	128.52	128.40	128.35
8000	149.04	148.57	147.30	146.88	146.74	146.69
9000	167.66	167.14	165.71	165.24	165.08	165.03
10000	186.29	185.71	184.12	183.60	183.42	183.36
11000	204.92	204.28	202.54	201.96	201.77	201.70
12000	223.55	222.85	220.95	220.32	220.11	220.04
13000	242.18	241.42	239.36	238.68	238.45	238.37
14000	260.81	259.99	257.77	257.04	256.79	256.71
15000	279.44	278.56	276.19	275.40	275.13	275.05
16000	298.07	297.13	294.60	293.76	293.48	293.38
17000	316.70	315.70	313.01	312.12	311.82	311.72
18000	335.33	334.27	331.42	330.48	330.16	330.05
19000	353.96	352.84	349.84	348.84	348.50	348.39
20000	372.59	371.41	368.25	367.20	366.85	366.73
21000	391.22	389.98	386.66	385.56	385.19	385.06
22000	409.85	408.55	405.07	403.92	403.53	403.40
23000	428.48	427.12	423.49	422.28	421.87	421.74
24000	447.10	445.69	441.90	440.64	440.21	440.07
25000	465.73	464.27	460.31	459.00	458.56	458.41
30000	558.88	557.12	552.37	550.80	550.27	550.09
35000	652.03	649.97	644.44	642.60	641.98	641.77
40000	745.17	742.82	736.50	734.39	733.69	733.45
45000	838.32	835.68	828.56	826.19	825.40	825.14
50000	931.47	928.53	920.62	917.99	917.11	916.82
55000	1024.61	1021.38	1012.68	1009.79	1008.82	1008.50
60000	1117.76	1114.24	1104.75	1101.59	1100.53	1100.18
65000	1210.91	1207.09	1196.81	1193.39	1192.25	1191.86
70000	1304.05	1299.94	1288.87	1285.19	1283.96	1283.54
75000	1397.20	1392.80	1380.93	1376.99	1375.67	1375.22
80000	1490.35	1485.65	1472.99	1468.79	1467.38	1466.91
85000	1583.49	1578.50	1565.06	1560.59	1559.09	1558.59
90000	1676.64	1671.35	1657.12	1652.39	1650.80	1650.27
95000	1769.79	1764.21	1749.18	1744.19	1742.51	1741.95
100000	1862.93	1857.06	1841.24	1835.98	1834.22	1833.63
200000	3725.87	3714.12	3682.48	3671.97	3668.45	3667.26
300000	5588.80	5571.18	5523.73	5507.95	5502.67	5500.90
400000	7451.73	7428.24	7364.97	7343.94	7336.90	7334.53
500000	9314.67	9285.30	9206.21	9179.92	9171.12	9168.16

22 1/2% MONTHLY PAYMENT

Necessary to amortize a loan

TERM / AMOUNT	1 YEAR	2 YEARS	3 YEARS	4 YEARS	5 YEARS	6 YEARS
500	46.92	26.06	19.22	15.89	13.95	12.71
600	56.30	31.28	23.07	19.07	16.74	15.25
700	65.68	36.49	26.91	22.24	19.53	17.80
800	75.07	41.70	30.76	25.42	22.32	20.34
900	84.45	46.91	34.60	28.60	25.11	22.88
1000	93.84	52.13	38.45	31.78	27.90	25.42
2000	187.67	104.25	76.90	63.56	55.81	50.85
3000	281.51	156.38	115.35	95.33	83.71	76.27
4000	375.34	208.50	153.80	127.11	111.62	101.70
5000	469.18	260.63	192.25	158.89	139.52	127.12
6000	563.01	312.75	230.70	190.67	167.42	152.54
7000	656.85	364.88	269.15	222.45	195.33	177.97
8000	750.68	417.00	307.60	254.23	223.23	203.39
9000	844.52	469.13	346.05	286.00	251.14	228.81
10000	938.35	521.26	384.50	317.78	279.04	254.24
11000	1032.19	573.38	422.95	349.56	306.94	279.66
12000	1126.02	625.51	461.40	381.34	334.85	305.09
13000	1219.86	677.63	499.85	413.12	362.75	330.51
14000	1313.70	729.76	538.30	444.90	390.66	355.93
15000	1407.53	781.88	576.75	476.67	418.56	381.36
16000	1501.37	834.01	615.20	508.45	446.46	406.78
17000	1595.20	886.13	653.64	540.23	474.37	432.21
18000	1689.04	938.26	692.09	572.01	502.27	457.63
19000	1782.87	990.39	730.54	603.79	530.18	483.05
20000	1876.71	1042.51	768.99	635.56	558.08	508.48
21000	1970.54	1094.64	807.44	667.34	585.98	533.90
22000	2064.38	1146.76	845.89	699.12	613.89	559.32
23000	2158.21	1198.89	884.34	730.90	641.79	584.75
24000	2252.05	1251.01	922.79	762.68	669.70	610.17
25000	2345.88	1303.14	961.24	794.46	697.60	635.60
30000	2815.06	1563.77	1153.49	953.35	837.12	762.71
35000	3284.24	1824.39	1345.74	1112.24	976.64	889.83
40000	3753.42	2085.02	1537.99	1271.13	1116.16	1016.95
45000	4222.59	2345.65	1730.24	1430.02	1255.68	1144.07
50000	4691.77	2606.28	1922.48	1588.91	1395.20	1271.19
55000	5160.95	2866.90	2114.73	1747.80	1534.72	1398.31
60000	5630.12	3127.53	2306.98	1906.69	1674.24	1525.43
65000	6099.30	3388.16	2499.23	2065.58	1813.76	1652.55
70000	6568.48	3648.79	2691.48	2224.47	1953.28	1779.67
75000	7037.65	3909.41	2883.73	2383.36	2092.80	1906.78
80000	7506.83	4170.04	3075.97	2542.26	2232.32	2033.90
85000	7976.01	4430.67	3268.22	2701.15	2371.84	2161.02
90000	8445.18	4691.30	3460.47	2860.04	2511.36	2288.14
95000	8914.36	4951.92	3652.72	3018.93	2650.88	2415.26
100000	9383.54	5212.55	3844.97	3177.82	2790.40	2542.38
200000	18767.10	10425.10	7689.93	6355.64	5580.80	5084.76
300000	28150.60	15637.70	11534.90	9533.46	8371.19	7627.14
400000	37534.20	20850.20	15379.90	12711.30	11161.60	10169.50
500000	46917.70	26062.80	19224.80	15889.10	13952.00	12711.90

MONTHLY PAYMENT

Necessary to amortize a loan

22 1/2%

TERM / AMOUNT	7 YEARS	8 YEARS	9 YEARS	10 YEARS	11 YEARS	12 YEARS
500	11.87	11.27	10.83	10.51	10.26	10.07
600	14.24	13.52	13.00	12.61	12.31	12.08
700	16.62	15.78	15.16	14.71	14.36	14.10
800	18.99	18.03	17.33	16.81	16.41	16.11
900	21.36	20.28	19.50	18.91	18.47	18.12
1000	23.74	22.54	21.66	21.01	20.52	20.14
2000	47.47	45.08	43.33	42.02	41.03	40.28
3000	71.21	67.61	64.99	63.03	61.55	60.41
4000	94.94	90.15	86.65	84.04	82.07	80.55
5000	118.68	112.69	108.32	105.06	102.58	100.69
6000	142.41	135.23	129.98	126.07	123.10	120.83
7000	166.15	157.77	151.65	147.08	143.62	140.96
8000	189.89	180.31	173.31	168.09	164.13	161.10
9000	213.62	202.84	194.97	189.10	184.65	181.24
10000	237.36	225.38	216.64	210.11	205.17	201.38
11000	261.09	247.92	238.30	231.12	225.69	221.51
12000	284.83	270.46	259.96	252.13	246.20	241.65
13000	308.56	293.00	281.63	273.15	266.72	261.79
14000	332.30	315.53	303.29	294.16	287.24	281.93
15000	356.04	338.07	324.95	315.17	307.75	302.06
16000	379.77	360.61	346.62	336.18	328.27	322.20
17000	403.51	383.15	368.28	357.19	348.79	342.34
18000	427.24	405.69	389.95	378.20	369.30	362.48
19000	450.98	428.23	411.61	399.21	389.82	382.62
20000	474.71	450.76	433.27	420.22	410.34	402.75
21000	498.45	473.30	454.94	441.24	430.85	422.89
22000	522.19	495.84	476.60	462.25	451.37	443.03
23000	545.92	518.38	498.26	483.26	471.89	463.17
24000	569.66	540.92	519.93	504.27	492.40	483.30
25000	593.39	563.45	541.59	525.28	512.92	503.44
30000	712.07	676.15	649.91	630.34	615.50	604.13
35000	830.75	788.84	758.23	735.39	718.09	704.82
40000	949.43	901.53	866.54	840.45	820.67	805.51
45000	1068.10	1014.22	974.86	945.50	923.26	906.19
50000	1186.78	1126.91	1083.18	1050.56	1025.84	1006.88
55000	1305.46	1239.60	1191.50	1155.62	1128.42	1107.57
60000	1424.14	1352.29	1299.82	1260.67	1231.01	1208.26
65000	1542.82	1464.98	1408.13	1365.73	1333.59	1308.95
70000	1661.50	1577.67	1516.45	1470.78	1436.18	1409.63
75000	1780.17	1690.36	1624.77	1575.84	1538.76	1510.32
80000	1898.85	1803.05	1733.09	1680.90	1641.34	1611.01
85000	2017.53	1915.74	1841.41	1785.95	1743.93	1711.70
90000	2136.21	2028.43	1949.72	1891.01	1846.51	1812.39
95000	2254.89	2141.13	2058.04	1996.06	1949.10	1913.07
100000	2373.57	2253.82	2166.36	2101.12	2051.68	2013.76
200000	4747.13	4507.63	4332.72	4202.24	4103.36	4027.53
300000	7120.70	6761.45	6499.08	6303.36	6155.04	6041.29
400000	9494.26	9015.26	8665.44	8404.48	8206.72	8055.05
500000	11867.80	11269.10	10831.80	10505.60	10258.40	10068.80

22 1/2% MONTHLY PAYMENT

Necessary to amortize a loan

TERM / AMOUNT	13 YEARS	14 YEARS	15 YEARS	16 YEARS	17 YEARS	18 YEARS
500	9.92	9.81	9.72	9.65	9.59	9.55
600	11.91	11.77	11.66	11.58	11.51	11.46
700	13.89	13.73	13.61	13.51	13.43	13.37
800	15.88	15.69	15.55	15.44	15.35	15.28
900	17.86	17.65	17.49	17.37	17.27	17.19
1000	19.84	19.62	19.44	19.30	19.18	19.10
2000	39.69	39.23	38.87	38.59	38.37	38.19
3000	59.53	58.85	58.31	57.89	57.55	57.29
4000	79.38	78.46	77.74	77.18	76.73	76.38
5000	99.22	98.08	97.18	96.48	95.92	95.48
6000	119.07	117.69	116.62	115.77	115.10	114.57
7000	138.91	137.31	136.05	135.07	134.29	133.67
8000	158.75	156.92	155.49	154.36	153.47	152.76
9000	178.60	176.54	174.93	173.66	172.65	171.86
10000	198.44	196.15	194.36	192.95	191.84	190.95
11000	218.29	215.77	213.80	212.25	211.02	210.05
12000	238.13	235.39	233.23	231.54	230.20	229.15
13000	257.97	255.00	252.67	250.84	249.39	248.24
14000	277.82	274.62	272.11	270.13	268.57	267.34
15000	297.66	294.23	291.54	289.43	287.76	286.43
16000	317.51	313.85	310.98	308.72	306.94	305.53
17000	337.35	333.46	330.42	328.02	326.12	324.62
18000	357.20	353.08	349.85	347.31	345.31	343.72
19000	377.04	372.69	369.29	366.61	364.49	362.81
20000	396.88	392.31	388.72	385.90	383.67	381.91
21000	416.73	411.92	408.16	405.20	402.86	401.00
22000	436.57	431.54	427.60	424.49	422.04	420.10
23000	456.42	451.16	447.03	443.79	441.22	439.19
24000	476.26	470.77	466.47	463.08	460.41	458.29
25000	496.10	490.39	485.91	482.38	479.59	477.39
30000	595.33	588.46	583.09	578.85	575.51	572.86
35000	694.55	686.54	680.27	675.33	671.43	668.34
40000	793.77	784.62	777.45	771.80	767.35	763.82
45000	892.99	882.70	874.63	868.28	863.26	859.29
50000	992.21	980.77	971.81	964.75	959.18	954.77
55000	1091.43	1078.85	1068.99	1061.23	1055.10	1050.25
60000	1190.65	1176.93	1166.17	1157.71	1151.02	1145.72
65000	1289.87	1275.00	1263.35	1254.18	1246.94	1241.20
70000	1389.09	1373.08	1360.53	1350.66	1342.86	1336.68
75000	1488.31	1471.16	1457.71	1447.13	1438.77	1432.16
80000	1587.53	1569.24	1554.89	1543.61	1534.69	1527.63
85000	1686.75	1667.31	1652.08	1640.08	1630.61	1623.11
90000	1785.98	1765.39	1749.26	1736.56	1726.53	1718.59
95000	1885.20	1863.47	1846.44	1833.03	1822.45	1814.06
100000	1984.42	1961.54	1943.62	1929.51	1918.37	1909.54
200000	3968.83	3923.09	3887.24	3859.02	3836.73	3819.08
300000	5953.25	5884.63	5830.86	5788.53	5755.09	5728.62
400000	7937.67	7846.18	7774.47	7718.03	7673.46	7638.16
500000	9922.09	9807.72	9718.09	9647.54	9591.83	9547.70

MONTHLY PAYMENT

Necessary to amortize a loan

22 1/2%

TERM / AMOUNT	19 YEARS	20 YEARS	25 YEARS	30 YEARS	35 YEARS	40 YEARS
500	9.51	9.48	9.41	9.39	9.38	9.38
600	11.42	11.38	11.29	11.26	11.25	11.25
700	13.32	13.28	13.18	13.14	13.13	13.13
800	15.22	15.18	15.06	15.02	15.01	15.00
900	17.12	17.07	16.94	16.90	16.88	16.88
1000	19.03	18.97	18.82	18.77	18.76	18.75
2000	38.05	37.94	37.64	37.55	37.52	37.51
3000	57.08	56.91	56.46	56.32	56.27	56.26
4000	76.10	75.88	75.29	75.09	75.03	75.01
5000	95.13	94.85	94.11	93.87	93.79	93.76
6000	114.15	113.82	112.93	112.64	112.55	112.52
7000	133.18	132.79	131.75	131.41	131.30	131.27
8000	152.20	151.76	150.57	150.19	150.06	150.02
9000	171.23	170.73	169.39	168.96	168.82	168.77
10000	190.25	189.70	188.22	187.73	187.58	187.53
11000	209.28	208.67	207.04	206.51	206.33	206.28
12000	228.30	227.64	225.86	225.28	225.09	225.03
13000	247.33	246.61	244.68	244.05	243.85	243.78
14000	266.36	265.58	263.50	262.83	262.61	262.54
15000	285.38	284.55	282.32	281.60	281.37	281.29
16000	304.41	303.52	301.14	300.37	300.12	300.03
17000	323.43	322.49	319.97	319.15	318.88	318.79
18000	342.46	341.46	338.79	337.92	337.64	337.55
19000	361.48	360.42	357.61	356.70	356.40	356.30
20000	380.51	379.39	376.43	375.47	375.15	375.05
21000	399.53	398.36	395.25	394.24	393.91	393.80
22000	418.56	417.33	414.07	413.02	412.67	412.56
23000	437.58	436.30	432.90	431.79	431.43	431.31
24000	456.61	455.27	451.72	450.56	450.18	450.06
25000	475.63	474.24	470.54	469.34	468.94	468.81
30000	570.76	569.09	564.65	563.20	562.73	562.58
35000	665.89	663.94	658.75	657.07	656.52	656.34
40000	761.02	758.79	752.86	750.94	750.31	750.10
45000	856.14	853.64	846.97	844.80	844.10	843.86
50000	951.27	948.49	941.08	938.67	937.88	937.63
55000	1046.40	1043.33	1035.18	1032.54	1031.67	1031.39
60000	1141.52	1138.18	1129.29	1126.40	1125.46	1125.15
65000	1236.65	1233.03	1223.40	1220.27	1219.25	1218.91
70000	1331.78	1327.88	1317.51	1314.14	1313.04	1312.68
75000	1426.90	1422.73	1411.61	1408.00	1406.83	1406.44
80000	1522.03	1517.58	1505.72	1501.87	1500.61	1500.20
85000	1617.16	1612.42	1599.83	1595.74	1594.40	1593.96
90000	1712.28	1707.27	1693.94	1689.61	1688.19	1687.73
95000	1807.41	1802.12	1788.04	1783.47	1781.98	1781.49
100000	1902.54	1896.97	1882.15	1877.34	1875.77	1875.25
200000	3805.07	3793.94	3764.30	3754.68	3751.53	3750.50
300000	5707.61	5690.91	5646.45	5632.02	5627.30	5625.75
400000	7610.15	7587.88	7528.60	7509.36	7503.07	7501.01
500000	9512.69	9484.85	9410.75	9386.70	9378.83	9376.26

23%

MONTHLY PAYMENT

Necessary to amortize a loan

TERM / AMOUNT	1 YEAR	2 YEARS	3 YEARS	4 YEARS	5 YEARS	6 YEARS
500	47.04	26.19	19.35	16.03	14.10	12.86
600	56.45	31.42	23.23	19.23	16.91	15.43
700	65.85	36.66	27.10	22.44	19.73	18.01
800	75.26	41.90	30.97	25.64	22.55	20.58
900	84.67	47.14	34.84	28.85	25.37	23.15
1000	94.08	52.37	38.71	32.05	28.19	25.72
2000	188.15	104.75	77.42	64.10	56.38	51.45
3000	282.23	157.12	116.13	96.15	84.57	77.17
4000	376.30	209.49	154.84	128.21	112.76	102.89
5000	470.38	261.87	193.55	160.26	140.95	128.62
6000	564.46	314.24	232.26	192.31	169.14	154.34
7000	658.53	366.61	270.97	224.36	197.33	180.06
8000	752.61	418.99	309.68	256.41	225.52	205.79
9000	846.69	471.36	348.39	288.46	253.71	231.51
10000	940.76	523.73	387.10	320.51	281.90	257.23
11000	1034.84	576.11	425.81	352.57	310.10	282.95
12000	1128.91	628.48	464.52	384.62	338.29	308.68
13000	1222.99	680.85	503.23	416.67	366.48	334.40
14000	1317.07	733.22	541.94	448.72	394.67	360.12
15000	1411.14	785.60	580.65	480.77	422.86	385.85
16000	1505.22	837.97	619.35	512.82	451.05	411.57
17000	1599.29	890.34	658.06	544.87	479.24	437.29
18000	1693.37	942.72	696.77	576.93	507.43	463.02
19000	1787.45	995.09	735.48	608.98	535.62	488.74
20000	1881.52	1047.46	774.19	641.03	563.81	514.46
21000	1975.60	1099.84	812.90	673.08	592.00	540.19
22000	2069.67	1152.21	851.61	705.13	620.19	565.91
23000	2163.75	1204.58	890.32	737.18	648.38	591.63
24000	2257.83	1256.96	929.03	769.23	676.57	617.35
25000	2351.90	1309.33	967.74	801.29	704.76	643.08
30000	2822.28	1571.20	1161.29	961.54	845.71	771.69
35000	3292.66	1833.06	1354.84	1121.80	986.67	900.31
40000	3763.04	2094.93	1548.39	1282.06	1127.62	1028.92
45000	4233.42	2356.79	1741.93	1442.31	1268.57	1157.54
50000	4703.80	2618.66	1935.48	1602.57	1409.52	1286.15
55000	5174.18	2880.52	2129.03	1762.83	1550.47	1414.77
60000	5644.56	3142.39	2322.58	1923.08	1691.43	1543.38
65000	6114.94	3404.26	2516.13	2083.34	1832.38	1672.00
70000	6585.33	3666.12	2709.68	2243.60	1973.33	1800.62
75000	7055.71	3927.99	2903.22	2403.86	2114.28	1929.23
80000	7526.09	4189.85	3096.77	2564.11	2255.23	2057.85
85000	7996.47	4451.72	3290.32	2724.37	2396.19	2186.46
90000	8466.85	4713.59	3483.87	2884.63	2537.14	2315.08
95000	8937.23	4975.45	3677.42	3044.88	2678.09	2443.69
100000	9407.61	5237.32	3870.96	3205.14	2819.04	2572.31
200000	18815.20	10474.60	7741.93	6410.28	5638.08	5144.61
300000	28222.80	15712.00	11612.90	9615.42	8457.13	7716.92
400000	37630.40	20949.30	15483.90	12820.60	11276.20	10289.20
500000	47038.00	26186.60	19354.80	16025.70	14095.20	12861.50

MONTHLY PAYMENT

Necessary to amortize a loan

23%

TERM / AMOUNT	7 YEARS	8 YEARS	9 YEARS	10 YEARS	11 YEARS	12 YEARS
500	12.02	11.43	11.00	10.68	10.43	10.25
600	14.43	13.72	13.20	12.81	12.52	12.30
700	16.83	16.00	15.40	14.95	14.61	14.35
800	19.24	18.29	17.60	17.08	16.70	16.40
900	21.64	20.58	19.80	19.22	18.78	18.45
1000	24.05	22.86	22.00	21.35	20.87	20.50
2000	48.09	45.72	43.99	42.71	41.74	41.00
3000	72.14	68.58	65.99	64.06	62.61	61.50
4000	96.19	91.44	87.99	85.42	83.48	81.99
5000	120.24	114.31	109.99	106.77	104.35	102.49
6000	144.28	137.17	131.98	128.13	125.22	122.99
7000	168.33	160.03	153.98	149.48	146.09	143.49
8000	192.38	182.89	175.98	170.84	166.96	163.99
9000	216.42	205.75	197.98	192.19	187.82	184.49
10000	240.47	228.61	219.97	213.55	208.69	204.98
11000	264.52	251.47	241.97	234.90	229.56	225.48
12000	288.57	274.33	263.97	256.26	250.43	245.98
13000	312.61	297.20	285.97	277.61	271.30	266.48
14000	336.66	320.06	307.96	298.97	292.17	286.98
15000	360.71	342.92	329.96	320.32	313.04	307.48
16000	384.76	365.78	351.96	341.68	333.91	327.97
17000	408.80	388.64	373.95	363.03	354.78	348.47
18000	432.85	411.50	395.95	384.39	375.65	368.97
19000	456.90	434.36	417.95	405.74	396.52	389.47
20000	480.94	457.22	439.95	427.10	417.39	409.97
21000	504.99	480.08	461.94	448.45	438.26	430.47
22000	529.04	502.95	483.94	469.81	459.13	450.96
23000	553.09	525.81	505.94	491.16	480.00	471.46
24000	577.13	548.67	527.94	512.51	500.87	491.96
25000	601.18	571.53	549.93	533.87	521.73	512.46
30000	721.42	685.84	659.92	640.64	626.08	614.95
35000	841.65	800.14	769.91	747.42	730.43	717.44
40000	961.89	914.45	879.89	854.19	834.78	819.94
45000	1082.12	1028.75	989.88	960.96	939.12	922.43
50000	1202.36	1143.06	1099.87	1067.74	1043.47	1024.92
55000	1322.59	1257.36	1209.85	1174.51	1147.82	1127.41
60000	1442.83	1371.67	1319.84	1281.29	1252.16	1229.90
65000	1563.07	1485.98	1429.82	1388.06	1356.51	1332.39
70000	1683.30	1600.28	1539.81	1494.83	1460.86	1434.89
75000	1803.54	1714.59	1649.80	1601.61	1565.20	1537.38
80000	1923.77	1828.89	1759.78	1708.38	1669.55	1639.87
85000	2044.01	1943.20	1869.77	1815.15	1773.90	1742.36
90000	2164.24	2057.50	1979.76	1921.93	1878.24	1844.85
95000	2284.48	2171.81	2089.74	2028.70	1982.59	1947.34
100000	2404.72	2286.12	2199.73	2135.48	2086.94	2049.84
200000	4809.43	4572.23	4399.46	4270.95	4173.87	4099.67
300000	7214.15	6858.35	6599.19	6406.43	6260.81	6149.51
400000	9618.86	9144.47	8798.92	8541.90	8347.75	8199.35
500000	12023.60	11430.60	10998.70	10677.40	10434.70	10249.20

23%

MONTHLY PAYMENT

Necessary to amortize a loan

TERM / AMOUNT	13 YEARS	14 YEARS	15 YEARS	16 YEARS	17 YEARS	18 YEARS
500	10.11	10.00	9.91	9.84	9.79	9.74
600	12.13	11.99	11.89	11.81	11.74	11.69
700	14.15	13.99	13.87	13.78	13.70	13.64
800	16.17	15.99	15.85	15.74	15.66	15.59
900	18.19	17.99	17.84	17.71	17.62	17.54
1000	20.21	19.99	19.82	19.68	19.57	19.49
2000	40.42	39.98	39.63	39.36	39.15	38.98
3000	60.64	59.97	59.45	59.04	58.72	58.47
4000	80.85	79.96	79.27	78.72	78.29	77.96
5000	101.06	99.95	99.08	98.40	97.87	97.45
6000	121.27	119.94	118.90	118.08	117.44	116.94
7000	141.49	139.93	138.72	137.77	137.02	136.43
8000	161.70	159.92	158.53	157.45	156.59	155.92
9000	181.91	179.91	178.35	177.13	176.16	175.41
10000	202.12	199.90	198.17	196.81	195.74	194.09
11000	222.34	219.89	217.98	216.49	215.31	214.38
12000	242.55	239.88	237.80	236.17	234.89	233.87
13000	262.76	259.87	257.62	255.85	254.46	253.36
14000	282.97	279.86	277.43	275.53	274.03	272.85
15000	303.18	299.85	297.25	295.21	293.61	292.34
16000	323.40	319.84	317.07	314.89	313.18	311.83
17000	343.61	339.83	336.88	334.57	332.75	331.32
18000	363.82	359.82	356.70	354.25	352.33	350.81
19000	384.03	379.81	376.52	373.93	371.90	370.30
20000	404.25	399.80	396.33	393.61	391.47	389.79
21000	424.46	419.79	416.15	413.29	411.05	409.28
22000	444.67	439.78	435.97	432.97	430.62	428.77
23000	464.88	459.77	455.78	452.66	450.20	448.26
24000	485.09	479.76	475.60	472.34	469.77	467.75
25000	505.31	499.75	495.42	492.02	489.34	487.24
30000	606.37	599.70	594.50	590.42	587.21	584.68
35000	707.43	699.65	693.58	688.82	685.08	682.13
40000	808.49	799.60	792.67	787.23	782.95	779.58
45000	909.55	899.55	891.75	885.63	880.82	877.02
50000	1010.61	999.50	990.83	984.03	978.69	974.47
55000	1111.67	1099.45	1089.91	1082.44	1076.55	1071.92
60000	1212.73	1199.40	1189.00	1180.84	1174.42	1169.36
65000	1313.80	1299.35	1288.08	1279.24	1272.29	1266.81
70000	1414.86	1399.31	1387.16	1377.65	1370.16	1364.26
75000	1515.92	1499.26	1486.25	1476.05	1468.03	1461.70
80000	1616.98	1599.21	1585.33	1574.45	1565.90	1559.15
85000	1718.04	1699.16	1684.41	1672.86	1663.77	1656.60
90000	1819.10	1799.11	1783.50	1771.26	1761.63	1754.04
95000	1920.16	1899.06	1882.58	1869.66	1859.50	1851.49
100000	2021.22	1999.01	1981.66	1968.07	1957.37	1948.94
200000	4042.45	3998.01	3963.33	3936.13	3914.74	3897.88
300000	6063.67	5997.02	5944.99	5904.20	5872.11	5846.82
400000	8084.90	7996.03	7926.65	7872.26	7829.49	7795.76
500000	10106.10	9995.04	9908.31	9840.33	9786.86	9744.69

MONTHLY PAYMENT

Necessary to amortize a loan

23%

TERM / AMOUNT	19 YEARS	20 YEARS	25 YEARS	30 YEARS	35 YEARS	40 YEARS
500	9.71	9.69	9.62	9.59	9.59	9.58
600	11.65	11.62	11.54	11.51	11.50	11.50
700	13.60	13.56	13.46	13.43	13.42	13.42
800	15.54	15.50	15.39	15.35	15.34	15.34
900	17.48	17.43	17.31	17.27	17.26	17.25
1000	19.42	19.37	19.23	19.19	19.17	19.17
2000	38.85	38.74	38.46	38.37	38.35	38.34
3000	58.27	58.11	57.69	57.56	57.52	57.51
4000	77.69	77.48	76.93	76.75	76.69	76.68
5000	97.11	96.85	96.16	95.94	95.87	95.84
6000	116.54	116.22	115.39	115.12	115.04	115.01
7000	135.96	135.59	134.62	134.31	134.21	134.18
8000	155.38	154.96	153.85	153.50	153.39	153.35
9000	174.81	174.33	173.08	172.69	172.56	172.52
10000	194.23	193.70	192.31	191.87	191.73	191.69
11000	213.65	213.07	211.54	211.06	210.91	210.86
12000	233.07	232.44	230.78	230.25	230.08	230.03
13000	252.50	251.81	250.01	249.44	249.25	249.19
14000	271.92	271.18	269.24	268.62	268.43	268.36
15000	291.34	290.55	288.47	287.81	287.60	287.53
16000	310.76	309.92	307.70	307.00	306.77	306.70
17000	330.19	329.29	326.93	326.18	325.95	325.87
18000	349.61	348.66	346.16	345.37	345.12	345.04
19000	369.03	368.03	365.40	364.56	364.29	364.21
20000	388.46	387.40	384.63	383.75	383.47	383.38
21000	407.88	406.77	403.86	402.93	402.64	402.54
22000	427.30	426.14	423.09	422.12	421.81	421.71
23000	446.72	445.51	442.32	441.31	440.99	440.88
24000	466.15	464.88	461.55	460.50	460.16	460.05
25000	485.57	484.25	480.78	479.68	479.33	479.22
30000	582.68	581.10	576.94	575.62	575.20	575.06
35000	679.80	677.95	673.10	671.56	671.06	670.91
40000	776.91	774.80	769.25	767.49	766.93	766.75
45000	874.02	871.65	865.41	863.43	862.80	862.60
50000	971.14	968.50	961.57	959.37	958.66	958.44
55000	1068.25	1065.35	1057.72	1055.30	1054.53	1054.28
60000	1165.37	1162.20	1153.88	1151.24	1150.40	1150.13
65000	1262.48	1259.05	1250.03	1247.18	1246.26	1245.97
70000	1359.59	1355.90	1346.19	1343.11	1342.13	1341.81
75000	1456.71	1452.75	1442.35	1439.05	1438.00	1437.66
80000	1553.82	1549.60	1538.50	1534.98	1533.86	1533.50
85000	1650.93	1646.45	1634.66	1630.92	1629.73	1629.35
90000	1748.05	1743.30	1730.82	1726.86	1725.59	1725.19
95000	1845.16	1840.15	1826.97	1822.79	1821.46	1821.03
100000	1942.28	1937.00	1923.13	1918.73	1917.33	1916.88
200000	3884.55	3874.01	3846.26	3837.46	3834.65	3833.76
300000	5826.83	5811.01	5769.39	5756.19	5751.98	5750.63
400000	7769.10	7748.01	7692.52	7674.92	7669.31	7667.51
500000	9711.38	9685.02	9615.65	9593.65	9586.63	9584.39

23 1/2%

MONTHLY PAYMENT
Necessary to amortize a loan

TERM / AMOUNT	1 YEAR	2 YEARS	3 YEARS	4 YEARS	5 YEARS	6 YEARS
500	47.16	26.31	19.49	16.16	14.24	13.01
600	56.59	31.57	23.38	19.40	17.09	15.61
700	66.02	36.84	27.28	22.63	19.93	18.22
800	75.45	42.10	31.18	25.86	22.78	20.82
900	84.89	47.36	35.07	29.09	25.63	23.42
1000	94.32	52.62	38.97	32.33	28.48	26.02
2000	188.64	105.24	77.94	64.65	56.96	52.05
3000	282.95	157.87	116.91	96.98	85.44	78.07
4000	377.27	210.49	155.88	129.30	113.91	104.10
5000	471.59	263.11	194.85	161.63	142.39	130.12
6000	565.91	315.73	233.83	193.96	170.87	156.15
7000	660.22	368.35	272.80	226.28	199.35	182.17
8000	754.54	420.98	311.77	258.61	227.83	208.19
9000	848.86	473.60	350.74	290.93	256.31	234.22
10000	943.18	526.22	389.71	323.26	284.79	260.24
11000	1037.49	578.84	428.68	355.59	313.26	286.27
12000	1131.81	631.46	467.65	387.91	341.74	312.29
13000	1226.13	684.08	506.62	420.24	370.22	338.31
14000	1320.45	736.71	545.59	452.56	398.70	364.34
15000	1414.77	789.33	584.56	484.89	427.18	390.36
16000	1509.08	841.95	623.53	517.22	455.66	416.39
17000	1603.40	894.57	662.50	549.54	484.13	442.41
18000	1697.72	947.19	701.47	581.87	512.61	468.43
19000	1792.04	999.82	740.45	614.19	541.09	494.46
20000	1886.35	1052.44	779.42	646.52	569.57	520.48
21000	1980.67	1105.06	818.39	678.85	598.05	546.51
22000	2074.99	1157.68	857.36	711.17	626.53	572.53
23000	2169.31	1210.30	896.33	743.50	655.01	598.56
24000	2263.62	1262.92	935.30	775.82	683.48	624.58
25000	2357.94	1315.55	974.27	808.15	711.96	650.60
30000	2829.53	1578.65	1169.12	969.78	854.35	780.72
35000	3301.12	1841.76	1363.98	1131.41	996.75	910.84
40000	3772.71	2104.87	1558.83	1293.04	1139.14	1040.96
45000	4244.30	2367.98	1753.69	1454.67	1281.53	1171.09
50000	4715.89	2631.09	1948.54	1616.30	1423.92	1301.21
55000	5187.47	2894.20	2143.39	1777.93	1566.32	1431.33
60000	5659.06	3157.31	2338.25	1939.56	1708.71	1561.45
65000	6130.65	3420.42	2533.10	2101.19	1851.10	1691.57
70000	6602.24	3683.53	2727.95	2262.82	1993.49	1821.69
75000	7073.83	3946.64	2922.81	2424.45	2135.89	1951.81
80000	7545.42	4209.75	3117.66	2586.08	2278.28	2081.93
85000	8017.00	4472.86	3312.52	2747.71	2420.67	2212.05
90000	8488.59	4735.96	3507.37	2909.34	2563.06	2342.17
95000	8960.18	4999.07	3702.22	3070.97	2705.45	2472.29
100000	9431.77	5262.18	3897.08	3232.60	2847.85	2602.41
200000	18863.50	10524.40	7794.16	6465.20	5695.69	5204.82
300000	28295.30	15786.50	11691.20	9697.80	8543.54	7807.24
400000	37727.10	21048.70	15588.30	12930.40	11391.40	10409.60
500000	47158.90	26310.90	19485.40	16163.00	14239.20	13012.10

MONTHLY PAYMENT

Necessary to amortize a loan

23 1/2%

TERM / AMOUNT	7 YEARS	8 YEARS	9 YEARS	10 YEARS	11 YEARS	12 YEARS
500	12.18	11.59	11.17	10.85	10.61	10.43
600	14.62	13.91	13.40	13.02	12.73	12.52
700	17.05	16.23	15.63	15.19	14.86	14.60
800	19.49	18.55	17.87	17.36	16.98	16.69
900	21.92	20.87	20.10	19.53	19.10	18.78
1000	24.36	23.19	22.33	21.70	21.22	20.86
2000	48.72	46.37	44.67	43.40	42.45	41.72
3000	73.08	69.56	67.00	65.10	63.67	62.58
4000	97.44	92.74	89.33	86.80	84.90	83.44
5000	121.80	115.93	111.67	108.50	106.12	104.31
6000	146.16	139.12	134.00	130.20	127.34	125.17
7000	170.52	162.30	156.33	151.90	148.57	146.03
8000	194.89	185.49	178.67	173.60	169.79	166.89
9000	219.25	208.68	201.00	195.30	191.02	187.75
10000	243.61	231.86	223.33	217.00	212.24	208.61
11000	267.97	255.05	245.66	238.71	233.46	229.47
12000	292.33	278.23	268.00	260.41	254.69	250.33
13000	316.69	301.42	290.33	282.11	275.91	271.20
14000	341.05	324.61	312.66	303.81	297.14	292.06
15000	365.41	347.79	335.00	325.51	318.36	312.92
16000	389.77	370.98	357.33	347.21	339.58	333.78
17000	414.13	394.17	379.66	368.91	360.81	354.64
18000	438.49	417.35	402.00	390.61	382.03	375.50
19000	462.85	440.54	424.33	412.31	403.26	396.36
20000	487.21	463.72	446.66	434.01	424.48	417.22
21000	511.57	486.91	469.00	455.71	445.71	438.08
22000	535.93	510.10	491.33	477.41	466.93	458.95
23000	560.29	533.28	513.66	499.11	488.15	479.81
24000	584.65	556.47	535.99	520.81	509.38	500.67
25000	609.02	579.66	558.33	542.51	530.60	521.53
30000	730.82	695.59	669.99	651.01	636.72	625.83
35000	852.62	811.52	781.66	759.52	742.84	730.14
40000	974.42	927.45	893.32	868.02	848.96	834.45
45000	1096.23	1043.38	1004.99	976.52	955.08	938.75
50000	1218.03	1159.31	1116.65	1085.02	1061.20	1043.06
55000	1339.83	1275.24	1228.32	1193.52	1167.32	1147.36
60000	1461.64	1391.17	1339.99	1302.03	1273.44	1251.67
65000	1583.44	1507.10	1451.65	1410.53	1379.56	1355.97
70000	1705.24	1623.03	1563.32	1519.03	1485.68	1460.28
75000	1827.04	1738.96	1674.98	1627.53	1591.80	1564.59
80000	1948.85	1854.89	1786.65	1736.03	1697.92	1668.89
85000	2070.65	1970.83	1898.31	1844.54	1804.04	1773.20
90000	2192.45	2086.76	2009.98	1953.04	1910.16	1877.50
95000	2314.26	2202.69	2121.64	2061.54	2016.28	1981.81
100000	2436.06	2318.62	2233.31	2170.04	2122.40	2086.11
200000	4872.12	4637.24	4466.62	4340.09	4244.80	4172.23
300000	7308.18	6955.86	6699.92	6510.13	6367.21	6258.34
400000	9744.23	9274.47	8933.23	8680.17	8489.61	8344.45
500000	12180.30	11593.10	11166.50	10850.20	10612.00	10430.60

23 1/2%

MONTHLY PAYMENT
Necessary to amortize a loan

TERM / AMOUNT	13 YEARS	14 YEARS	15 YEARS	16 YEARS	17 YEARS	18 YEARS
500	10.29	10.18	10.10	10.03	9.98	9.94
600	12.35	12.22	12.12	12.04	11.98	11.93
700	14.41	14.26	14.14	14.05	13.98	13.92
800	16.47	16.29	16.16	16.05	15.97	15.91
900	18.52	18.33	18.18	18.06	17.97	17.90
1000	20.58	20.37	20.20	20.07	19.97	19.88
2000	41.16	40.73	40.40	40.14	39.93	39.77
3000	61.75	61.10	60.60	60.20	59.90	59.65
4000	82.33	81.47	80.80	80.27	79.86	79.54
5000	102.91	101.83	100.99	100.34	99.83	99.42
6000	123.49	122.20	121.19	120.41	119.79	119.31
7000	144.08	142.57	141.39	140.48	139.76	139.19
8000	164.66	162.93	161.59	160.54	159.72	159.08
9000	185.24	183.30	181.79	180.61	179.69	178.96
10000	205.82	203.67	201.99	200.68	199.65	198.85
11000	226.41	224.03	222.19	220.75	219.62	218.73
12000	246.99	244.40	242.39	240.82	239.58	238.62
13000	267.57	264.77	262.59	260.88	259.55	258.50
14000	288.15	285.13	282.78	280.95	279.51	278.39
15000	308.73	305.50	302.98	301.02	299.48	298.27
16000	329.32	325.87	323.18	321.09	319.45	318.16
17000	349.90	346.23	343.38	341.15	339.41	338.04
18000	370.48	366.60	363.58	361.22	359.38	357.93
19000	391.06	386.97	383.78	381.29	379.34	377.81
20000	411.65	407.33	403.98	401.36	399.31	397.70
21000	432.23	427.70	424.18	421.43	419.27	417.58
22000	452.81	448.07	444.38	441.49	439.24	437.47
23000	473.39	468.43	464.57	461.56	459.20	457.35
24000	493.98	488.80	484.77	481.63	479.17	477.24
25000	514.16	509.16	504.97	501.70	499.13	497.12
30000	617.47	611.00	605.97	602.04	598.96	596.54
35000	720.38	712.83	706.96	702.38	698.79	695.97
40000	823.29	814.66	807.95	802.72	798.61	795.39
45000	926.20	916.50	908.95	903.06	898.44	894.82
50000	1029.11	1018.33	1009.94	1003.39	998.27	994.24
55000	1132.03	1120.16	1110.94	1103.73	1098.09	1093.66
60000	1234.94	1221.99	1211.93	1204.07	1197.92	1193.09
65000	1337.85	1323.83	1312.92	1304.41	1297.75	1292.51
70000	1440.76	1425.66	1413.92	1404.75	1397.57	1391.93
75000	1543.67	1527.49	1514.91	1505.09	1497.40	1491.36
80000	1646.58	1629.33	1615.91	1605.43	1597.22	1590.78
85000	1749.49	1731.16	1716.90	1705.77	1697.05	1690.21
90000	1852.41	1832.99	1817.90	1806.11	1796.88	1789.63
95000	1955.32	1934.83	1918.89	1906.45	1896.70	1889.05
100000	2058.23	2036.66	2019.88	2006.79	1996.53	1988.48
200000	4116.46	4073.32	4039.77	4013.58	3993.06	3976.96
300000	6174.69	6109.97	6059.65	6020.36	5989.59	5965.43
400000	8232.92	8146.63	8079.54	8027.15	7986.12	7953.91
500000	10291.10	10183.30	10099.40	10033.90	9982.66	9942.39

MONTHLY PAYMENT

Necessary to amortize a loan

23 1/2%

TERM AMOUNT	19 YEARS	20 YEARS	25 YEARS	30 YEARS	35 YEARS	40 YEARS
500	9.91	9.89	9.82	9.80	9.79	9.79
600	11.89	11.86	11.79	11.76	11.75	11.75
700	13.88	13.84	13.75	13.72	13.71	13.71
800	15.86	15.82	15.71	15.68	15.67	15.67
900	17.84	17.79	17.68	17.64	17.63	17.63
1000	19.82	19.77	19.64	19.60	19.59	19.59
2000	39.64	39.54	39.28	39.20	39.18	39.17
3000	59.46	59.31	58.93	58.80	58.77	58.76
4000	79.29	79.09	78.57	78.41	78.36	78.34
5000	99.11	98.86	98.21	98.01	97.95	97.93
6000	118.93	118.63	117.85	117.61	117.53	117.51
7000	138.75	138.40	137.49	137.21	137.12	137.10
8000	158.57	158.17	157.13	156.81	156.71	156.68
9000	178.39	177.94	176.78	176.41	176.30	176.27
10000	198.21	197.72	196.42	196.02	195.89	195.85
11000	218.04	217.49	216.06	215.62	215.48	215.44
12000	237.86	237.26	235.70	235.22	235.07	235.02
13000	257.68	257.03	255.34	254.82	254.66	254.61
14000	277.50	276.80	274.98	274.42	274.25	274.19
15000	297.32	296.57	294.63	294.02	293.84	293.78
16000	317.14	316.34	314.27	313.63	313.42	313.36
17000	336.96	336.12	333.91	333.23	333.01	332.95
18000	356.79	355.89	353.55	352.83	352.60	352.53
19000	376.61	375.66	373.19	372.43	372.19	372.12
20000	396.43	395.43	392.84	392.03	391.78	391.70
21000	416.25	415.20	412.48	411.63	411.37	411.29
22000	436.07	434.97	432.12	431.23	430.96	430.87
23000	455.89	454.75	451.76	450.84	450.55	450.46
24000	475.71	474.52	471.40	470.44	470.14	470.04
25000	495.54	494.29	491.04	490.04	489.73	489.63
30000	594.64	593.15	589.25	588.05	587.67	587.55
35000	693.75	692.00	687.46	686.05	685.62	685.48
40000	792.86	790.86	785.67	784.06	783.56	783.40
45000	891.96	889.72	883.88	882.07	881.51	881.33
50000	991.07	988.58	982.09	980.08	979.45	979.26
55000	1090.18	1087.43	1080.29	1078.08	1077.40	1077.18
60000	1189.29	1186.29	1178.50	1176.09	1175.34	1175.11
65000	1288.39	1285.15	1276.71	1274.10	1273.29	1273.03
70000	1387.50	1384.01	1374.92	1372.11	1371.23	1370.96
75000	1486.61	1482.86	1473.13	1470.12	1469.18	1468.88
80000	1585.71	1581.72	1571.34	1568.12	1567.12	1566.81
85000	1684.82	1680.58	1669.55	1666.13	1665.07	1664.73
90000	1783.93	1779.44	1767.76	1764.14	1763.01	1762.66
95000	1883.04	1878.29	1865.96	1862.15	1860.96	1860.59
100000	1982.14	1977.15	1964.17	1960.15	1958.90	1958.51
200000	3964.29	3954.30	3928.35	3920.31	3917.80	3917.02
300000	5946.43	5931.46	5892.52	5880.46	5876.70	5875.53
400000	7928.57	7908.61	7856.69	7840.61	7835.61	7834.04
500000	9910.71	9885.76	9820.86	9800.77	9794.51	9792.55

24%

MONTHLY PAYMENT

Necessary to amortize a loan

TERM / AMOUNT	1 YEAR	2 YEARS	3 YEARS	4 YEARS	5 YEARS	6 YEARS
500	47.28	26.44	19.62	16.30	14.38	13.16
600	56.74	31.72	23.54	19.56	17.26	15.80
700	66.19	37.01	27.46	22.82	20.14	18.43
800	75.65	42.30	31.39	26.08	23.01	21.06
900	85.10	47.58	35.31	29.34	25.89	23.69
1000	94.56	52.87	39.23	32.60	28.77	26.33
2000	189.12	105.74	78.47	65.20	57.54	52.65
3000	283.68	158.61	117.70	97.81	86.30	78.98
4000	378.24	211.49	156.93	130.41	115.07	105.31
5000	472.80	264.36	196.17	163.01	143.84	131.63
6000	567.36	317.23	235.40	195.61	172.61	157.96
7000	661.92	370.10	274.63	228.21	201.38	184.29
8000	756.48	422.97	313.86	260.82	230.14	210.62
9000	851.04	475.84	353.10	293.42	258.91	236.94
10000	945.60	528.71	392.33	326.02	287.68	263.27
11000	1040.16	581.58	431.56	358.62	316.45	289.60
12000	1134.72	634.45	470.80	391.22	345.22	315.92
13000	1229.28	687.33	510.03	423.83	373.98	342.25
14000	1323.84	740.20	549.26	456.43	402.75	368.58
15000	1418.40	793.07	588.49	489.03	431.51	394.90
16000	1512.96	845.94	627.73	521.63	460.29	421.23
17000	1607.52	898.81	666.96	554.23	489.06	447.56
18000	1702.08	951.68	706.19	586.83	517.82	473.88
19000	1796.64	1004.55	745.43	619.44	546.59	500.21
20000	1891.20	1057.42	784.66	652.04	575.36	526.54
21000	1985.76	1110.30	823.89	684.64	604.13	552.86
22000	2080.32	1163.17	863.12	717.24	632.90	579.19
23000	2174.88	1216.04	902.36	749.84	661.66	605.52
24000	2269.44	1268.91	941.59	782.45	690.43	631.85
25000	2364.00	1321.78	980.82	815.05	719.20	658.17
30000	2836.79	1586.14	1176.99	978.06	863.04	789.81
35000	3309.59	1850.49	1373.15	1141.07	1006.88	921.44
40000	3782.39	2114.85	1569.32	1304.08	1150.72	1053.07
45000	4255.19	2379.20	1765.48	1467.09	1294.56	1184.71
50000	4727.99	2643.56	1961.65	1630.09	1438.40	1316.34
55000	5200.79	2907.92	2157.81	1793.10	1582.24	1447.98
60000	5673.59	3172.27	2353.98	1956.11	1726.08	1579.61
65000	6146.39	3436.63	2550.14	2119.12	1869.92	1711.25
70000	6619.19	3700.98	2746.30	2282.13	2013.76	1842.88
75000	7091.99	3965.34	2942.47	2445.14	2157.60	1974.51
80000	7564.79	4229.70	3138.63	2608.15	2301.44	2106.15
85000	8037.59	4494.05	3334.80	2771.16	2445.28	2237.78
90000	8510.38	4758.41	3530.96	2934.17	2589.12	2369.42
95000	8983.18	5022.76	3727.13	3097.18	2732.96	2501.05
100000	9455.98	5287.12	3923.29	3260.19	2876.80	2632.69
200000	18912.00	10574.20	7846.59	6520.38	5753.60	5265.37
300000	28367.90	15861.40	11769.90	9780.57	8630.40	7898.06
400000	37823.90	21148.50	15693.20	13040.80	11507.20	10530.70
500000	47279.90	26435.60	19616.50	16300.90	14384.00	13163.40

MONTHLY PAYMENT

Necessary to amortize a loan

24%

TERM / AMOUNT	7 YEARS	8 YEARS	9 YEARS	10 YEARS	11 YEARS	12 YEARS
500	12.34	11.76	11.34	11.02	10.79	10.61
600	14.81	14.11	13.60	13.23	12.95	12.74
700	17.27	16.46	15.87	15.43	15.11	14.86
800	19.74	18.81	18.14	17.64	17.26	16.98
900	22.21	21.16	20.40	19.84	19.42	19.10
1000	24.68	23.51	22.67	22.05	21.58	21.23
2000	49.35	47.03	45.34	44.10	43.16	42.45
3000	74.03	70.54	68.01	66.14	64.74	63.68
4000	98.70	94.05	90.68	88.19	86.32	84.90
5000	123.38	117.57	113.35	110.24	107.90	106.13
6000	148.06	141.08	136.03	132.29	129.48	127.36
7000	172.73	164.59	158.70	154.34	151.07	148.58
8000	197.41	188.11	181.37	176.39	172.65	169.81
9000	222.08	211.62	204.04	198.43	194.23	191.03
10000	246.76	235.13	226.71	220.48	215.81	212.26
11000	271.43	258.65	249.38	242.53	237.39	233.49
12000	296.11	282.16	272.05	264.58	258.97	254.71
13000	320.79	305.67	294.72	286.63	280.55	275.94
14000	345.46	329.18	317.39	308.67	302.13	297.16
15000	370.14	352.70	340.06	330.72	323.71	318.39
16000	394.81	376.21	362.73	352.77	345.29	339.61
17000	419.49	399.72	385.41	374.82	366.87	360.84
18000	444.17	423.24	408.08	396.87	388.45	382.07
19000	468.84	446.75	430.75	418.91	410.03	403.29
20000	493.52	470.26	453.42	440.96	431.61	424.52
21000	518.19	493.78	476.09	463.01	453.19	445.74
22000	542.87	517.29	498.76	485.06	474.78	466.97
23000	567.54	540.80	521.43	507.11	496.36	488.20
24000	592.22	564.32	544.10	529.16	517.94	509.42
25000	616.90	587.83	566.77	551.20	539.52	530.65
30000	740.28	705.39	680.13	661.44	647.42	636.78
35000	863.65	822.96	793.48	771.68	755.32	742.91
40000	987.03	940.53	906.84	881.92	863.23	849.04
45000	1110.41	1058.09	1020.19	992.17	971.13	955.16
50000	1233.79	1175.66	1133.54	1102.41	1079.03	1061.29
55000	1357.17	1293.22	1246.90	1212.65	1186.94	1167.42
60000	1480.55	1410.79	1360.25	1322.89	1294.84	1273.55
65000	1603.93	1528.35	1473.61	1433.13	1402.74	1379.68
70000	1727.31	1645.92	1586.96	1543.37	1510.65	1485.81
75000	1850.69	1763.49	1700.31	1653.61	1618.55	1591.94
80000	1974.07	1881.05	1813.67	1763.85	1726.45	1698.07
85000	2097.45	1998.62	1927.02	1874.09	1834.36	1804.20
90000	2220.83	2116.18	2040.38	1984.33	1942.26	1910.33
95000	2344.20	2233.75	2153.73	2094.57	2050.17	2016.46
100000	2467.58	2351.31	2267.09	2204.81	2158.07	2122.59
200000	4935.17	4702.63	4534.17	4409.62	4316.14	4245.17
300000	7402.75	7053.94	6801.26	6614.43	6474.21	6367.76
400000	9870.33	9405.26	9068.35	8819.25	8632.27	8490.35
500000	12337.90	11756.60	11335.40	11024.10	10790.30	10612.90

24%

MONTHLY PAYMENT

Necessary to amortize a loan

TERM / AMOUNT	13 YEARS	14 YEARS	15 YEARS	16 YEARS	17 YEARS	18 YEARS
500	10.48	10.37	10.29	10.23	10.18	10.14
600	12.57	12.45	12.35	12.27	12.22	12.17
700	14.67	14.52	14.41	14.32	14.25	14.20
800	16.76	16.60	16.47	16.37	16.29	16.23
900	18.86	18.67	18.52	18.41	18.32	18.25
1000	20.95	20.74	20.58	20.46	20.36	20.28
2000	41.91	41.49	41.17	40.91	40.72	40.56
3000	62.86	62.23	61.75	61.37	61.08	60.84
4000	83.82	82.98	82.33	81.83	81.43	81.13
5000	104.77	103.72	102.91	102.28	101.79	101.41
6000	125.73	124.47	123.50	122.74	122.15	121.69
7000	146.68	145.21	144.08	143.20	142.51	141.97
8000	167.63	165.96	164.66	163.65	162.87	162.25
9000	188.59	186.70	185.25	184.11	183.23	182.53
10000	209.54	207.45	205.83	204.57	203.58	202.82
11000	230.50	228.19	226.41	225.02	223.94	223.10
12000	251.45	248.94	246.99	245.48	244.30	243.38
13000	272.41	269.68	267.58	265.94	264.66	263.66
14000	293.36	290.43	288.16	286.39	285.02	283.94
15000	314.31	311.17	308.74	306.85	305.38	304.22
16000	335.27	331.92	329.32	327.31	325.73	324.50
17000	356.22	352.66	349.91	347.76	346.09	344.79
18000	377.18	373.41	370.49	368.22	366.45	365.07
19000	398.13	394.15	391.07	388.68	386.81	385.35
20000	419.08	414.90	411.66	409.13	407.17	405.63
21000	440.04	435.64	432.24	429.59	427.53	425.91
22000	460.99	456.39	452.82	450.05	447.88	446.19
23000	481.95	477.13	473.40	470.50	468.24	466.47
24000	502.90	497.88	493.99	490.96	488.60	486.76
25000	523.86	518.62	514.57	511.42	508.96	507.04
30000	628.63	622.35	617.48	613.70	610.75	608.45
35000	733.40	726.07	720.40	715.98	712.54	709.85
40000	838.17	829.80	823.31	818.27	814.33	811.26
45000	942.94	933.52	926.22	920.55	916.13	912.67
50000	1047.71	1037.24	1029.14	1022.83	1017.92	1014.07
55000	1152.48	1140.97	1132.05	1125.12	1119.71	1115.48
60000	1257.25	1244.69	1234.96	1227.40	1221.50	1216.89
65000	1362.02	1348.42	1337.88	1329.68	1323.29	1318.30
70000	1466.80	1452.14	1440.79	1431.97	1425.08	1419.70
75000	1571.57	1555.87	1543.71	1534.25	1526.88	1521.11
80000	1676.34	1659.59	1646.62	1636.53	1628.67	1622.52
85000	1781.11	1763.31	1749.53	1738.82	1730.46	1723.93
90000	1885.88	1867.04	1852.45	1841.10	1832.25	1825.33
95000	1990.65	1970.76	1955.36	1943.38	1934.04	1926.74
100000	2095.42	2074.49	2058.27	2045.67	2035.84	2028.15
200000	4190.84	4148.98	4116.55	4091.33	4071.67	4056.30
300000	6286.27	6223.46	6174.82	6137.00	6107.51	6084.45
400000	8381.69	8297.95	8233.10	8182.67	8143.34	8112.60
500000	10477.10	10372.40	10291.40	10228.30	10179.20	10140.70

MONTHLY PAYMENT

Necessary to amortize a loan

24%

TERM / AMOUNT	19 YEARS	20 YEARS	25 YEARS	30 YEARS	35 YEARS	40 YEARS
500	10.11	10.09	10.03	10.01	10.00	10.00
600	12.13	12.10	12.03	12.01	12.00	12.00
700	14.15	14.12	14.04	14.01	14.00	14.00
800	16.18	16.14	16.04	16.01	16.00	16.00
900	18.20	18.16	18.05	18.01	18.00	18.00
1000	20.22	20.17	20.05	20.02	20.00	20.00
2000	40.44	40.35	40.11	40.03	40.01	40.00
3000	60.66	60.52	60.16	60.05	60.01	60.00
4000	80.89	80.70	80.21	80.06	80.02	80.01
5000	101.11	100.87	100.26	100.08	100.02	100.01
6000	121.33	121.05	120.32	120.10	120.03	120.01
7000	141.55	141.22	140.37	140.11	140.03	140.01
8000	161.77	161.39	160.42	160.13	160.04	160.01
9000	181.99	181.57	180.48	180.14	180.04	180.01
10000	202.21	201.74	200.53	200.16	200.05	200.02
11000	222.43	221.92	220.58	220.18	220.05	220.02
12000	242.66	242.09	240.63	240.19	240.06	240.02
13000	262.88	262.26	260.69	260.21	260.06	260.02
14000	283.10	282.44	280.74	280.23	280.07	280.02
15000	303.32	302.61	300.79	300.24	300.07	300.02
16000	323.54	322.79	320.84	320.26	320.08	320.02
17000	343.76	342.96	340.90	340.27	340.08	340.03
18000	363.98	363.13	360.95	360.29	360.09	360.03
19000	384.21	383.31	381.00	380.31	380.09	380.03
20000	404.43	403.48	401.06	400.32	400.10	400.03
21000	424.65	423.66	421.11	420.34	420.10	420.03
22000	444.87	443.83	441.16	440.35	440.11	440.03
23000	465.09	464.00	461.21	460.37	460.11	460.03
24000	485.31	484.18	481.27	480.39	480.12	480.04
25000	505.53	504.35	501.32	500.40	500.12	500.04
30000	606.64	605.22	601.58	600.48	600.15	600.05
35000	707.75	706.09	701.85	700.56	700.17	700.05
40000	808.85	806.96	802.11	800.64	800.20	800.06
45000	909.96	907.83	902.37	900.72	900.22	900.07
50000	1011.06	1008.70	1002.64	1000.80	1000.24	1000.07
55000	1112.17	1109.57	1102.90	1100.88	1100.27	1100.08
60000	1213.28	1210.45	1203.16	1200.96	1200.29	1200.09
65000	1314.38	1311.32	1303.43	1301.04	1300.32	1300.10
70000	1415.49	1412.19	1403.69	1401.12	1400.34	1400.10
75000	1516.60	1513.06	1503.96	1501.20	1500.37	1500.11
80000	1617.70	1613.93	1604.22	1601.28	1600.39	1600.12
85000	1718.81	1714.80	1704.48	1701.36	1700.42	1700.13
90000	1819.92	1815.67	1804.75	1801.44	1800.44	1800.13
95000	1921.02	1916.54	1905.01	1901.52	1900.46	1900.14
100000	2022.13	2017.41	2005.27	2001.60	2000.49	2000.15
200000	4044.26	4034.82	4010.55	4003.21	4000.98	4000.30
300000	6066.39	6052.22	6015.82	6004.81	6001.47	6000.45
400000	8088.52	8069.63	8021.09	8006.42	8001.95	8000.60
500000	10110.60	10087.00	10026.40	10008.00	10002.40	10000.70

24 1/2%

MONTHLY PAYMENT

Necessary to amortize a loan

TERM / AMOUNT	1 YEAR	2 YEARS	3 YEARS	4 YEARS	5 YEARS	6 YEARS
500	47.40	26.56	19.75	16.44	14.53	13.32
600	56.88	31.87	23.70	19.73	17.44	15.98
700	66.36	37.18	27.65	23.02	20.34	18.64
800	75.84	42.50	31.60	26.30	23.25	21.31
900	85.32	47.81	35.55	29.59	26.15	23.97
1000	94.80	53.12	39.50	32.88	29.06	26.63
2000	189.60	106.24	78.99	65.76	58.12	53.26
3000	284.41	159.36	118.49	98.64	87.18	79.89
4000	379.21	212.48	157.98	131.52	116.24	106.53
5000	474.01	265.61	197.48	164.39	145.30	133.16
6000	568.81	318.73	236.98	197.27	174.35	159.79
7000	663.61	371.85	276.47	230.15	203.41	186.42
8000	758.42	424.97	315.07	263.03	232.47	213.05
9000	853.22	478.09	355.46	295.91	201.53	239.68
10000	948.02	531.21	394.96	328.79	290.59	266.31
11000	1042.82	584.33	434.46	361.67	319.65	292.94
12000	1137.62	637.45	473.95	394.55	348.71	319.57
13000	1232.42	690.57	513.45	427.43	377.77	346.21
14000	1327.23	743.70	552.94	460.31	406.83	372.84
15000	1422.03	796.82	592.44	493.18	435.88	399.47
16000	1516.83	849.94	631.93	526.06	464.94	426.10
17000	1611.63	903.06	671.43	558.94	494.00	452.73
18000	1706.43	956.18	710.93	591.82	523.06	479.36
19000	1801.24	1009.30	750.42	624.70	552.12	505.99
20000	1896.04	1062.42	789.92	657.58	581.18	532.62
21000	1990.84	1115.54	829.41	690.46	610.24	559.26
22000	2085.64	1168.66	868.91	723.34	639.30	585.89
23000	2180.44	1221.78	908.41	756.22	668.36	612.52
24000	2275.24	1274.90	947.90	789.09	697.41	639.15
25000	2370.05	1328.03	987.40	821.97	726.47	665.78
30000	2844.06	1593.63	1184.88	986.37	871.77	798.94
35000	3318.06	1859.24	1382.36	1150.76	1017.06	932.09
40000	3792.07	2124.84	1579.84	1315.16	1162.36	1065.25
45000	4266.08	2390.45	1777.32	1479.55	1307.65	1198.40
50000	4740.09	2656.05	1974.79	1643.94	1452.95	1331.56
55000	5214.10	2921.66	2172.27	1808.34	1598.24	1464.72
60000	5688.11	3187.26	2369.75	1972.73	1743.54	1597.87
65000	6162.12	3452.87	2567.23	2137.13	1888.83	1731.03
70000	6636.13	3718.47	2764.71	2301.52	2034.13	1864.18
75000	7110.14	3984.08	2962.19	2465.92	2179.42	1997.34
80000	7584.15	4249.68	3159.67	2630.31	2324.71	2130.50
85000	8058.16	4515.29	3357.15	2794.71	2470.01	2263.65
90000	8532.17	4780.89	3554.63	2959.10	2615.30	2396.81
95000	9006.18	5046.50	3752.11	3123.49	2760.60	2529.96
100000	9480.19	5312.10	3949.59	3287.89	2905.89	2663.12
200000	18960.40	10624.20	7899.18	6575.78	5811.79	5326.24
300000	28440.60	15936.30	11848.80	9863.67	8717.68	7989.36
400000	37920.70	21248.40	15798.40	13151.60	11623.60	10652.50
500000	47400.90	26560.50	19747.90	16439.40	14529.50	13315.60

MONTHLY PAYMENT

Necessary to amortize a loan

24 1/2%

TERM / AMOUNT	7 YEARS	8 YEARS	9 YEARS	10 YEARS	11 YEARS	12 YEARS
500	12.50	11.92	11.51	11.20	10.97	10.80
600	15.00	14.31	13.81	13.44	13.16	12.96
700	17.50	16.69	16.11	15.68	15.36	15.11
800	19.99	19.07	18.41	17.92	17.55	17.27
900	22.49	21.46	20.71	20.16	19.75	19.43
1000	24.99	23.84	23.01	22.40	21.94	21.59
2000	49.99	47.68	46.02	44.80	43.88	43.19
3000	74.98	71.53	69.03	67.19	65.82	64.78
4000	99.97	95.37	92.04	89.59	87.76	86.37
5000	124.96	119.21	115.05	111.99	109.70	107.96
6000	149.96	143.05	138.06	134.39	131.64	129.56
7000	174.95	166.89	161.07	156.78	153.58	151.15
8000	199.94	190.74	184.09	179.18	175.51	172.74
9000	224.94	214.58	207.10	201.58	197.45	194.33
10000	249.93	238.42	230.11	223.98	219.39	215.93
11000	274.92	262.26	253.12	246.38	241.33	237.52
12000	299.91	286.10	276.13	268.77	263.27	259.11
13000	324.91	309.95	299.14	291.17	285.21	280.70
14000	349.90	333.79	322.15	313.57	307.15	302.30
15000	374.89	357.63	345.16	335.97	329.09	323.89
16000	399.89	381.47	368.17	358.36	351.03	345.48
17000	424.88	405.31	391.18	380.76	372.97	367.07
18000	449.87	429.16	414.19	403.16	394.91	388.67
19000	474.86	453.00	437.20	425.56	416.85	410.26
20000	499.86	476.84	460.21	447.96	438.79	431.85
21000	524.85	500.68	483.22	470.35	460.73	453.44
22000	549.84	524.52	506.23	492.75	482.66	475.04
23000	574.84	548.37	529.24	515.15	504.60	496.63
24000	599.83	572.21	552.25	537.55	526.54	518.22
25000	624.82	596.05	575.26	559.94	548.48	539.81
30000	749.79	715.26	690.32	671.93	658.18	647.77
35000	874.75	834.47	805.37	783.92	767.88	755.74
40000	999.71	953.68	920.42	895.91	877.57	863.70
45000	1124.68	1072.89	1035.48	1007.90	987.27	971.66
50000	1249.64	1192.10	1150.53	1119.89	1096.96	1079.62
55000	1374.61	1311.31	1265.58	1231.88	1206.66	1187.59
60000	1499.57	1430.52	1380.63	1343.86	1316.36	1295.55
65000	1624.53	1549.73	1495.69	1455.85	1426.05	1403.51
70000	1749.50	1668.94	1610.74	1567.84	1535.75	1511.47
75000	1874.46	1788.15	1725.79	1679.83	1645.45	1619.44
80000	1999.43	1907.36	1840.85	1791.82	1755.14	1727.40
85000	2124.39	2026.57	1955.90	1903.81	1864.84	1835.36
90000	2249.36	2145.78	2070.95	2015.80	1974.53	1943.32
95000	2374.32	2264.99	2186.00	2127.79	2084.23	2051.29
100000	2499.28	2384.20	2301.06	2239.77	2193.93	2159.25
200000	4998.57	4768.39	4602.11	4479.55	4387.85	4318.50
300000	7497.85	7152.59	6903.17	6719.32	6581.78	6477.74
400000	9997.14	9536.79	9204.23	8959.10	8775.71	8636.99
500000	12496.40	11921.00	11505.30	11198.90	10969.60	10796.20

24 1/2%

MONTHLY PAYMENT

Necessary to amortize a loan

TERM / AMOUNT	13 YEARS	14 YEARS	15 YEARS	16 YEARS	17 YEARS	18 YEARS
500	10.66	10.56	10.48	10.42	10.38	10.34
600	12.80	12.67	12.58	12.51	12.45	12.41
700	14.93	14.79	14.68	14.59	14.53	14.48
800	17.06	16.90	16.77	16.68	16.60	16.54
900	19.20	19.01	18.87	18.76	18.68	18.61
1000	21.33	21.12	20.97	20.85	20.75	20.68
2000	42.66	42.25	41.94	41.69	41.51	41.36
3000	63.98	63.37	62.90	62.54	62.26	62.04
4000	85.31	84.50	83.87	83.39	83.01	82.72
5000	106.64	105.62	104.84	104.24	103.76	103.40
6000	127.97	126.75	125.81	125.08	124.52	124.08
7000	149.30	147.87	146.78	145.93	145.27	144.76
8000	170.62	169.00	167.75	166.78	166.02	165.44
9000	191.95	190.12	188.71	187.62	186.78	186.12
10000	213.28	211.25	209.68	208.47	207.53	206.79
11000	234.61	232.37	230.65	229.32	228.28	227.47
12000	255.94	253.50	251.62	250.16	249.03	248.15
13000	277.26	274.62	272.59	271.01	269.79	268.83
14000	298.59	295.75	293.56	291.86	290.54	289.51
15000	319.92	316.87	314.52	312.70	311.29	310.19
16000	341.25	338.00	335.49	333.55	332.04	330.87
17000	362.58	359.12	356.46	354.40	352.80	351.55
18000	383.90	380.25	377.43	375.25	373.55	372.23
19000	405.23	401.37	398.40	396.09	394.30	392.91
20000	426.56	422.50	419.37	416.94	415.06	413.59
21000	447.89	443.62	440.33	437.79	435.81	434.27
22000	469.22	464.75	461.30	458.63	456.56	454.95
23000	490.54	485.87	482.27	479.48	477.31	475.63
24000	511.87	507.00	503.24	500.33	498.07	496.31
25000	533.20	528.12	524.21	521.17	518.82	516.99
30000	639.84	633.75	629.05	625.41	622.58	620.38
35000	746.48	739.37	733.89	729.64	726.35	723.78
40000	853.12	845.00	838.73	833.88	830.11	827.18
45000	959.76	950.62	943.57	938.11	933.87	930.58
50000	1066.40	1056.24	1048.41	1042.35	1037.64	1033.97
55000	1173.04	1161.87	1153.25	1146.58	1141.40	1137.37
60000	1279.68	1267.49	1258.09	1250.82	1245.17	1240.77
65000	1386.32	1373.12	1362.94	1355.05	1348.93	1344.16
70000	1492.96	1478.74	1467.78	1459.29	1452.69	1447.56
75000	1599.60	1584.37	1572.62	1563.52	1556.46	1550.96
80000	1706.24	1689.99	1677.46	1667.76	1660.22	1654.36
85000	1812.88	1795.62	1782.30	1771.99	1763.98	1757.75
90000	1919.52	1901.24	1887.14	1876.23	1867.75	1861.15
95000	2026.16	2006.86	1991.98	1980.46	1971.51	1964.55
100000	2132.80	2112.49	2096.82	2084.70	2075.28	2067.94
200000	4265.59	4224.98	4193.65	4169.39	4150.55	4135.89
300000	6398.39	6337.47	6290.47	6254.09	6225.83	6203.83
400000	8531.18	8449.96	8387.30	8338.78	8301.10	8271.78
500000	10664.00	10562.40	10484.10	10423.50	10376.40	10339.70

MONTHLY PAYMENT

Necessary to amortize a loan

24 1/2%

TERM / AMOUNT	19 YEARS	20 YEARS	25 YEARS	30 YEARS	35 YEARS	40 YEARS
500	10.31	10.29	10.23	10.22	10.21	10.21
600	12.37	12.35	12.28	12.26	12.25	12.25
700	14.44	14.40	14.33	14.30	14.29	14.29
800	16.50	16.46	16.37	16.34	16.34	16.33
900	18.56	18.52	18.42	18.39	18.38	18.38
1000	20.62	20.58	20.46	20.43	20.42	20.42
2000	41.24	41.16	40.93	40.86	40.84	40.84
3000	61.87	61.73	61.39	61.29	61.26	61.25
4000	82.49	82.31	81.86	81.72	81.68	81.67
5000	103.11	102.89	102.32	102.15	102.10	102.09
6000	123.73	123.47	122.79	122.59	122.53	122.51
7000	144.36	144.04	143.25	143.02	142.95	142.93
8000	164.98	164.62	163.71	163.45	163.37	163.34
9000	185.60	185.20	184.18	183.88	183.79	183.76
10000	206.22	205.78	204.64	204.31	204.21	204.18
11000	226.85	226.35	225.11	224.74	224.63	224.60
12000	247.47	246.93	245.57	245.17	245.05	245.02
13000	268.09	267.51	266.04	265.60	265.47	265.43
14000	288.71	288.09	286.50	286.03	285.89	285.85
15000	309.33	308.67	306.96	306.46	306.31	306.27
16000	329.96	329.24	327.43	326.89	326.73	326.69
17000	350.58	349.82	347.89	347.32	347.16	347.11
18000	371.20	370.40	368.36	367.75	367.58	367.52
19000	391.82	390.98	388.82	388.19	388.00	387.94
20000	412.45	411.55	409.29	408.62	408.42	408.36
21000	433.07	432.13	429.75	429.05	428.84	428.78
22000	453.69	452.71	450.21	449.48	449.26	449.19
23000	474.31	473.29	470.68	469.91	469.68	469.61
24000	494.94	493.86	491.14	490.34	490.10	490.03
25000	515.56	514.44	511.61	510.77	510.52	510.45
30000	618.67	617.33	613.93	612.92	612.63	612.54
35000	721.78	720.22	716.25	715.08	714.73	714.63
40000	824.89	823.11	818.57	817.23	816.84	816.72
45000	928.00	925.99	920.89	919.39	918.94	918.81
50000	1031.11	1028.88	1023.21	1021.54	1021.04	1020.90
55000	1134.23	1131.77	1125.54	1123.69	1123.15	1122.99
60000	1237.34	1234.66	1227.86	1225.85	1225.25	1225.08
65000	1340.45	1337.55	1330.18	1328.00	1327.36	1327.16
70000	1443.56	1440.44	1432.50	1430.16	1429.46	1429.25
75000	1546.67	1543.32	1534.82	1532.31	1531.57	1531.34
80000	1649.78	1646.21	1637.14	1634.46	1633.67	1633.43
85000	1752.89	1749.10	1739.46	1736.62	1735.77	1735.52
90000	1856.01	1851.99	1841.79	1838.77	1837.88	1837.61
95000	1959.12	1954.88	1944.11	1940.93	1939.98	1939.70
100000	2062.23	2057.77	2046.43	2043.08	2042.09	2041.79
200000	4124.46	4115.53	4092.86	4086.16	4084.17	4083.58
300000	6186.69	6173.30	6139.28	6129.24	6126.26	6125.38
400000	8248.91	8231.06	8185.71	8172.32	8168.35	8167.17
500000	10311.10	10288.80	10232.10	10215.40	10210.40	10209.00

25%

MONTHLY PAYMENT

Necessary to amortize a loan

TERM / AMOUNT	1 YEAR	2 YEARS	3 YEARS	4 YEARS	5 YEARS	6 YEARS
500	47.52	26.69	19.88	16.58	14.68	13.47
600	57.03	32.02	23.86	19.89	17.61	16.16
700	66.53	37.36	27.83	23.21	20.55	18.86
800	76.04	42.70	31.81	26.53	23.48	21.55
900	85.54	48.03	35.78	29.84	26.42	24.24
1000	95.04	53.37	39.76	33.16	29.35	26.94
2000	190.09	106.74	79.52	66.31	58.70	53.87
3000	285.13	160.11	119.28	99.47	88.05	80.81
4000	380.18	213.49	159.04	132.63	117.41	107.75
5000	475.22	266.86	198.80	165.79	146.76	134.69
6000	570.26	320.23	238.56	198.94	176.11	161.62
7000	665.31	373.60	278.32	232.10	205.46	188.56
8000	760.35	426.97	318.08	265.26	234.81	215.50
9000	855.40	480.34	357.84	298.41	264.16	242.43
10000	950.44	533.71	397.60	331.57	293.51	269.37
11000	1045.48	587.09	437.36	364.73	322.86	296.31
12000	1140.53	640.46	477.12	397.89	352.22	323.25
13000	1235.57	693.83	516.88	431.04	381.57	350.18
14000	1330.62	747.20	556.64	464.20	410.92	377.12
15000	1425.66	800.57	596.40	497.36	440.27	404.06
16000	1520.70	853.94	636.16	530.51	469.62	430.99
17000	1615.75	907.31	675.92	563.67	498.97	457.93
18000	1710.79	960.69	715.68	596.83	528.32	484.87
19000	1805.84	1014.06	755.44	629.98	557.67	511.81
20000	1900.88	1067.43	795.20	663.14	587.03	538.74
21000	1995.92	1120.80	834.96	696.30	616.38	565.68
22000	2090.97	1174.17	874.71	729.46	645.73	592.62
23000	2186.01	1227.54	914.47	762.61	675.08	619.55
24000	2281.06	1280.91	954.23	795.77	704.43	646.49
25000	2376.10	1334.29	993.99	828.93	733.78	673.43
30000	2851.32	1601.14	1192.79	994.71	880.54	808.11
35000	3326.54	1868.00	1391.59	1160.50	1027.29	942.80
40000	3801.76	2134.86	1590.39	1326.28	1174.05	1077.49
45000	4276.98	2401.71	1789.19	1492.07	1320.81	1212.17
50000	4752.20	2668.57	1987.99	1657.85	1467.56	1346.86
55000	5227.42	2935.43	2186.79	1823.64	1614.32	1481.54
60000	5702.64	3202.28	2385.59	1989.42	1761.08	1616.23
65000	6177.86	3469.14	2584.38	2155.21	1907.83	1750.91
70000	6653.08	3736.00	2783.18	2321.00	2054.59	1885.60
75000	7128.30	4002.86	2981.98	2486.78	2201.35	2020.29
80000	7603.52	4269.71	3180.78	2652.57	2348.10	2154.97
85000	8078.74	4536.57	3379.58	2818.35	2494.86	2289.66
90000	8553.96	4803.43	3578.38	2984.14	2641.62	2424.34
95000	9029.18	5070.28	3777.18	3149.92	2788.37	2559.03
100000	9504.40	5337.14	3975.97	3315.71	2935.13	2693.71
200000	19008.80	10674.30	7951.95	6631.41	5870.26	5387.43
300000	28513.20	16011.40	11927.90	9947.12	8805.38	8081.14
400000	38017.60	21348.60	15903.90	13262.80	11740.50	10774.90
500000	47522.00	26685.70	19879.90	16578.50	14675.60	13468.60

MONTHLY PAYMENT

Necessary to amortize a loan

25%

TERM / AMOUNT	7 YEARS	8 YEARS	9 YEARS	10 YEARS	11 YEARS	12 YEARS
500	12.66	12.09	11.68	11.37	11.15	10.98
600	15.19	14.50	14.01	13.65	13.38	13.18
700	17.72	16.92	16.35	15.92	15.61	15.37
800	20.25	19.34	18.68	18.20	17.84	17.57
900	22.78	21.76	21.02	20.47	20.07	19.76
1000	25.31	24.17	23.35	22.75	22.30	21.96
2000	50.62	48.35	46.70	45.50	44.60	43.92
3000	75.93	72.52	70.06	68.25	66.90	65.88
4000	101.25	96.69	93.41	91.00	89.20	87.84
5000	126.56	120.86	116.76	113.75	111.50	109.81
6000	151.87	145.04	140.11	136.50	133.80	131.77
7000	177.18	169.21	163.47	159.25	156.10	153.73
8000	202.49	193.38	186.82	181.99	178.40	175.69
9000	227.80	217.55	210.17	204.74	200.70	197.65
10000	253.12	241.73	233.52	227.49	223.00	219.61
11000	278.43	265.90	256.87	250.24	245.30	241.57
12000	303.74	290.07	280.23	272.99	267.60	263.53
13000	329.05	314.24	303.58	295.74	289.90	285.49
14000	354.36	338.42	326.93	318.49	312.20	307.45
15000	379.67	362.59	350.28	341.24	334.50	329.41
16000	404.99	386.76	373.64	363.99	356.80	351.38
17000	430.30	410.94	396.99	386.74	379.10	373.34
18000	455.61	435.11	420.34	409.49	401.40	395.30
19000	480.92	459.28	443.69	432.24	423.70	417.26
20000	506.23	483.45	467.04	454.99	446.00	439.22
21000	531.54	507.63	490.40	477.74	468.30	461.18
22000	556.86	531.80	513.75	500.48	490.60	483.14
23000	582.17	555.97	537.10	523.23	512.89	505.10
24000	607.48	580.14	560.45	545.98	535.19	527.06
25000	632.79	604.32	583.81	568.73	557.49	549.02
30000	759.35	725.18	700.57	682.48	668.99	658.83
35000	885.91	846.04	817.33	796.23	780.49	768.63
40000	1012.46	966.91	934.09	909.97	891.99	878.44
45000	1139.02	1087.77	1050.85	1023.72	1003.49	988.24
50000	1265.58	1208.63	1167.61	1137.46	1114.99	1098.05
55000	1392.14	1329.50	1284.37	1251.21	1226.49	1207.85
60000	1518.70	1450.36	1401.13	1364.96	1337.99	1317.66
65000	1645.25	1571.22	1517.89	1478.70	1449.48	1427.46
70000	1771.81	1692.09	1634.65	1592.45	1560.98	1537.26
75000	1898.37	1812.95	1751.41	1706.20	1672.48	1647.07
80000	2024.93	1933.81	1868.17	1819.94	1783.98	1756.87
85000	2151.49	2054.67	1984.94	1933.69	1895.48	1866.68
90000	2278.04	2175.54	2101.70	2047.44	2006.98	1976.48
95000	2404.60	2296.40	2218.46	2161.18	2118.48	2086.29
100000	2531.16	2417.26	2335.22	2274.93	2229.98	2196.09
200000	5062.32	4834.53	4670.44	4549.86	4459.95	4392.18
300000	7593.48	7251.79	7005.65	6824.78	6689.93	6588.28
400000	10124.60	9669.06	9340.87	9099.71	8919.90	8784.37
500000	12655.80	12086.30	11676.10	11374.60	11149.90	10980.50

MONTHLY PAYMENT

Necessary to amortize a loan

TERM / AMOUNT	13 YEARS	14 YEARS	15 YEARS	16 YEARS	17 YEARS	18 YEARS
500	10.85	10.75	10.68	10.62	10.57	10.54
600	13.02	12.90	12.81	12.74	12.69	12.65
700	15.19	15.05	14.95	14.87	14.80	14.76
800	17.36	17.21	17.08	16.99	16.92	16.86
900	19.53	19.36	19.22	19.11	19.03	18.97
1000	21.70	21.51	21.36	21.24	21.15	21.08
2000	43.41	43.01	42.71	42.48	42.30	42.16
3000	65.11	64.52	64.07	63.72	63.45	63.24
4000	86.81	86.03	85.42	84.95	84.59	84.31
5000	108.52	107.53	106.78	106.19	105.74	105.39
6000	130.22	129.04	128.13	127.43	126.89	126.47
7000	151.92	150.55	149.49	148.67	148.04	147.55
8000	173.63	172.05	170.84	169.91	169.19	168.63
9000	195.33	193.56	192.20	191.15	190.34	189.71
10000	217.03	215.07	213.55	212.39	211.49	210.79
11000	238.74	236.57	234.91	233.63	232.63	231.86
12000	260.44	258.08	256.26	254.86	253.78	252.94
13000	282.15	279.59	277.62	276.10	274.93	274.02
14000	303.85	301.09	298.97	297.34	296.08	295.10
15000	325.55	322.60	320.33	318.58	317.23	316.18
16000	347.26	344.11	341.69	339.82	338.38	337.26
17000	368.96	365.61	363.04	361.06	359.52	358.34
18000	390.66	387.12	384.40	382.30	380.67	379.41
19000	412.37	408.62	405.75	403.53	401.82	400.49
20000	434.07	430.13	427.11	424.77	422.97	421.57
21000	455.77	451.64	448.46	446.01	444.12	442.65
22000	477.48	473.14	469.82	467.25	465.27	463.73
23000	499.18	494.65	491.17	488.49	486.42	484.81
24000	520.88	516.16	512.53	509.73	507.56	505.89
25000	542.59	537.66	533.88	530.97	528.71	526.96
30000	651.10	645.20	640.66	637.16	634.45	632.36
35000	759.62	752.73	747.44	743.35	740.20	737.75
40000	868.14	860.26	854.21	849.55	845.94	843.14
45000	976.65	967.80	960.99	955.74	951.68	948.54
50000	1085.17	1075.33	1067.76	1061.93	1057.42	1053.93
55000	1193.69	1182.86	1174.54	1168.13	1163.17	1159.32
60000	1302.21	1290.39	1281.32	1274.32	1268.91	1264.71
65000	1410.72	1397.93	1388.09	1380.51	1374.65	1370.11
70000	1519.24	1505.46	1494.87	1486.71	1480.39	1475.50
75000	1627.76	1612.99	1601.65	1592.90	1586.13	1580.89
80000	1736.27	1720.52	1708.42	1699.09	1691.88	1686.29
85000	1844.79	1828.06	1815.20	1805.29	1797.62	1791.68
90000	1953.31	1935.59	1921.98	1911.48	1903.36	1897.07
95000	2061.83	2043.12	2028.75	2017.67	2009.10	2002.46
100000	2170.34	2150.65	2135.53	2123.86	2114.85	2107.86
200000	4340.69	4301.31	4271.06	4247.73	4229.69	4215.71
300000	6511.03	6451.96	6406.58	6371.59	6344.54	6323.57
400000	8681.37	8602.62	8542.11	8495.46	8459.38	8431.43
500000	10851.70	10753.30	10677.60	10619.30	10574.20	10539.30

MONTHLY PAYMENT

Necessary to amortize a loan

25%

TERM / AMOUNT	19 YEARS	20 YEARS	25 YEARS	30 YEARS	35 YEARS	40 YEARS
500	10.51	10.49	10.44	10.42	10.42	10.42
600	12.61	12.59	12.53	12.51	12.50	12.50
700	14.72	14.69	14.61	14.59	14.59	14.58
800	16.82	16.79	16.70	16.68	16.67	16.67
900	18.92	18.88	18.79	18.76	18.75	18.75
1000	21.02	20.98	20.88	20.85	20.84	20.83
2000	42.05	41.96	41.75	41.69	41.67	41.67
3000	63.07	62.95	62.63	62.54	62.51	62.50
4000	84.10	83.93	83.51	83.38	83.35	83.34
5000	105.12	104.91	104.38	104.23	104.19	104.17
6000	126.15	125.89	125.26	125.08	125.02	125.01
7000	147.17	146.88	146.13	145.92	145.86	145.84
8000	168.20	167.86	167.01	166.77	166.70	166.68
9000	189.22	188.84	187.89	187.61	187.53	187.51
10000	210.24	209.82	208.76	208.46	208.37	208.34
11000	231.27	230.80	229.64	229.30	229.21	229.18
12000	252.29	251.79	250.52	250.15	250.04	250.01
13000	273.32	272.77	271.39	271.00	270.88	270.85
14000	294.34	293.75	292.27	291.84	291.72	291.68
15000	315.37	314.73	313.15	312.69	312.55	312.52
16000	336.39	335.72	334.02	333.53	333.39	333.35
17000	357.41	356.70	354.90	354.38	354.23	354.18
18000	378.44	377.68	375.77	375.22	375.07	375.02
19000	399.46	398.66	396.65	396.07	395.90	395.85
20000	420.49	419.64	417.53	416.92	416.74	416.69
21000	441.51	440.63	438.40	437.76	437.58	437.52
22000	462.54	461.61	459.28	458.61	458.41	458.36
23000	483.56	482.59	480.16	479.45	479.25	479.19
24000	504.58	503.57	501.03	500.30	500.09	500.03
25000	525.61	524.55	521.91	521.15	520.92	520.86
30000	630.73	629.47	626.29	625.37	625.11	625.03
35000	735.85	734.38	730.67	729.60	729.29	729.20
40000	840.97	839.29	835.05	833.83	833.48	833.38
45000	946.10	944.20	939.43	938.06	937.66	937.55
50000	1051.22	1049.11	1043.82	1042.29	1041.85	1041.72
55000	1156.34	1154.02	1148.20	1146.52	1146.03	1145.89
60000	1261.46	1258.93	1252.58	1250.75	1250.22	1250.06
65000	1366.58	1363.84	1356.96	1354.98	1354.40	1354.23
70000	1471.70	1468.75	1461.34	1459.21	1458.59	1458.41
75000	1576.82	1573.66	1565.72	1563.43	1562.77	1562.58
80000	1681.95	1678.57	1670.10	1667.66	1666.96	1666.75
85000	1787.07	1783.48	1774.49	1771.89	1771.14	1770.92
90000	1892.19	1888.39	1878.87	1876.12	1875.33	1875.09
95000	1997.31	1993.31	1983.25	1980.35	1979.51	1979.27
100000	2102.43	2098.22	2087.63	2084.58	2083.69	2083.44
200000	4204.86	4196.43	4175.26	4169.16	4167.39	4166.88
300000	6307.30	6294.65	6262.89	6253.74	6251.08	6250.31
400000	8409.73	8392.86	8350.52	8338.31	8334.78	8333.75
500000	10512.20	10491.10	10438.20	10422.90	10418.50	10417.20

NOTES:

NOTES:

NOTES:

NOTES:

NOTES:

NOTES: